A Kodansha Comics Trade Paperback Original
Star-Crossed!! 3 copyright © 2020 Junko
English translation copyright © 2021 Junko

Published in the United States by Kodansha Comics, an imprint of
Kodansha USA Publishing, LLC, New York.

Publication rights for this English edition arranged through
Kodansha Ltd., Tokyo.

First published in Japan in 2020 by Kodansha Ltd., Tokyo
as *Wota Doru, Oshiga watashide watashiga oshide*, volume 3.

ISBN 978-1-64651-215-7

Original cover design by HASEPRO

Printed in the United States of America.

www.kodansha.us

9 8 7 6 5 4 3 2 1
Translation: Barbara Vincent / amimaru
Lettering: Mohit Dhiman / amimaru
Production assistants: Dani Brockman, Monika Hegedusova, Adam Jankowski / amimaru
Additional lettering and layout: Scott O. Brown
Editing: Vanessa Tenazas
Kodansha Comics edition cover design by Phil Balsman

Publisher: Kiichiro Sugawara

Director of publishing services: Ben Applegate
Associate director of operations: Stephen Pakula
Publishing services managing editors: Alanna Ruse, Madison Salters
Production managers: Emi Lotto, Angela Zurlo
Logo and character art ©Kodansha USA Publishing, LLC

Yuri Is My Job!

miman

Hime is a picture-perfect high school princess, so when she accidentally injures a café manager named Mai, she's willing to cover some shifts to keep her façade intact. To Hime's surprise, the café is themed after a private school where the all-female staff always puts on their best act for their loyal customers. However, under the guidance of the most graceful girl there, Hime can't help but blush and blunder! Beneath all the frills and laughter, Hime feels tension brewing as she finds out more about her new job and her budding feelings...

KC/ KODANSHA COMICS

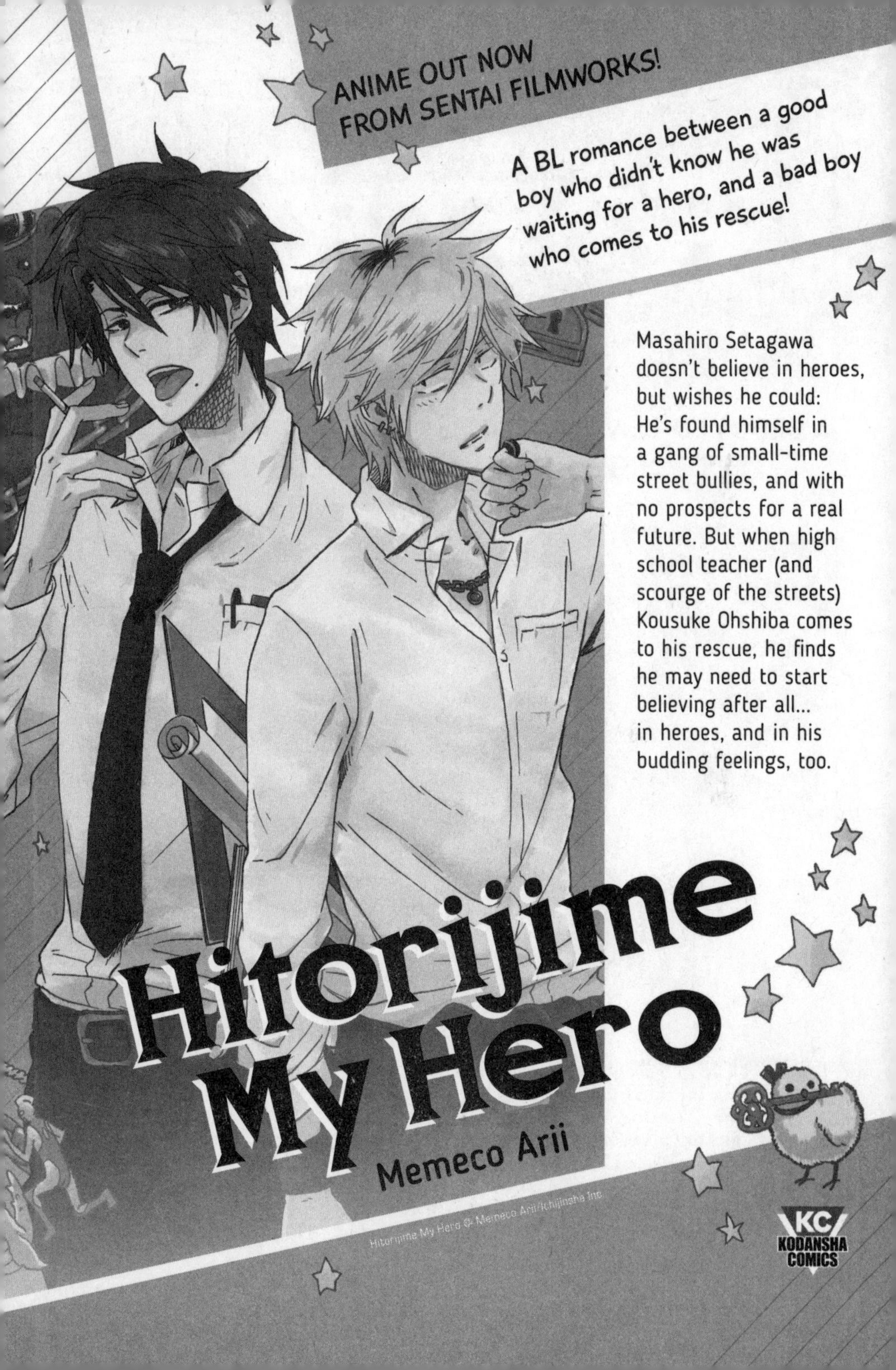
ANIME OUT NOW FROM SENTAI FILMWORKS!
A BL romance between a good boy who didn't know he was waiting for a hero, and a bad boy who comes to his rescue!
Masahiro Setagawa doesn't believe in heroes, but wishes he could: He's found himself in a gang of small-time street bullies, and with no prospects for a real future. But when high school teacher (and scourge of the streets) Kousuke Ohshiba comes to his rescue, he finds he may need to start believing after all... in heroes, and in his budding feelings, too.
Hitorijime My Hero
Memeco Arii
Hitorijime My Hero © Memeco Arii/Ichijinsha Inc.
KC KODANSHA COMICS

MAGIC · KNIGHT RAYEARTH

25TH ANNIVERSARY EDITION

CLAMP

A BELOVED CLASSIC MAKES ITS STUNNING RETURN IN THIS GORGEOUS, LIMITED EDITION BOX SET!

This tale of three Tokyo teenagers who cross through a magical portal and become the champions of another world is a modern manga classic. The box set includes three volumes of manga covering the entire first series of *Magic Knight Rayearth*, plus the series's super-rare full-color art book companion, all printed at a larger size than ever before on premium paper, featuring a newly-revised translation and lettering, and exquisite foil-stamped covers.

A strictly limited edition, this will be gone in a flash!

The art-deco cyberpunk classic from the creators of *xxxHOLiC* and *Cardcaptor Sakura!*

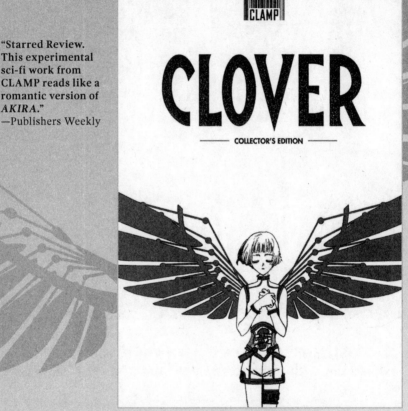

CLOVER © CLAMP·ShigatsuTsuitachi CO.,LTD./Kodansha Ltd.

Su was born into a bleak future, where the government keeps tight control over children with magical powers—codenamed "Clovers." With Su being the only "four-leaf" Clover in the world, she has been kept isolated nearly her whole life. Can ex-military agent Kazuhiko deliver her to the happiness she seeks? Experience the complete series in this hardcover edition, which also includes over twenty pages of ravishing color art!

KC
KODANSHA
COMICS

The beloved characters from
Cardcaptor Sakura return in a brand new, reimagined fantasy adventure!

"[*Tsubasa*] takes readers on a fantastic ride that only gets more exhilarating with each successive chapter." —Anime News Network

In the Kingdom of Clow, an archaeological dig unleashes an incredible power, causing Princess Sakura to lose her memories. To save her, her childhood friend Syaoran must follow the orders of the Dimension Witch and travel alongside Kurogane, an unrivaled warrior; Fai, a powerful magician; and Mokona, a curiously strange creature, to retrieve Sakura's dispersed memories!

"Clever, sassy, and original....*xxxHOLiC* has the inherent hallmarks of a runaway hit."
—NewType magazine

Beautifully seductive artwork and uniquely Japanese depictions of the supernatural will hypnotize CLAMP fans!

xxxHOLiC © CLAMP ShigatsuTsuitachi CO.,LTD./Kodansha Ltd.
xxxHOLiC Rei © CLAMP ShigatsuTsuitachi CO.,LTD./Kodansha Ltd.

Kimihiro Watanuki is haunted by visions of ghosts and spirits. He seeks help from a mysterious woman named Yuko, who claims she can help. However, Watanuki must work for Yuko in order to pay for her aid. Soon Watanuki finds himself employed in Yuko's shop, where he sees things and meets customers that are stranger than anything he could have ever imagined.

KC
KODANSHA
COMICS

Chobits © CLAMP·ShigatsuTsuitachi CO.,LTD./Kodansha Ltd.

Poor college student Hideki is down on his luck. All he wants is a good job, a girlfriend, and his very own "persocom"—the latest and greatest in humanoid computer technology. Hideki's luck changes one night when he finds Chi—a persocom thrown out in a pile of trash. But Hideki soon discovers that there's much more to his cute new persocom than meets the eye.

KC KODANSHA COMICS

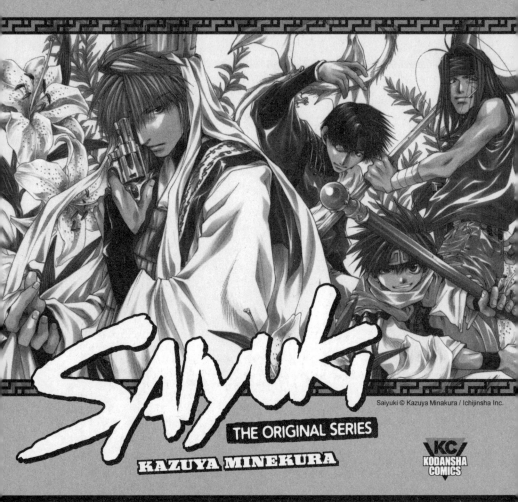

Young characters and steampunk setting, like *Howl's Moving Castle* and *Battle Angel Alita*

A boy with a talent for machines and a mysterious girl whose wings he's fixed will take you beyond the clouds! In the tradition of the high-flying, resonant adventure stories of Studio Ghibli comes a gorgeous tale about the longing of young hearts for adventure and friendship!

THE SWEET SCENT OF LOVE IS IN THE AIR! FOR FANS OF OFFBEAT ROMANCES LIKE *WOTAKOI*

Sweat and Soap © Kintetsu Yamada / Kodansha Ltd.

In an office romance, there's a fine line between sexy and awkward... and that line is where Asako — a woman who sweats copiously — meets Koutarou — a perfume developer who can't get enough of Asako's, er, scent. Don't miss a romcom manga like no other!

STAR⇌CROSSED!!

03

JUNKO

CONTENTS

STORY

Azusa is a hardcore idol fangirl, but when she's caught in a freak accident with her favorite idol Chikashi, they end up swapping bodies! To cover up this fact, Chikashi's manager Matsumoto has Chikashi transfer into Azusa's school and move in next door, instructing Azusa to act as Matsumoto's trainee... but Azusa herself, still trapped in Chikashi's body, has to take dance lessons with the other P4U members! The training goes off without a hitch, but the post-lesson bath is another story. Unable to cope with the stimulation of being surrounded by the three other P4U members in the buff, Azusa-Chikashi promptly passes out! And then she's kissed by Haru, the leader?!

CHARACTER

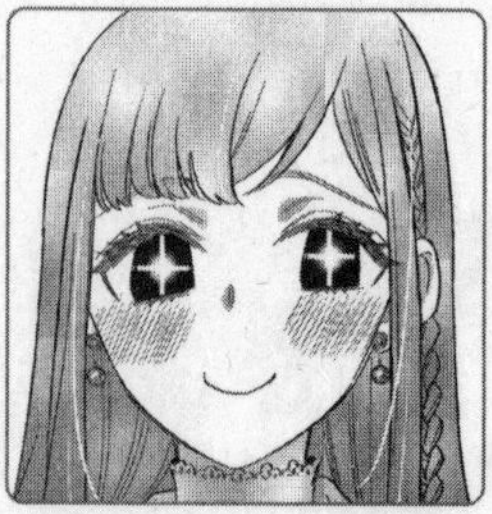

Azusa Asahina

A picture-perfect high school girl—with the looks, grades, and student council president title to match. In reality, she's a rabid fangirl who's crafted an elaborate image to be a worthy superfan of her favorite idol, Chikashi Chida.

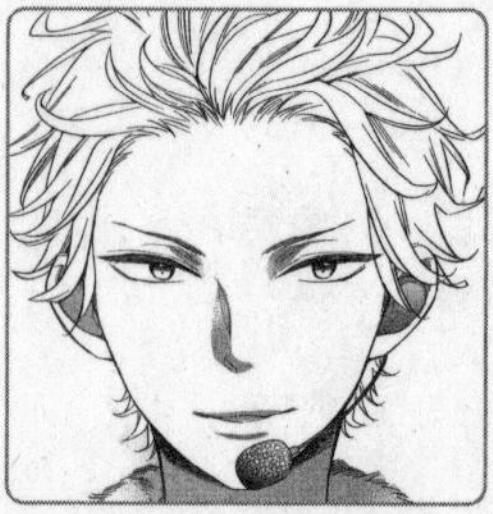

Chikashi Chida (Chika)

A member of the four-man idol group P4U, and Azusa's favorite. He died in an accident during a concert, but was restored to life by God. He's put off by Azusa's idol obsession.

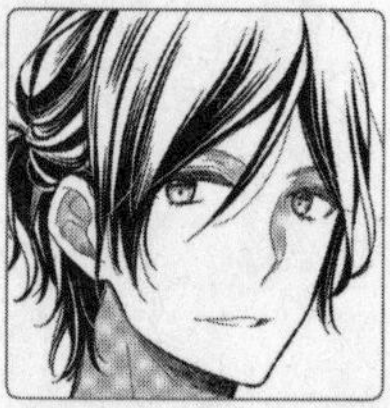

Haruki Haijima (Haru)

P4U's leader. He has feelings for Chikashi?!

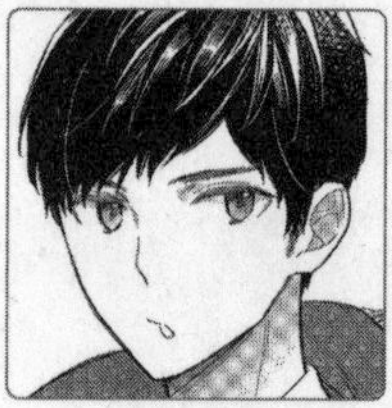

Fumi

Azusa's hapless childhood friend who is zealously and obnoxiously in love with her.

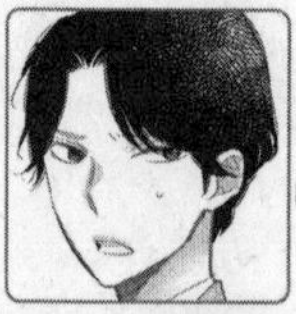

Matsumoto

P4U's manager. Loves cats.

P4U

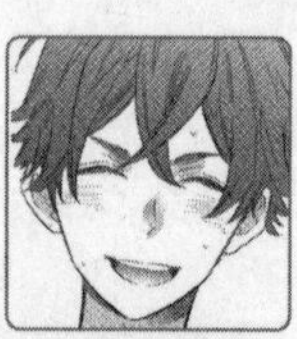

Mariya Manaka (Mari)

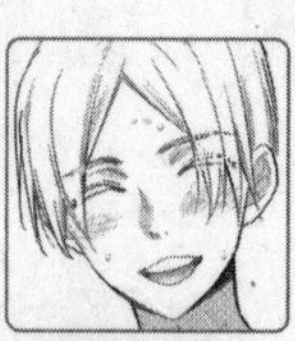

Mikito Miyama (Miki)

R⇄CROSS

D!! STAR

AR⇄CROS

CROSSED

⇄CROSSE

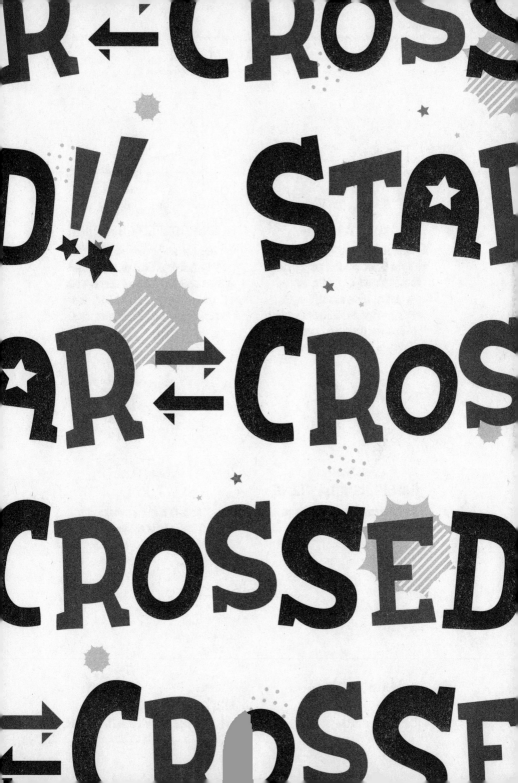

STAGE. 7 | STANS CAN'T BE FRIENDS

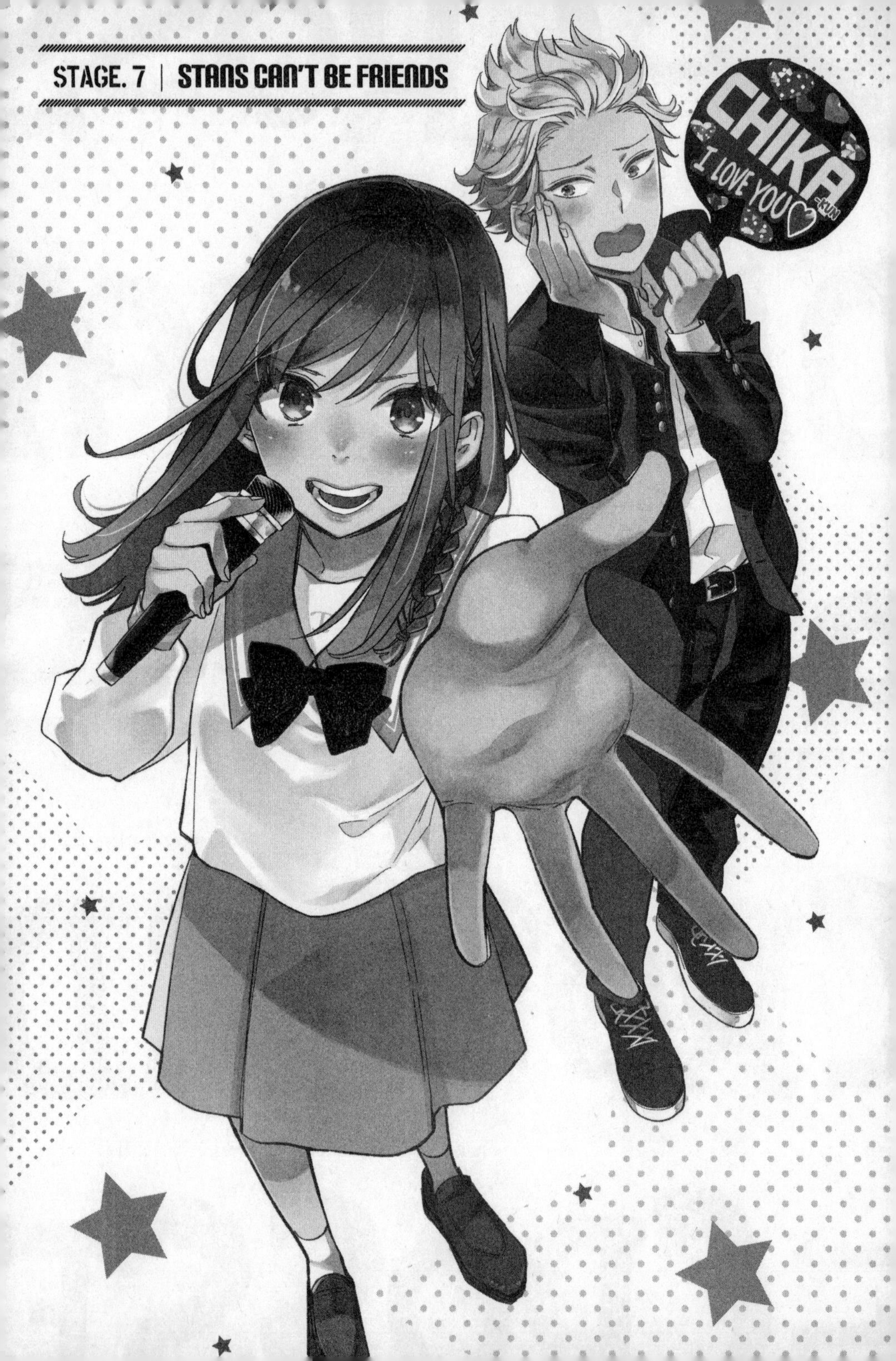
CHIKA-KUN
I LOVE YOU♡

R⇄CROSS

D!! STAI

AR⇄CROS

CROSSED

⇄CROSSE

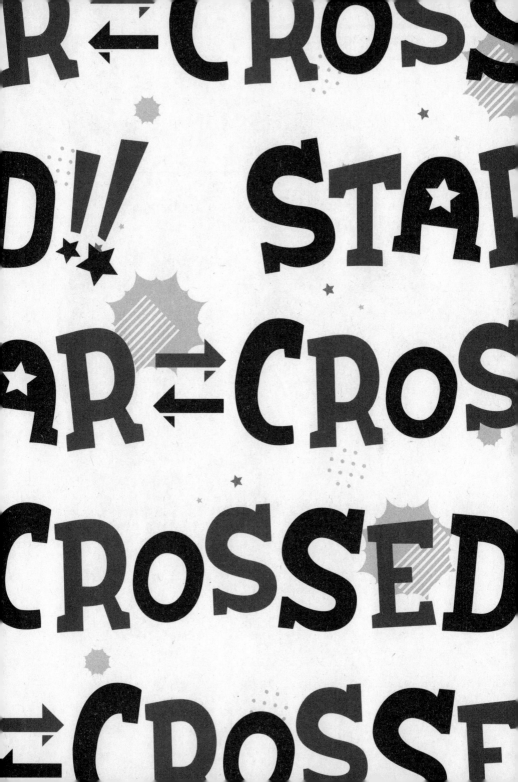

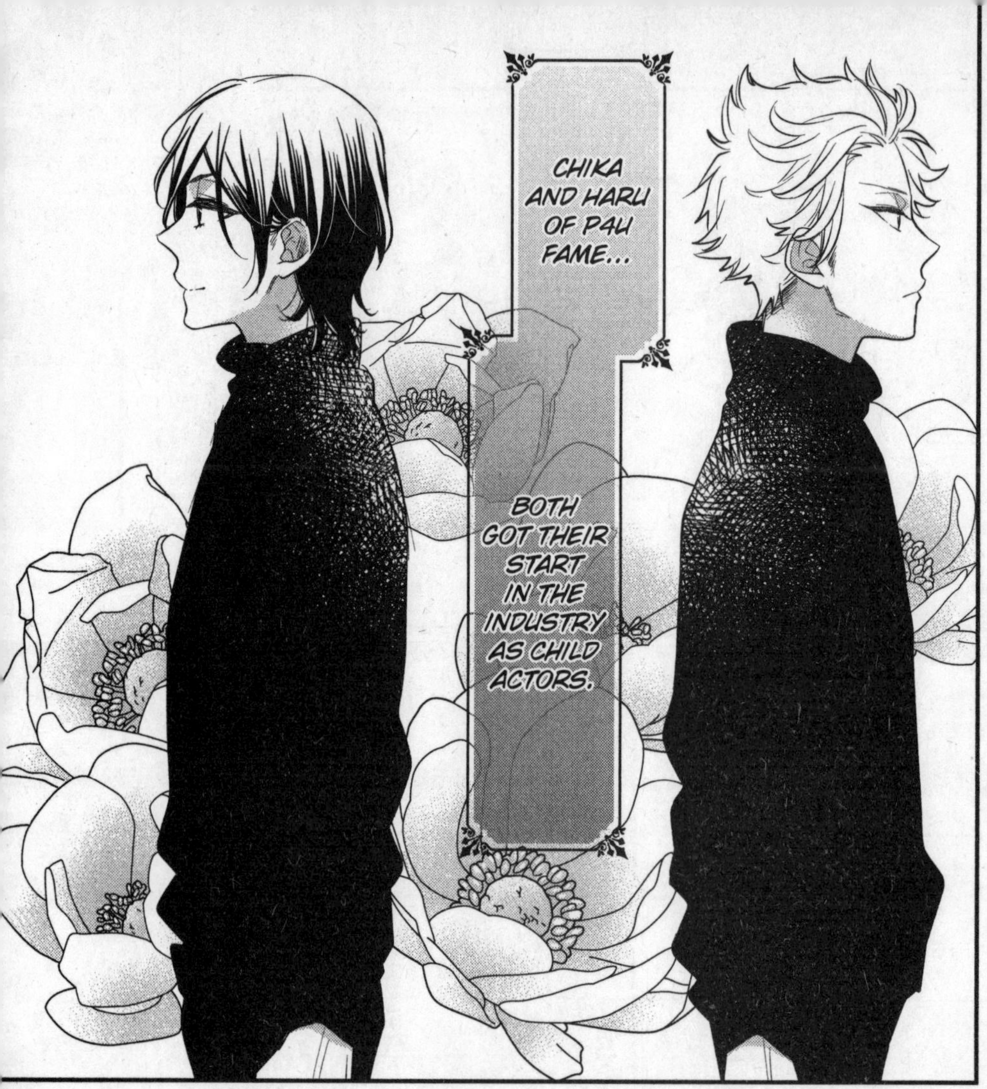
CHIKA AND HARU OF P4U FAME...
BOTH GOT THEIR START IN THE INDUSTRY AS CHILD ACTORS.

STAR⇄CROSSED!!

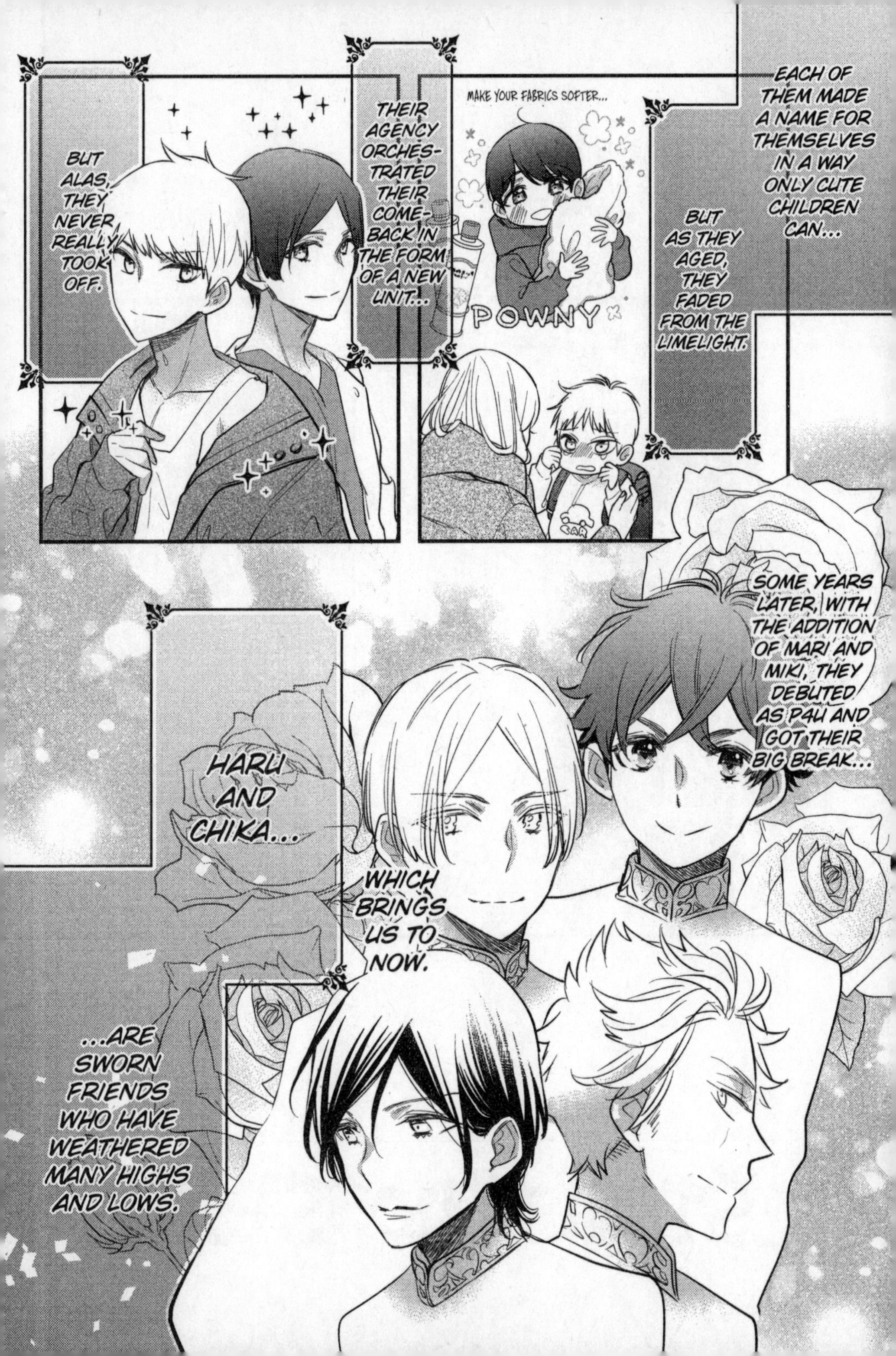
EACH OF THEM MADE A NAME FOR THEMSELVES IN A WAY ONLY CUTE CHILDREN CAN...
BUT AS THEY AGED, THEY FADED FROM THE LIMELIGHT.
MAKE YOUR FABRICS SOFTER...
POWNY
THEIR AGENCY ORCHES-TRATED THEIR COME-BACK IN THE FORM OF A NEW UNIT...
BUT ALAS, THEY NEVER REALLY TOOK OFF.
SOME YEARS LATER, WITH THE ADDITION OF MARI AND MIKI, THEY DEBUTED AS P4U AND GOT THEIR BIG BREAK...
WHICH BRINGS US TO NOW.
HARU AND CHIKA...
...ARE SWORN FRIENDS WHO HAVE WEATHERED MANY HIGHS AND LOWS.

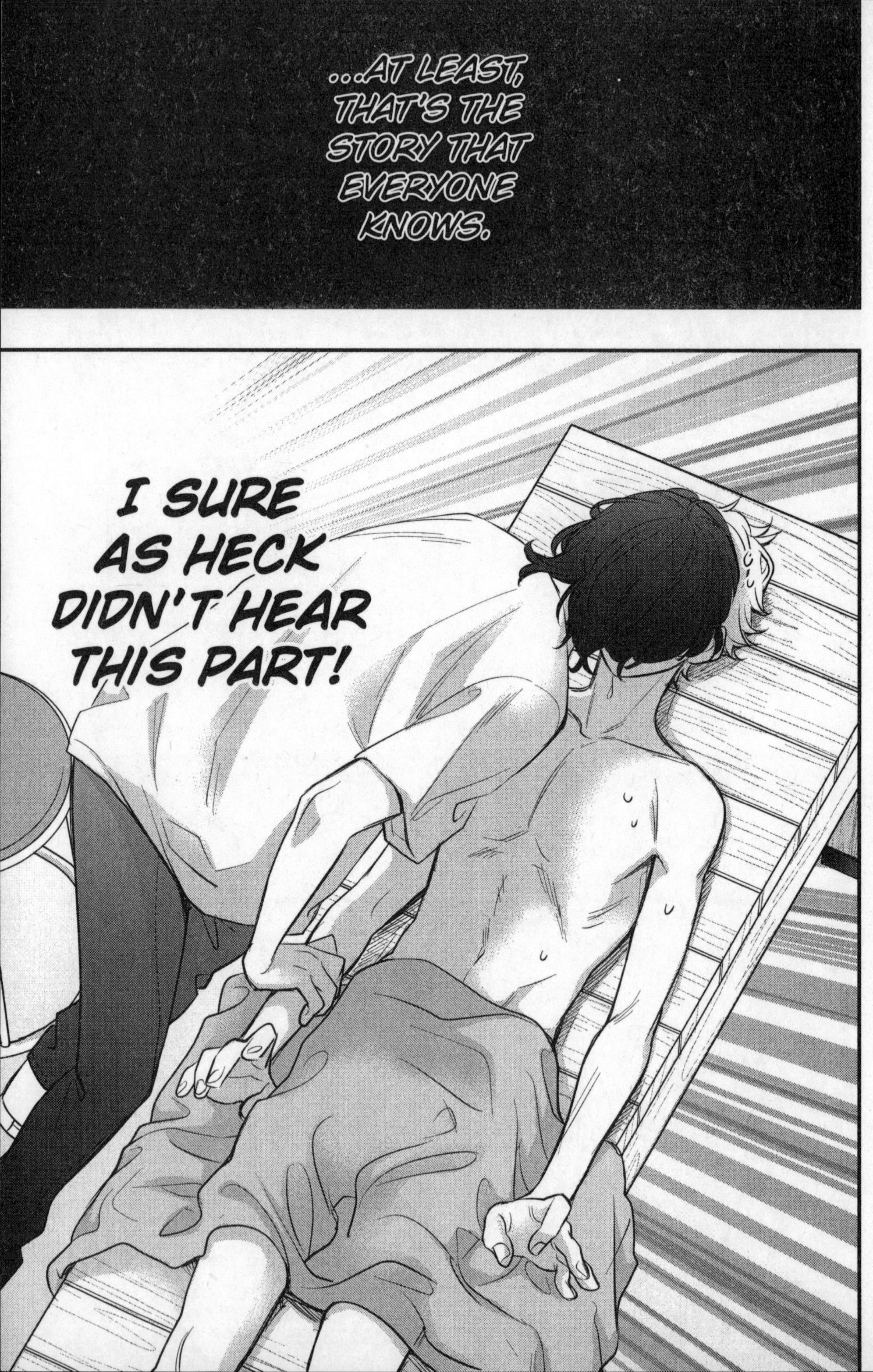
...AT LEAST, THAT'S THE STORY THAT EVERYONE KNOWS.
I SURE AS HECK DIDN'T HEAR THIS PART!

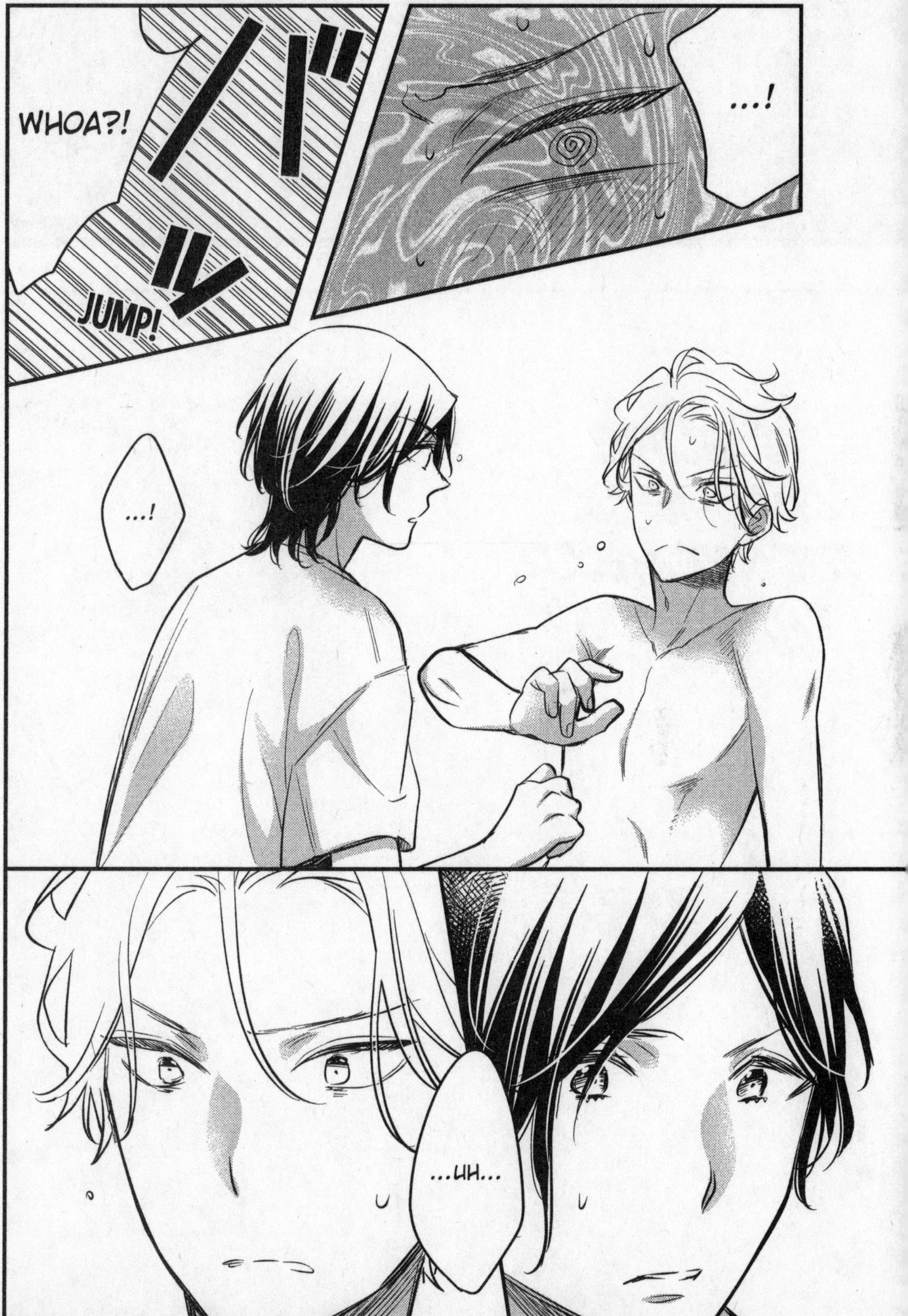
...!
WHOA?!
JUMP!
...!
...UH...

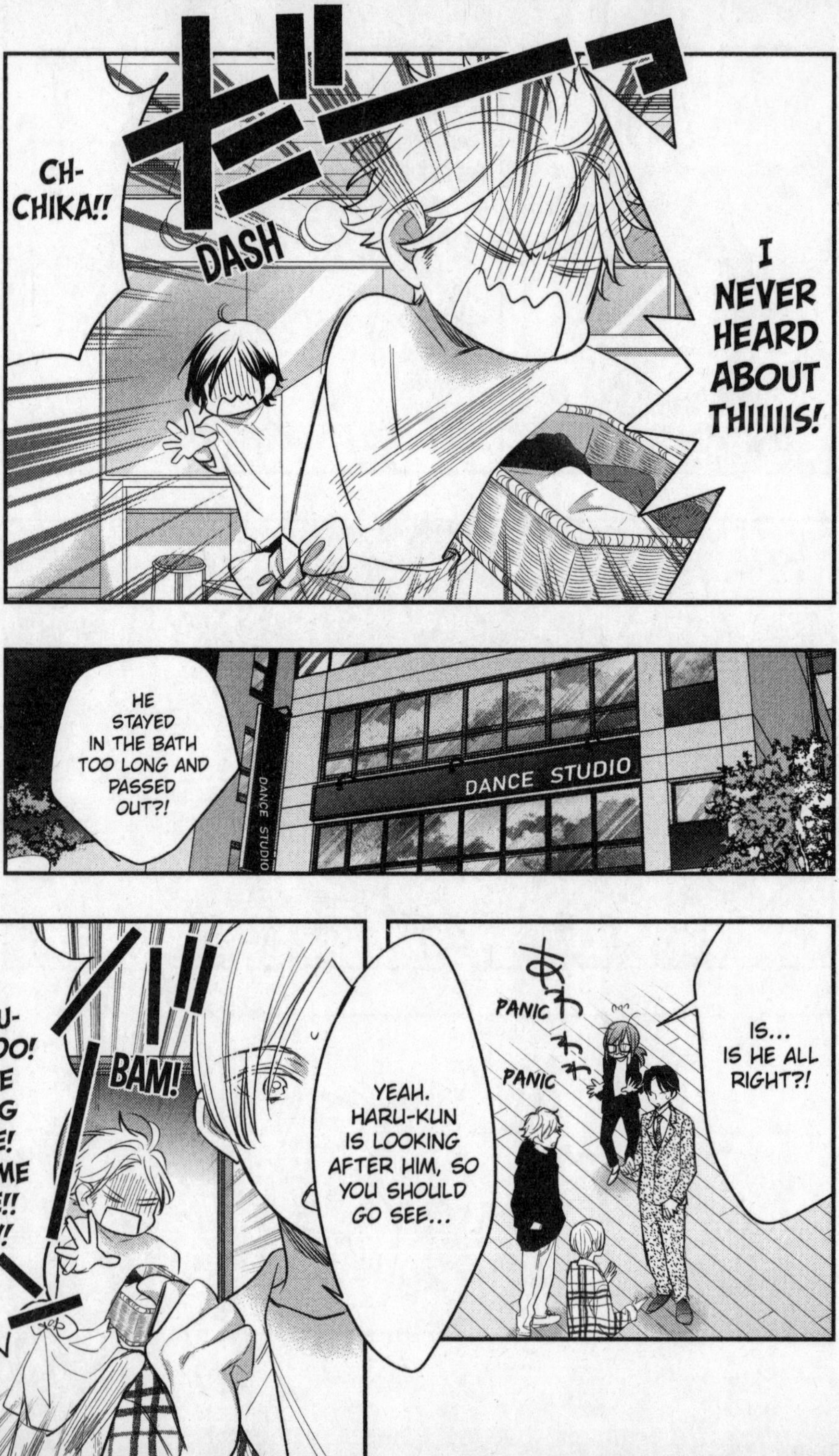
I NEVER HEARD ABOUT THIIIIIS!
DASH
CH-CHIKA!!
HE STAYED IN THE BATH TOO LONG AND PASSED OUT?!
DANCE STUDIO
DANCE STUDIO
IS... IS HE ALL RIGHT?!
あわわ
PANIC
PANIC
YEAH. HARU-KUN IS LOOKING AFTER HIM, SO YOU SHOULD GO SEE...
BAM!
MATSU-MOTOOO! WE'RE GOING HOME! TAKE ME HOME!! NOW!

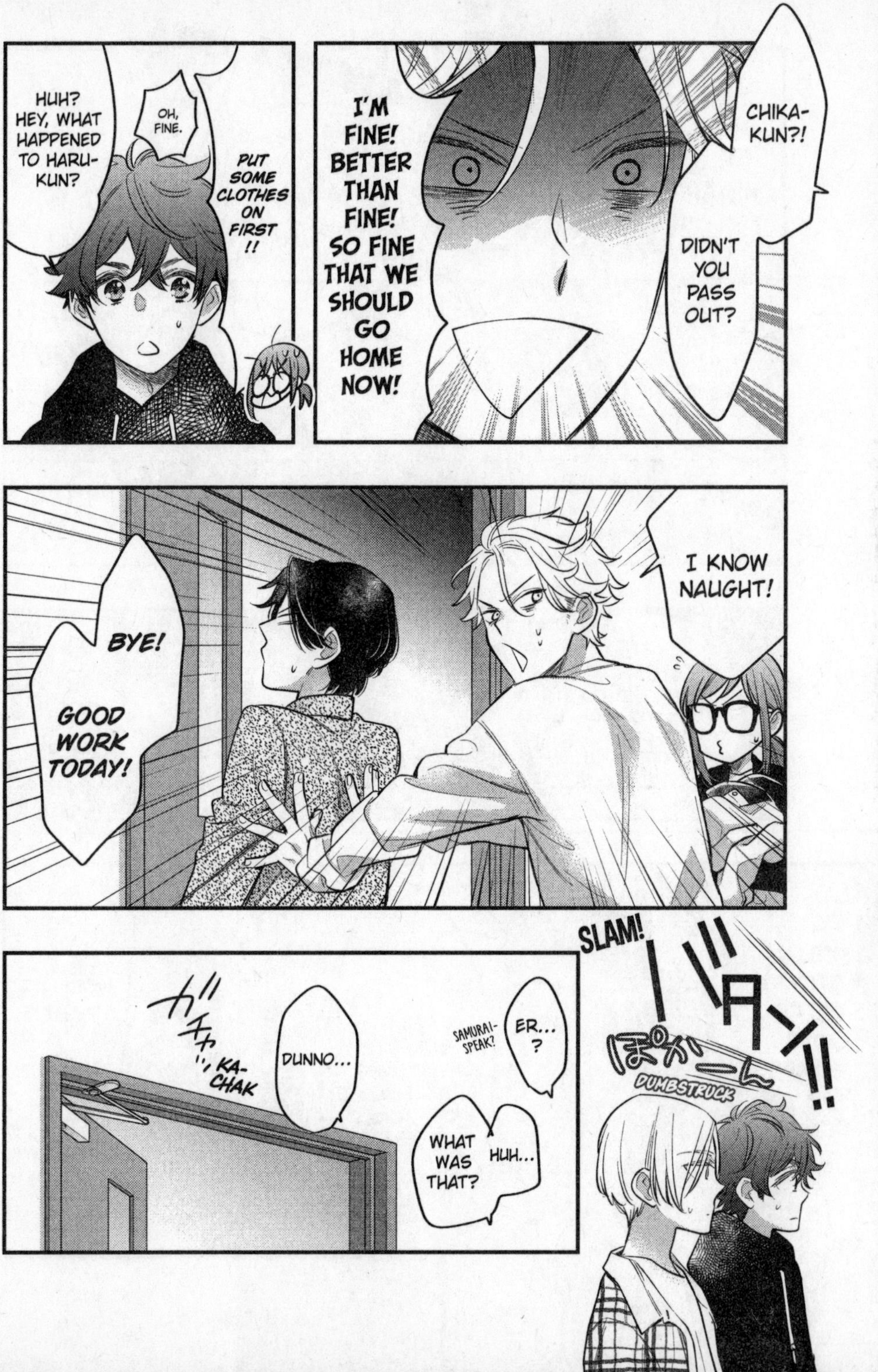
CHIKA-KUN?!
DIDN'T YOU PASS OUT?
I'M FINE! BETTER THAN FINE! SO FINE THAT WE SHOULD GO HOME NOW!
OH, FINE.
PUT SOME CLOTHES ON FIRST !!
HUH? HEY, WHAT HAPPENED TO HARU-KUN?
I KNOW NAUGHT!
BYE!
GOOD WORK TODAY!
SLAM!
バタン!!
ぽか〜ん
DUMBSTRUCK
ER... ?
SAMURAI-SPEAK?
HUH...
WHAT WAS THAT?
DUNNO...
ガチャ
KA-CHAK

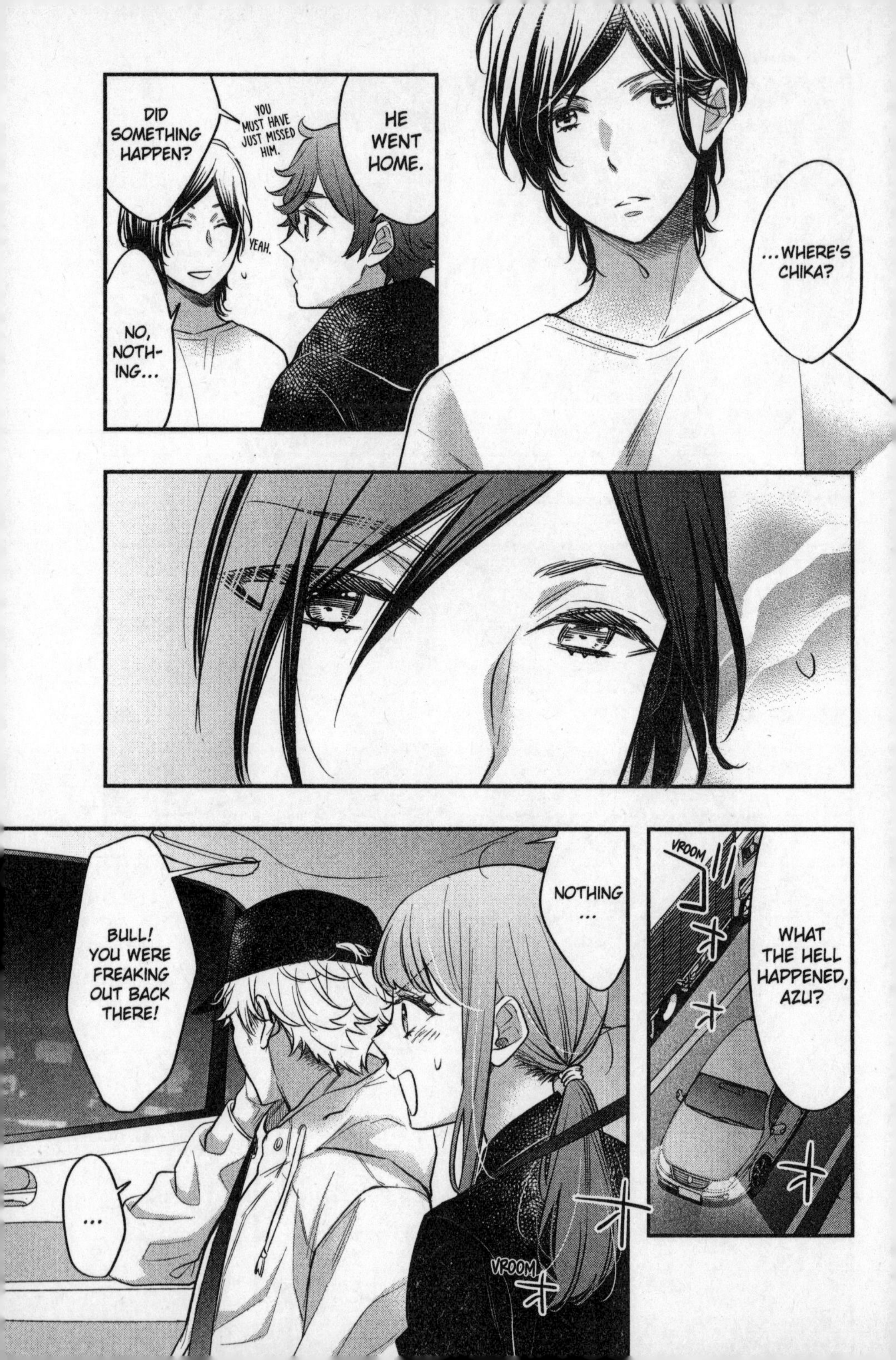
...WHERE'S CHIKA?
HE WENT HOME.
YOU MUST HAVE JUST MISSED HIM.
DID SOMETHING HAPPEN?
YEAH.
NO, NOTHING...
VROOM
WHAT THE HELL HAPPENED, AZU?
NOTHING...
BULL! YOU WERE FREAKING OUT BACK THERE!
...
VROOM

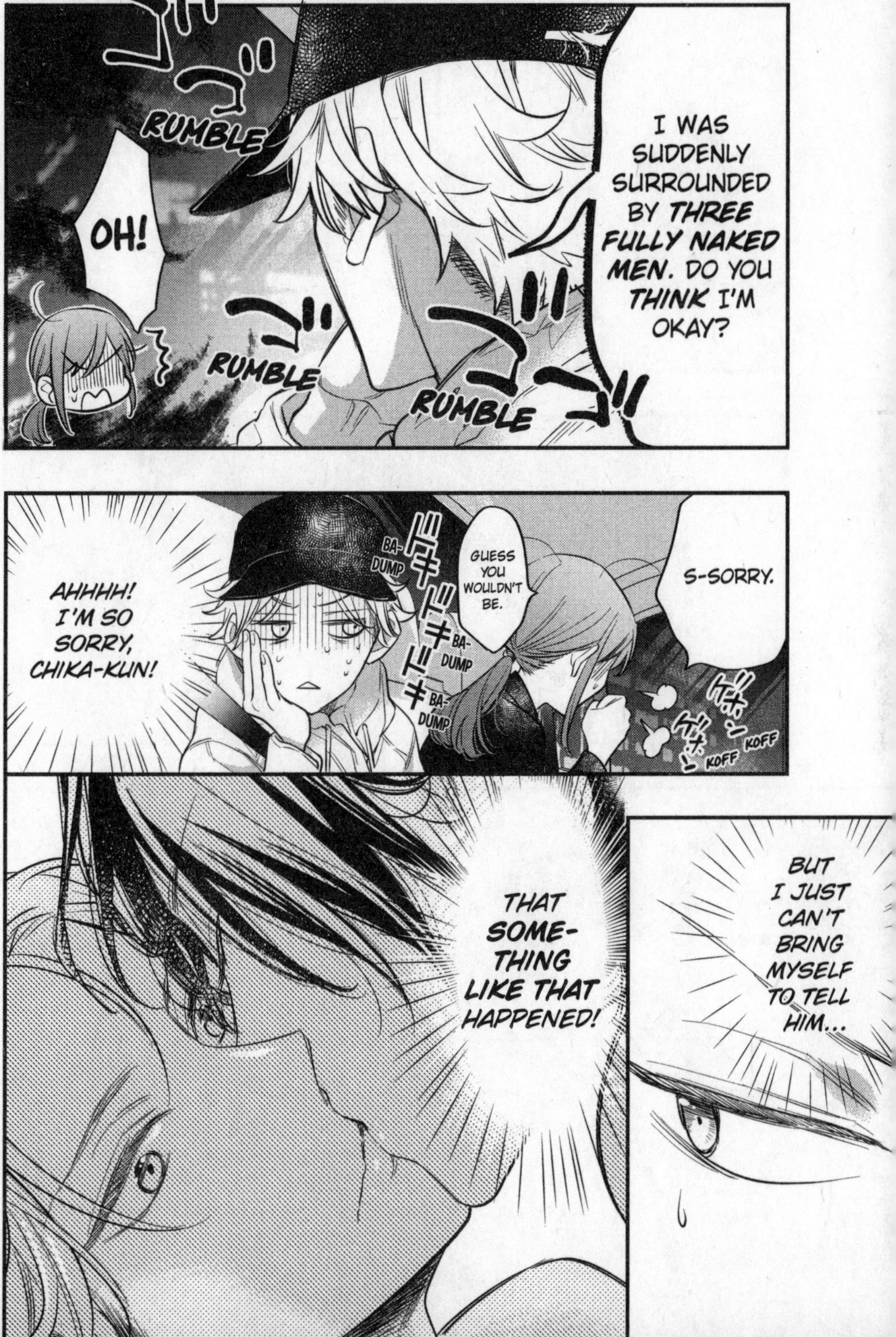
I WAS SUDDENLY SURROUNDED BY THREE FULLY NAKED MEN. DO YOU THINK I'M OKAY?
RUMBLE
OH!
RUMBLE
RUMBLE
S-SORRY.
KOFF
KOFF
GUESS YOU WOULDN'T BE.
BA-DUMP
BA-DUMP
BA-DUMP
AHHHH! I'M SO SORRY, CHIKA-KUN!
BUT I JUST CAN'T BRING MYSELF TO TELL HIM...
THAT SOME-THING LIKE THAT HAPPENED!

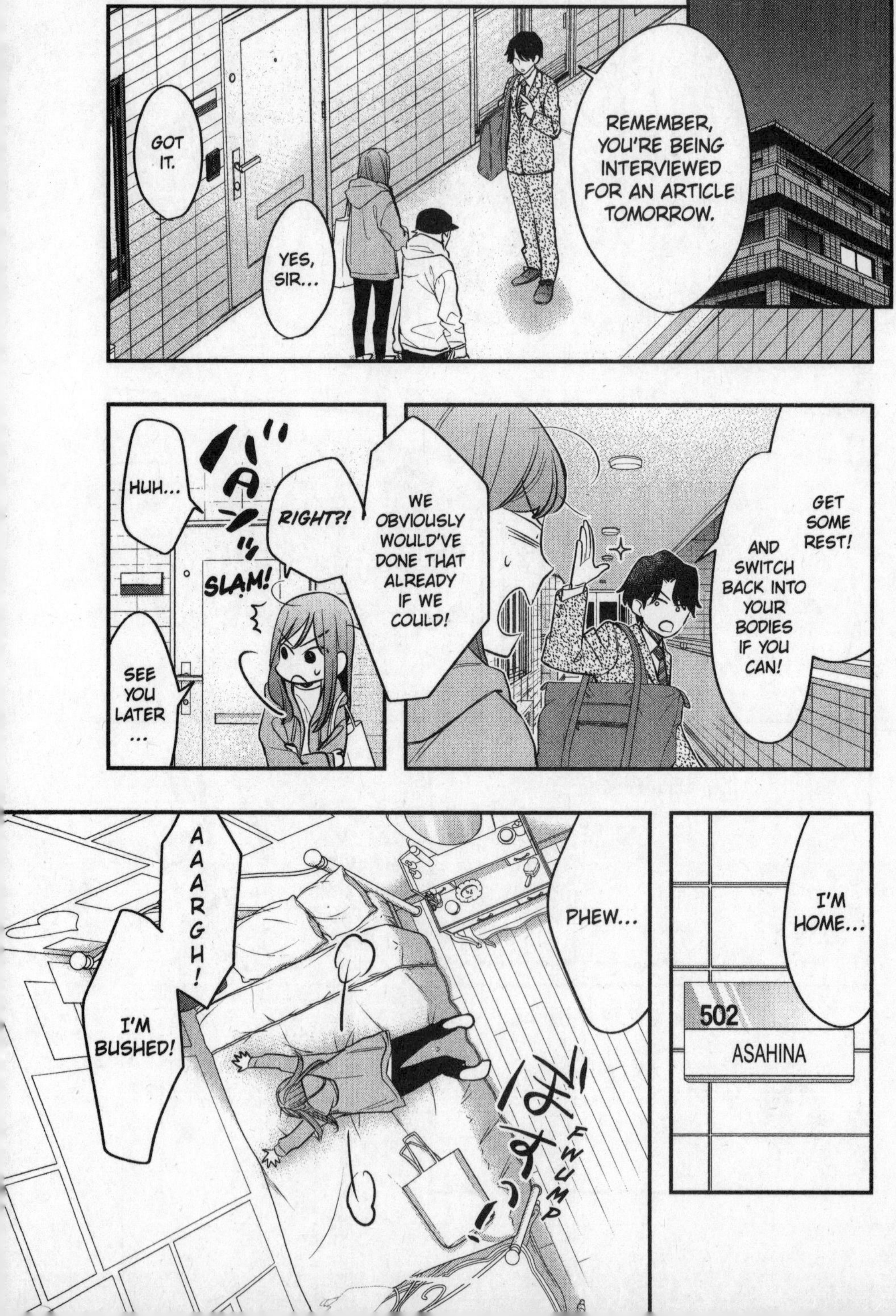
REMEMBER, YOU'RE BEING INTERVIEWED FOR AN ARTICLE TOMORROW.
YES, SIR...
GOT IT.
GET SOME REST!
AND SWITCH BACK INTO YOUR BODIES IF YOU CAN!
WE OBVIOUSLY WOULD'VE DONE THAT ALREADY IF WE COULD!
RIGHT?!
SLAM!
HUH...
SEE YOU LATER...
I'M HOME...
502
ASAHINA
PHEW...
FWUMP
AAAARGH!
I'M BUSHED!

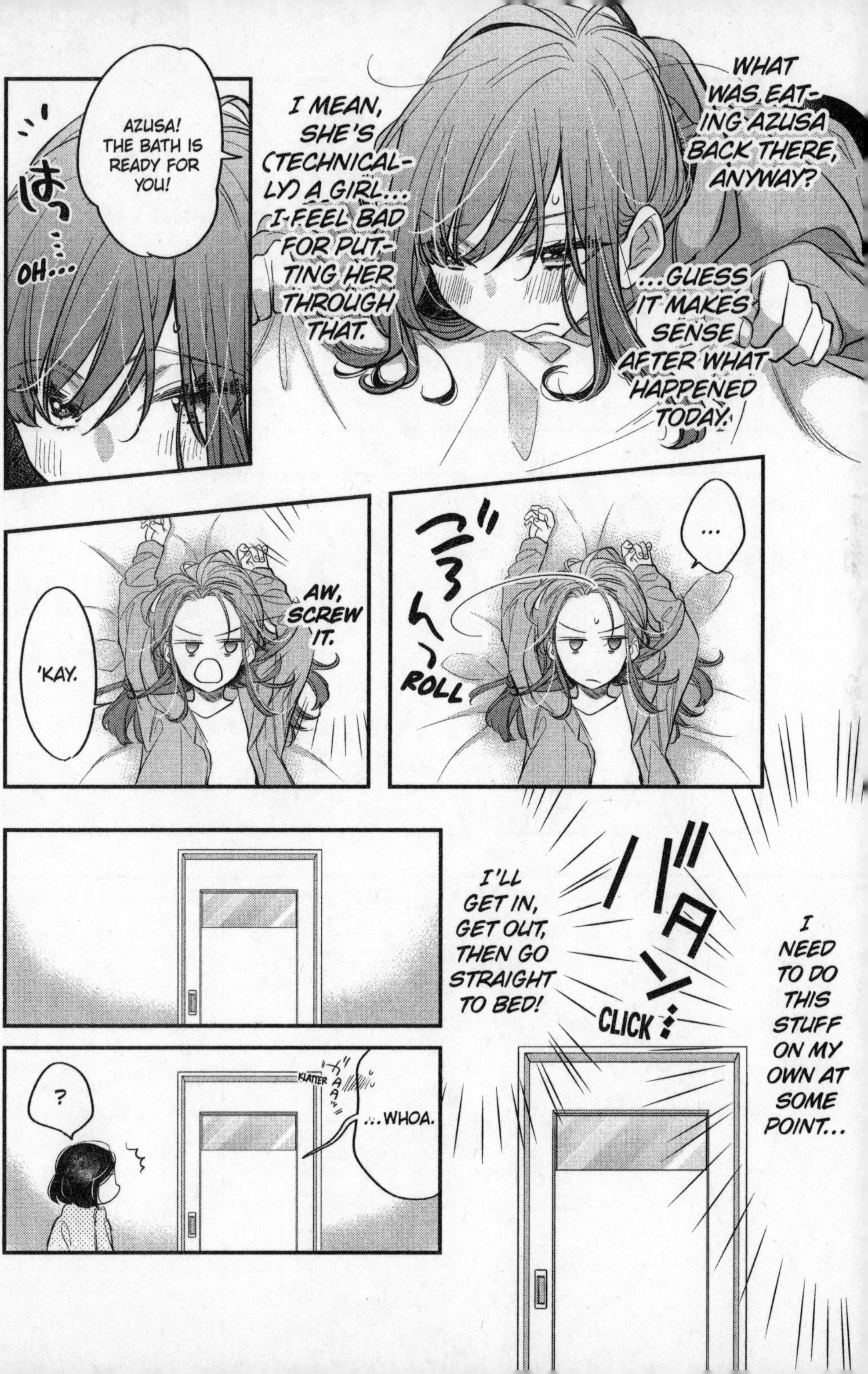
WHAT WAS EATING AZUSA BACK THERE, ANYWAY?
...GUESS IT MAKES SENSE AFTER WHAT HAPPENED TODAY.
I MEAN, SHE'S (TECHNICALLY) A GIRL... I FEEL BAD FOR PUTTING HER THROUGH THAT.
AZUSA! THE BATH IS READY FOR YOU!
はっ
OH...
...
ごろん
ROLL
AW, SCREW IT.
'KAY.
I NEED TO DO THIS STUFF ON MY OWN AT SOME POINT...
バタン
CLICK
I'LL GET IN, GET OUT, THEN GO STRAIGHT TO BED!
KLATTER
...WHOA.
?

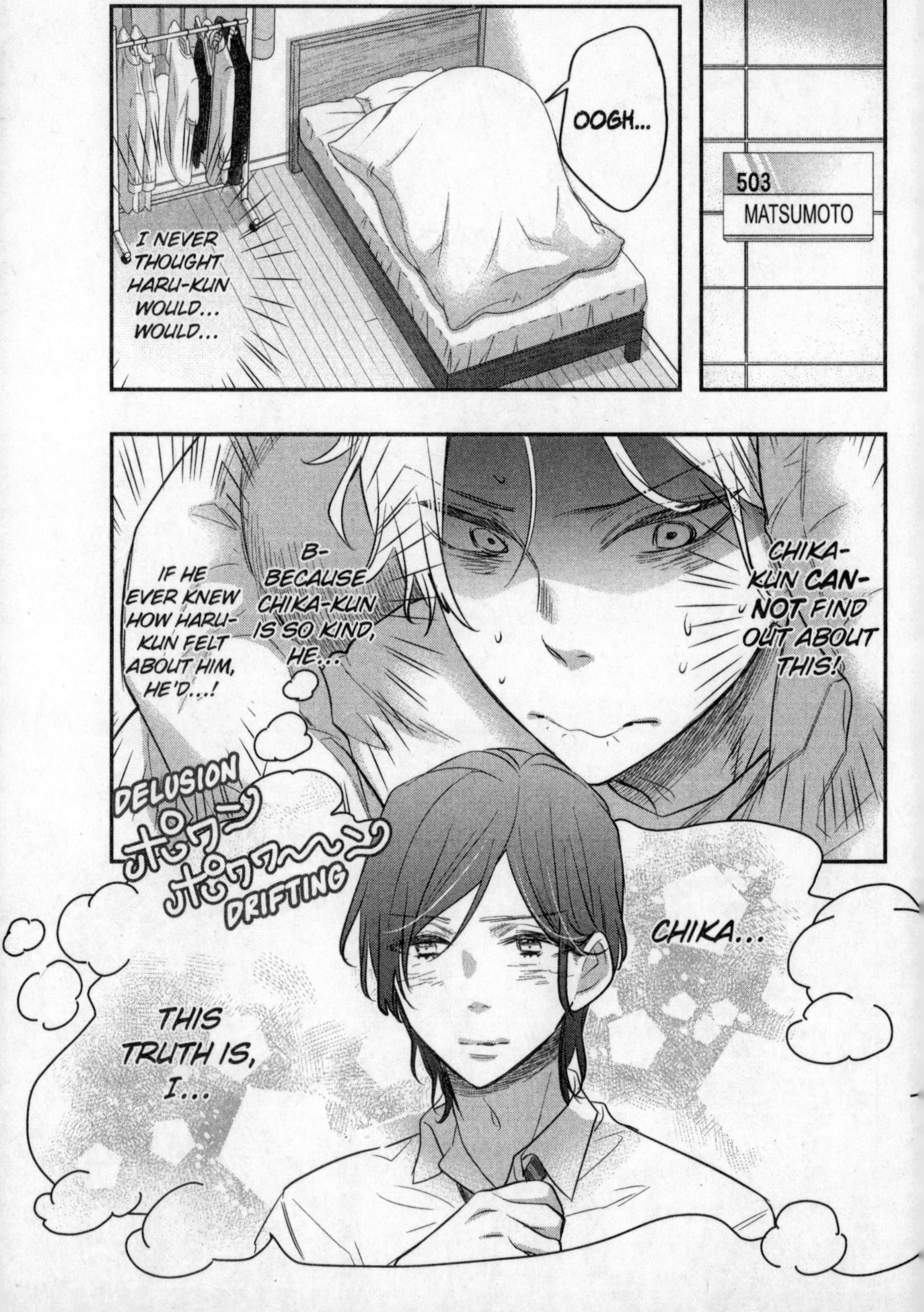
503
MATSUMOTO
OOGH...
I NEVER THOUGHT HARU-KUN WOULD... WOULD...
CHIKA-KUN CANNOT FIND OUT ABOUT THIS!
B-BECAUSE CHIKA-KUN IS SO KIND, HE...
IF HE EVER KNEW HOW HARU-KUN FELT ABOUT HIM, HE'D...!
DELUSION
DRIFTING
CHIKA...
THIS TRUTH IS, I...

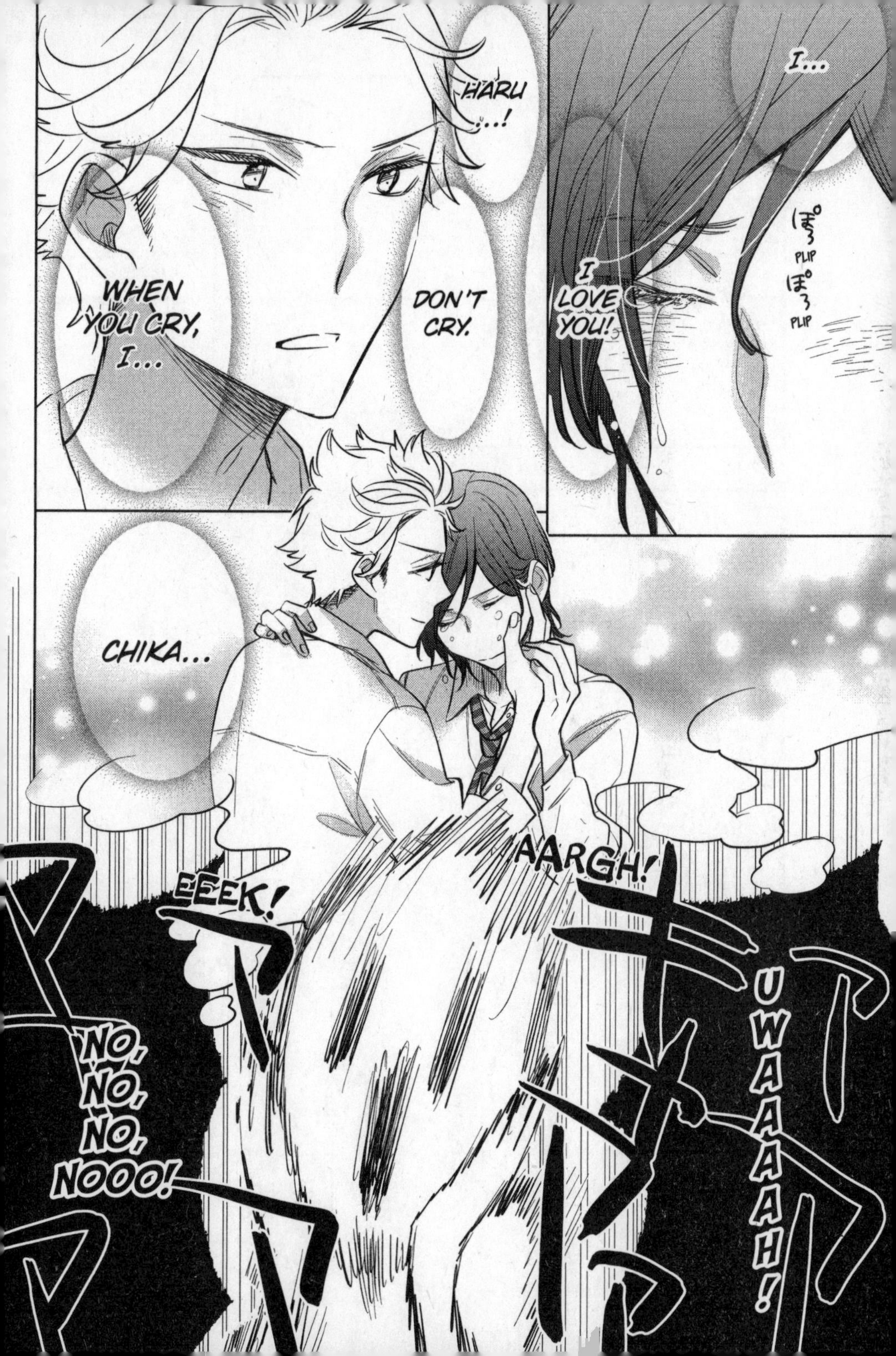
I...
I LOVE YOU!
ぽろ
PLIP
ぽろ
PLIP
HARU ...!
DON'T CRY.
WHEN YOU CRY, I...
CHIKA...
UWAAAAAH!
AARGH!
EEEK!
NO, NO, NO, NOOO!

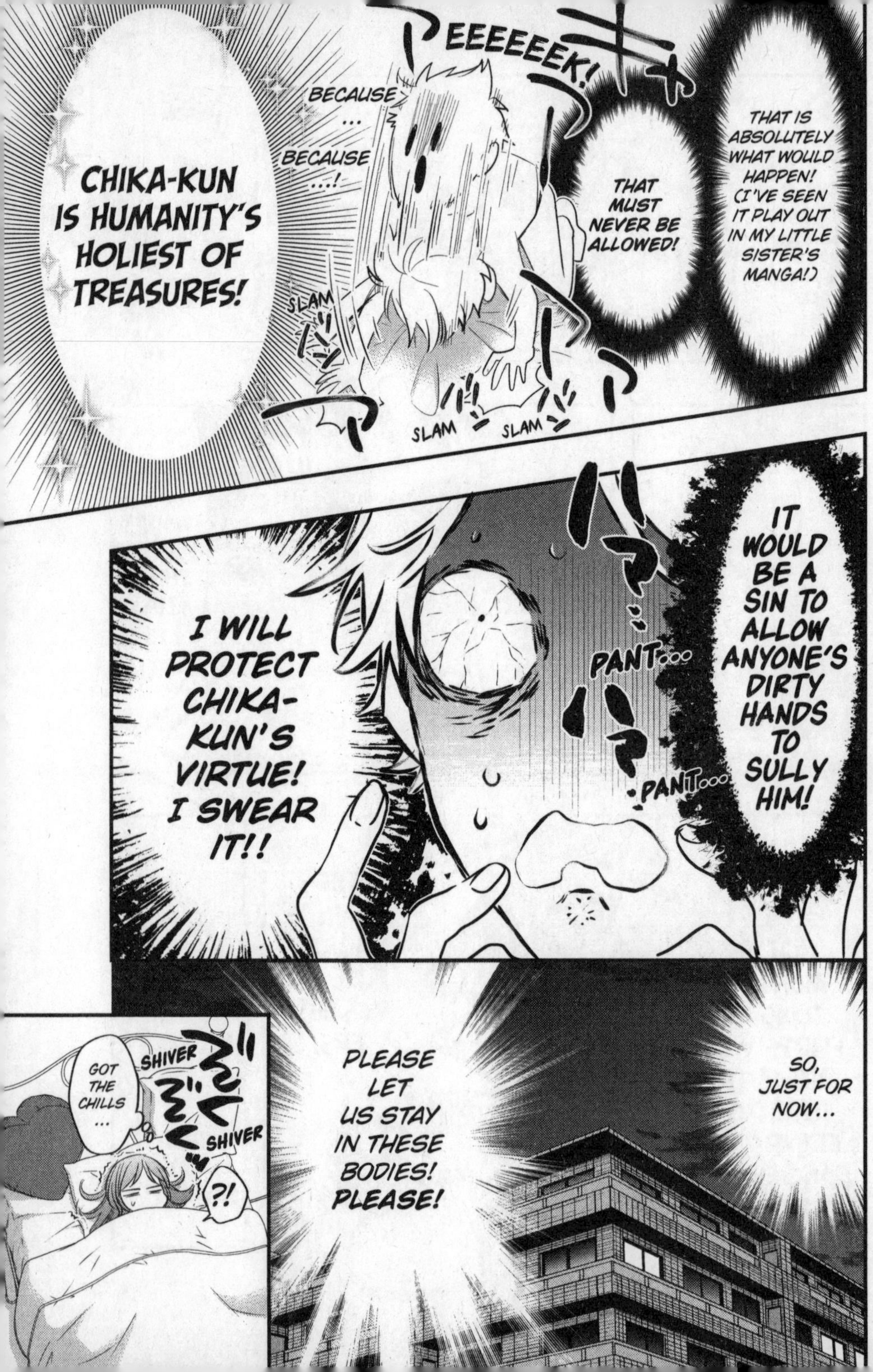
PEEEEEEEK!
THAT IS ABSOLUTELY WHAT WOULD HAPPEN! (I'VE SEEN IT PLAY OUT IN MY LITTLE SISTER'S MANGA!)
THAT MUST NEVER BE ALLOWED!
BECAUSE ... BECAUSE ...!
SLAM
SLAM
SLAM
CHIKA-KUN IS HUMANITY'S HOLIEST OF TREASURES!
IT WOULD BE A SIN TO ALLOW ANYONE'S DIRTY HANDS TO SULLY HIM!
PANT...
PANT...
I WILL PROTECT CHIKA-KUN'S VIRTUE! I SWEAR IT!!
SO, JUST FOR NOW...
PLEASE LET US STAY IN THESE BODIES! PLEASE!
SHIVER
SHIVER
GOT THE CHILLS ...
?!

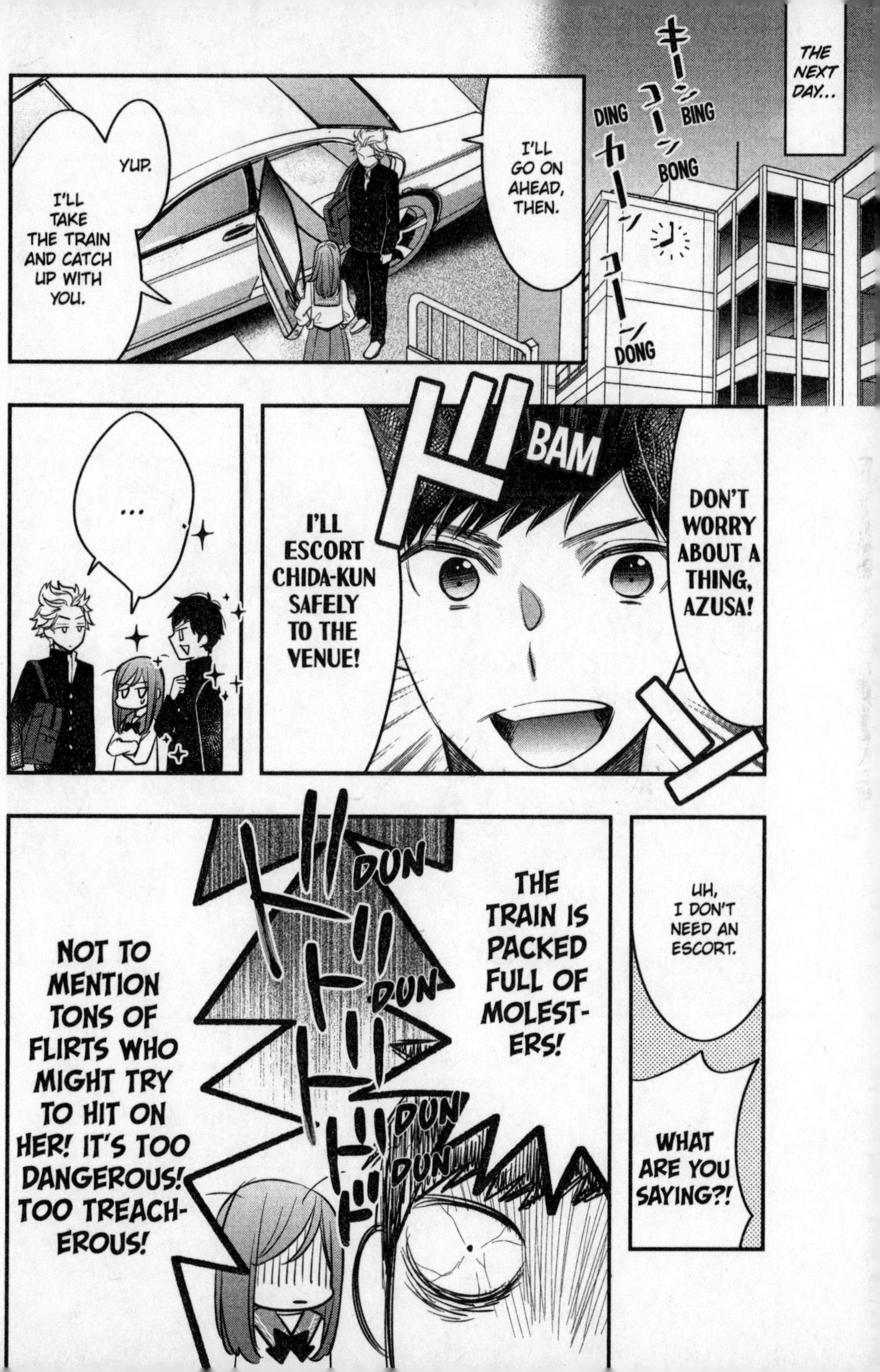
THE NEXT DAY...
DING
BING
BONG
DONG
I'LL GO ON AHEAD, THEN.
YUP.
I'LL TAKE THE TRAIN AND CATCH UP WITH YOU.
BAM
DON'T WORRY ABOUT A THING, AZUSA!
I'LL ESCORT CHIDA-KUN SAFELY TO THE VENUE!
...
UH, I DON'T NEED AN ESCORT.
WHAT ARE YOU SAYING?!
THE TRAIN IS PACKED FULL OF MOLEST-ERS!
NOT TO MENTION TONS OF FLIRTS WHO MIGHT TRY TO HIT ON HER! IT'S TOO DANGEROUS! TOO TREACH-EROUS!
DUN
DUN
DUN
DUN

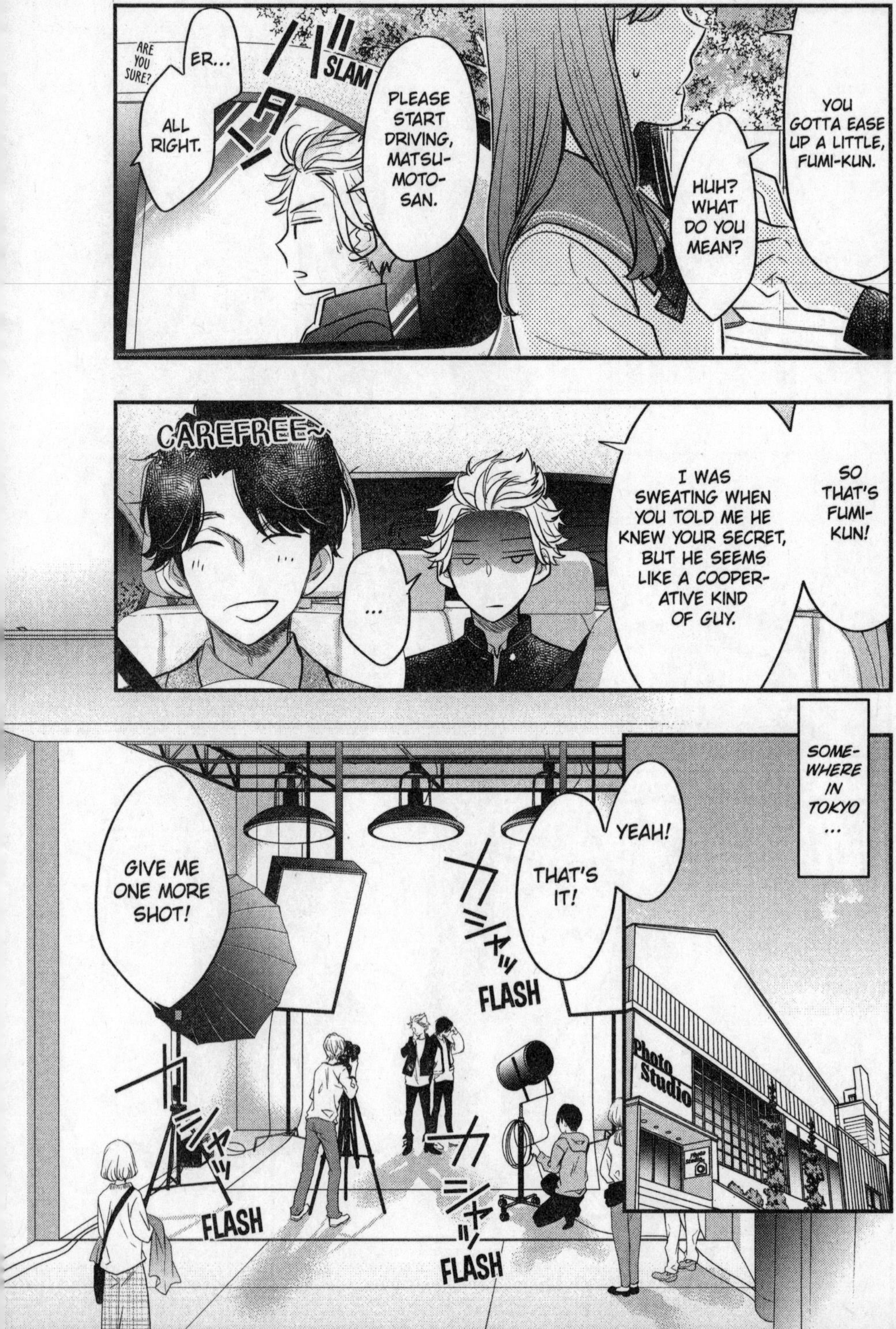
YOU GOTTA EASE UP A LITTLE, FUMI-KUN.
HUH? WHAT DO YOU MEAN?
PLEASE START DRIVING, MATSU-MOTO-SAN.
SLAM
ER...
ALL RIGHT.
ARE YOU SURE?
SO THAT'S FUMI-KUN!
I WAS SWEATING WHEN YOU TOLD ME HE KNEW YOUR SECRET, BUT HE SEEMS LIKE A COOPER-ATIVE KIND OF GUY.
...
CAREFREE~
SOME-WHERE IN TOKYO ...
Photo Studio
YEAH!
THAT'S IT!
FLASH
GIVE ME ONE MORE SHOT!
FLASH
FLASH

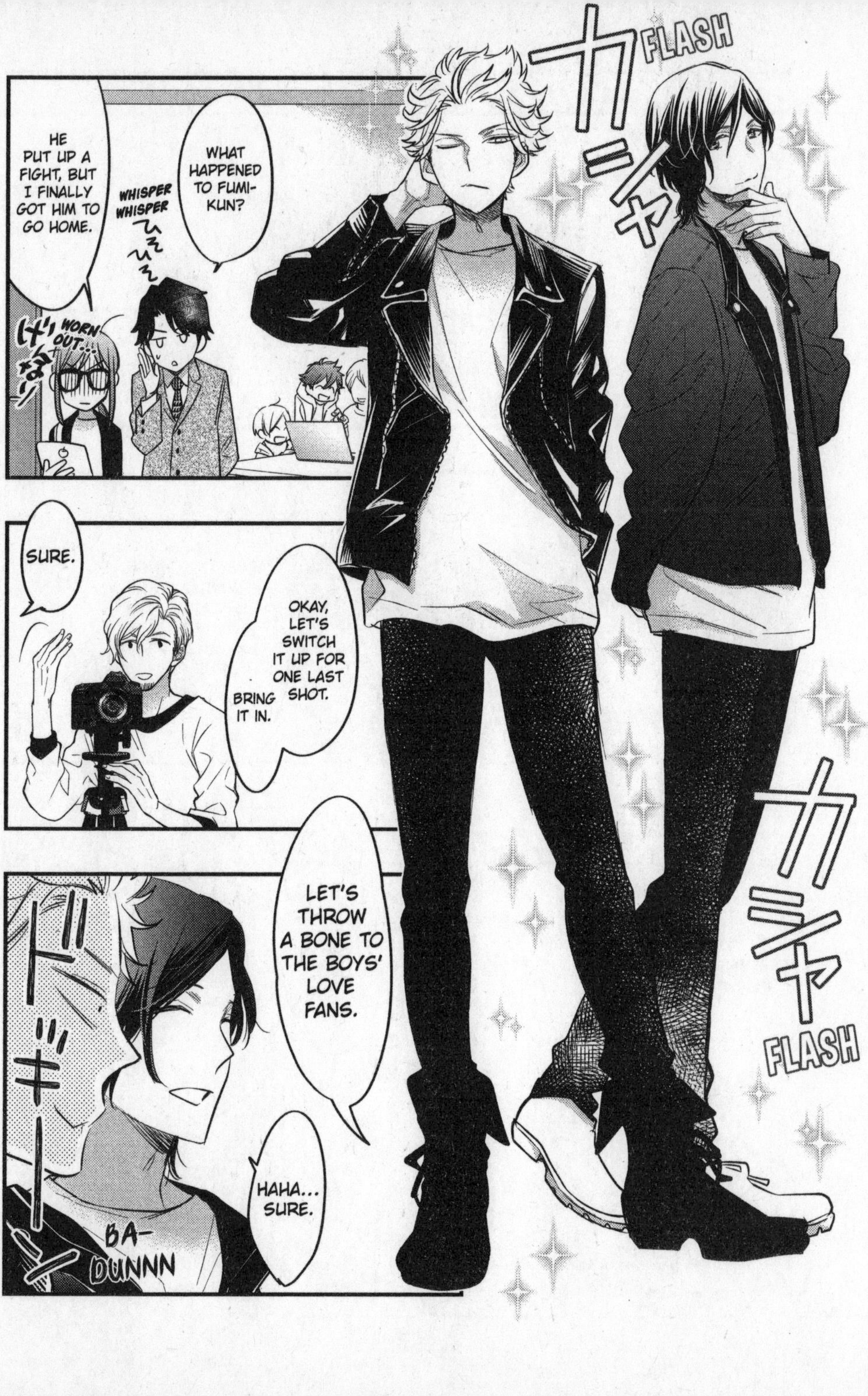
FLASH
FLASH
WHAT HAPPENED TO FUMI-KUN?
WHISPER WHISPER
HE PUT UP A FIGHT, BUT I FINALLY GOT HIM TO GO HOME.
WORN OUT...
OKAY, LET'S SWITCH IT UP FOR ONE LAST SHOT.
BRING IT IN.
SURE.
LET'S THROW A BONE TO THE BOYS' LOVE FANS.
HAHA... SURE.
BA-DUNNN

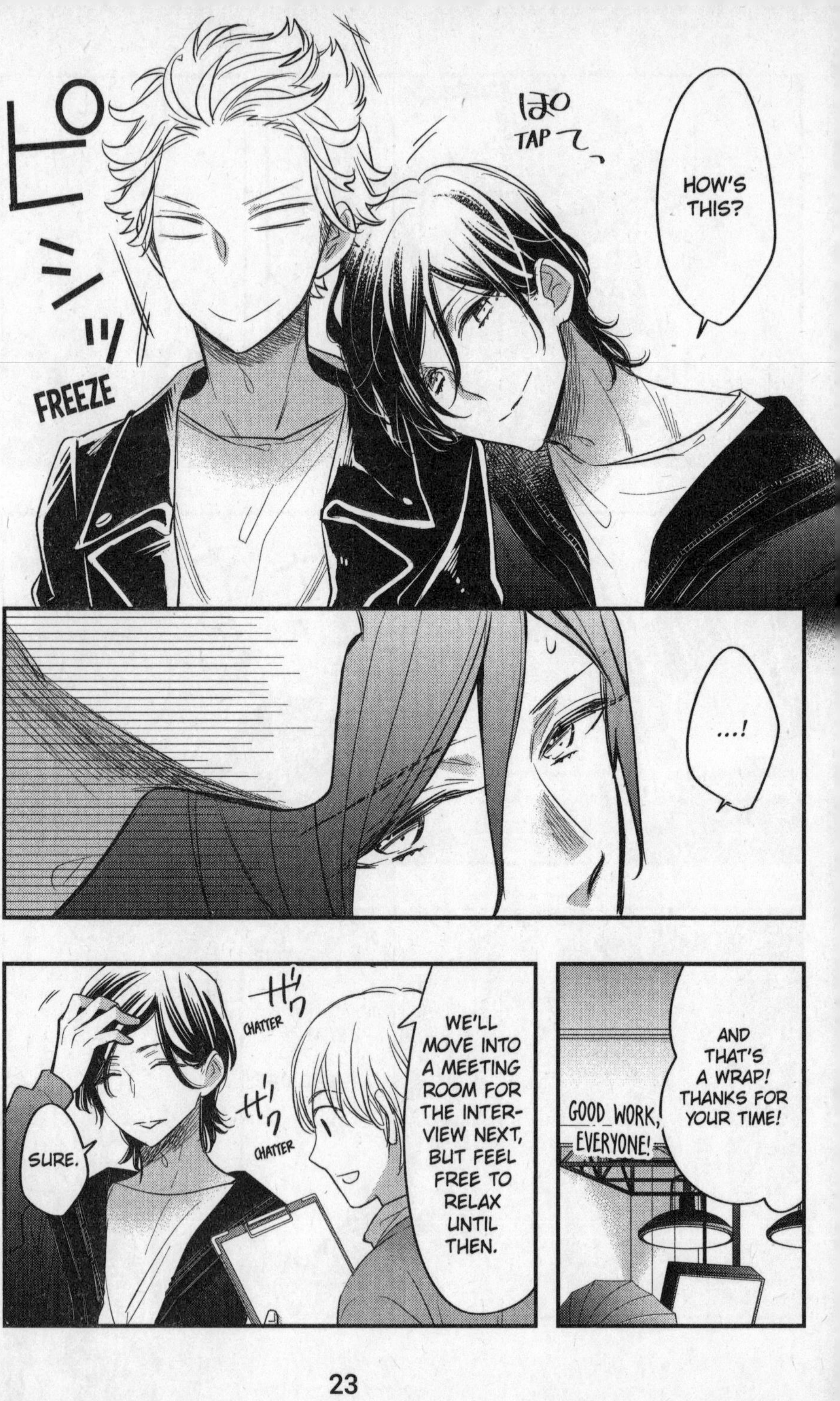

HOW'S THIS?
ぽ TAP て
ピシッ
FREEZE
...!
AND THAT'S A WRAP! THANKS FOR YOUR TIME!
GOOD WORK, EVERYONE!
WE'LL MOVE INTO A MEETING ROOM FOR THE INTER-VIEW NEXT, BUT FEEL FREE TO RELAX UNTIL THEN.
ザワ CHATTER
ザワ CHATTER
SURE.

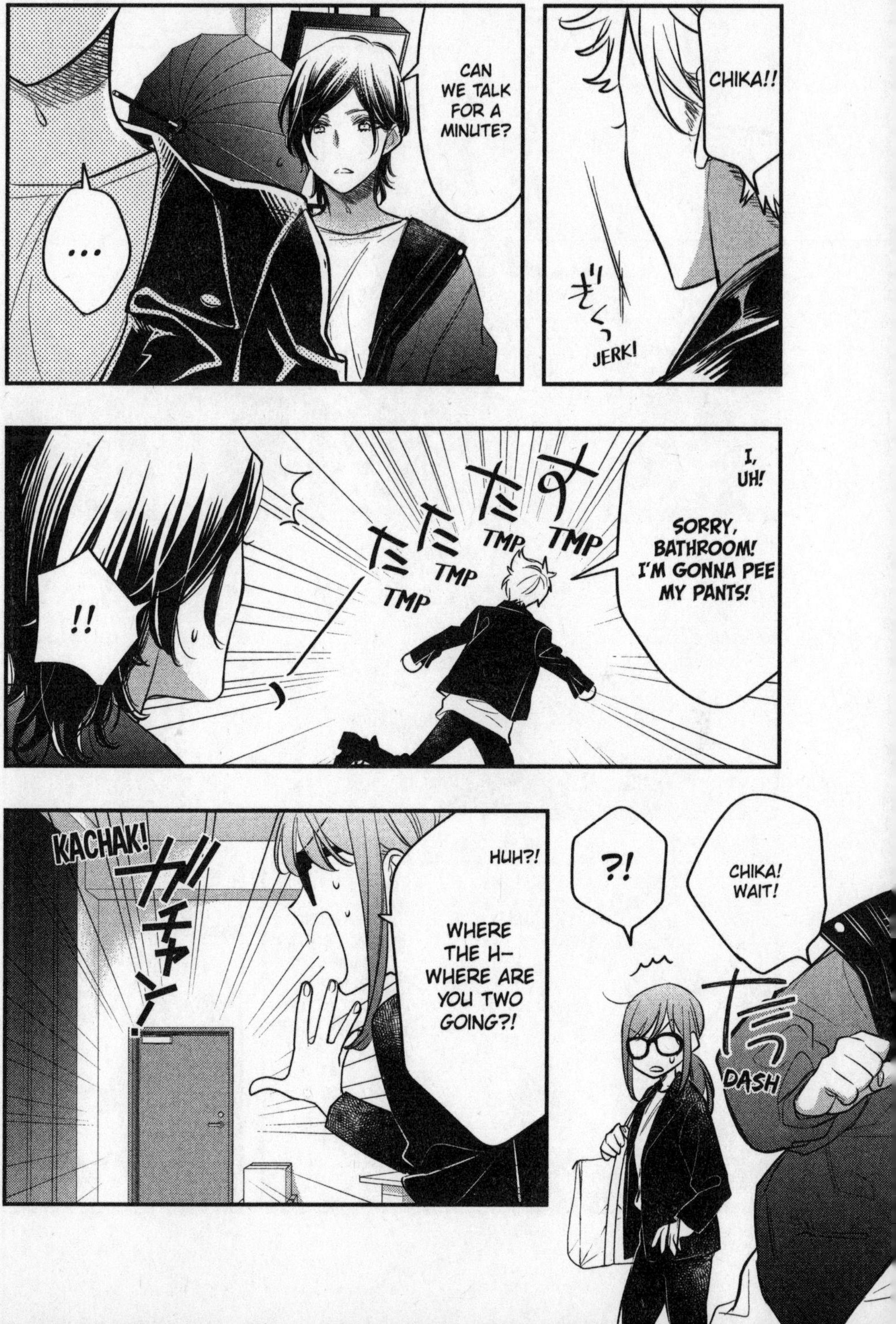
CHIKA!!
ぎくっ
JERK!
CAN WE TALK FOR A MINUTE?
...
I, UH!
SORRY, BATHROOM! I'M GONNA PEE MY PANTS!
TMP TMP
TMP
TMP
!!
CHIKA! WAIT!
?!
たっ
DASH
HUH?!
WHERE THE H— WHERE ARE YOU TWO GOING?!
KACHAK!
ガチャン

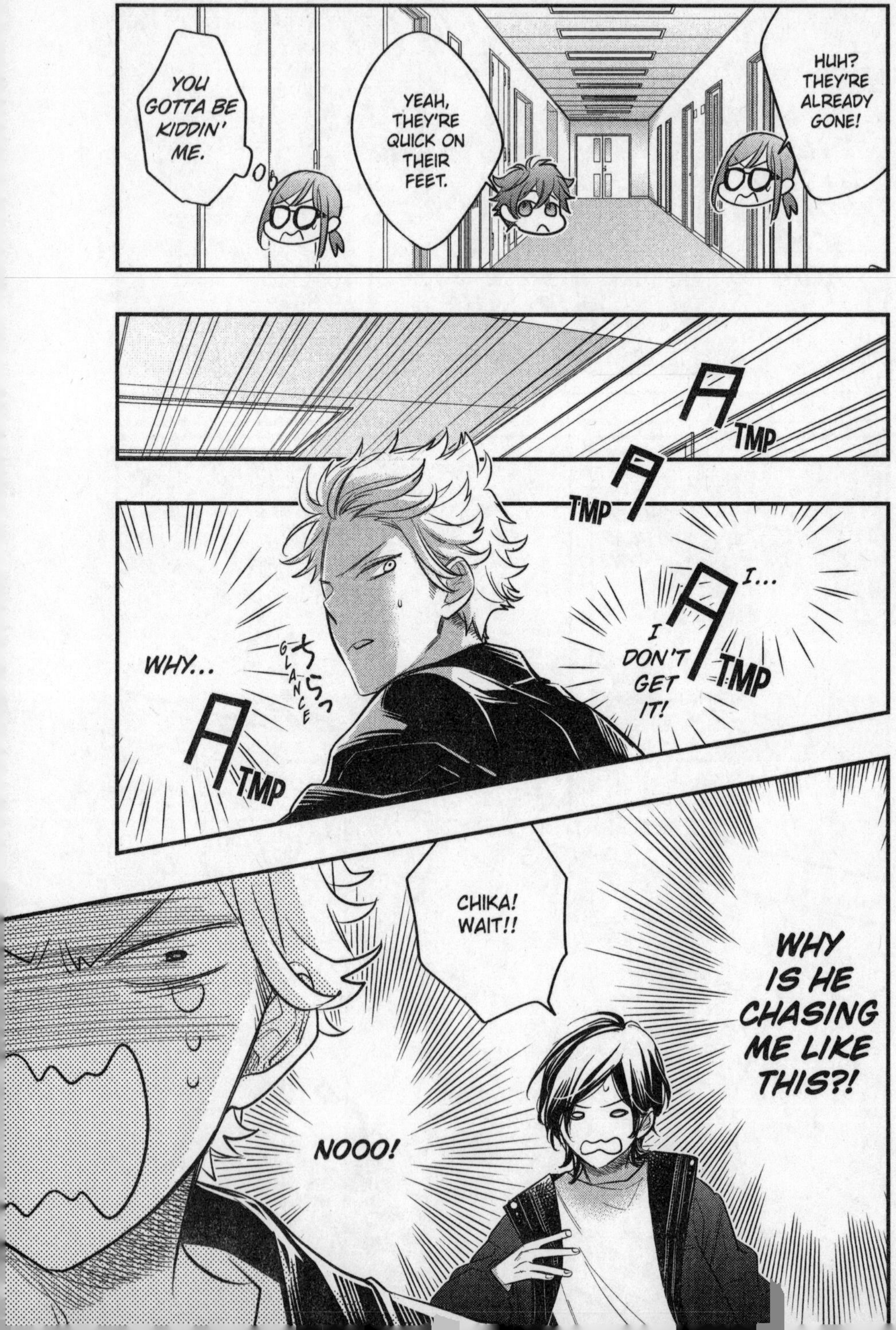
HUH? THEY'RE ALREADY GONE!
YEAH, THEY'RE QUICK ON THEIR FEET.
YOU GOTTA BE KIDDIN' ME.
TMP
TMP
I...
I DON'T GET IT!
TMP
GLANCE
WHY...
TMP
WHY IS HE CHASING ME LIKE THIS?!
CHIKA! WAIT!!
NOOO!

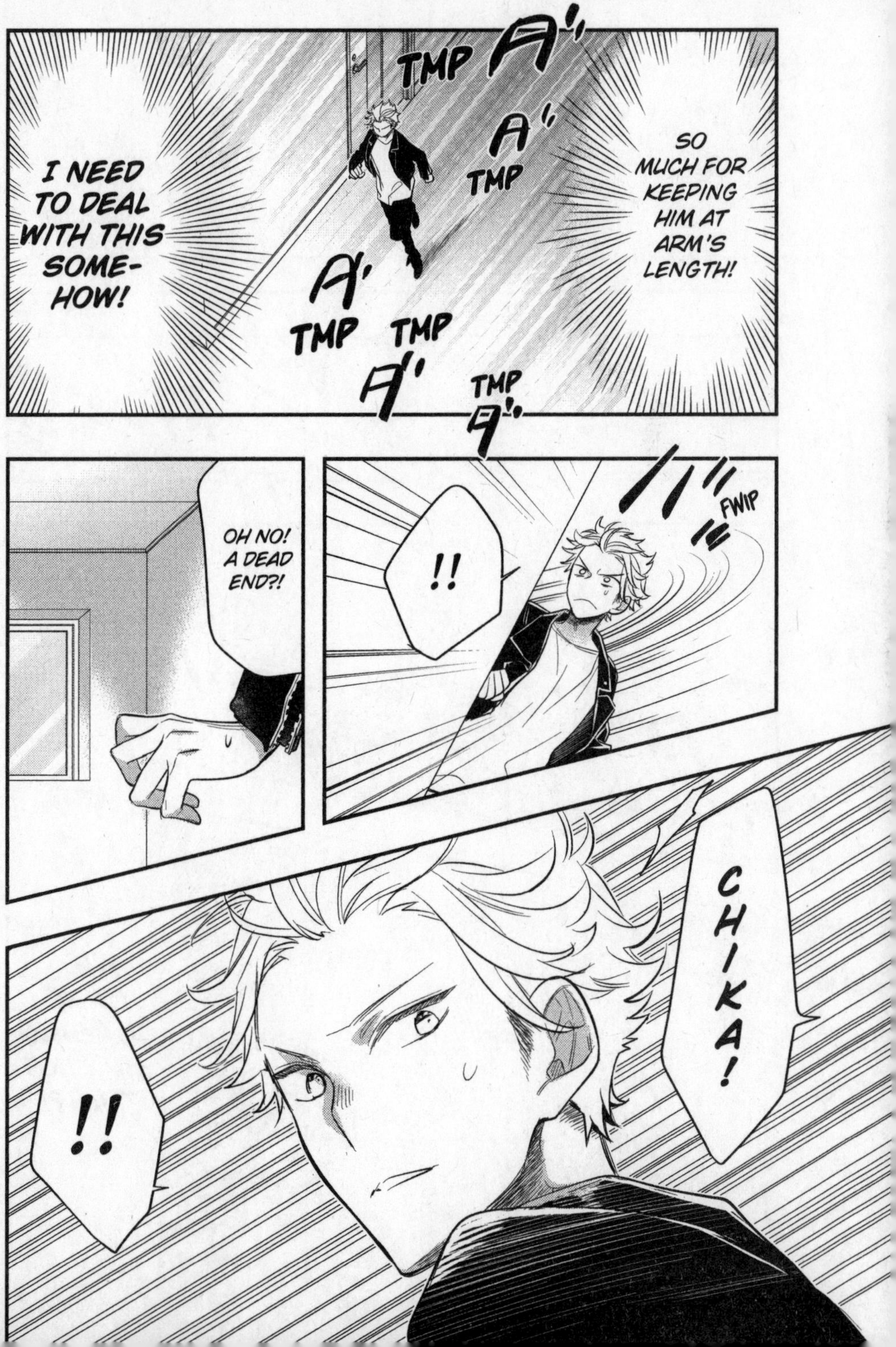
SO MUCH FOR KEEPING HIM AT ARM'S LENGTH!
TMP
TMP
TMP
TMP
TMP
I NEED TO DEAL WITH THIS SOME-HOW!
FWIP
!!
OH NO! A DEAD END?!
CHIKA!
!!

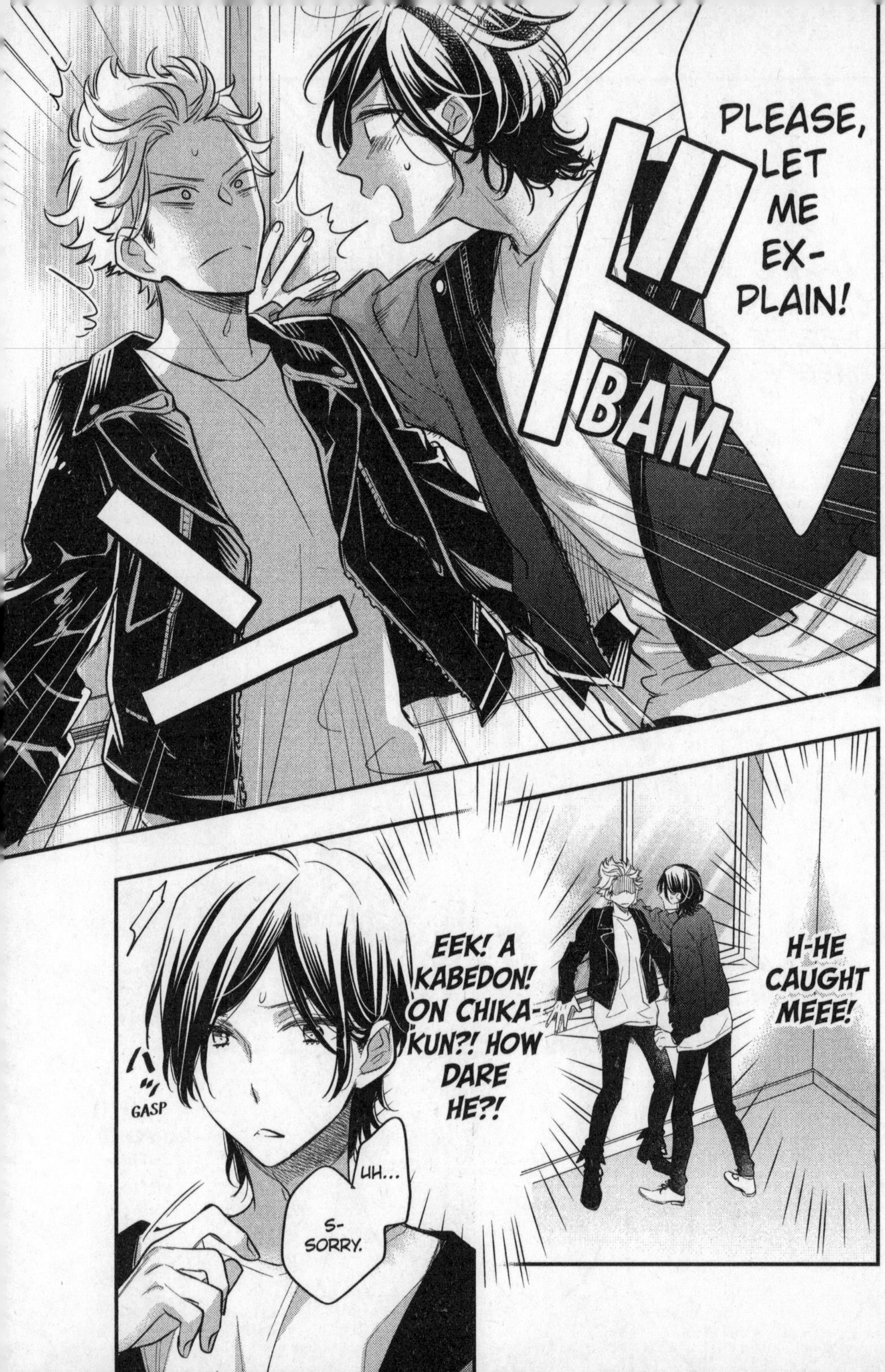
PLEASE, LET ME EX- PLAIN!
BAM
H-HE CAUGHT MEEE!
EEK! A KABEDON! ON CHIKA-KUN?! HOW DARE HE?!
GASP
UH...
S- SORRY.

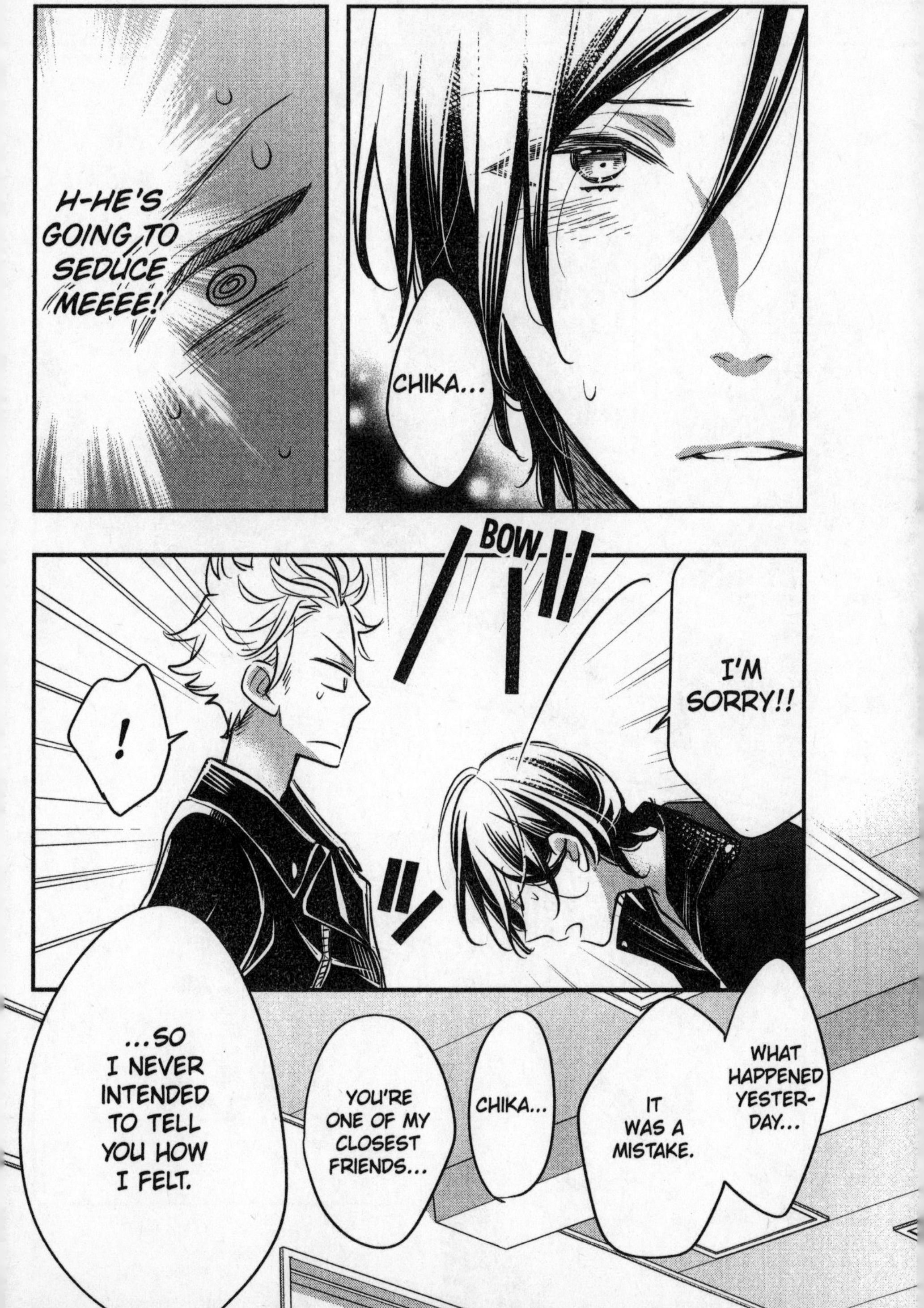
CHIKA...
H-HE'S GOING TO SEDUCE MEEEE!
I'M SORRY!!
BOW
!
WHAT HAPPENED YESTER-DAY...
IT WAS A MISTAKE.
CHIKA...
YOU'RE ONE OF MY CLOSEST FRIENDS...
...SO I NEVER INTENDED TO TELL YOU HOW I FELT.

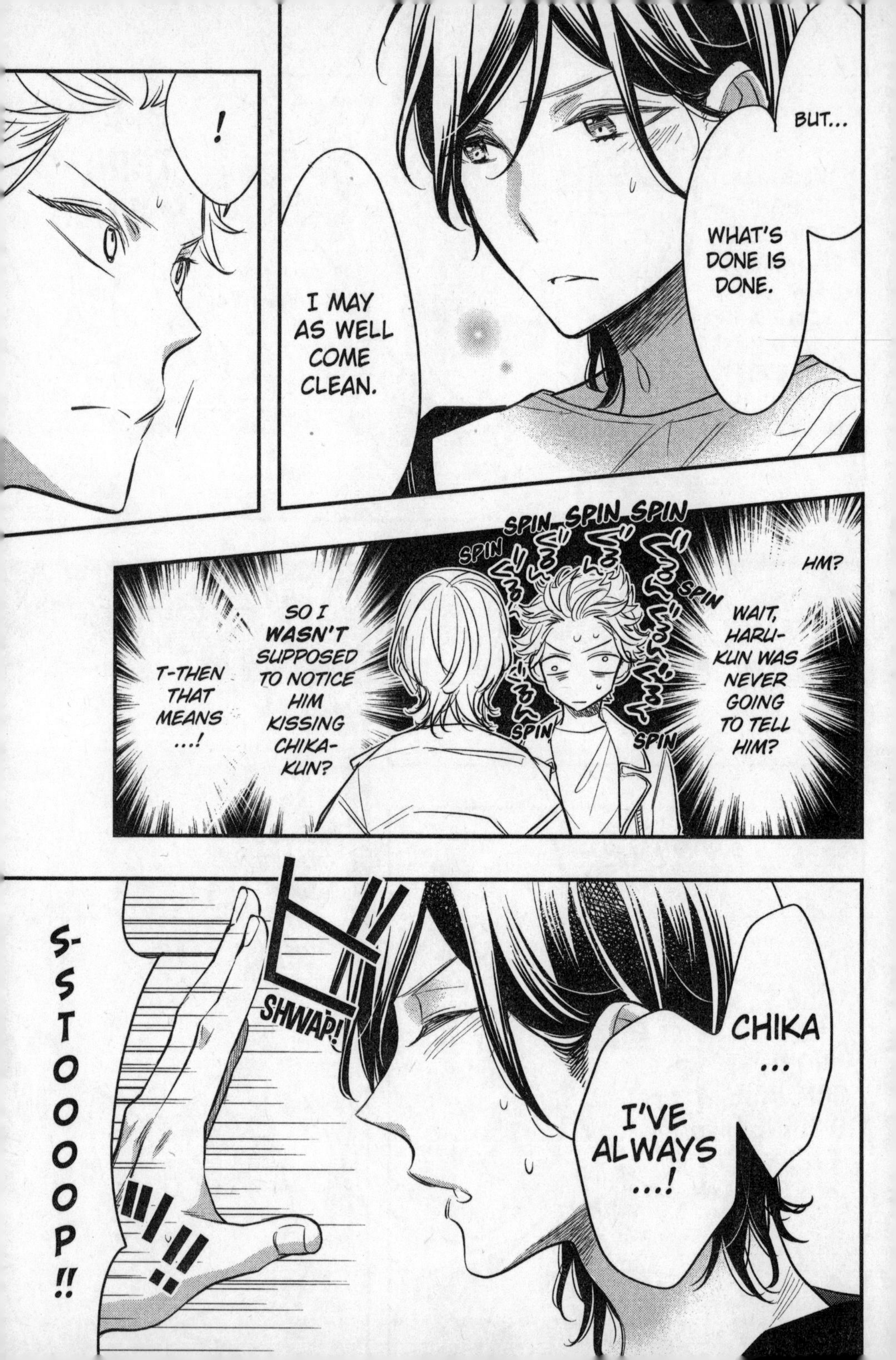
BUT...
WHAT'S DONE IS DONE.
I MAY AS WELL COME CLEAN.
!
HM?
WAIT, HARU-KUN WAS NEVER GOING TO TELL HIM?
SPIN SPIN SPIN SPIN SPIN SPIN SPIN
SO I WASN'T SUPPOSED TO NOTICE HIM KISSING CHIKA-KUN?
T-THEN THAT MEANS ...!
CHIKA ...
I'VE ALWAYS ...!
SHWAP!
S-STOOOOOP!!

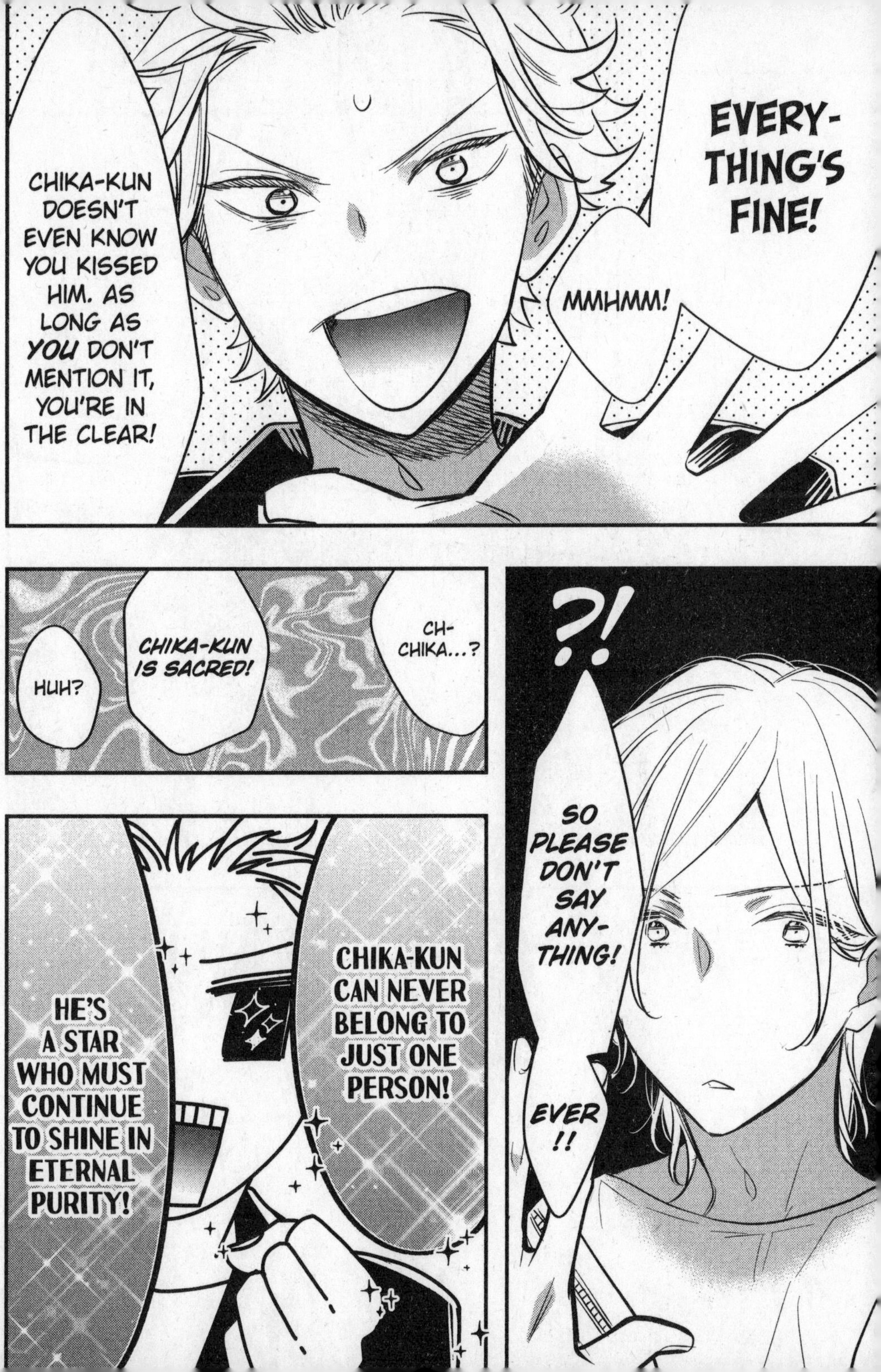
EVERY-THING'S FINE!
MMHMM!
CHIKA-KUN DOESN'T EVEN KNOW YOU KISSED HIM. AS LONG AS *YOU* DON'T MENTION IT, YOU'RE IN THE CLEAR!
?!
SO PLEASE DON'T SAY ANY-THING!
EVER !!
CH-CHIKA...?
CHIKA-KUN IS SACRED!
HUH?
CHIKA-KUN CAN NEVER BELONG TO JUST ONE PERSON!
HE'S A STAR WHO MUST CONTINUE TO SHINE IN ETERNAL PURITY!

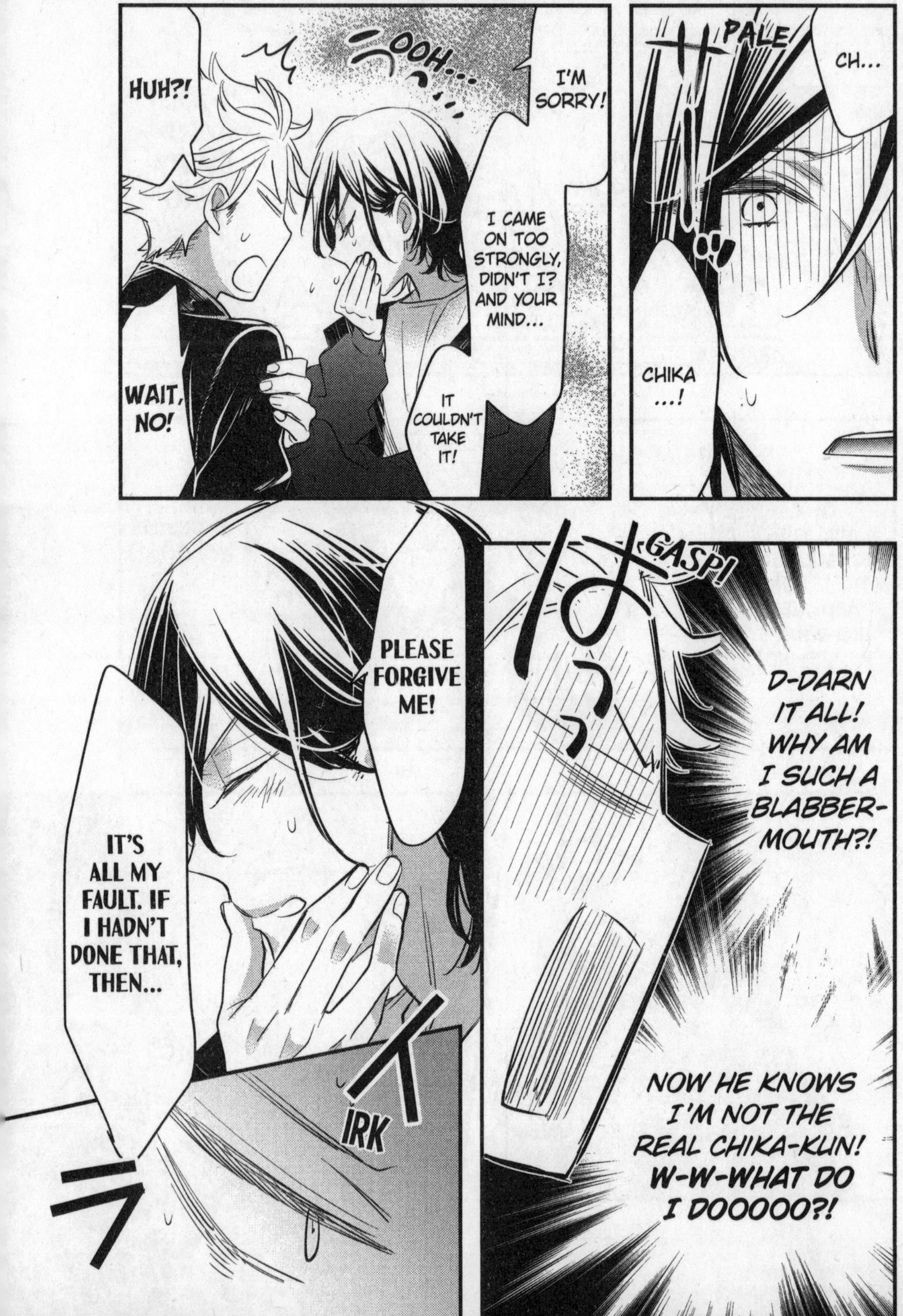
PALE
CH...
CHIKA ...!
I'M SORRY!
OOOH...
HUH?!
I CAME ON TOO STRONGLY, DIDN'T I? AND YOUR MIND...
IT COULDN'T TAKE IT!
WAIT, NO!
GASP!
D-DARN IT ALL! WHY AM I SUCH A BLABBER-MOUTH?!
NOW HE KNOWS I'M NOT THE REAL CHIKA-KUN! W-W-WHAT DO I DOOOOO?!
PLEASE FORGIVE ME!
IT'S ALL MY FAULT. IF I HADN'T DONE THAT, THEN...
IRK

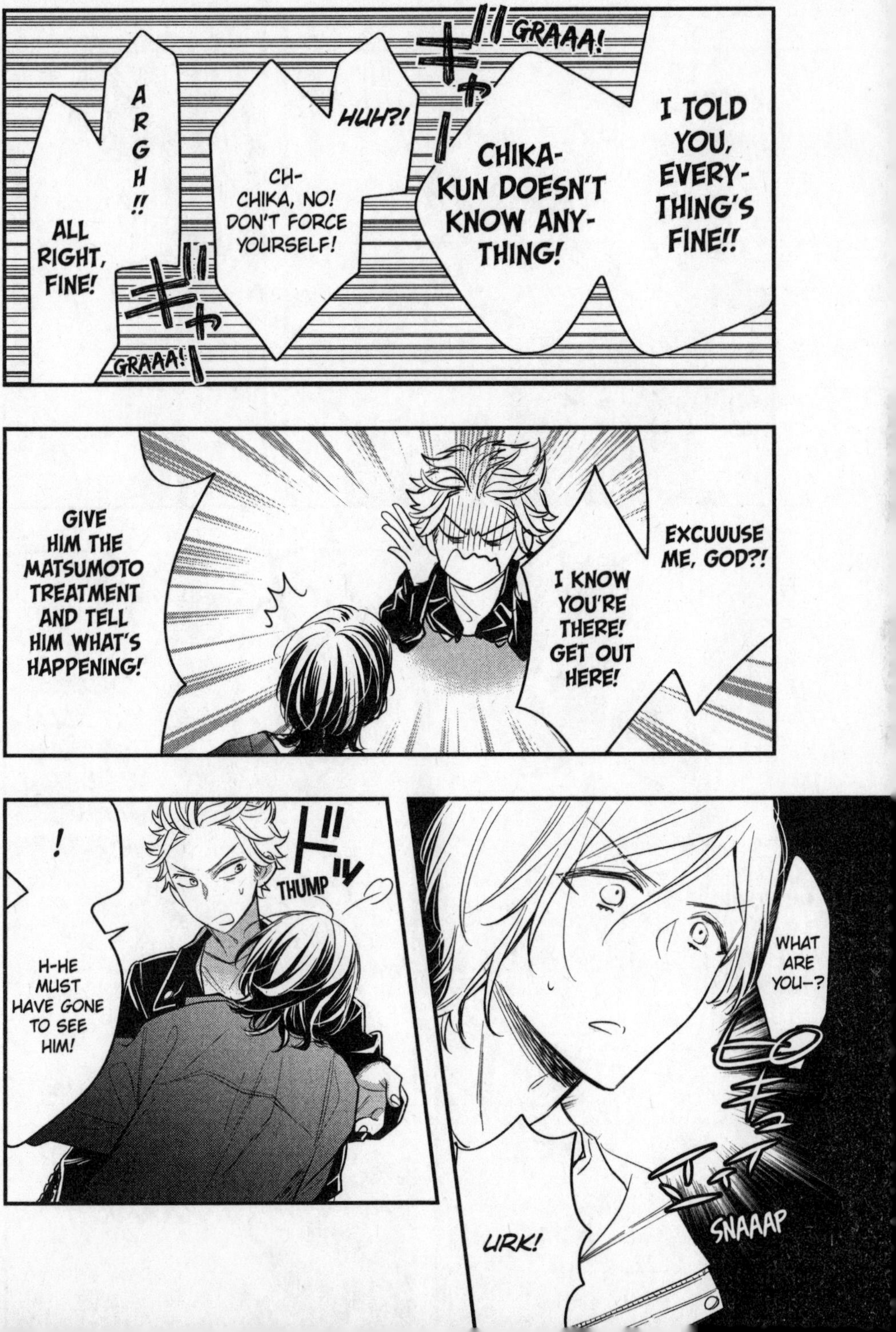
GRAAA!
I TOLD YOU, EVERY-THING'S FINE!!
CHIKA-KUN DOESN'T KNOW ANY-THING!
HUH?!
CH-CHIKA, NO! DON'T FORCE YOURSELF!
ARGH!!
ALL RIGHT, FINE!
GRAAA!
EXCUUUSE ME, GOD?!
I KNOW YOU'RE THERE! GET OUT HERE!
GIVE HIM THE MATSUMOTO TREATMENT AND TELL HIM WHAT'S HAPPENING!
WHAT ARE YOU–?
SNAAAP
URK!
THUMP
!
H-HE MUST HAVE GONE TO SEE HIM!

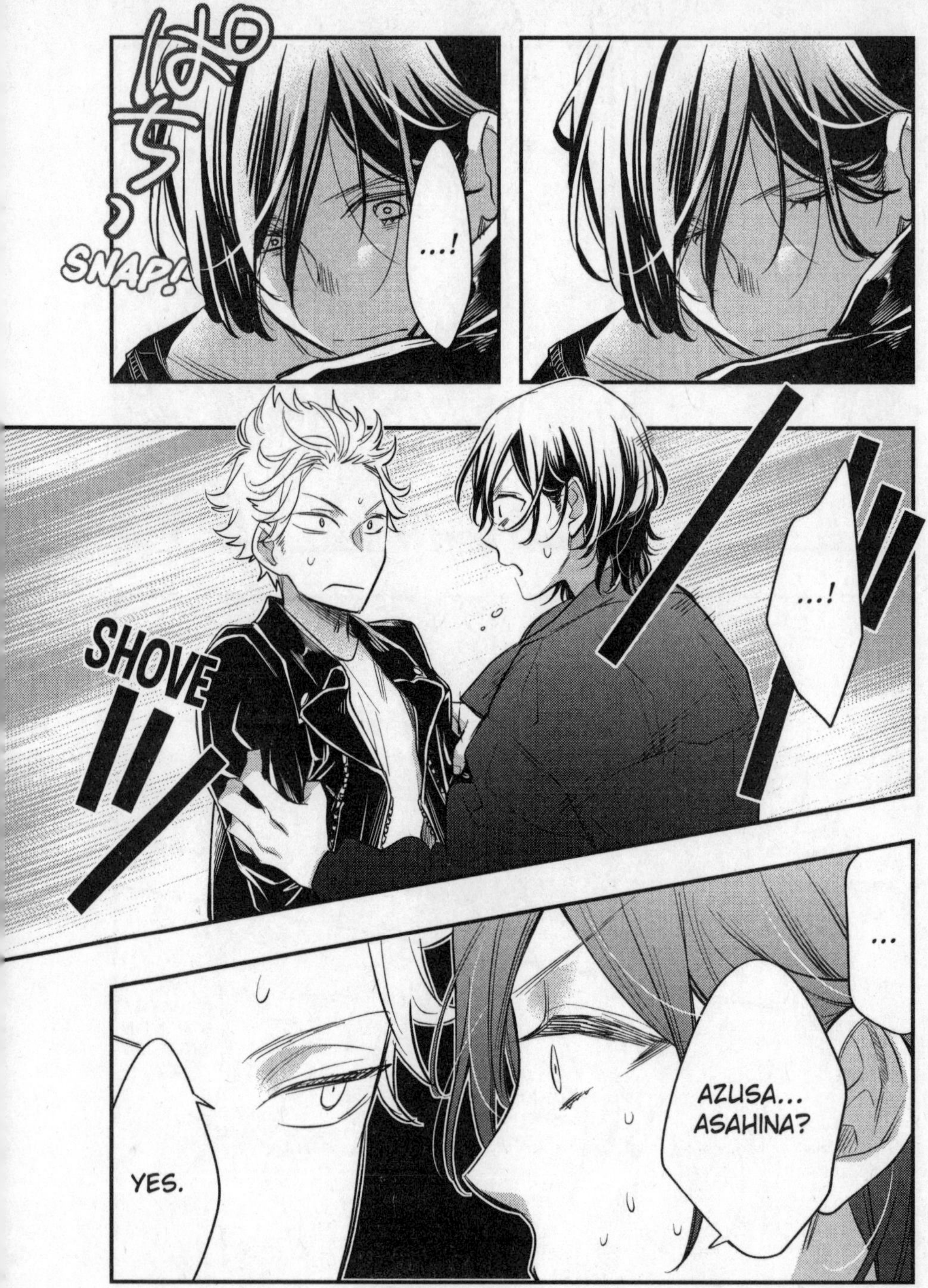
...!
ぱちっ
SNAP!
...!
SHOVE
...
AZUSA... ASAHINA?
YES.

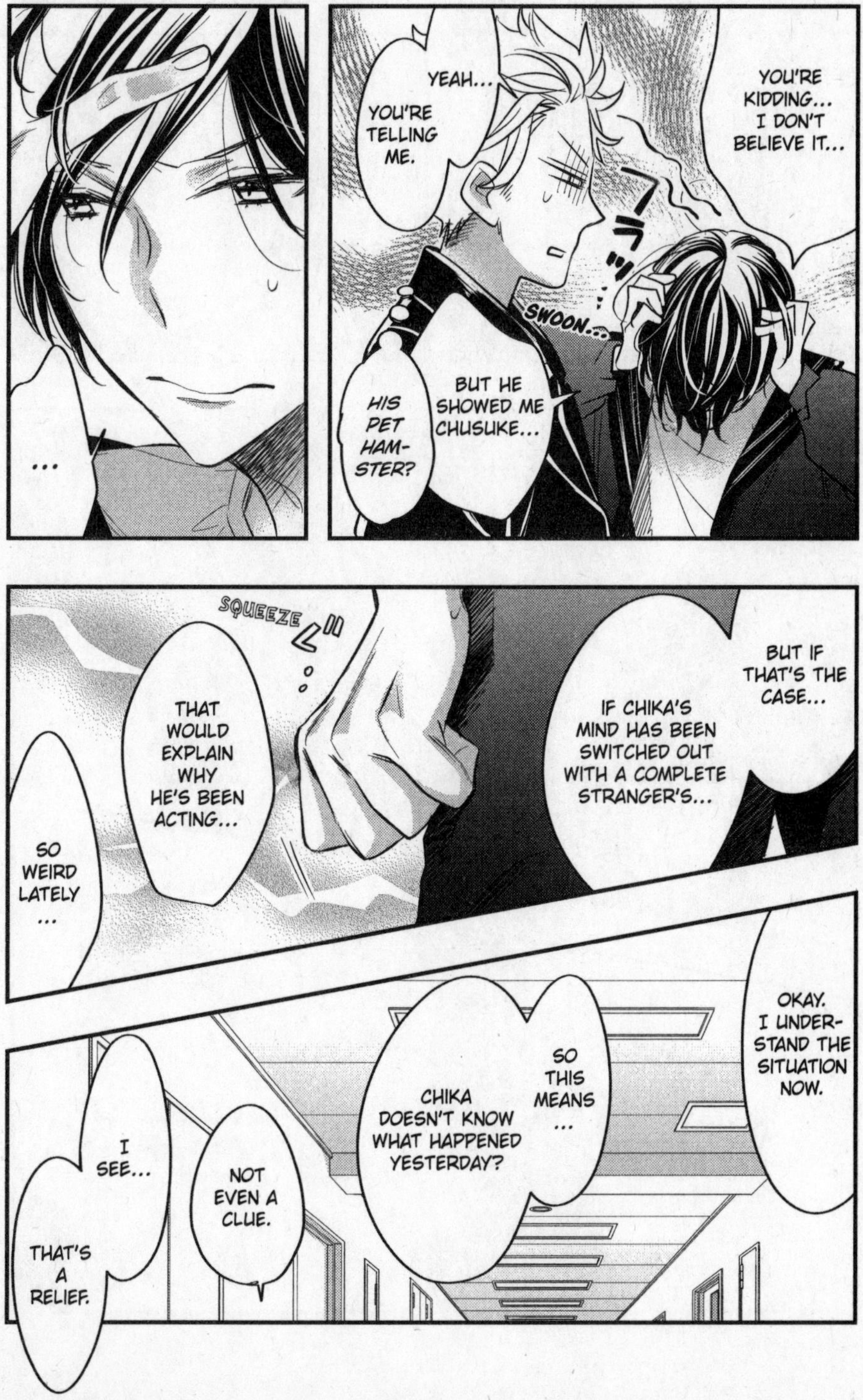
YOU'RE KIDDING... I DON'T BELIEVE IT...
YEAH...
YOU'RE TELLING ME.
SWOON...
BUT HE SHOWED ME CHUSUKE...
HIS PET HAMSTER?
...
BUT IF THAT'S THE CASE...
IF CHIKA'S MIND HAS BEEN SWITCHED OUT WITH A COMPLETE STRANGER'S...
SQUEEZE
THAT WOULD EXPLAIN WHY HE'S BEEN ACTING...
SO WEIRD LATELY...
OKAY. I UNDER-STAND THE SITUATION NOW.
SO THIS MEANS...
CHIKA DOESN'T KNOW WHAT HAPPENED YESTERDAY?
NOT EVEN A CLUE.
I SEE...
THAT'S A RELIEF.

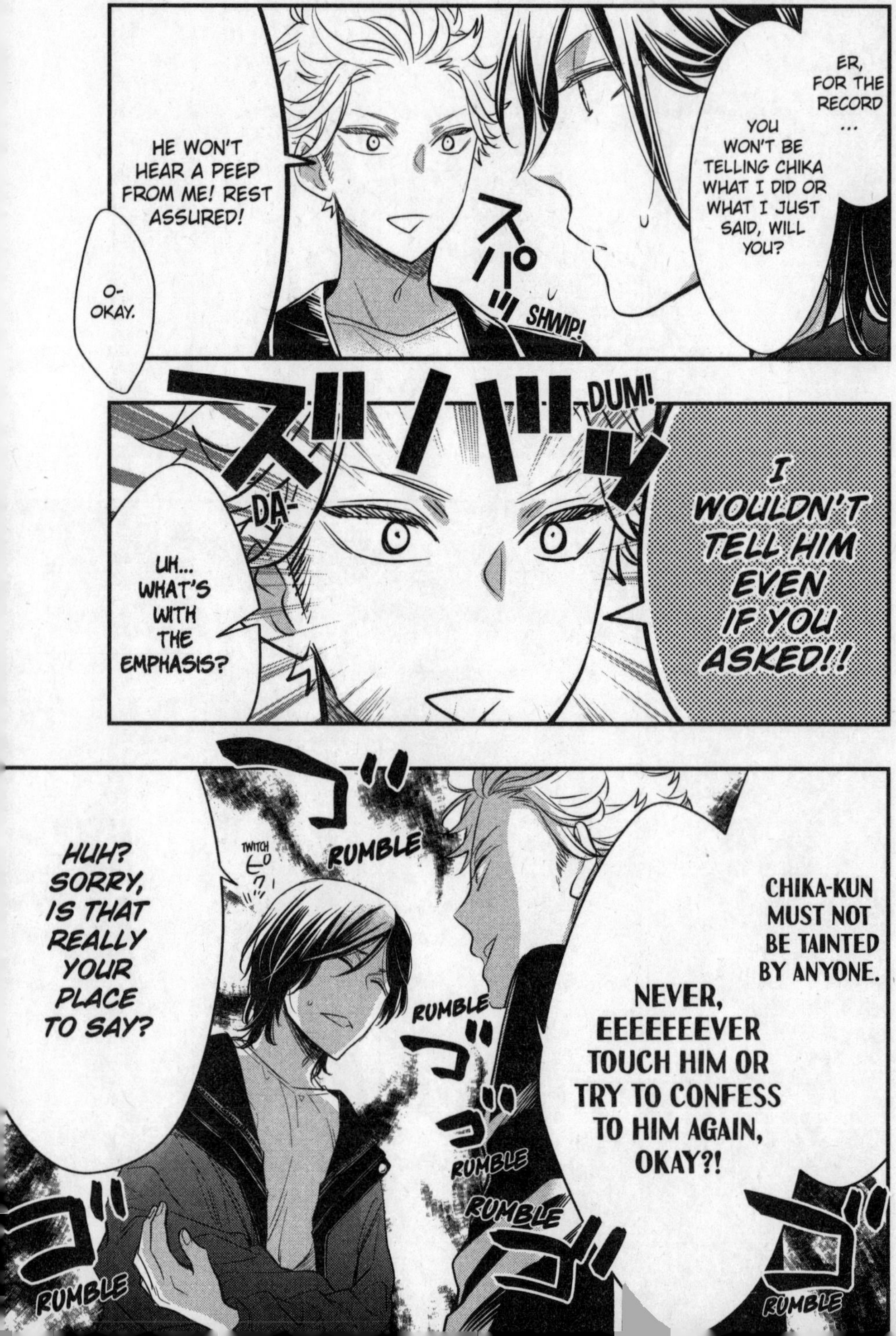
ER, FOR THE RECORD ... YOU WON'T BE TELLING CHIKA WHAT I DID OR WHAT I JUST SAID, WILL YOU?
SHWIP!
HE WON'T HEAR A PEEP FROM ME! REST ASSURED!
O-OKAY.
DUM!
I WOULDN'T TELL HIM EVEN IF YOU ASKED!!
DA-
UH... WHAT'S WITH THE EMPHASIS?
CHIKA-KUN MUST NOT BE TAINTED BY ANYONE.
NEVER, EEEEEEEVER TOUCH HIM OR TRY TO CONFESS TO HIM AGAIN, OKAY?!
RUMBLE
RUMBLE
RUMBLE
RUMBLE
RUMBLE
TWITCH
HUH? SORRY, IS THAT REALLY YOUR PLACE TO SAY?
RUMBLE
RUMBLE

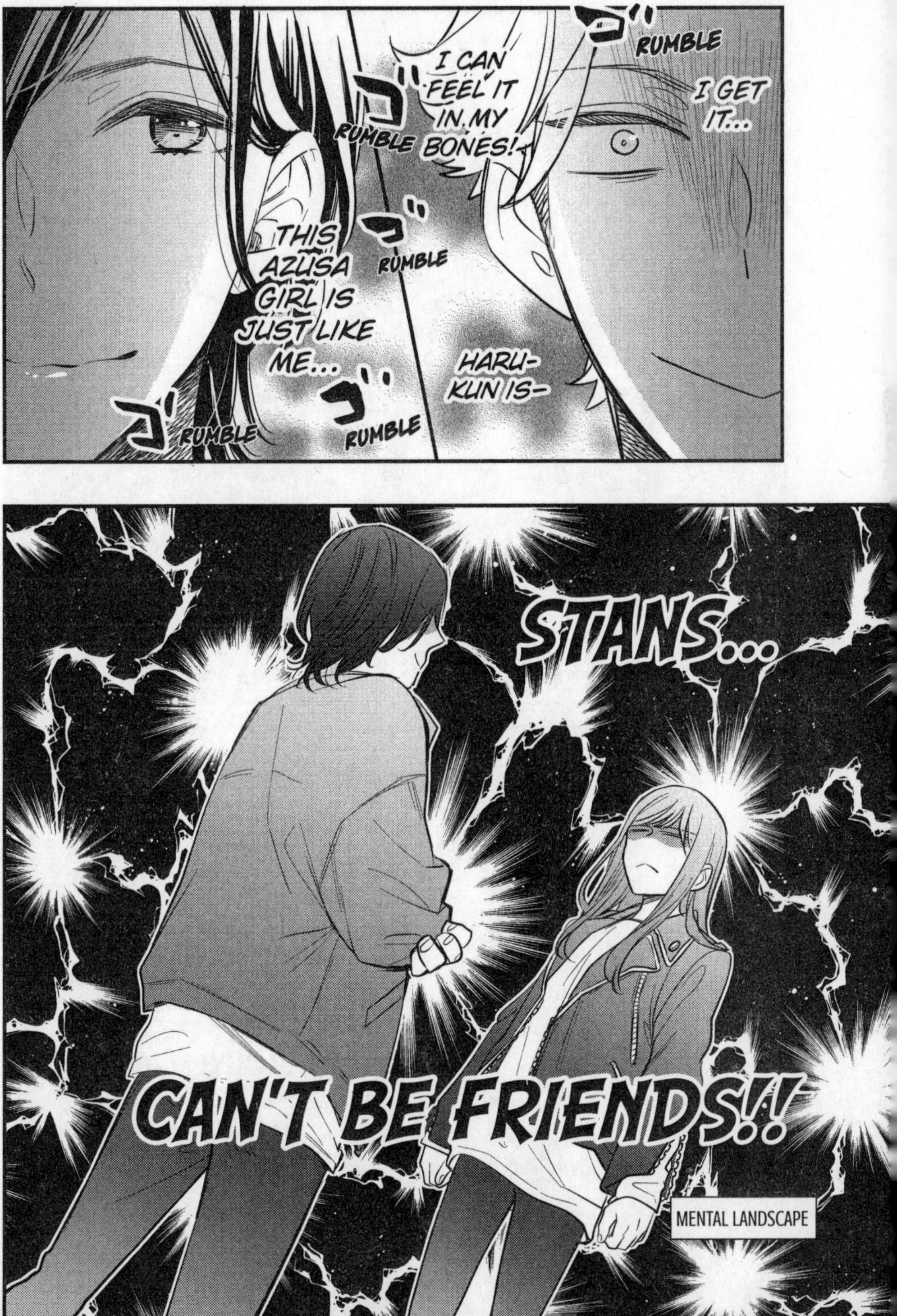
RUMBLE
I GET IT...
I CAN FEEL IT IN MY BONES!
RUMBLE
RUMBLE
HARU-KUN IS-
THIS AZUSA GIRL IS JUST LIKE ME...
RUMBLE
RUMBLE
STANS...
CAN'T BE FRIENDS!!
MENTAL LANDSCAPE

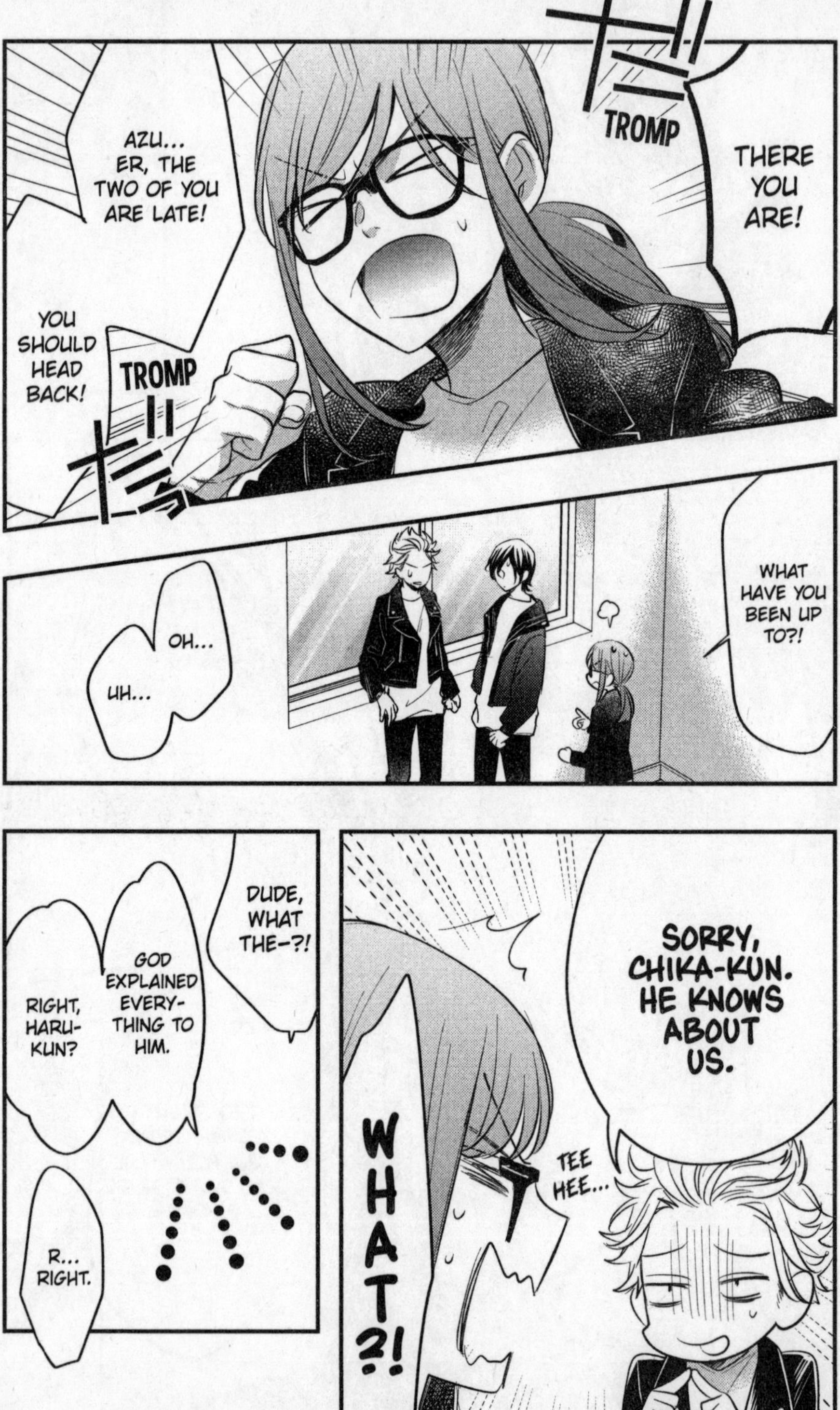
TROMP
THERE YOU ARE!
AZU... ER, THE TWO OF YOU ARE LATE!
YOU SHOULD HEAD BACK!
TROMP
WHAT HAVE YOU BEEN UP TO?!
OH...
UH...
SORRY, CHIKA-KUN. HE KNOWS ABOUT US.
TEE HEE...
WHAT?!
DUDE, WHAT THE-?!
GOD EXPLAINED EVERY-THING TO HIM.
RIGHT, HARU-KUN?
R... RIGHT.

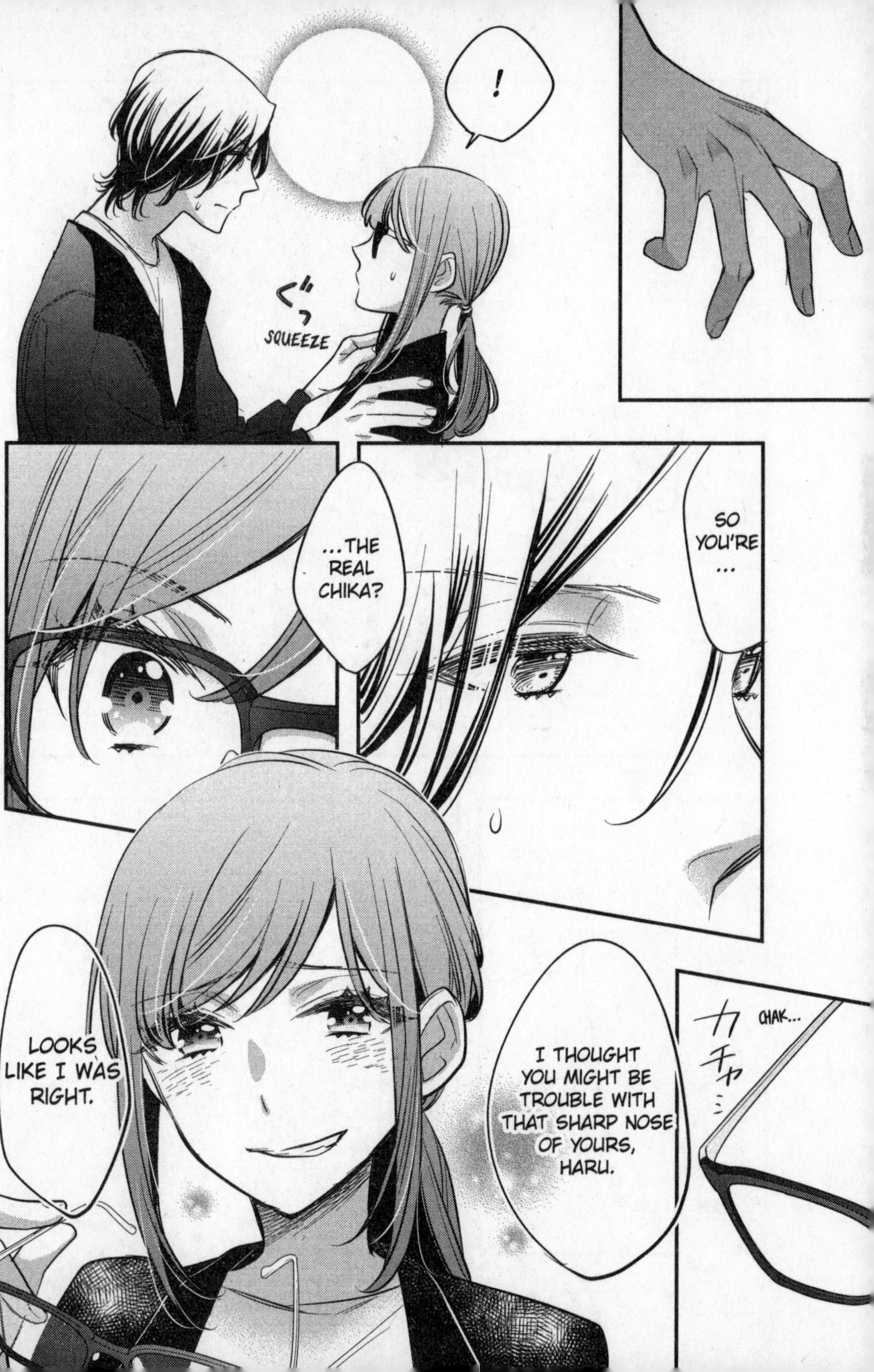
!
ぐっ
SQUEEZE
SO YOU'RE ...
...THE REAL CHIKA?
カチャ
CHAK...
I THOUGHT YOU MIGHT BE TROUBLE WITH THAT SHARP NOSE OF YOURS, HARU.
LOOKS LIKE I WAS RIGHT.

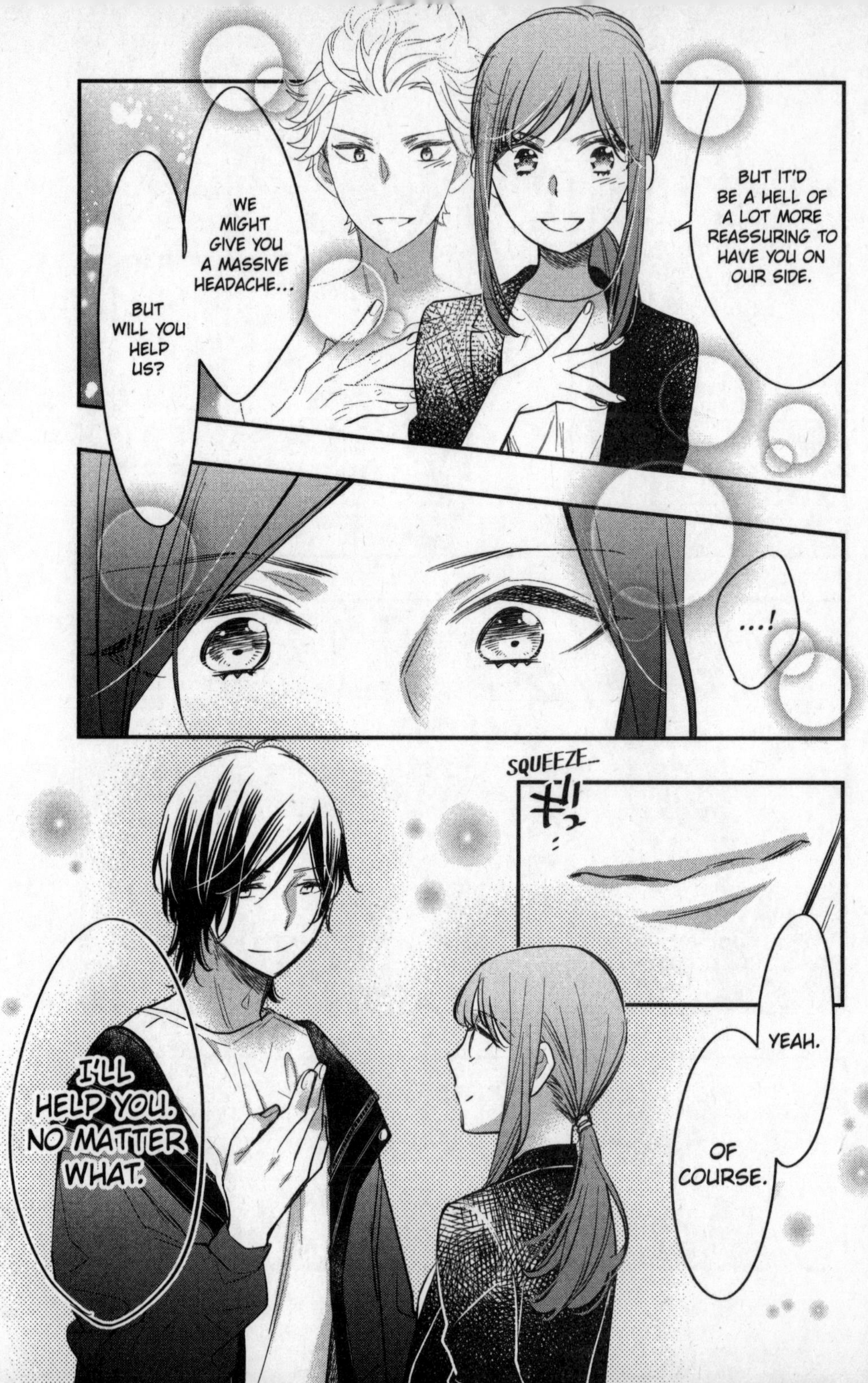
BUT IT'D BE A HELL OF A LOT MORE REASSURING TO HAVE YOU ON OUR SIDE.
WE MIGHT GIVE YOU A MASSIVE HEADACHE...
BUT WILL YOU HELP US?
...!
SQUEEZE...
YEAH.
OF COURSE.
I'LL HELP YOU. NO MATTER WHAT.

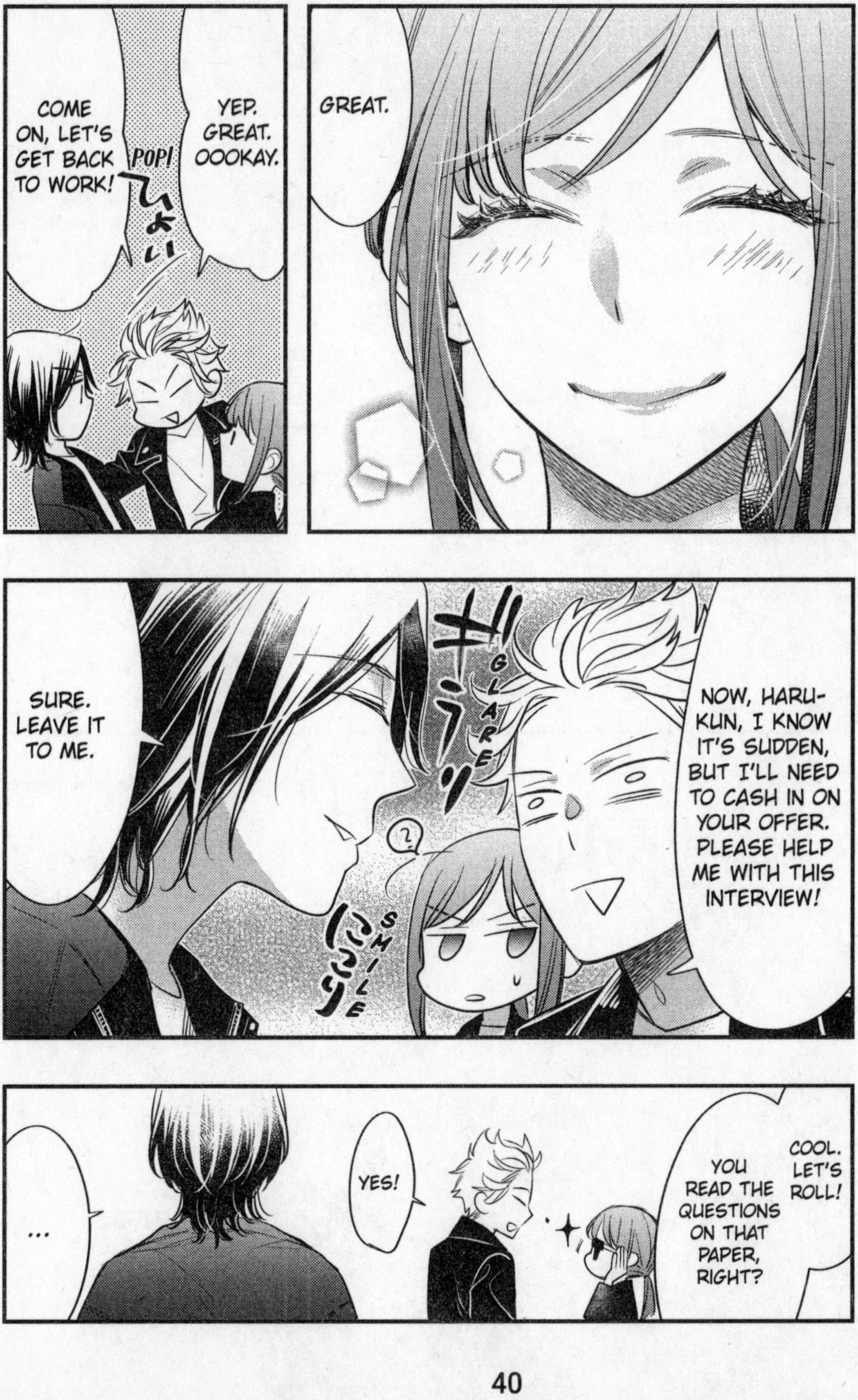
GREAT.
YEP. GREAT. OOOKAY.
POP!
ひょい
COME ON, LET'S GET BACK TO WORK!
NOW, HARU-KUN, I KNOW IT'S SUDDEN, BUT I'LL NEED TO CASH IN ON YOUR OFFER. PLEASE HELP ME WITH THIS INTERVIEW!
ギラッ
GLARE
にこっ
SMILE
SURE. LEAVE IT TO ME.
COOL. LET'S ROLL!
YOU READ THE QUESTIONS ON THAT PAPER, RIGHT?
YES!
...

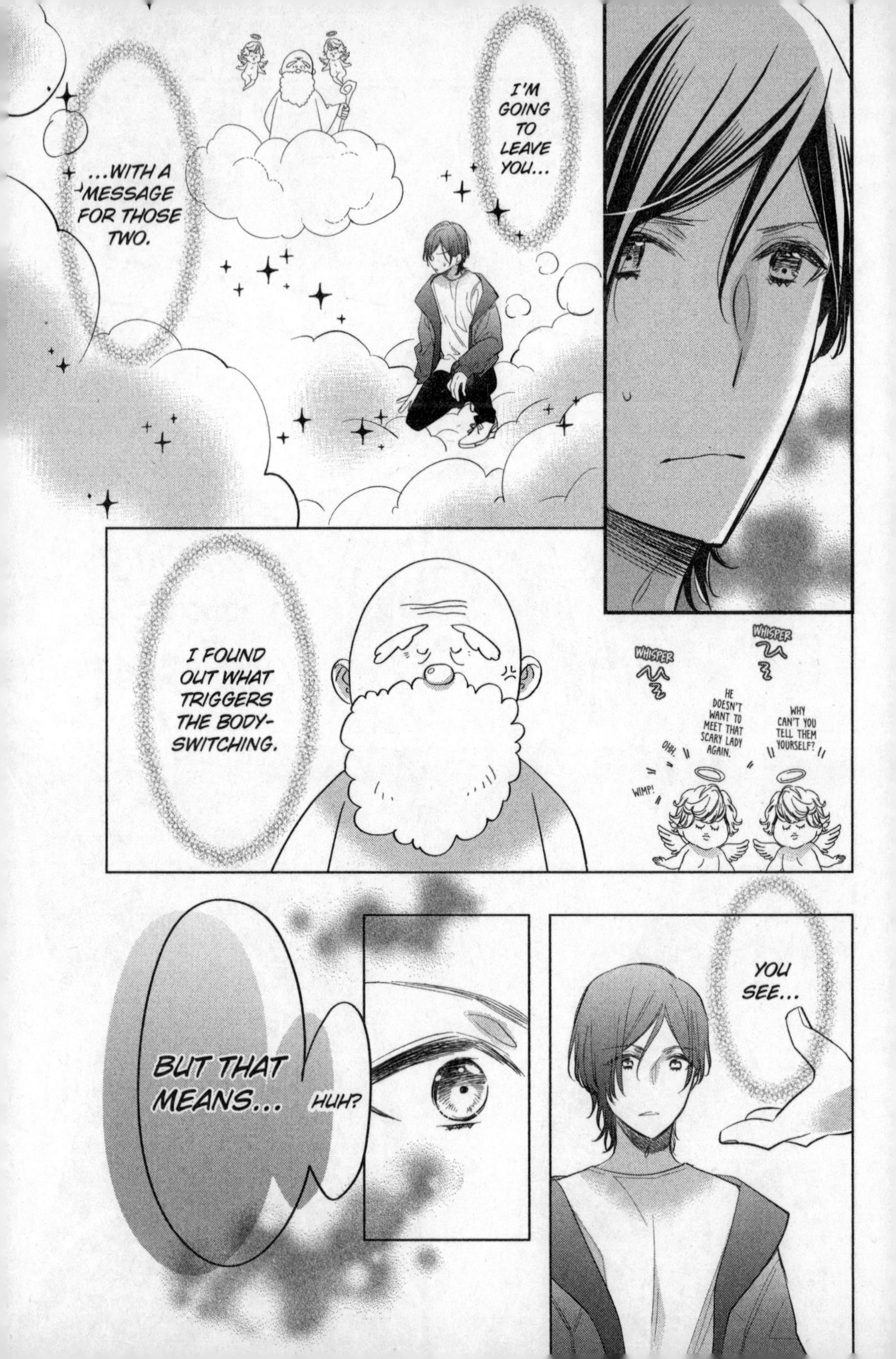
I'M GOING TO LEAVE YOU...
...WITH A MESSAGE FOR THOSE TWO.
WHISPER
WHISPER
WHY CAN'T YOU TELL THEM YOURSELF?
HE DOESN'T WANT TO MEET THAT SCARY LADY AGAIN.
OHH.
WIMP!
I FOUND OUT WHAT TRIGGERS THE BODY-SWITCHING.
YOU SEE...
HUH?
BUT THAT MEANS...

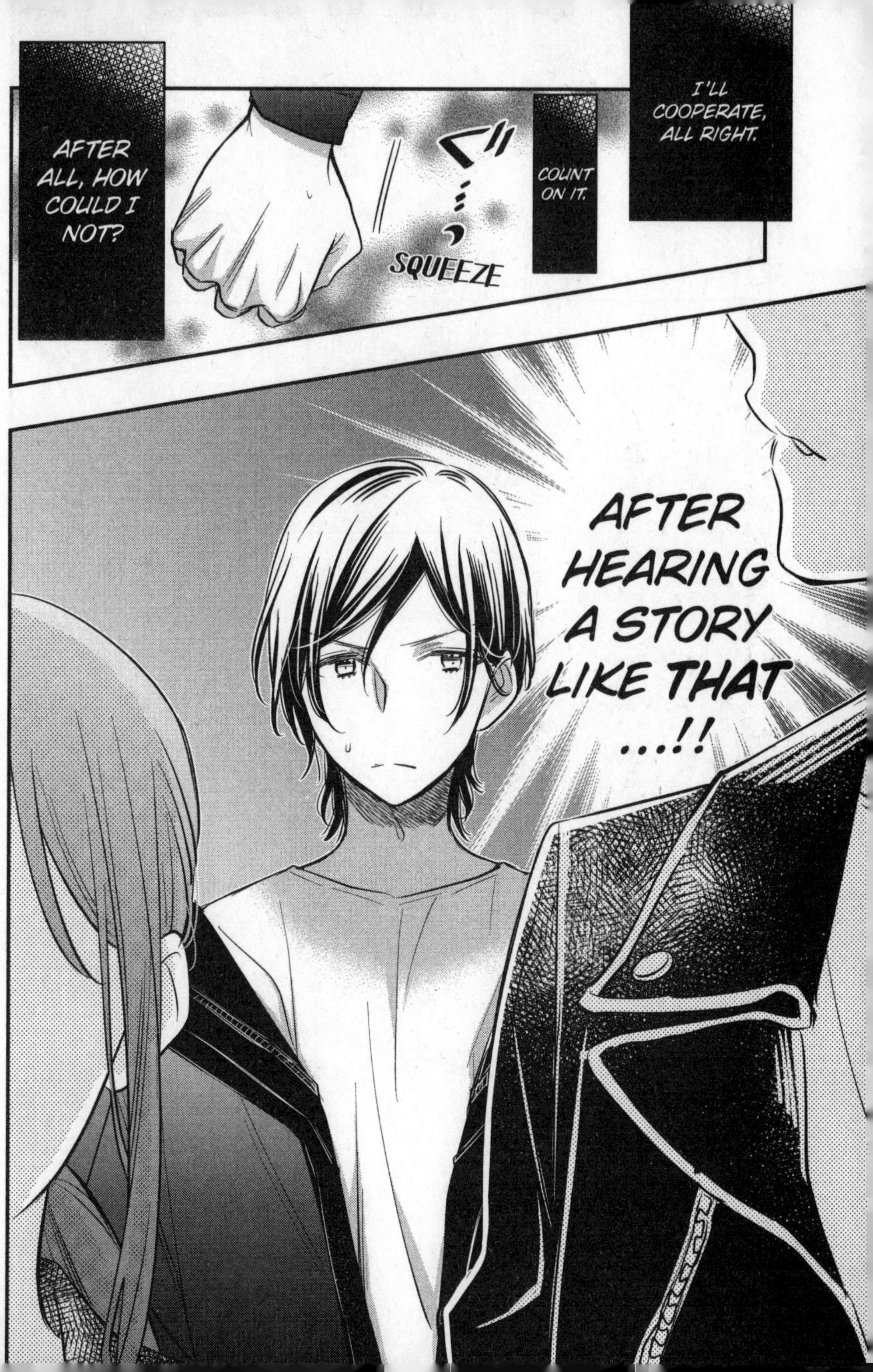
I'LL COOPERATE, ALL RIGHT.
COUNT ON IT.
SQUEEZE
AFTER ALL, HOW COULD I NOT?
AFTER HEARING A STORY LIKE THAT ...!!

R⇄CROSS

D!! STAR

AR⇄CROS

CROSSED

⇄CROSSE

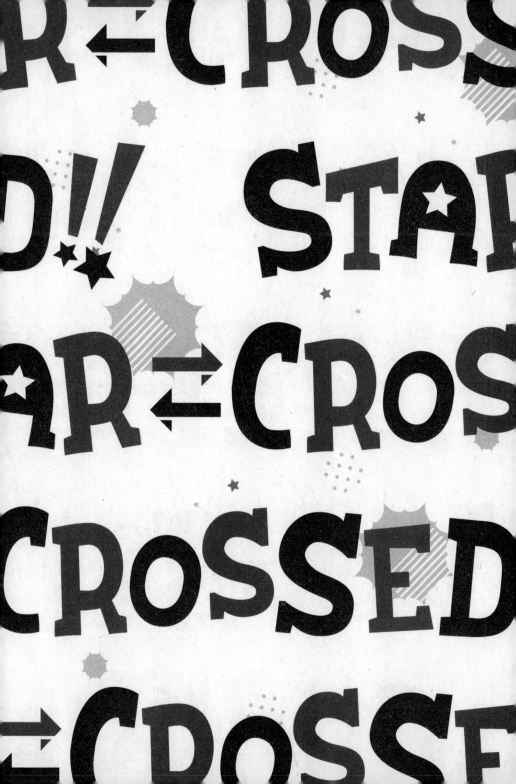

R⇄CROSS

D!! STAR

AR⇄CROS

CROSSED

⇄CROSSE

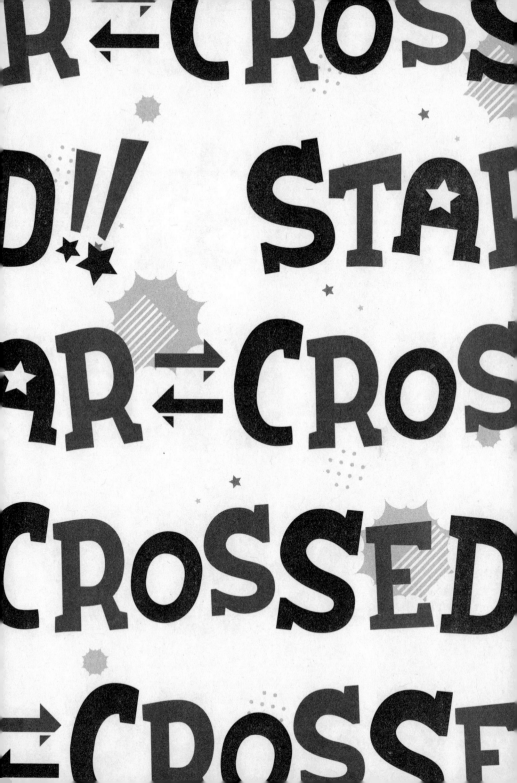

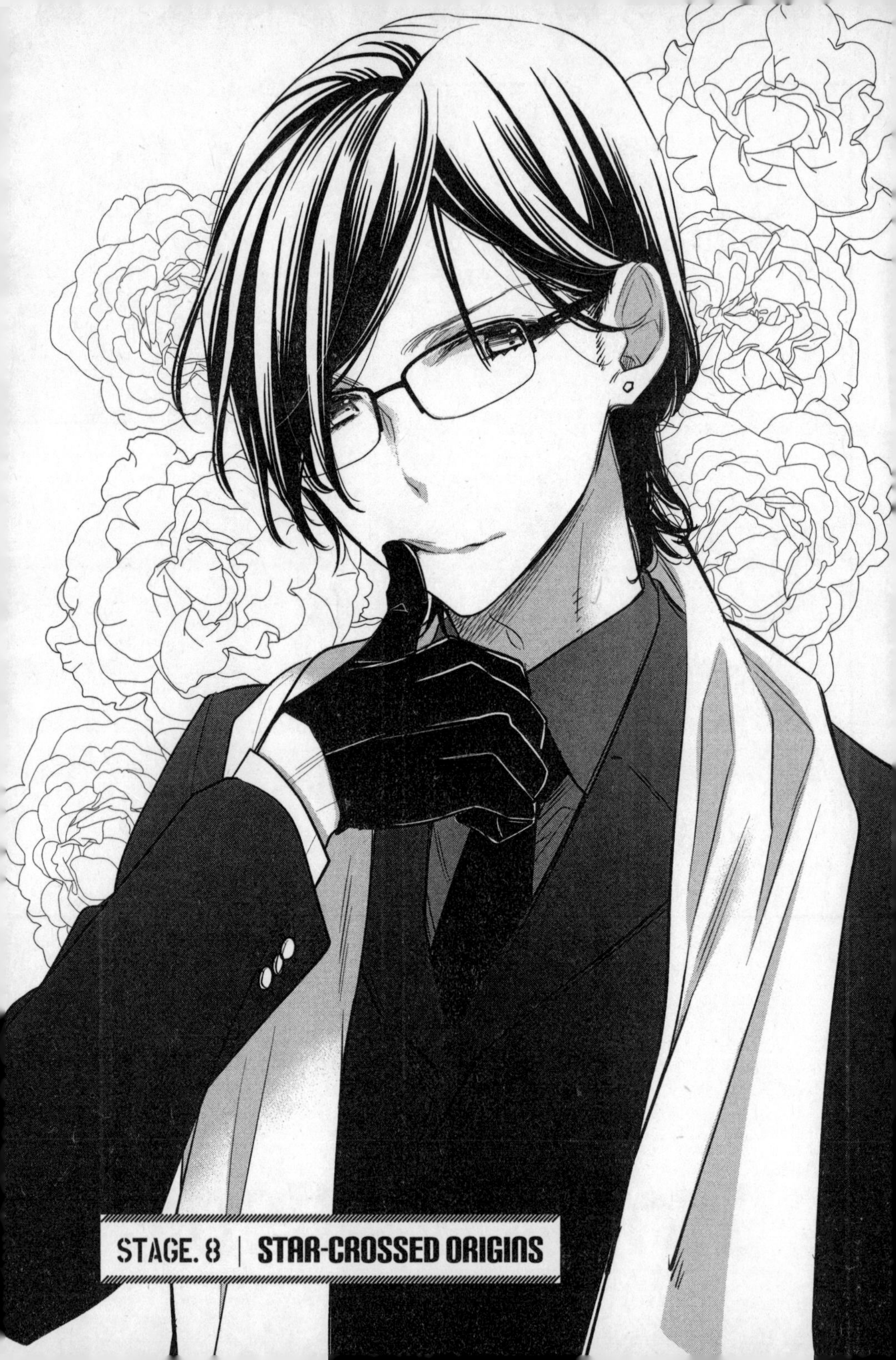

STAGE. 8 | STAR-CROSSED ORIGINS

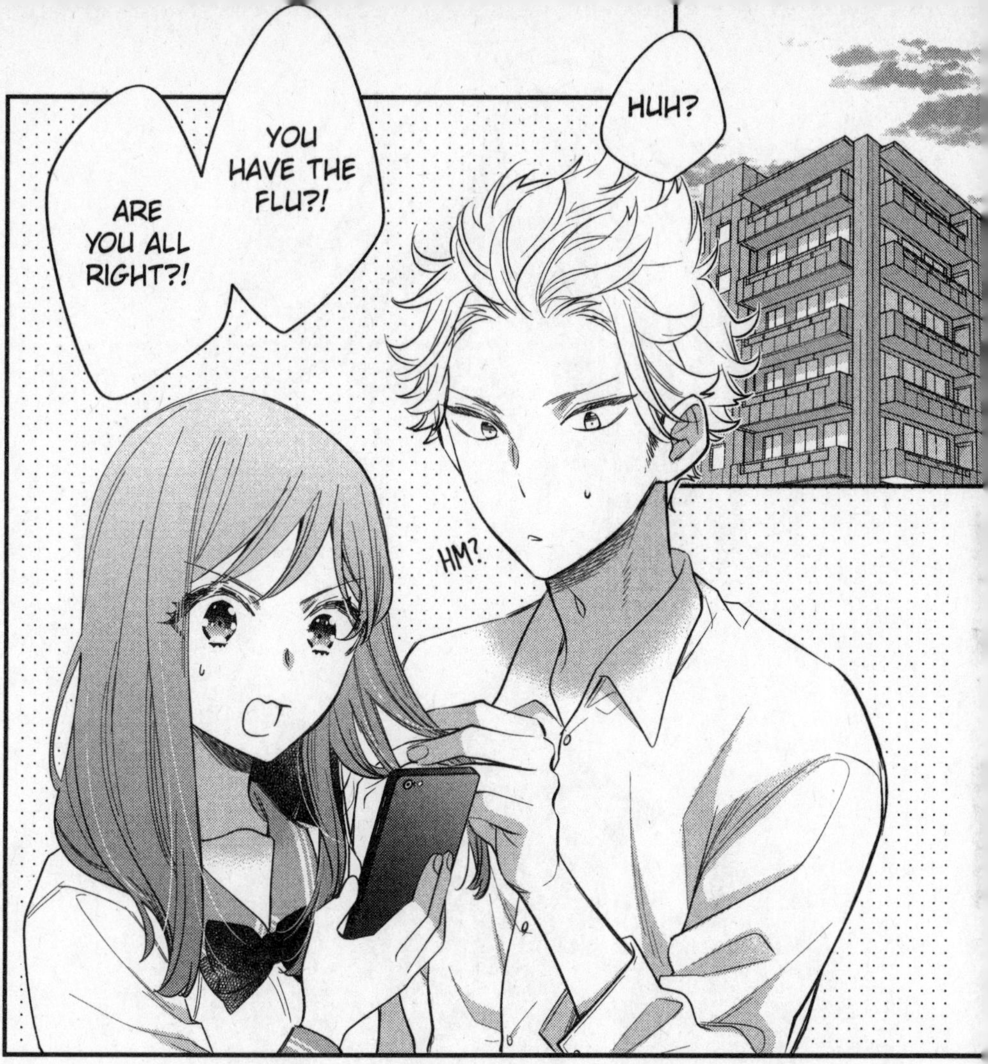
HUH?
YOU HAVE THE FLU?!
ARE YOU ALL RIGHT?!
HM?

STAR⇄CROSSED!!

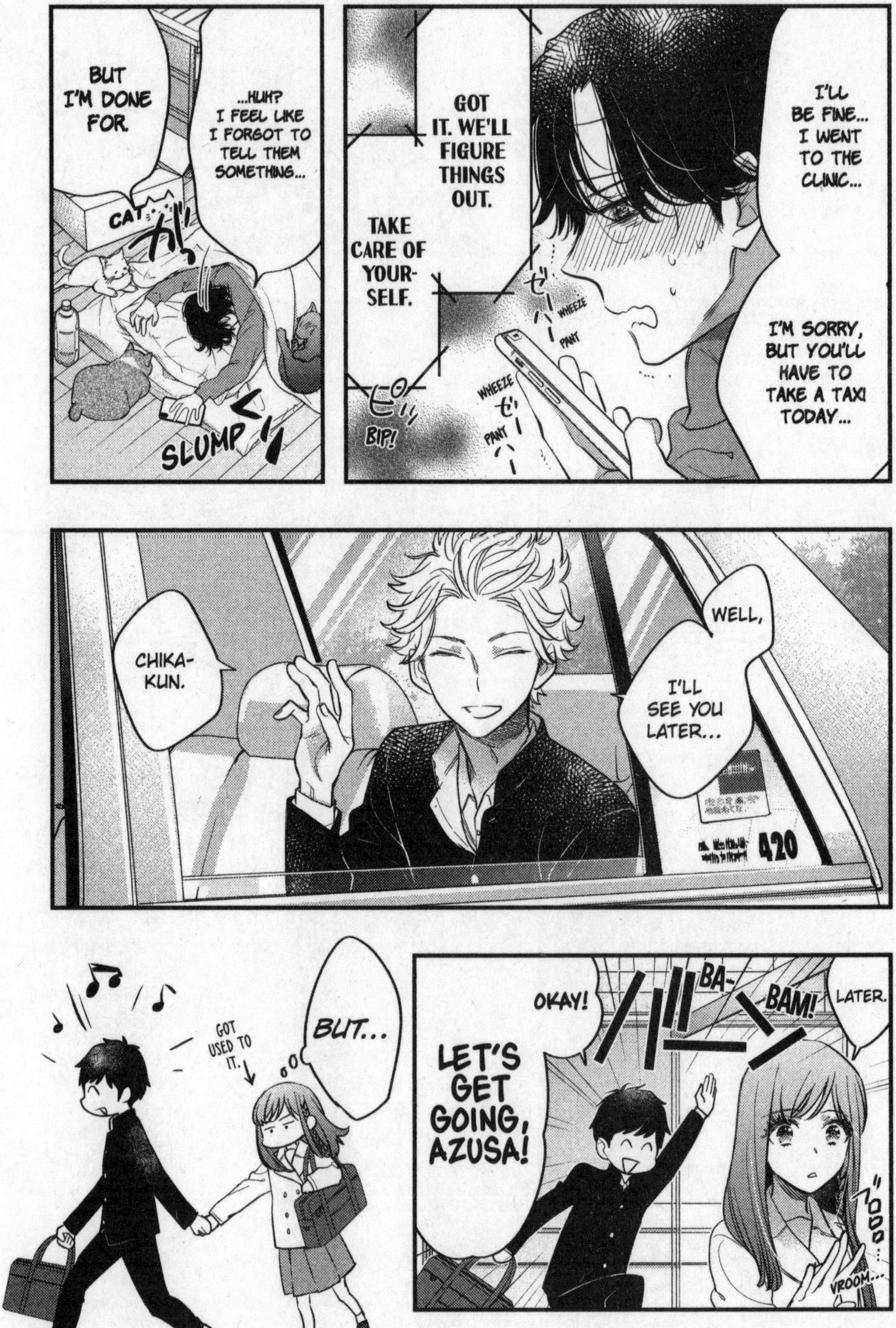
I'LL BE FINE... I WENT TO THE CLINIC...
I'M SORRY, BUT YOU'LL HAVE TO TAKE A TAXI TODAY...
WHEEZE
PANT
WHEEZE
PANT
GOT IT. WE'LL FIGURE THINGS OUT.
TAKE CARE OF YOURSELF.
BIP!
...HUH? I FEEL LIKE I FORGOT TO TELL THEM SOMETHING...
BUT I'M DONE FOR.
CAT
SLUMP
WELL,
I'LL SEE YOU LATER...
CHIKA-KUN.
LATER.
BA-BAM!
OKAY!
LET'S GET GOING, AZUSA!
VROOM...
BUT...
GOT USED TO IT.

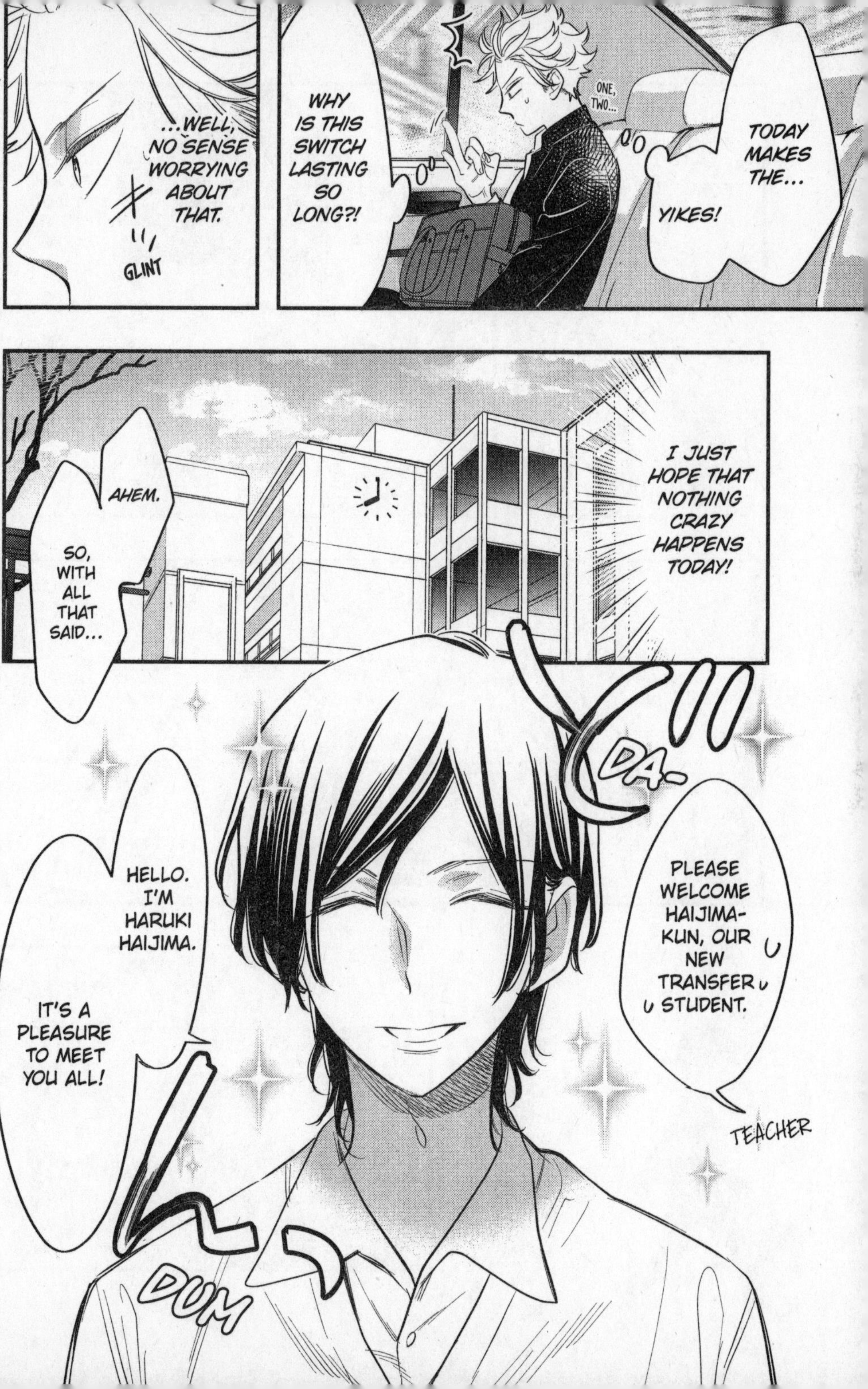
TODAY MAKES THE...
YIKES!
ONE, TWO...
WHY IS THIS SWITCH LASTING SO LONG?!
...WELL, NO SENSE WORRYING ABOUT THAT.
GLINT
I JUST HOPE THAT NOTHING CRAZY HAPPENS TODAY!
AHEM.
SO, WITH ALL THAT SAID...
DA-
PLEASE WELCOME HAIJIMA-KUN, OUR NEW TRANSFER STUDENT.
TEACHER
HELLO. I'M HARUKI HAIJIMA.
IT'S A PLEASURE TO MEET YOU ALL!
DUM

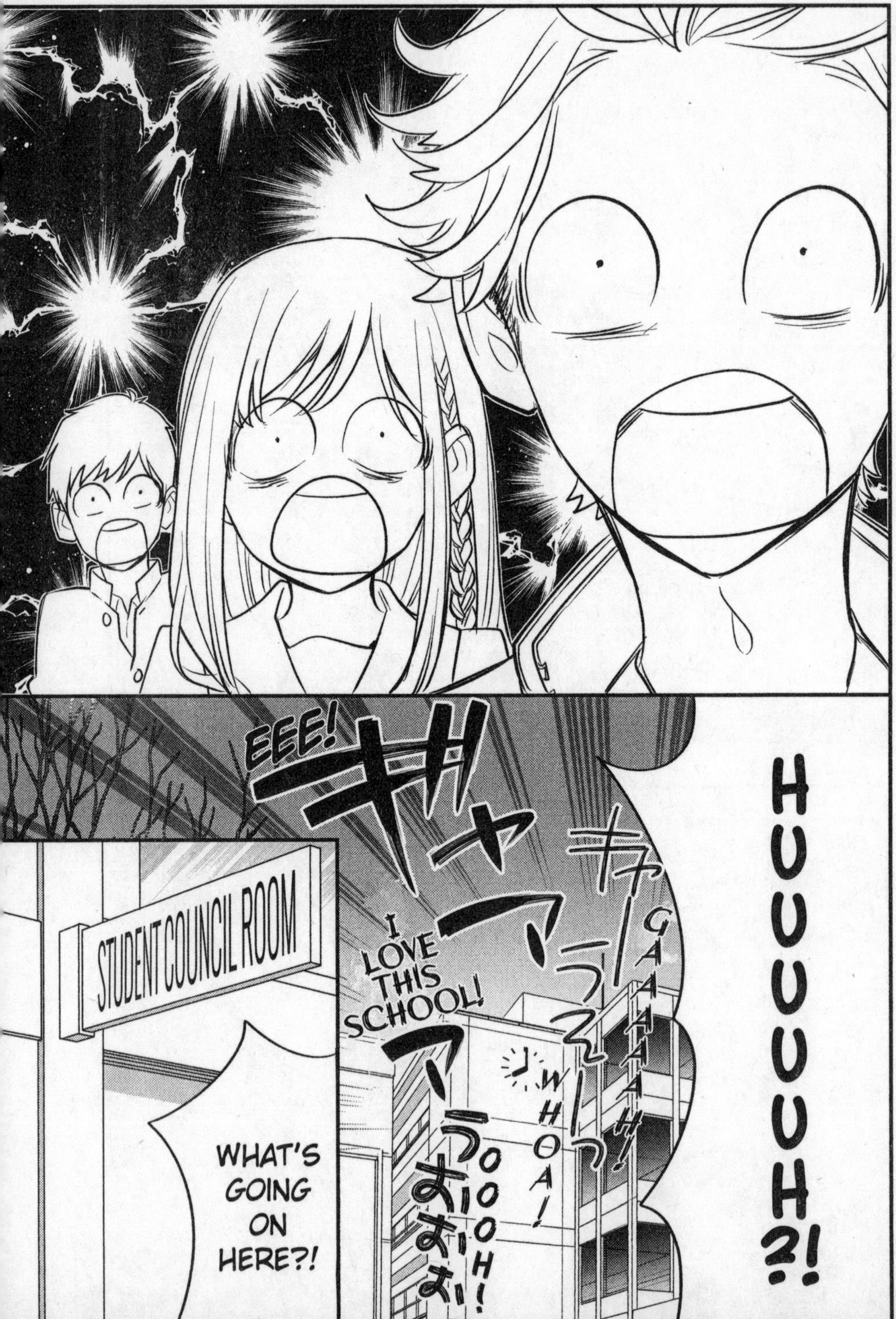
HUUUUUH?!
EEE!
GAAAAAH!
WHOA!
OOOOH!
I LOVE THIS SCHOOL!
STUDENT COUNCIL ROOM
WHAT'S GOING ON HERE?!

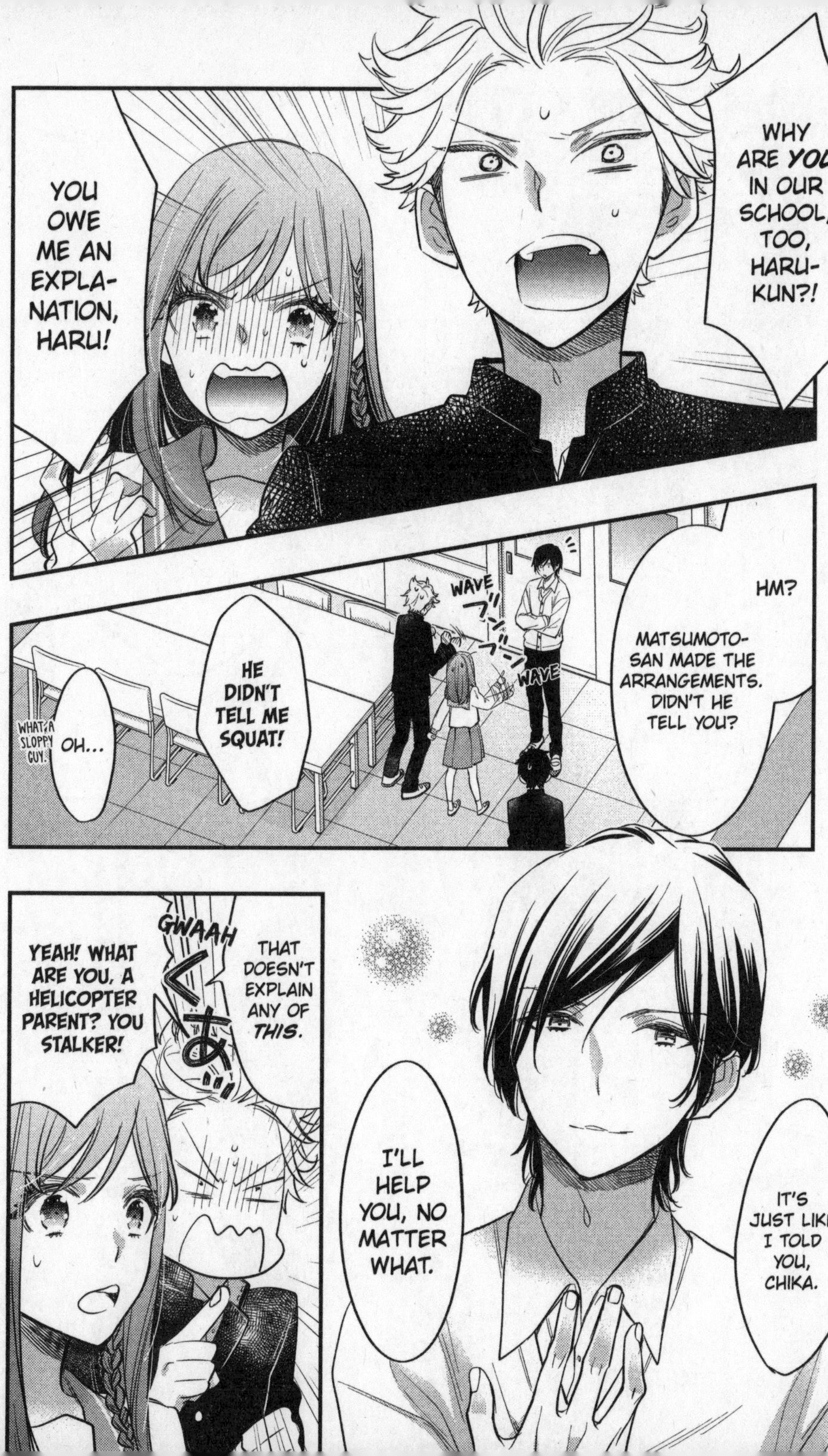

WHY ARE YOU IN OUR SCHOOL, TOO, HARU-KUN?!
YOU OWE ME AN EXPLANATION, HARU!
HM?
MATSUMOTO-SAN MADE THE ARRANGEMENTS. DIDN'T HE TELL YOU?
WAVE
WAVE
HE DIDN'T TELL ME SQUAT!
OH...
WHAT A SLOPPY GUY.
IT'S JUST LIKE I TOLD YOU, CHIKA.
I'LL HELP YOU, NO MATTER WHAT.
THAT DOESN'T EXPLAIN ANY OF THIS.
GWAAH
YEAH! WHAT ARE YOU, A HELICOPTER PARENT? YOU STALKER!

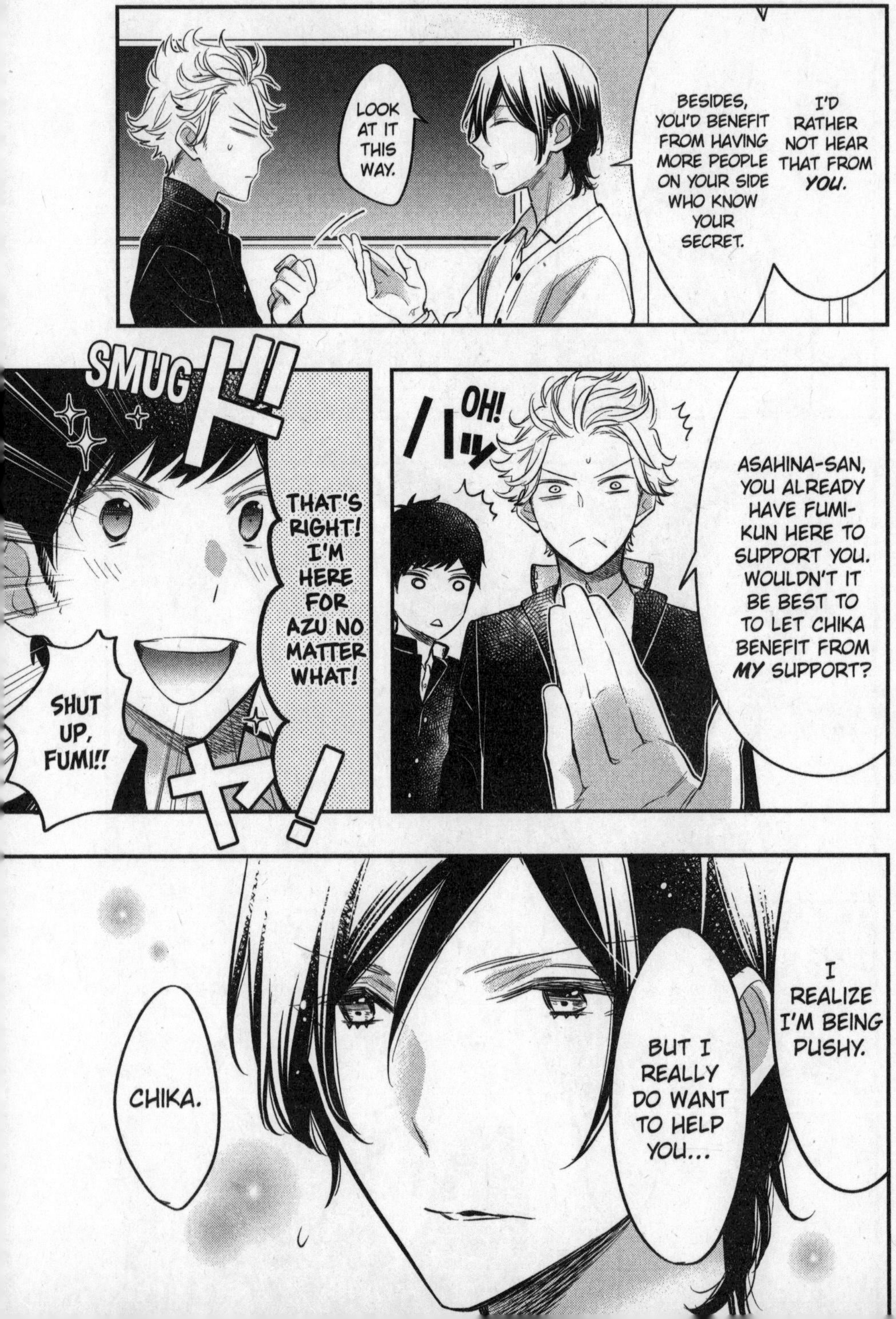
I'D RATHER NOT HEAR THAT FROM *YOU*.
BESIDES, YOU'D BENEFIT FROM HAVING MORE PEOPLE ON YOUR SIDE WHO KNOW YOUR SECRET.
LOOK AT IT THIS WAY.
ASAHINA-SAN, YOU ALREADY HAVE FUMI-KUN HERE TO SUPPORT YOU. WOULDN'T IT BE BEST TO TO LET CHIKA BENEFIT FROM *MY* SUPPORT?
OH!
ハッ
SMUG
ド!!
THAT'S RIGHT! I'M HERE FOR AZU NO MATTER WHAT!
SHUT UP, FUMI!!
ヤ!
I REALIZE I'M BEING PUSHY.
BUT I REALLY DO WANT TO HELP YOU...
CHIKA.

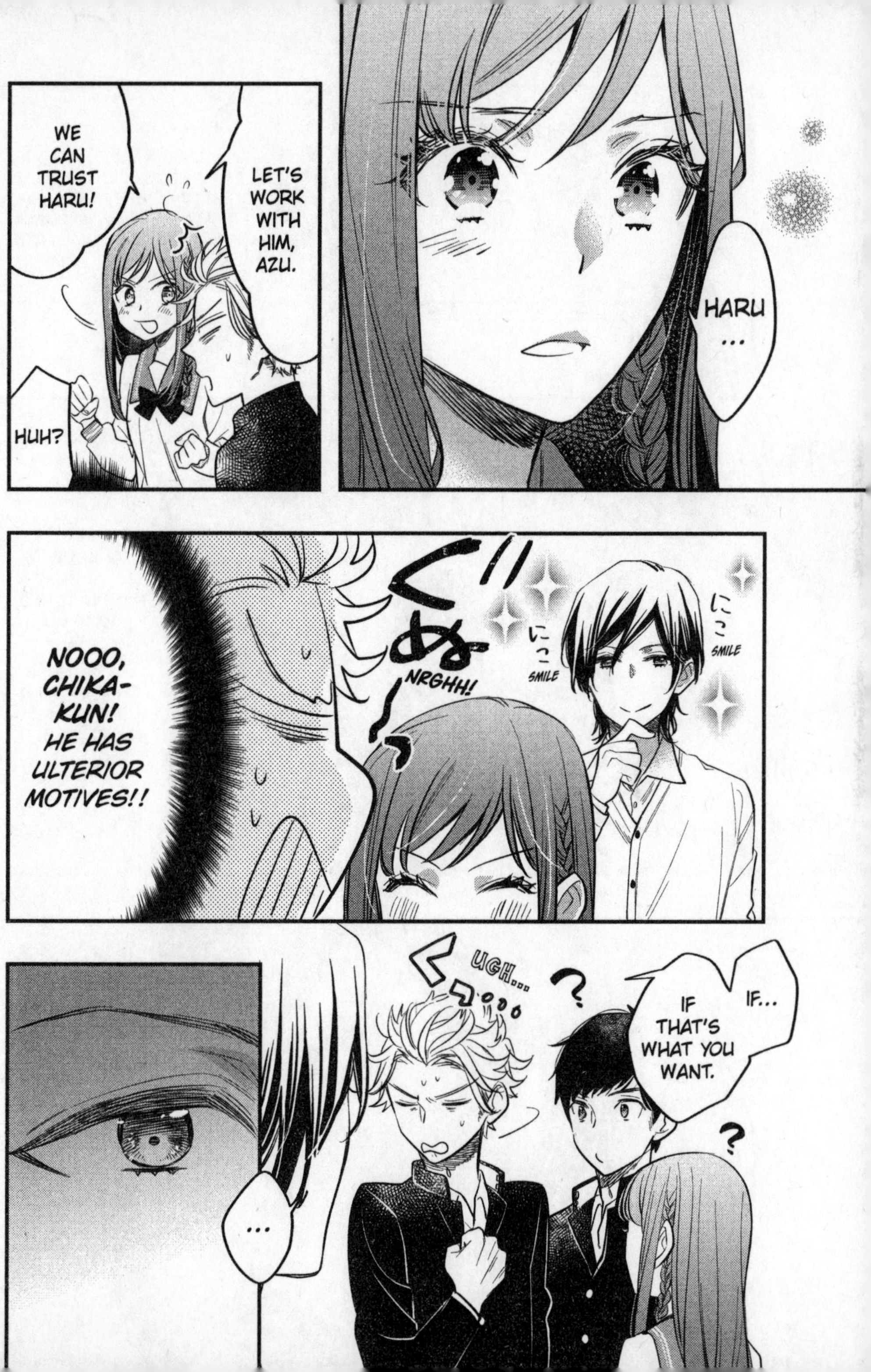
HARU...
LET'S WORK WITH HIM, AZU.
WE CAN TRUST HARU!
HUH?
にこ
SMILE
にこ
SMILE
くぬ
NRGHH!
NOOO, CHIKA-KUN! HE HAS ULTERIOR MOTIVES!!
IF...
IF THAT'S WHAT YOU WANT.
?
?
くっ
UGH...
...

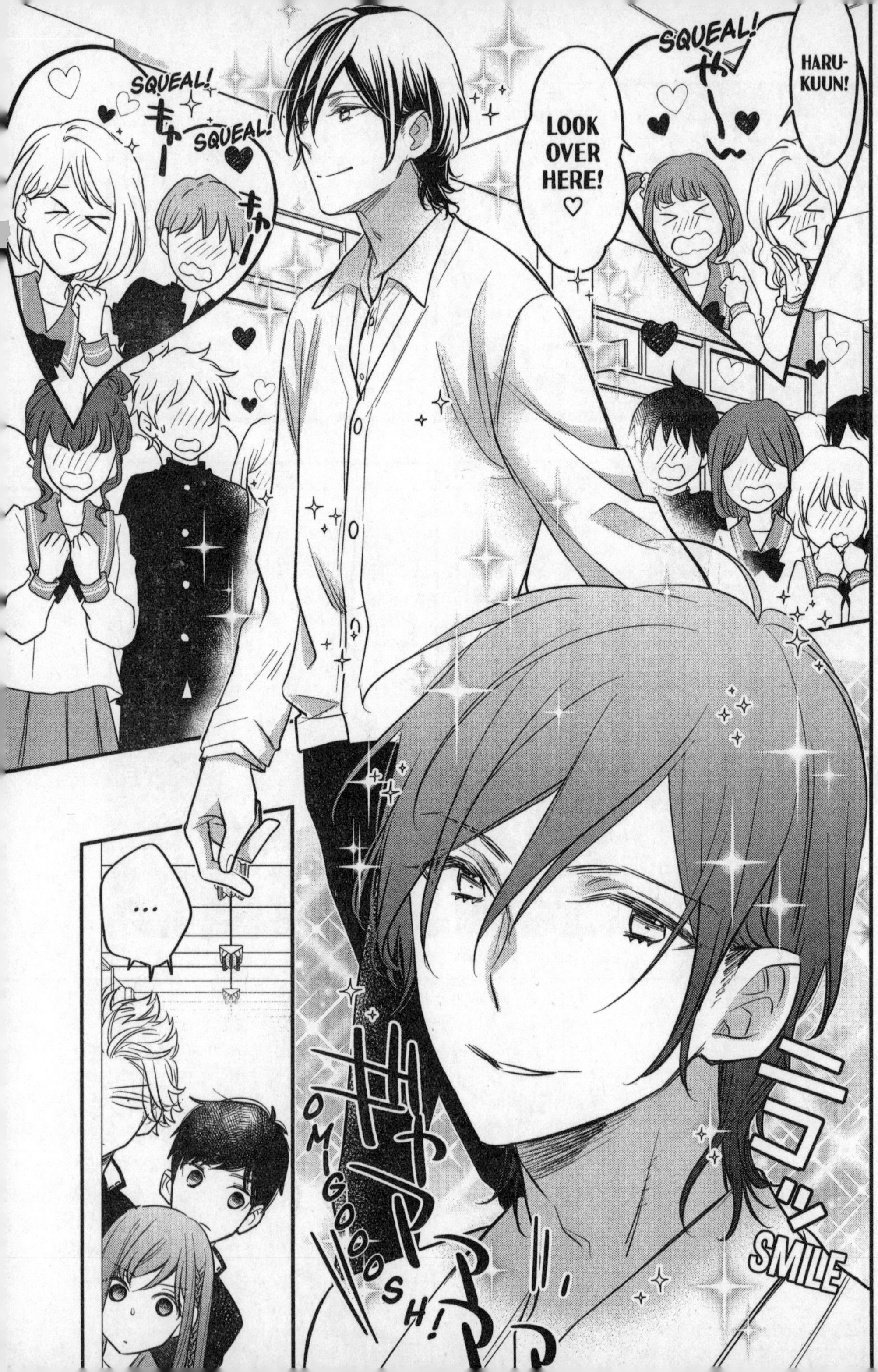

HARU-KUUN!
SQUEAL!
LOOK OVER HERE! ♡
SQUEAL!
SQUEAL!
SMILE
OMIGOOOOSH!
...

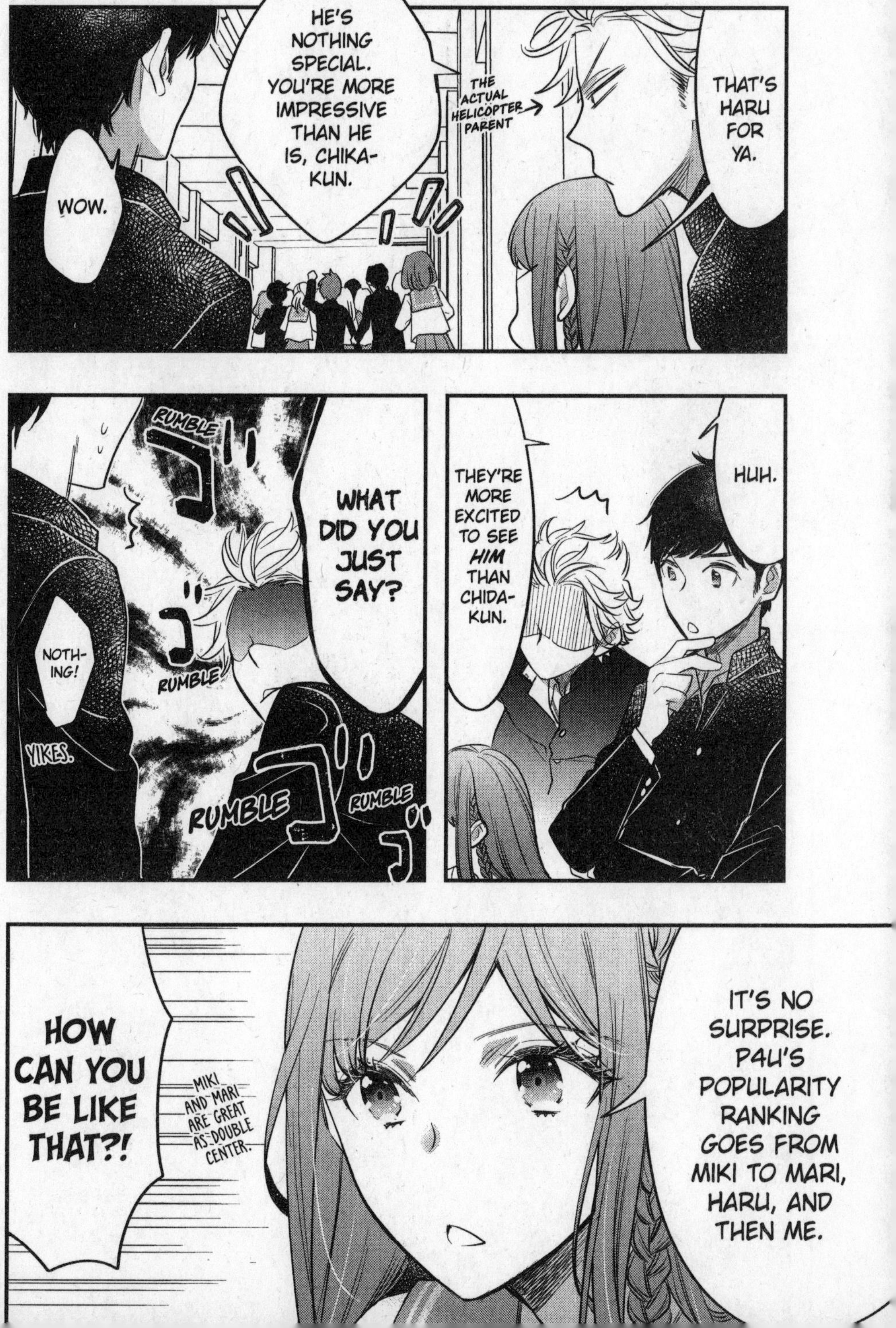
THAT'S HARU FOR YA.
THE ACTUAL HELICOPTER PARENT
HE'S NOTHING SPECIAL. YOU'RE MORE IMPRESSIVE THAN HE IS, CHIKA-KUN.
WOW.
HUH.
THEY'RE MORE EXCITED TO SEE HIM THAN CHIDA-KUN.
WHAT DID YOU JUST SAY?
RUMBLE
RUMBLE
NOTH-ING!
YIKES.
RUMBLE
RUMBLE
IT'S NO SURPRISE. P4U'S POPULARITY RANKING GOES FROM MIKI TO MARI, HARU, AND THEN ME.
MIKI AND MARI ARE GREAT AS DOUBLE CENTER.
HOW CAN YOU BE LIKE THAT?!

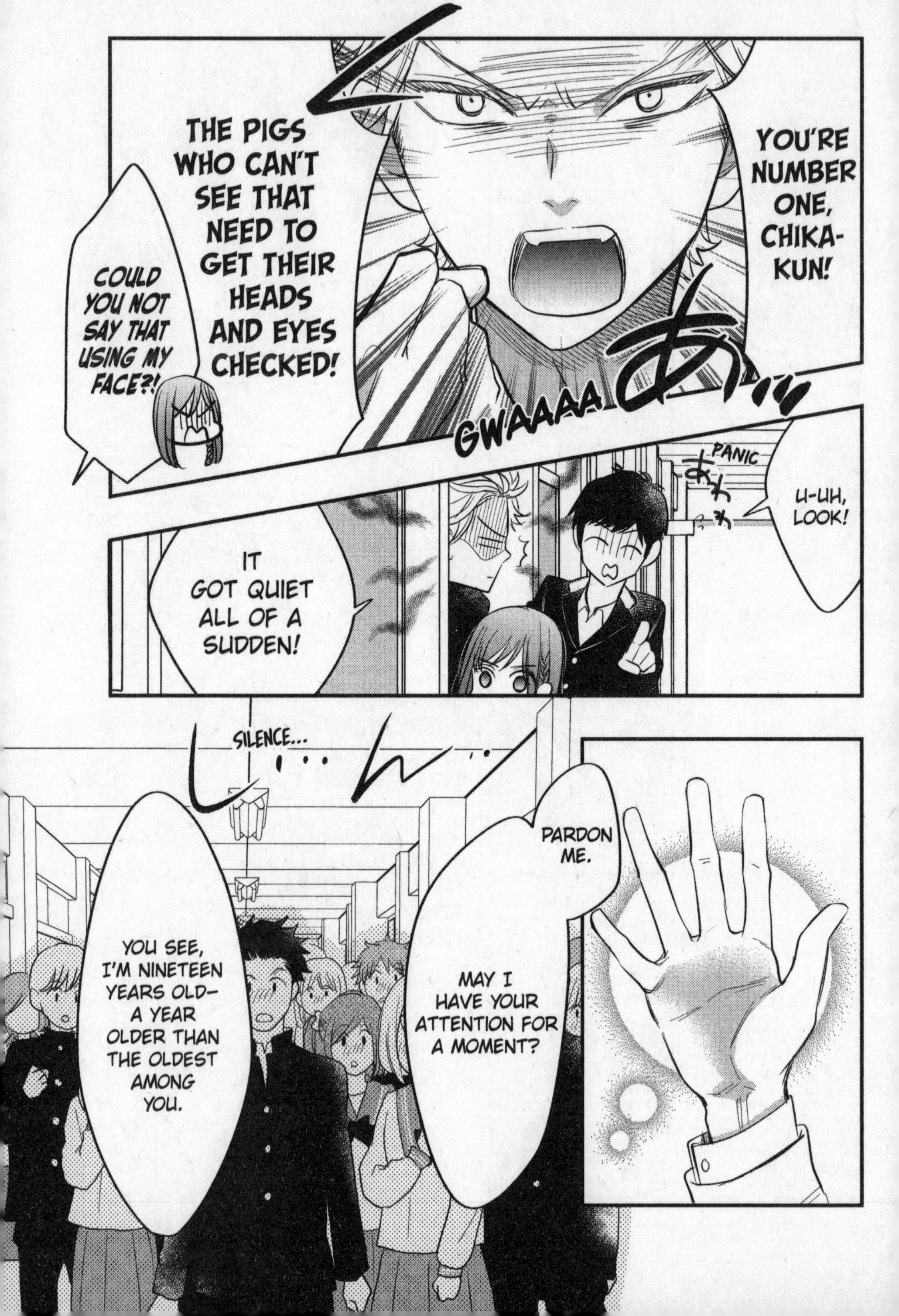
YOU'RE NUMBER ONE, CHIKA-KUN!
THE PIGS WHO CAN'T SEE THAT NEED TO GET THEIR HEADS AND EYES CHECKED!
GWAAAA
COULD YOU NOT SAY THAT USING MY FACE?!
PANIC
U-UH, LOOK!
IT GOT QUIET ALL OF A SUDDEN!
PARDON ME.
MAY I HAVE YOUR ATTENTION FOR A MOMENT?
SILENCE...
YOU SEE, I'M NINETEEN YEARS OLD–A YEAR OLDER THAN THE OLDEST AMONG YOU.

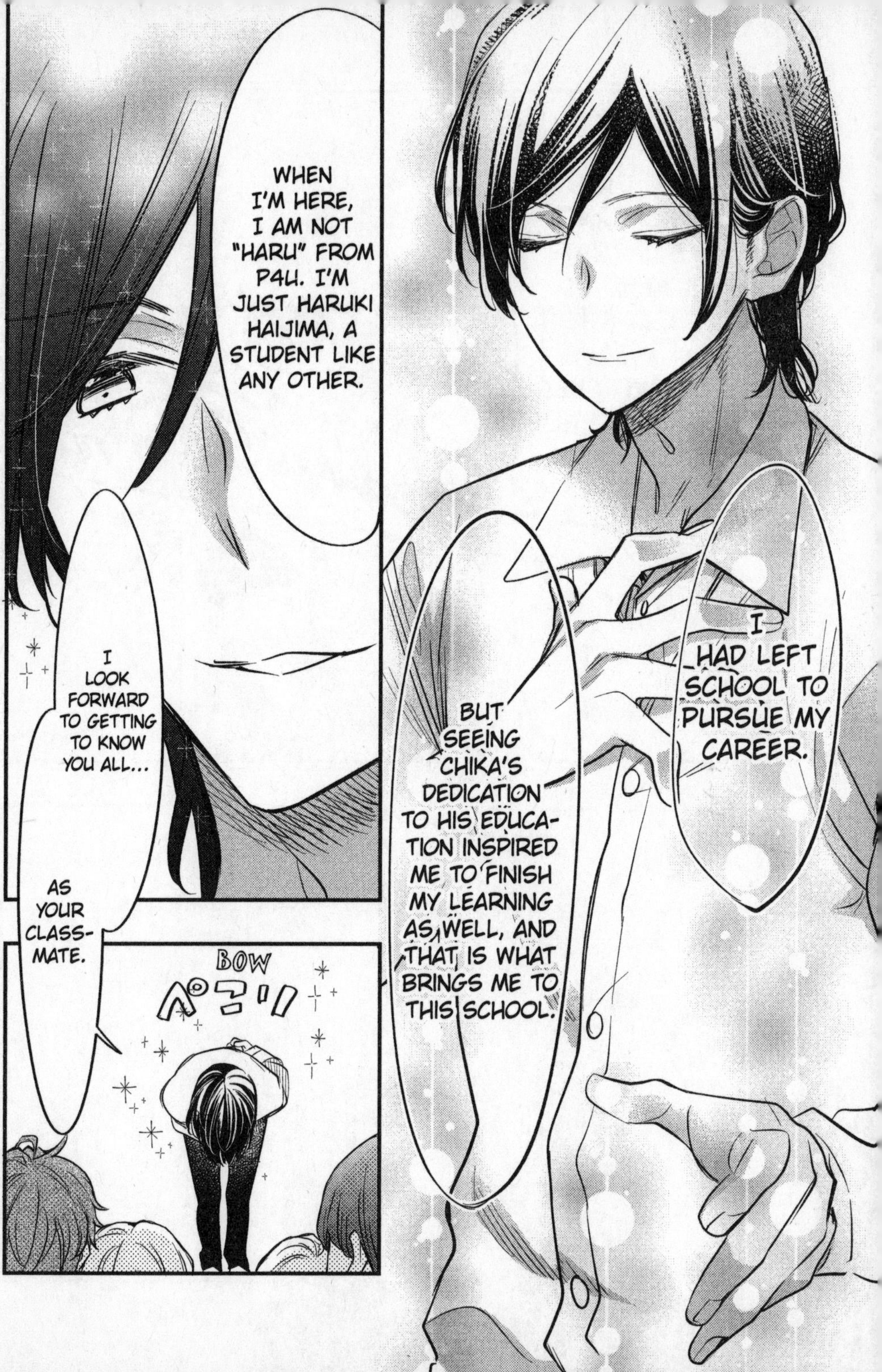
I HAD LEFT SCHOOL TO PURSUE MY CAREER.
BUT SEEING CHIKA'S DEDICATION TO HIS EDUCATION INSPIRED ME TO FINISH MY LEARNING AS WELL, AND THAT IS WHAT BRINGS ME TO THIS SCHOOL.
WHEN I'M HERE, I AM NOT "HARU" FROM P4U. I'M JUST HARUKI HAIJIMA, A STUDENT LIKE ANY OTHER.
I LOOK FORWARD TO GETTING TO KNOW YOU ALL...
AS YOUR CLASSMATE.
BOW
ペコリ

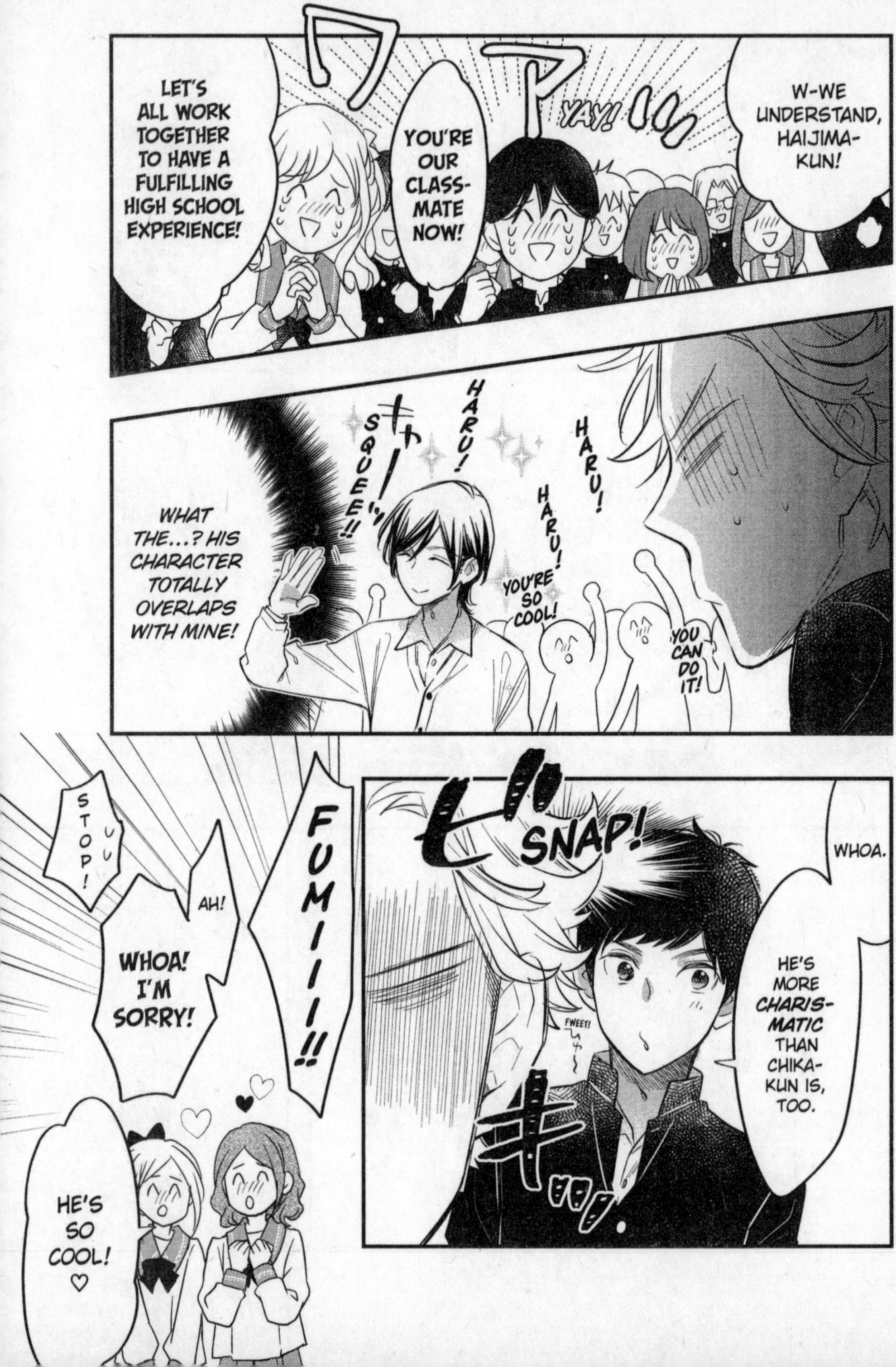
W-WE UNDERSTAND, HAIJIMA-KUN!
YAY!
YOU'RE OUR CLASSMATE NOW!
LET'S ALL WORK TOGETHER TO HAVE A FULFILLING HIGH SCHOOL EXPERIENCE!
HARU!
HARU!
HARU!
SQUEE!!
YOU'RE SO COOL!
YOU CAN DO IT!
WHAT THE…? HIS CHARACTER TOTALLY OVERLAPS WITH MINE!
WHOA.
SNAP!
HE'S MORE CHARISMATIC THAN CHIKA-KUN IS, TOO.
FWEET!
FUMIIIII!!
STOP!
AH!
WHOA! I'M SORRY!
HE'S SO COOL! ♡

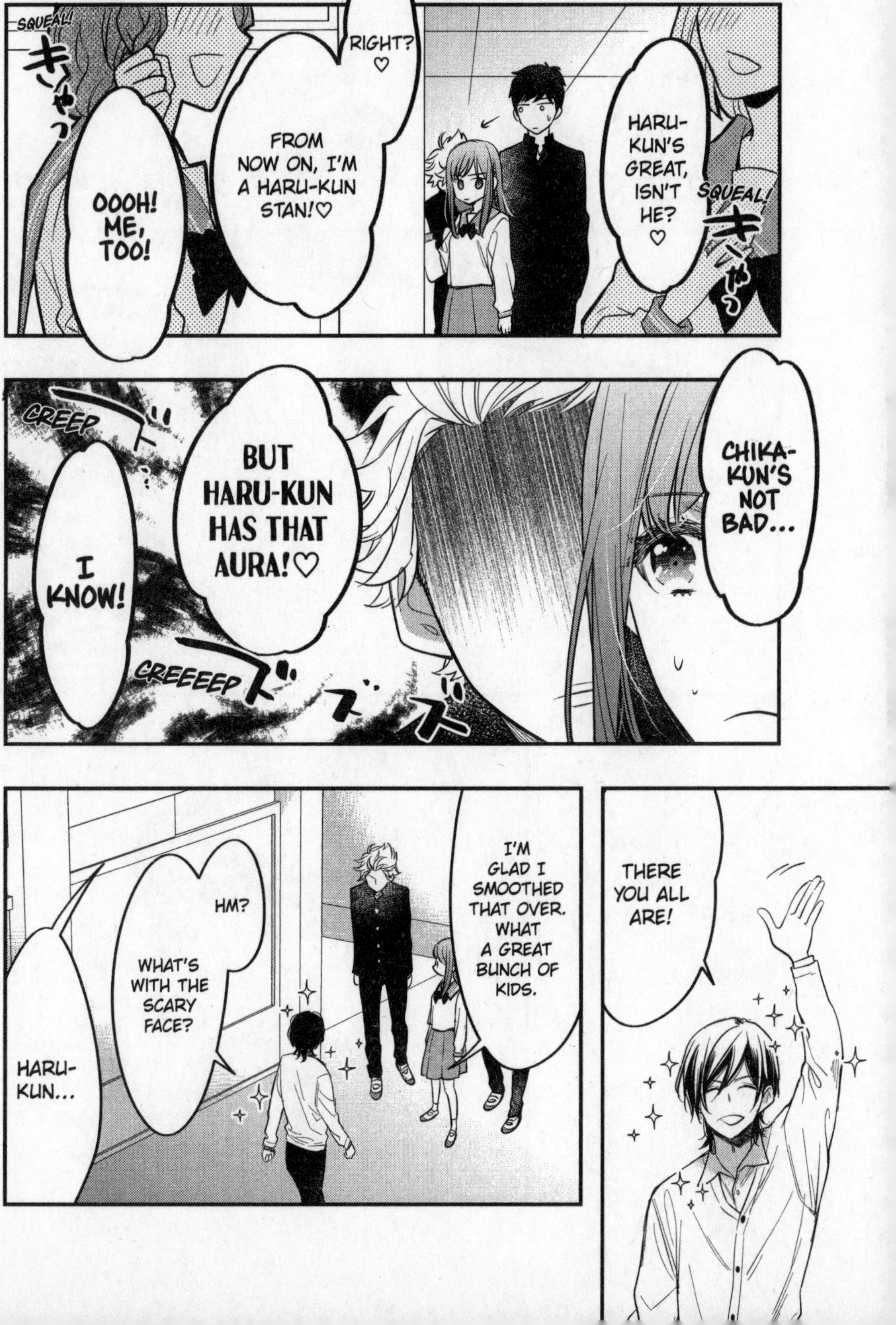
HARU-KUN'S GREAT, ISN'T HE? ♡
SQUEAL!
RIGHT? ♡
FROM NOW ON, I'M A HARU-KUN STAN!♡
OOOH! ME, TOO!
SQUEAL!
CHIKA-KUN'S NOT BAD...
BUT HARU-KUN HAS THAT AURA!♡
I KNOW!
CREEP
CREEEEEP
THERE YOU ALL ARE!
I'M GLAD I SMOOTHED THAT OVER. WHAT A GREAT BUNCH OF KIDS.
HM?
WHAT'S WITH THE SCARY FACE?
HARU-KUN...

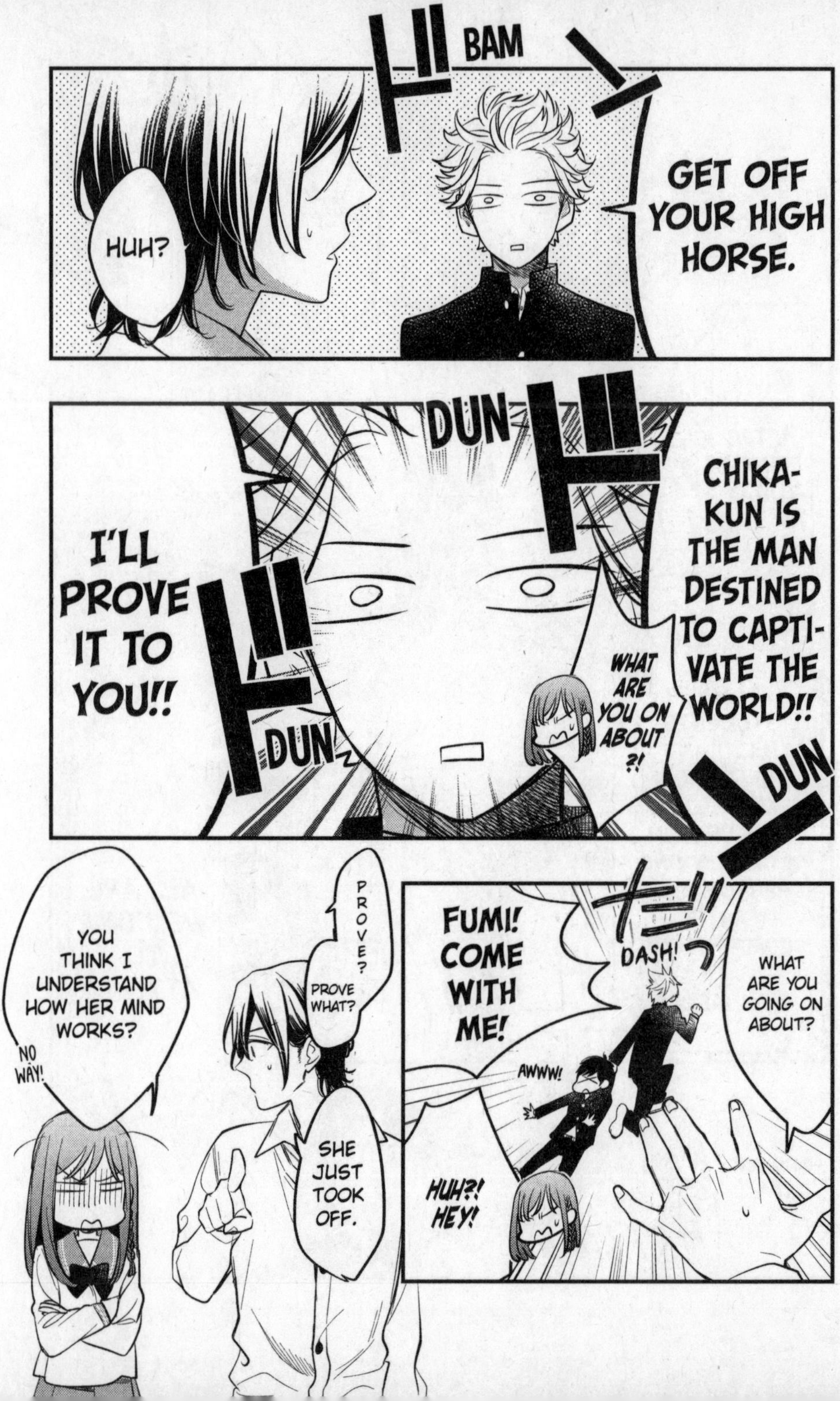
BAM
GET OFF YOUR HIGH HORSE.
HUH?
DUN
CHIKA-KUN IS THE MAN DESTINED TO CAPTI-VATE THE WORLD!!
DUN
WHAT ARE YOU ON ABOUT?!
I'LL PROVE IT TO YOU!!
DUN
DASH!
WHAT ARE YOU GOING ON ABOUT?
FUMI! COME WITH ME!
AWWW!
HUH?! HEY!
PROVE? PROVE WHAT?
SHE JUST TOOK OFF.
YOU THINK I UNDERSTAND HOW HER MIND WORKS?
NO WAY!

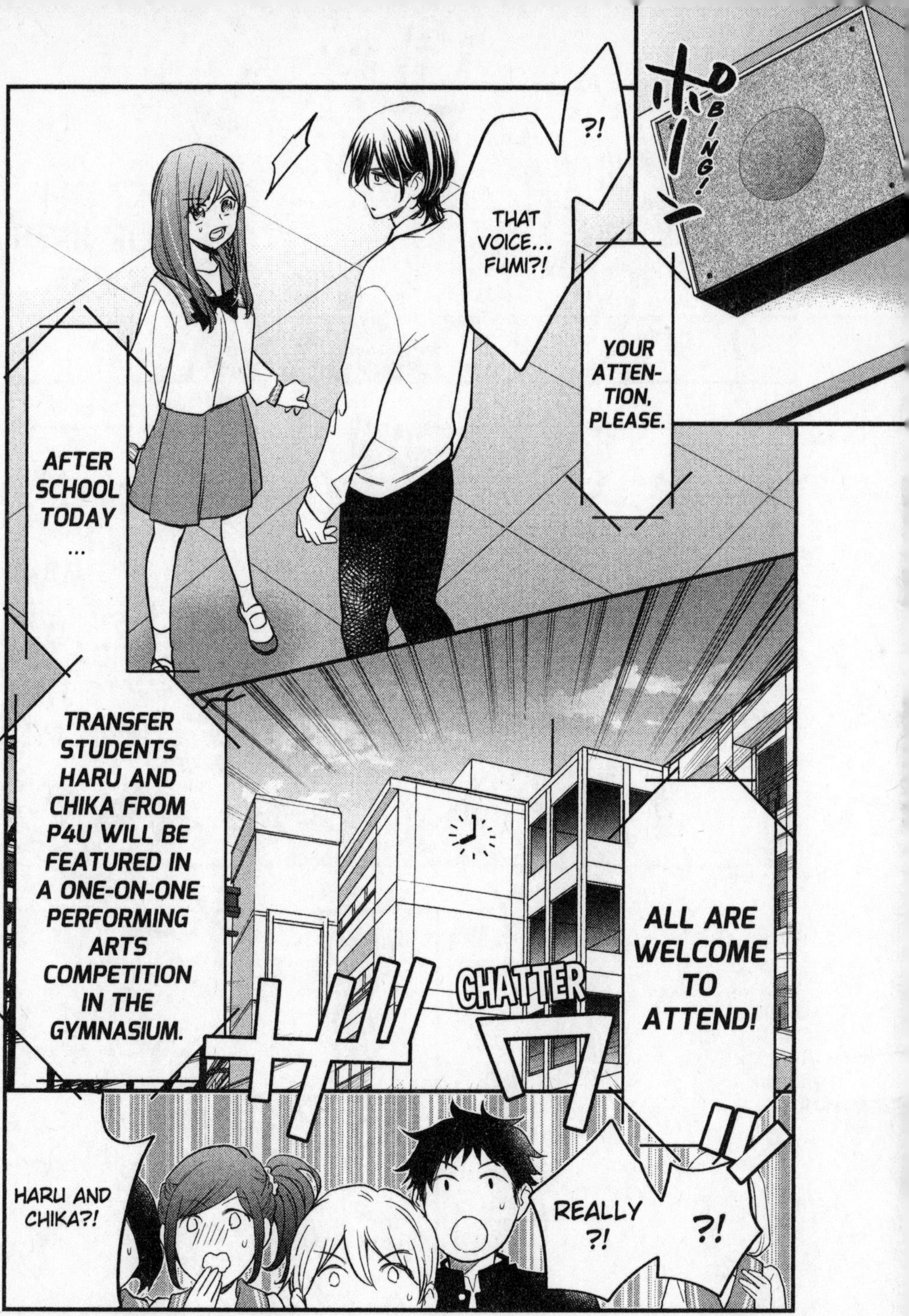
BING!
YOUR ATTENTION, PLEASE.
?!
THAT VOICE... FUMI?!
AFTER SCHOOL TODAY ...
ALL ARE WELCOME TO ATTEND!
CHATTER
TRANSFER STUDENTS HARU AND CHIKA FROM P4U WILL BE FEATURED IN A ONE-ON-ONE PERFORMING ARTS COMPETITION IN THE GYMNASIUM.
?!
REALLY ?!
HARU AND CHIKA?!

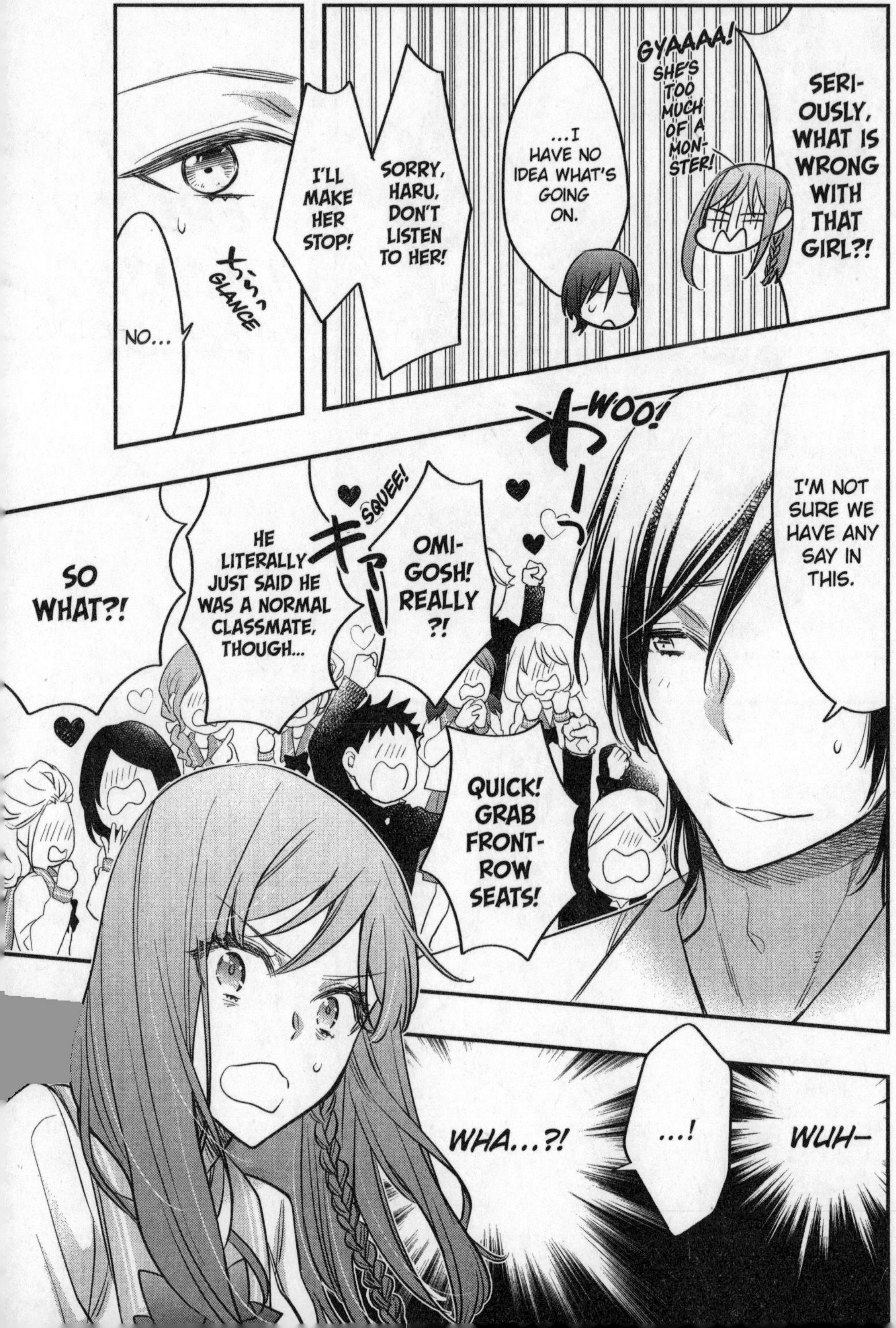
SERI-OUSLY, WHAT IS WRONG WITH THAT GIRL?!
GYAAAA! SHE'S TOO MUCH OF A MON-STER!
...I HAVE NO IDEA WHAT'S GOING ON.
SORRY, HARU, DON'T LISTEN TO HER!
I'LL MAKE HER STOP!
GLANCE
NO...
-WOO!
I'M NOT SURE WE HAVE ANY SAY IN THIS.
SQUEE!
OMI-GOSH! REALLY?!
HE LITERALLY JUST SAID HE WAS A NORMAL CLASSMATE, THOUGH...
SO WHAT?!
QUICK! GRAB FRONT-ROW SEATS!
WUH-
...!
WHA...?!

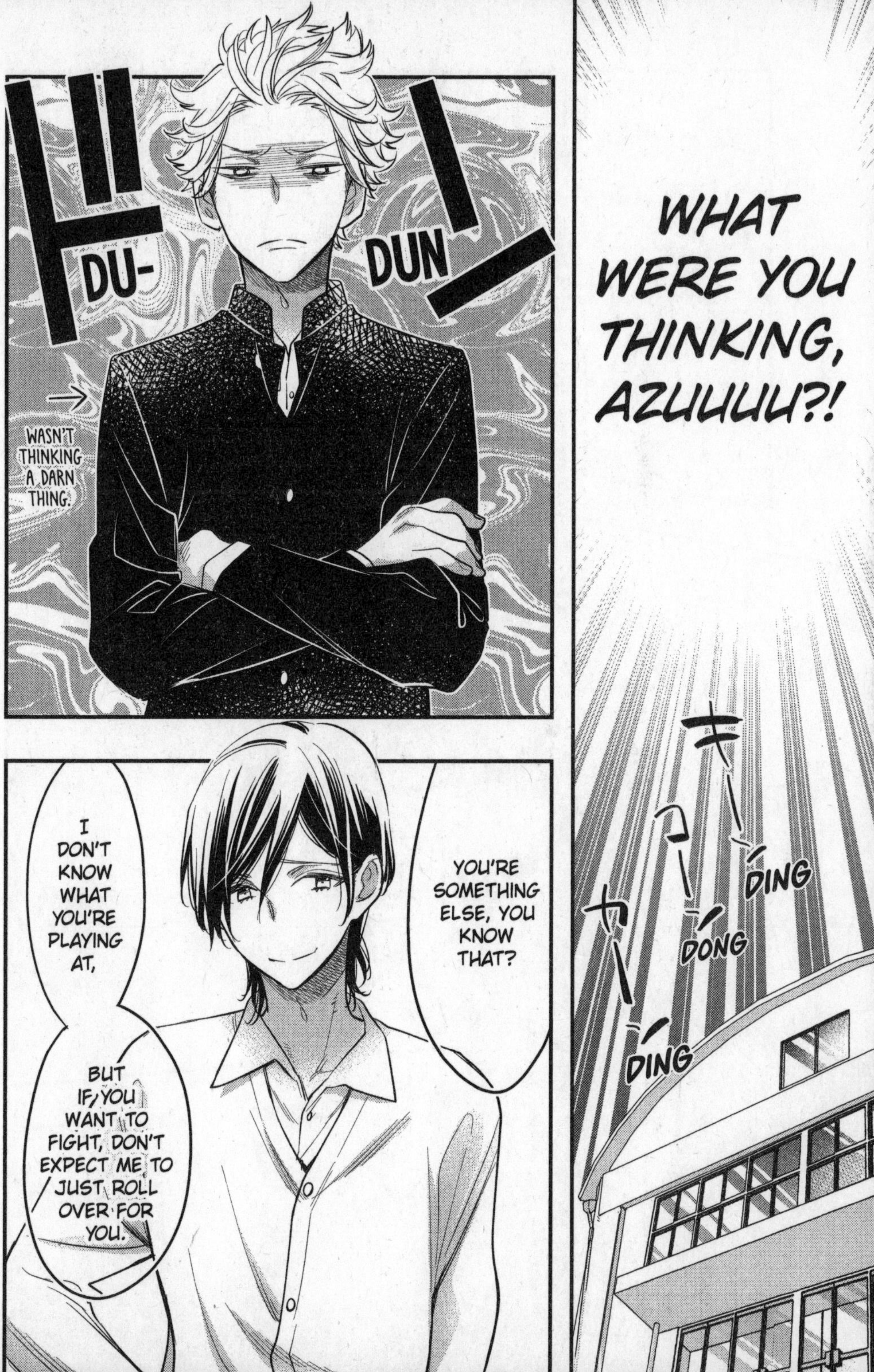
WHAT WERE YOU THINKING, AZUUUUU?!
DING
DONG
DING
DU-
DUN
WASN'T THINKING A DARN THING.
YOU'RE SOMETHING ELSE, YOU KNOW THAT?
I DON'T KNOW WHAT YOU'RE PLAYING AT,
BUT IF YOU WANT TO FIGHT, DON'T EXPECT ME TO JUST ROLL OVER FOR YOU.

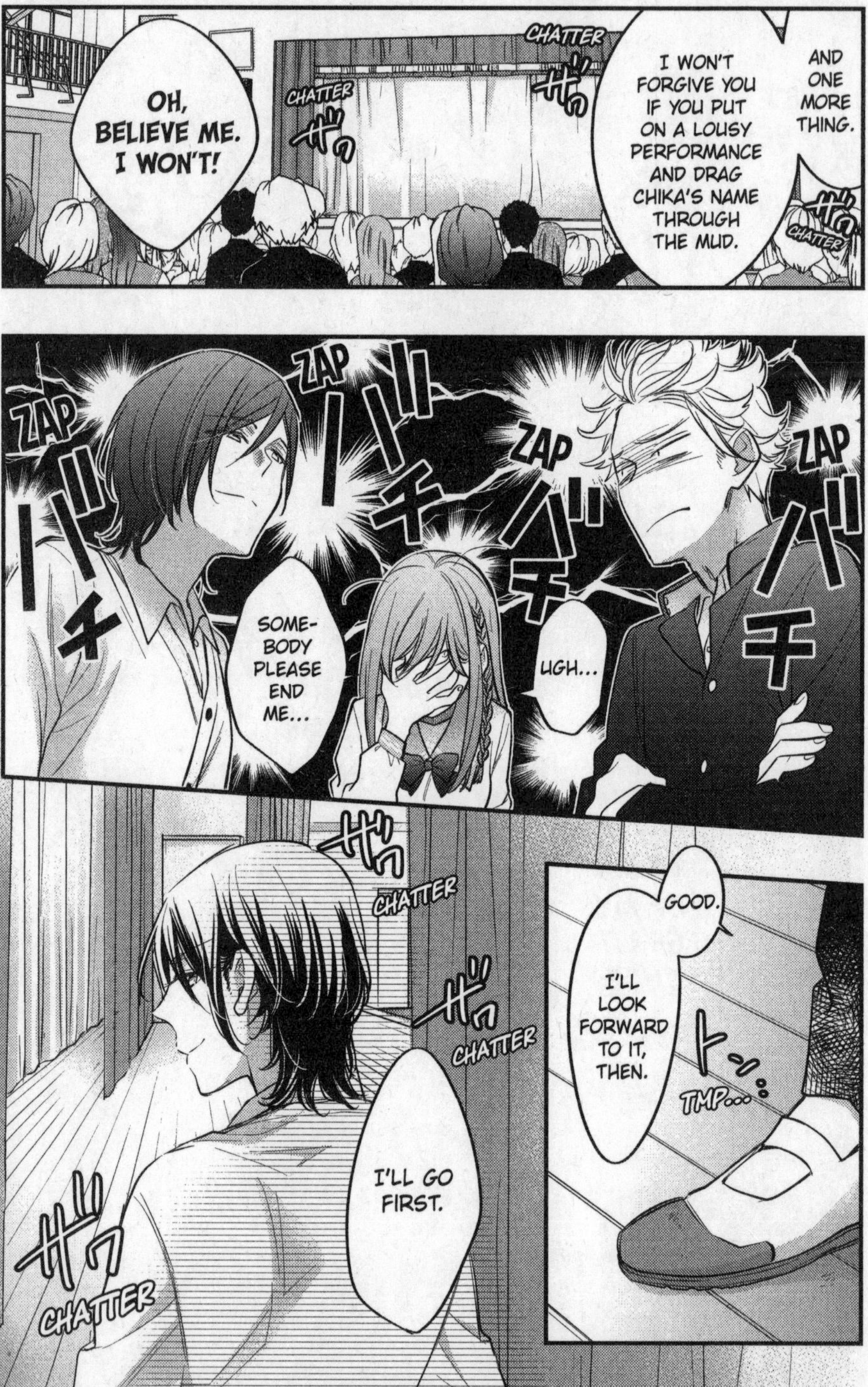
AND ONE MORE THING.
I WON'T FORGIVE YOU IF YOU PUT ON A LOUSY PERFORMANCE AND DRAG CHIKA'S NAME THROUGH THE MUD.
CHATTER
CHATTER
CHATTER
OH, BELIEVE ME. I WON'T!
ZAP
ZAP
ZAP
ZAP
UGH...
SOME-BODY PLEASE END ME...
GOOD.
I'LL LOOK FORWARD TO IT, THEN.
TMP...
CHATTER
CHATTER
I'LL GO FIRST.
CHATTER

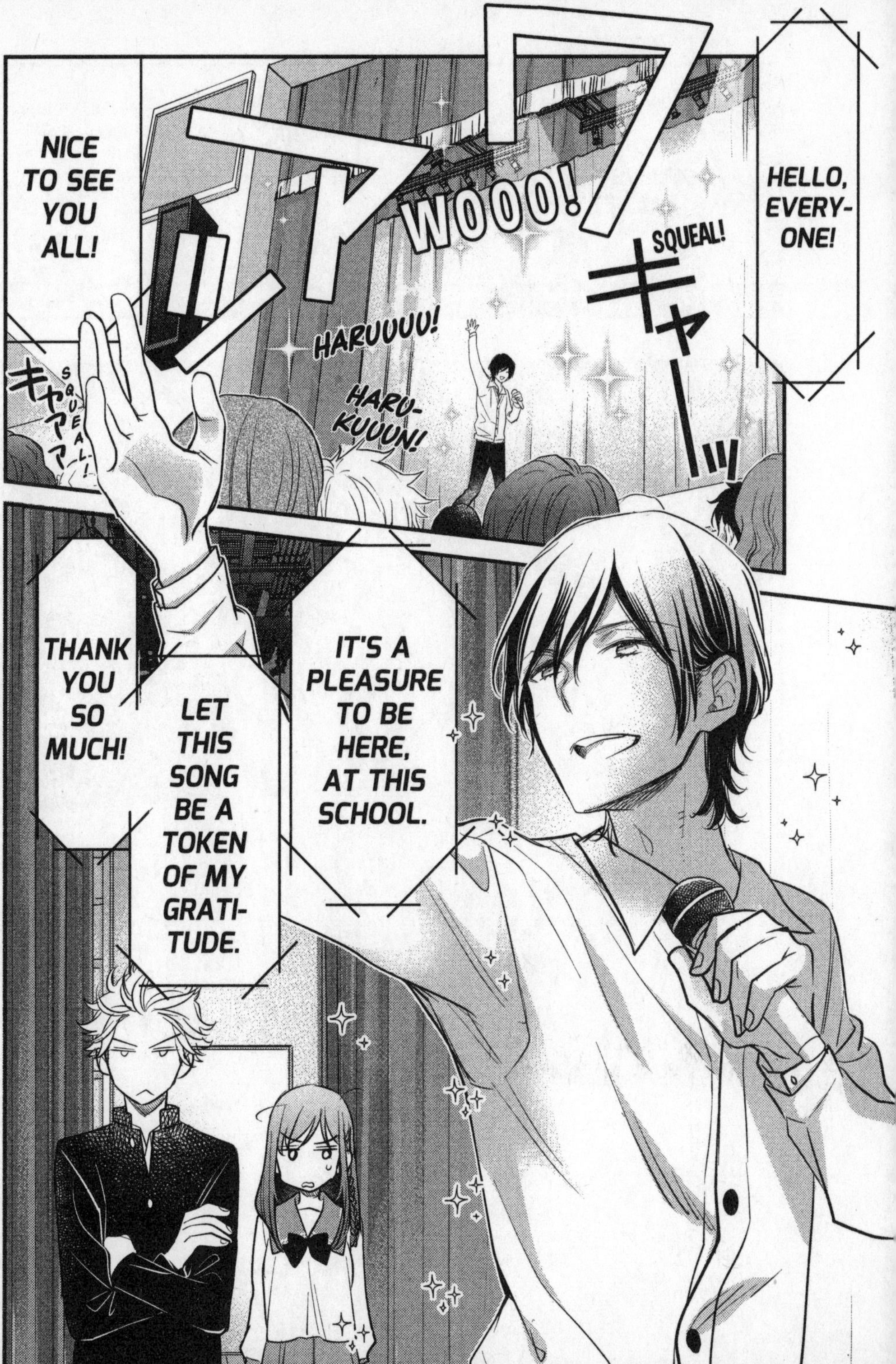

HELLO, EVERYONE!
キャーッ
SQUEAL!
ワァーッ
WOOO!
HARUUUU!
HARU-KUUUN!
キャアアー
SQUEAL!
NICE TO SEE YOU ALL!
IT'S A PLEASURE TO BE HERE, AT THIS SCHOOL.
LET THIS SONG BE A TOKEN OF MY GRATITUDE.
THANK YOU SO MUCH!

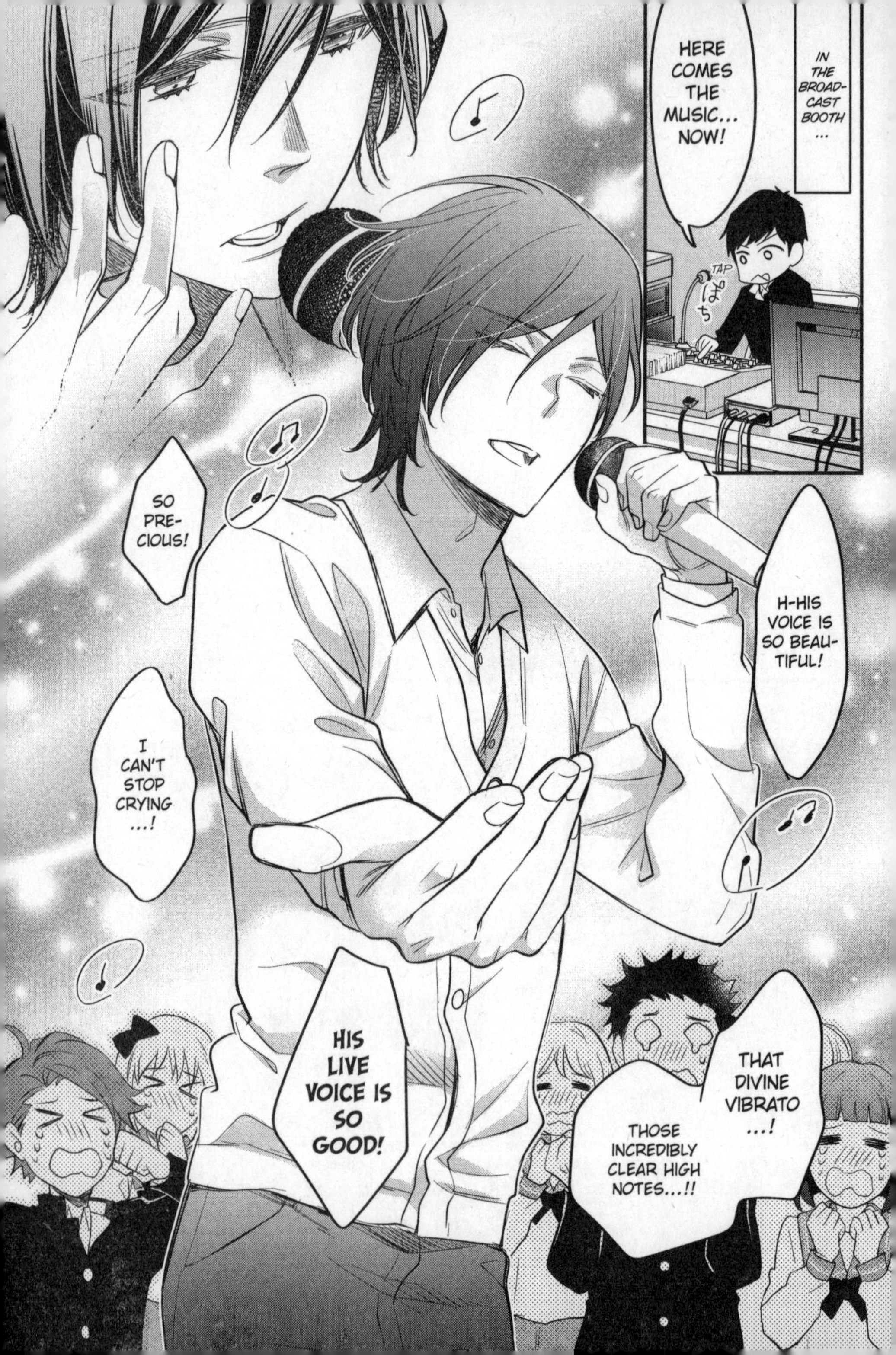
IN THE BROAD-CAST BOOTH...
HERE COMES THE MUSIC... NOW!
TAP
H-HIS VOICE IS SO BEAU-TIFUL!
SO PRE-CIOUS!
I CAN'T STOP CRYING ...!
THAT DIVINE VIBRATO ...!
THOSE INCREDIBLY CLEAR HIGH NOTES...!!
HIS LIVE VOICE IS SO GOOD!

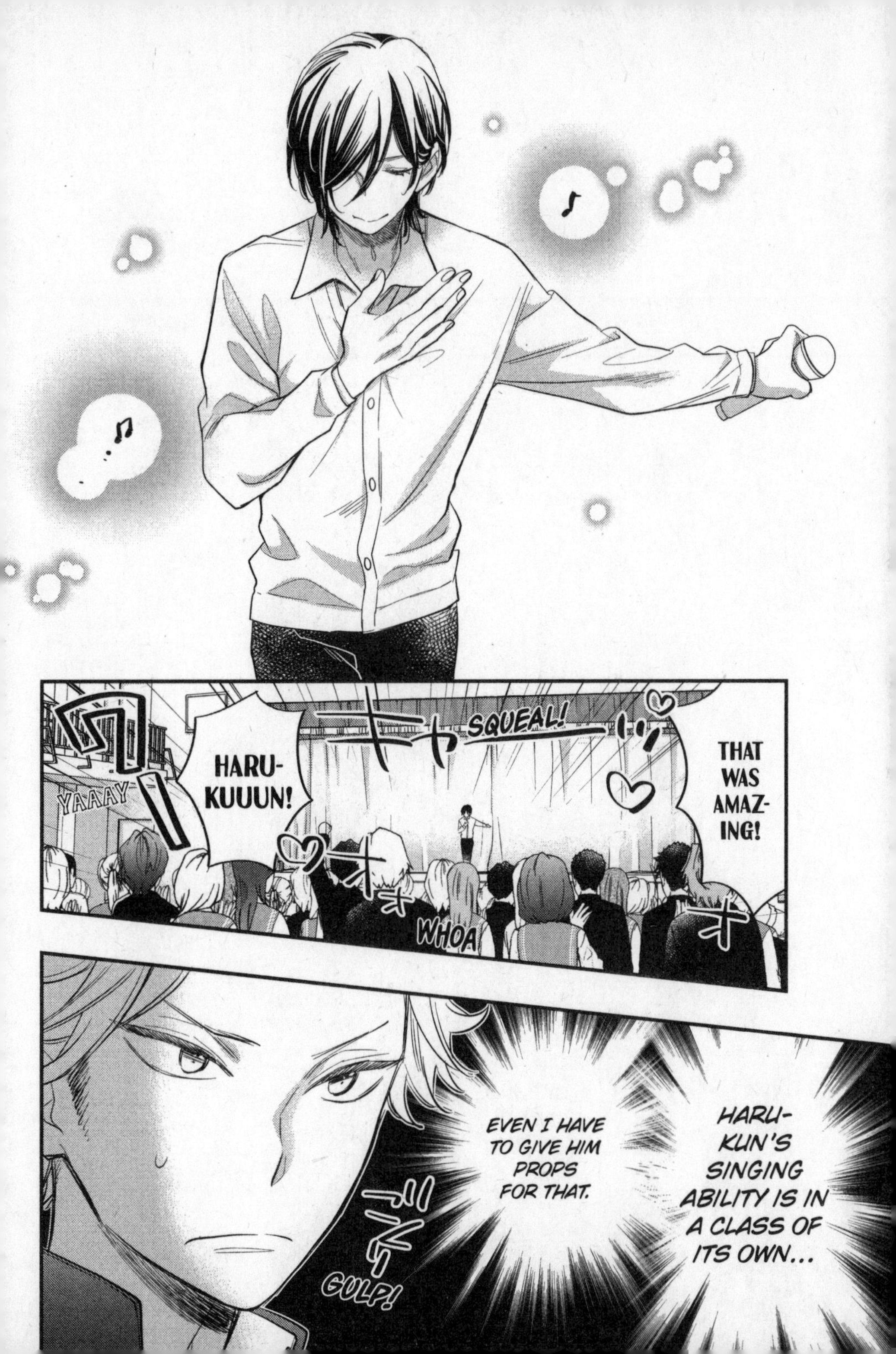
THAT WAS AMAZ-ING!
SQUEAL!
HARU-KUUUN!
YAAAY
WHOA
HARU-KUN'S SINGING ABILITY IS IN A CLASS OF ITS OWN...
EVEN I HAVE TO GIVE HIM PROPS FOR THAT.
GULP!

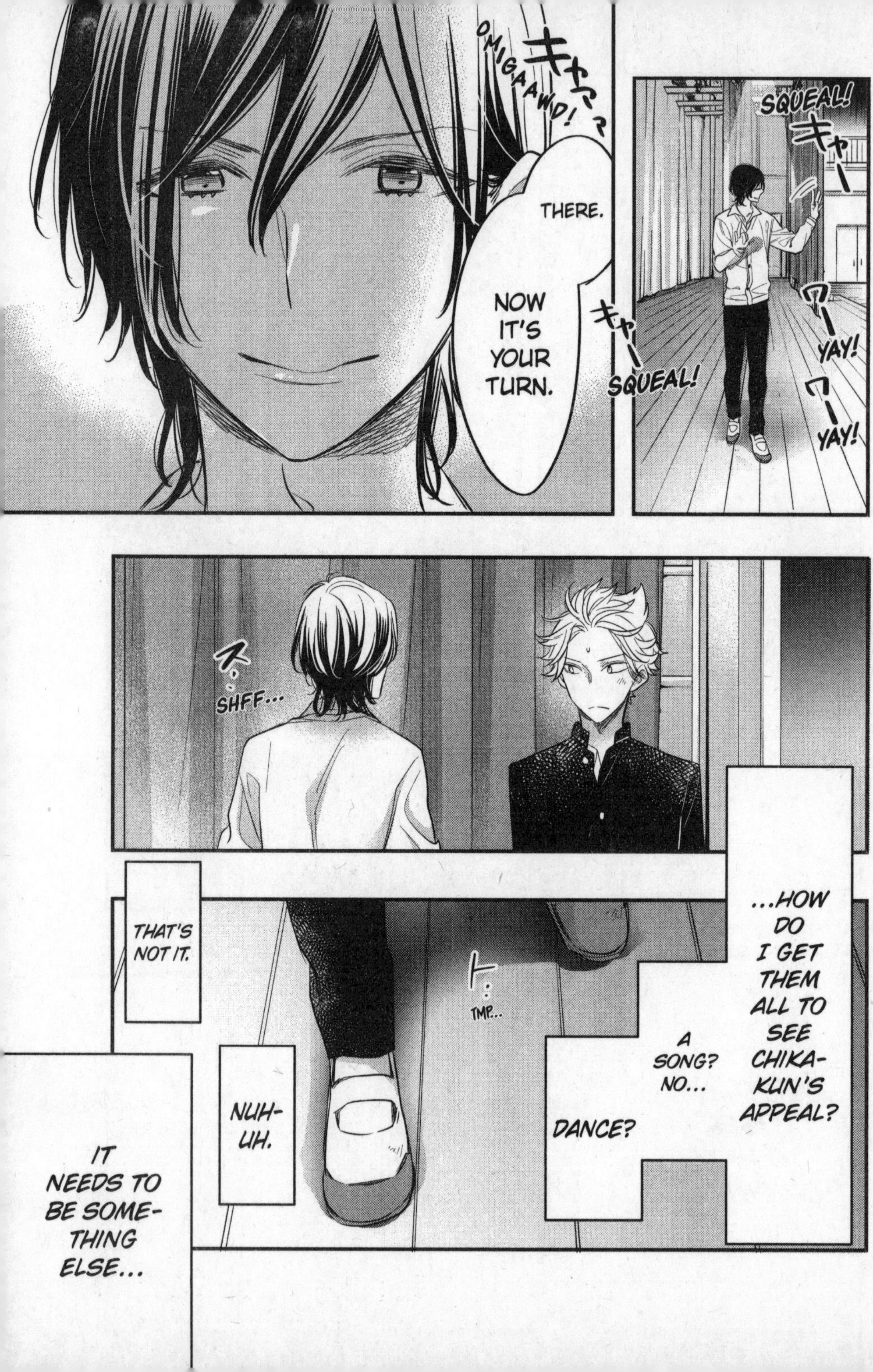

SQUEAL! キャー
ワー YAY!
ワー YAY!
OMIGAAWD! キャ～
THERE.
NOW IT'S YOUR TURN.
キャー SQUEAL!
ス… SHFF...
...HOW DO I GET THEM ALL TO SEE CHIKA-KUN'S APPEAL?
A SONG? NO...
DANCE?
ト… TMP...
THAT'S NOT IT.
NUH-UH.
IT NEEDS TO BE SOME-THING ELSE...

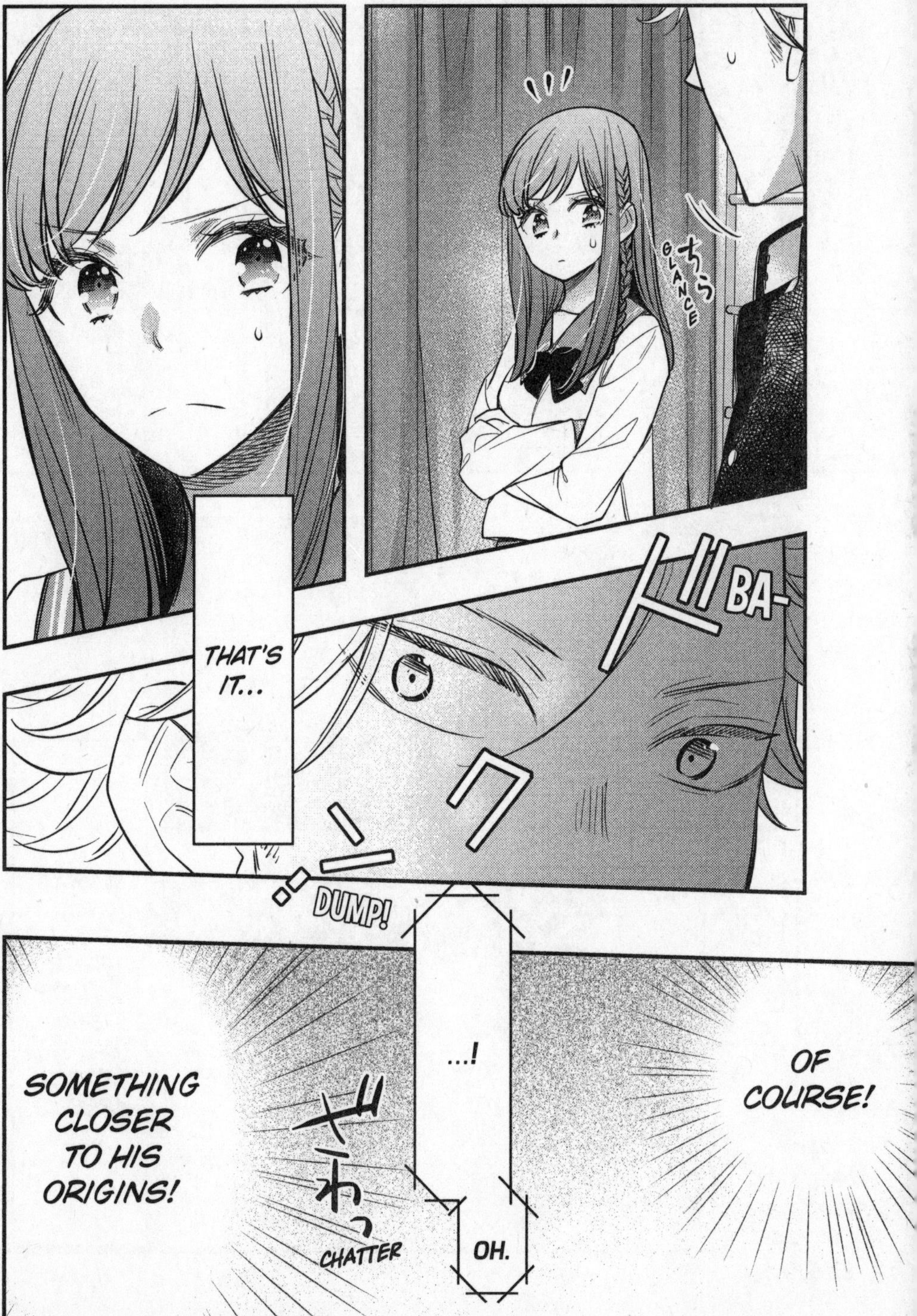
ちら
GLANCE
THAT'S IT...
BA-
DUMP!
OF COURSE!
...!
OH.
CHATTER
SOMETHING CLOSER TO HIS ORIGINS!

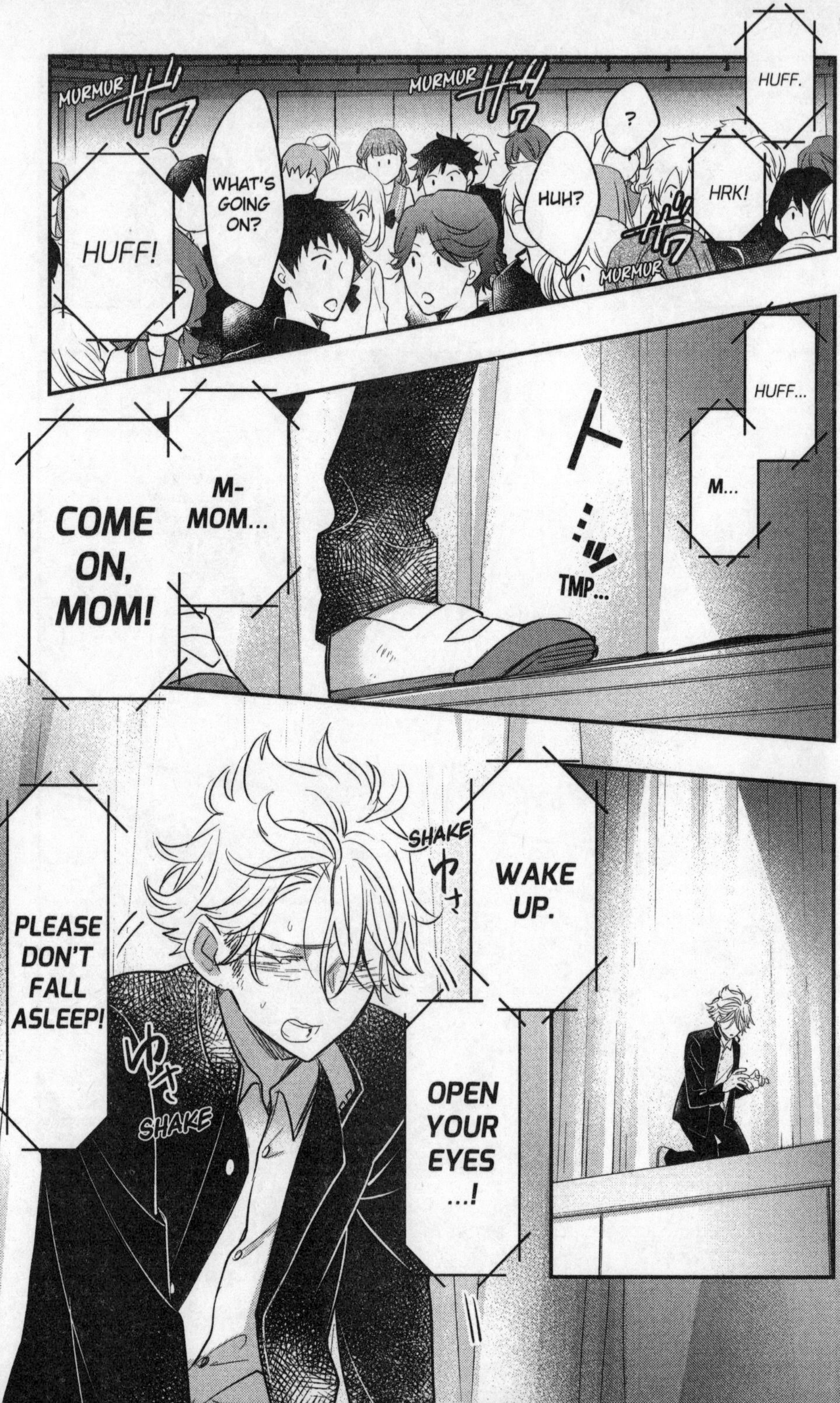

HUFF.
HRK!
MURMUR ザワ
?
HUH?
MURMUR ザワ
WHAT'S GOING ON?
MURMUR ザワ
HUFF!
HUFF...
M...
TMP...
M- MOM...
COME ON, MOM!
WAKE UP.
SHAKE ゆさ
OPEN YOUR EYES ...!
PLEASE DON'T FALL ASLEEP!
ゆさ SHAKE

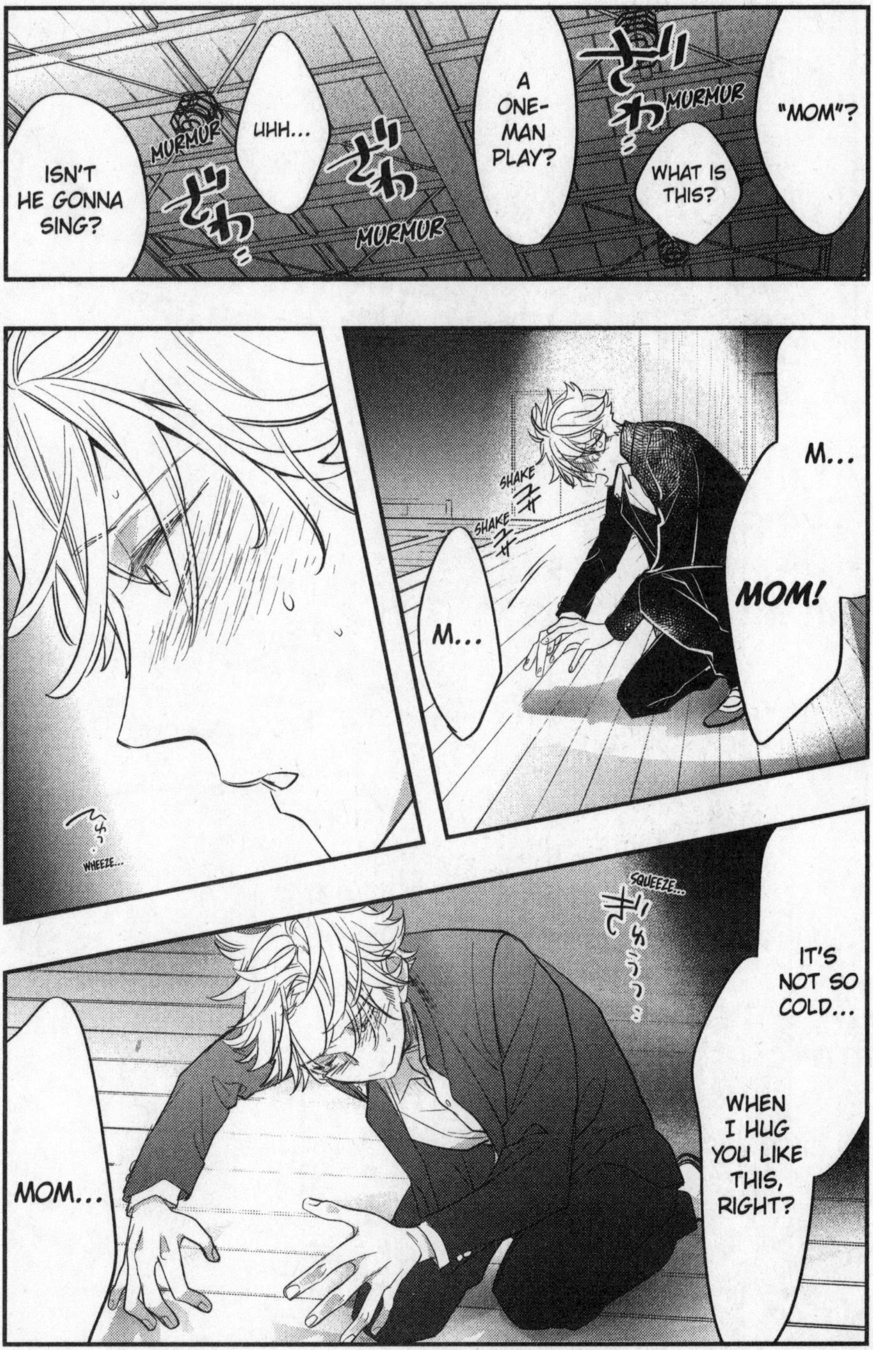

"MOM"?
WHAT IS THIS?
MURMUR
A ONE-MAN PLAY?
UHH...
MURMUR
MURMUR
ISN'T HE GONNA SING?
M... MOM!
SHAKE
SHAKE
M...
WHEEZE...
SQUEEZE...
IT'S NOT SO COLD... WHEN I HUG YOU LIKE THIS, RIGHT?
MOM...

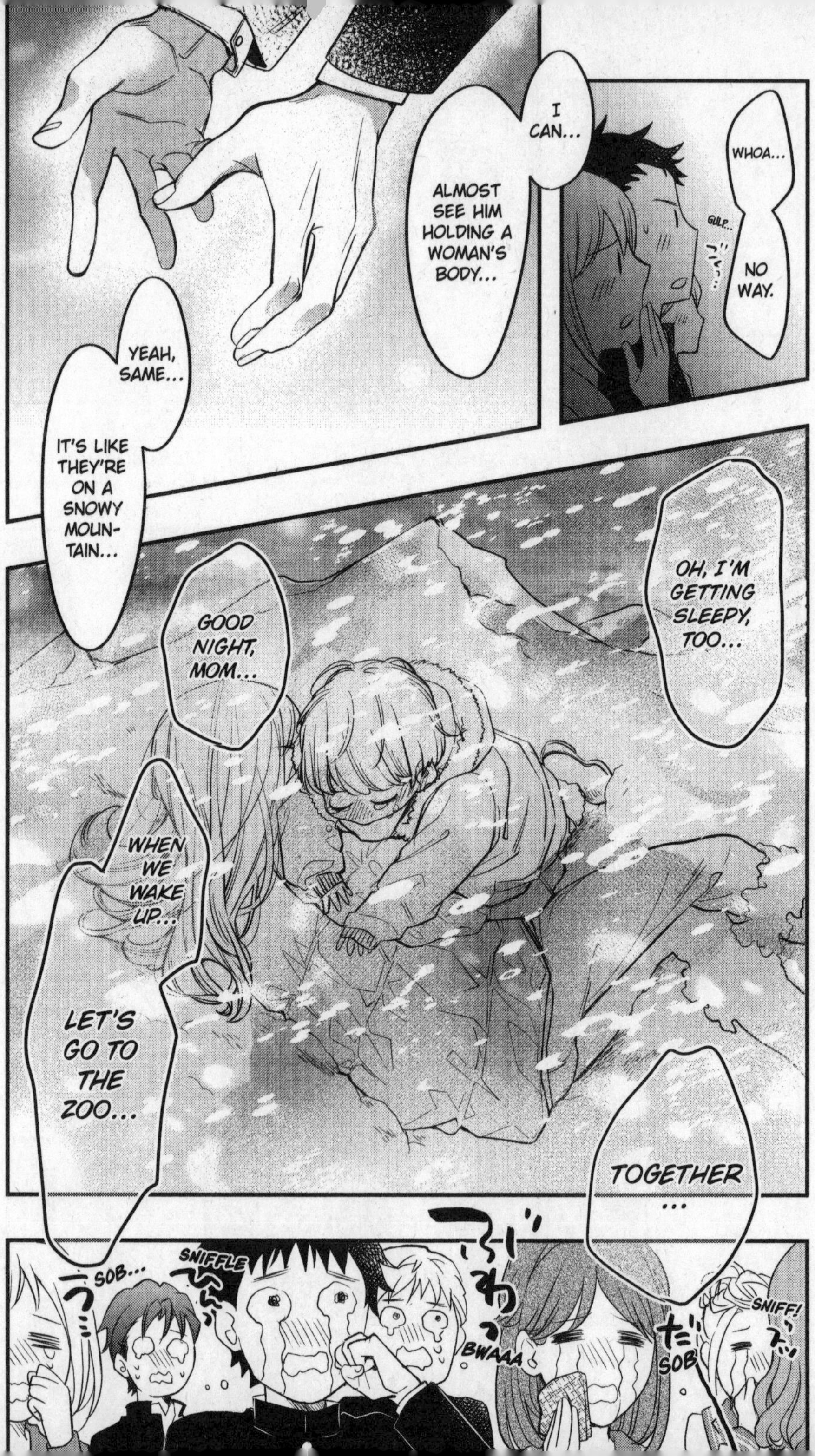
WHOA...
GULP...
NO WAY.
I CAN...
ALMOST SEE HIM HOLDING A WOMAN'S BODY...
YEAH, SAME...
IT'S LIKE THEY'RE ON A SNOWY MOUN-TAIN...
OH, I'M GETTING SLEEPY, TOO...
GOOD NIGHT, MOM...
WHEN WE WAKE UP...
LET'S GO TO THE ZOO...
TOGETHER...
SNIFF!
SOB
BWAAA
SNIFFLE
SOB...

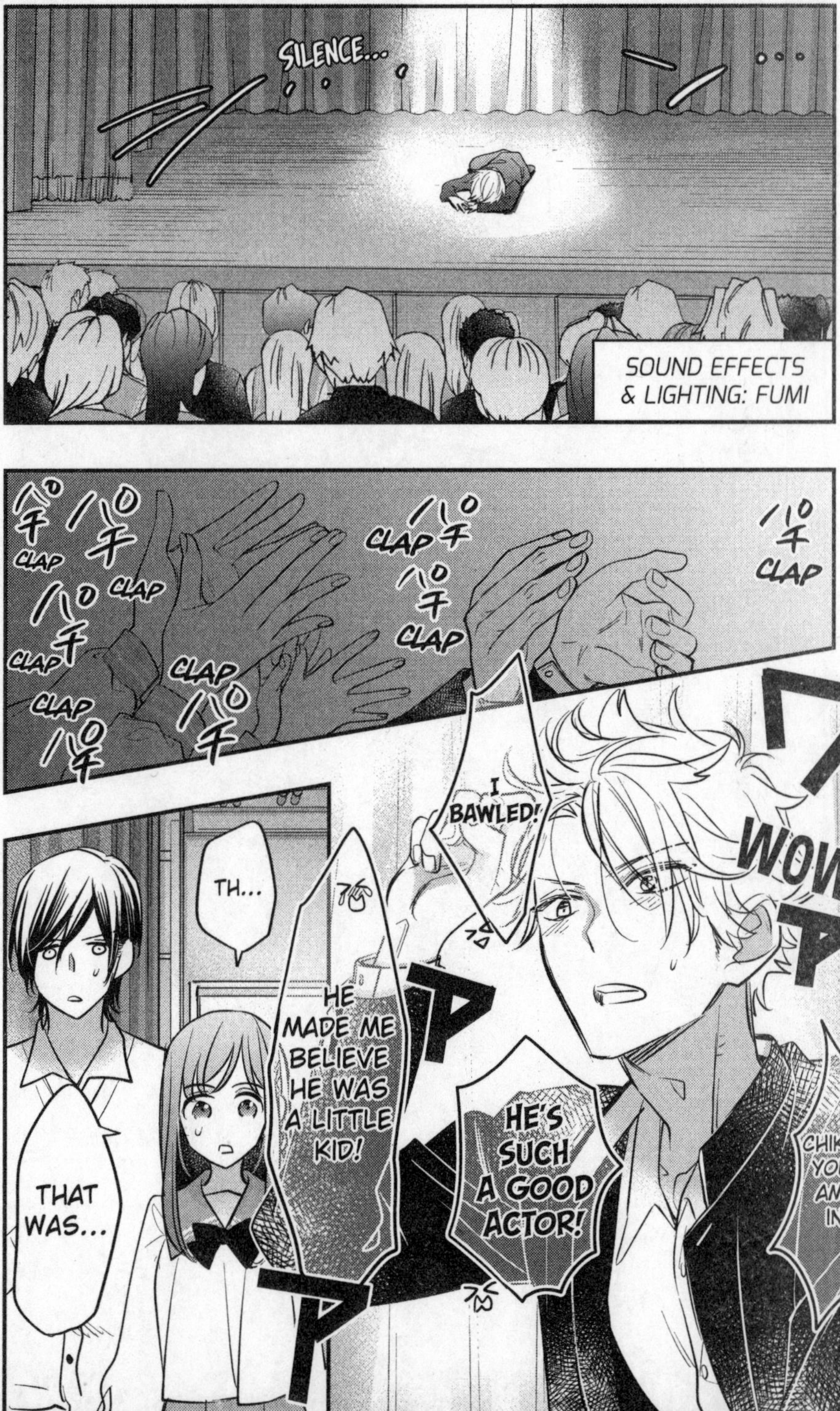
...
SILENCE...
SOUND EFFECTS & LIGHTING: FUMI
パチ CLAP
パチ CLAP
パチ CLAP
パチ CLAP
パチ CLAP
パチ CLAP
パチ CLAP
パチ CLAP
パチ CLAP
WOW!
I BAWLED!
CHIKAAA! YOU'RE AMAZ-ING!
HE'S SUCH A GOOD ACTOR!
HE MADE ME BELIEVE HE WAS A LITTLE KID!
TH...
THAT WAS...

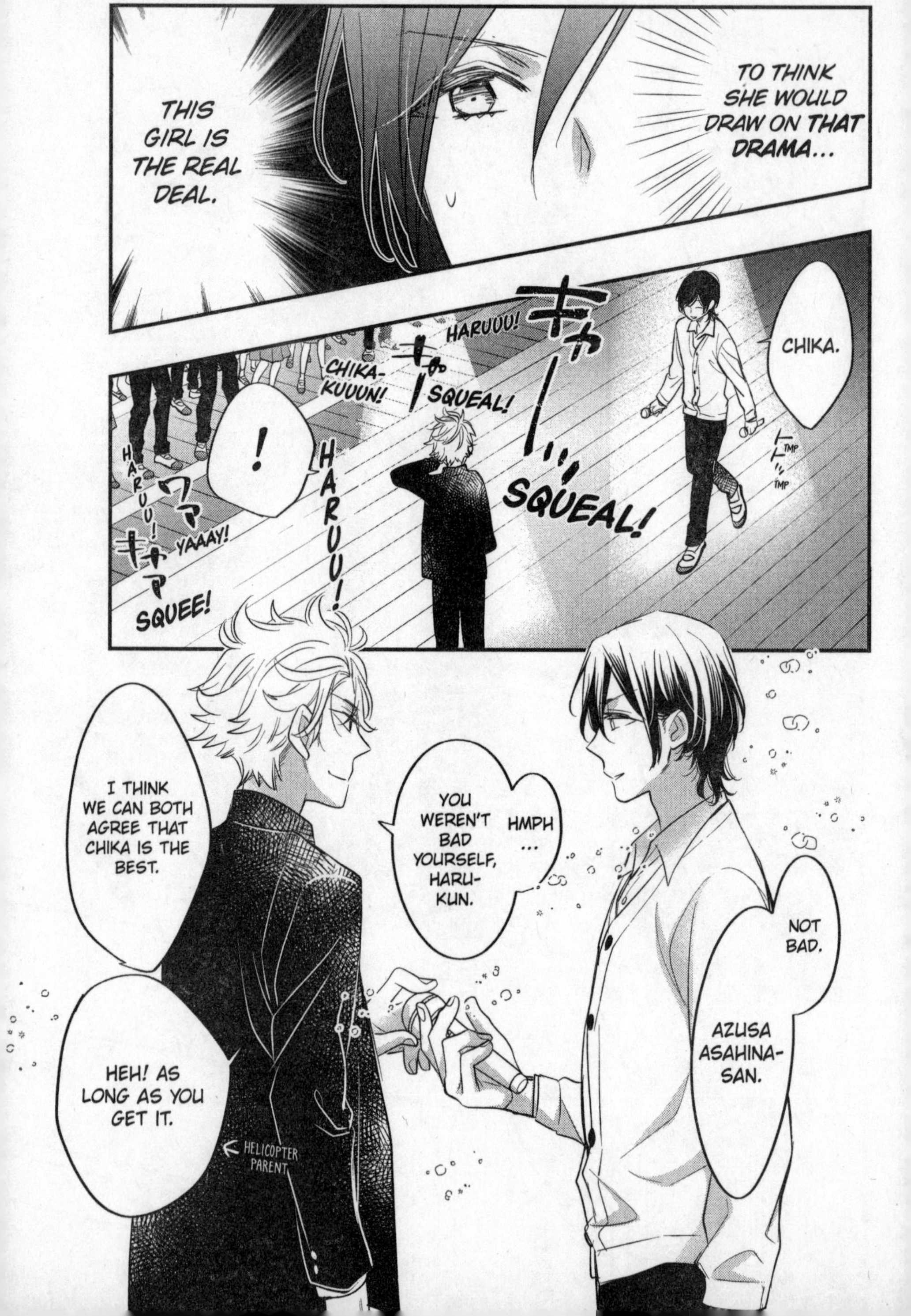

TO THINK SHE WOULD DRAW ON THAT DRAMA...
THIS GIRL IS THE REAL DEAL.
CHIKA.
TMP TMP
SQUEAL!
HARUUU!
SQUEAL!
CHIKA-KUUUN!
!
HARUUU!
HARUU!
YAAAY!
SQUEE!
NOT BAD.
AZUSA ASAHINA-SAN.
HMPH...
YOU WEREN'T BAD YOURSELF, HARU-KUN.
I THINK WE CAN BOTH AGREE THAT CHIKA IS THE BEST.
HEH! AS LONG AS YOU GET IT.
HELICOPTER PARENT

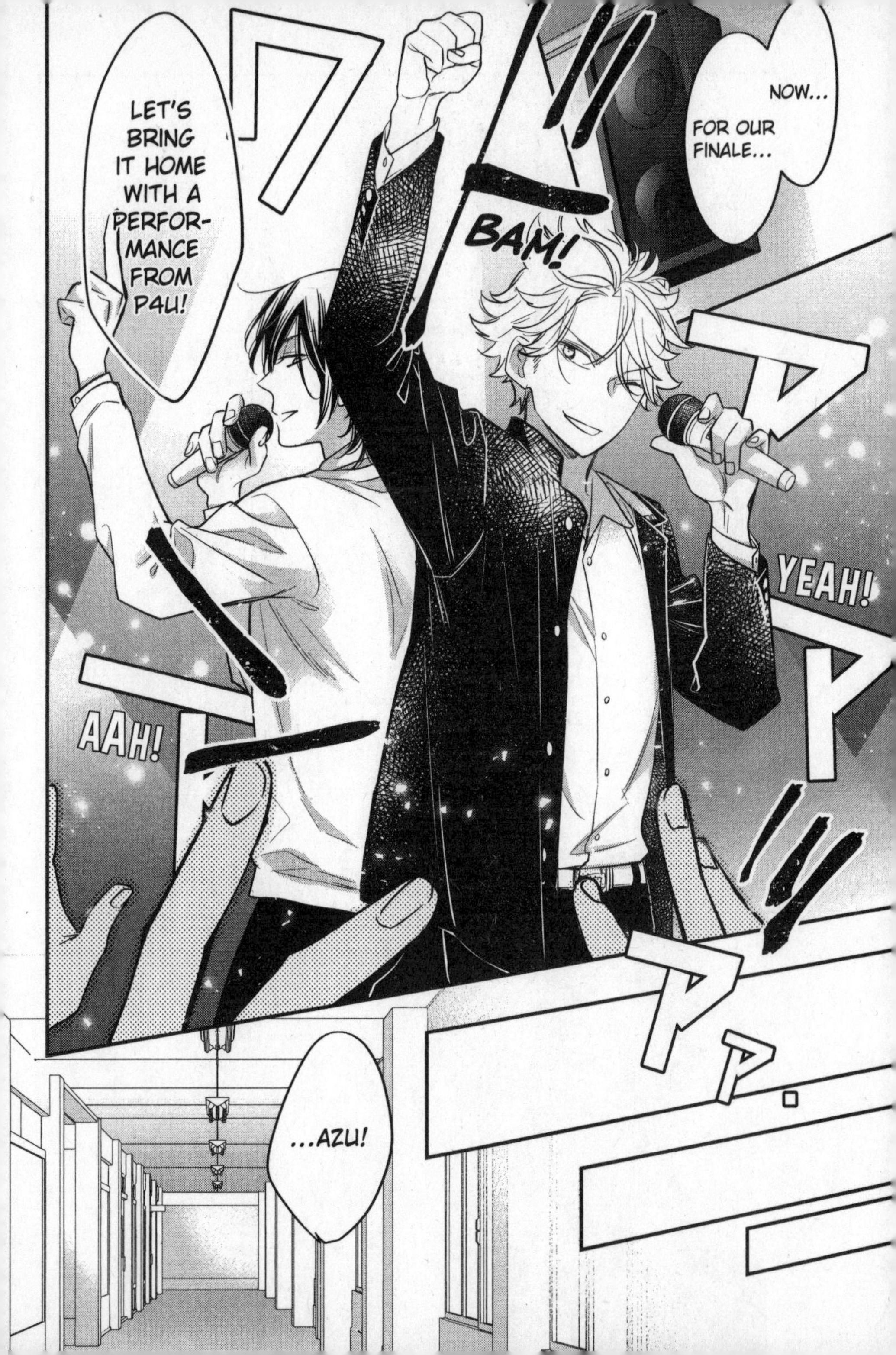
NOW...
FOR OUR FINALE...
LET'S BRING IT HOME WITH A PERFORMANCE FROM P4U!
BAM!
YEAH!
AAH!
...AZU!

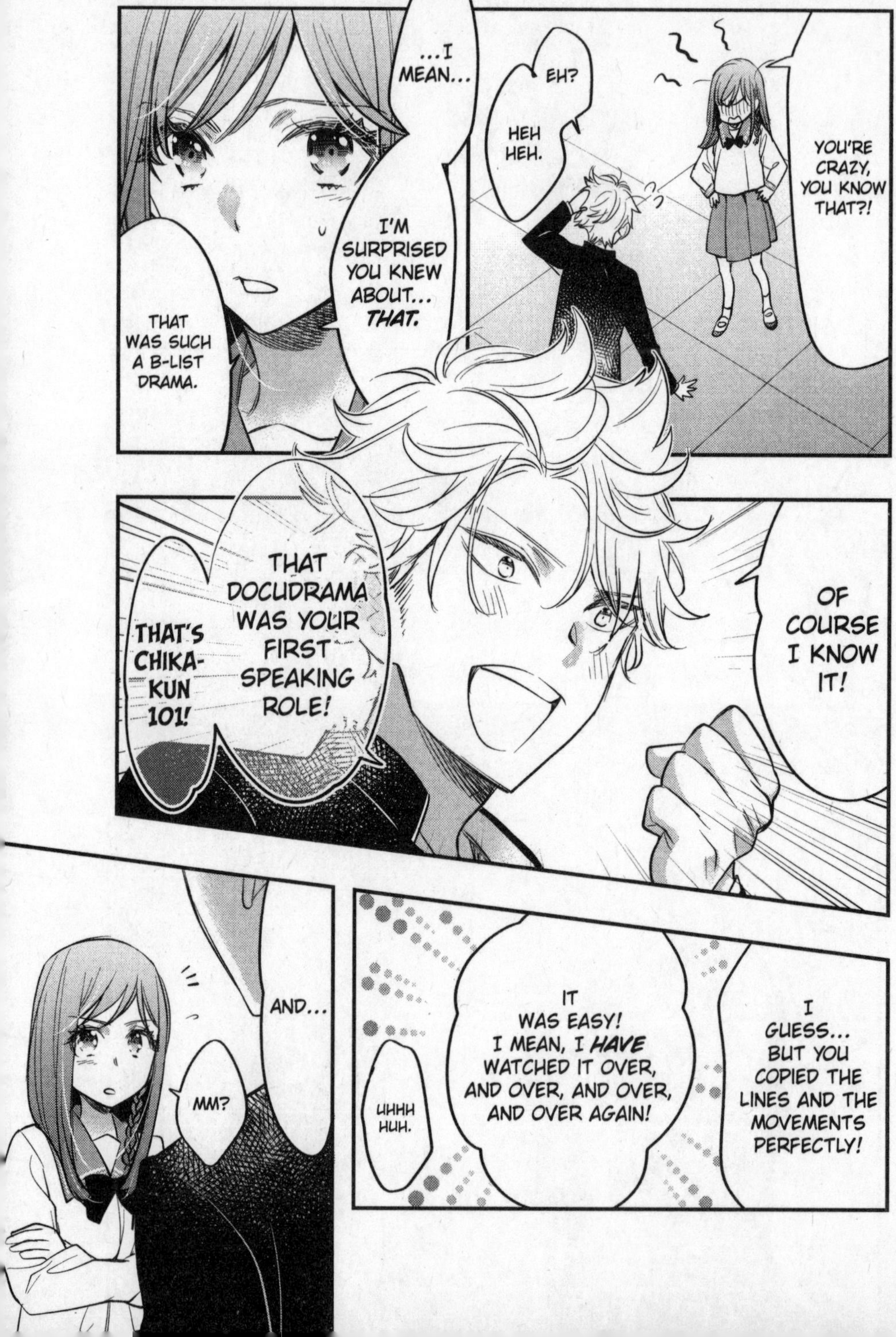
YOU'RE CRAZY, YOU KNOW THAT?!
EH?
HEH HEH.
...I MEAN...
I'M SURPRISED YOU KNEW ABOUT... *THAT.*
THAT WAS SUCH A B-LIST DRAMA.
OF COURSE I KNOW IT!
THAT DOCUDRAMA WAS YOUR FIRST SPEAKING ROLE!
THAT'S CHIKA-KUN 101!
I GUESS... BUT YOU COPIED THE LINES AND THE MOVEMENTS PERFECTLY!
IT WAS EASY! I MEAN, I *HAVE* WATCHED IT OVER, AND OVER, AND OVER, AND OVER AGAIN!
UHHH HUH.
AND...
MM?

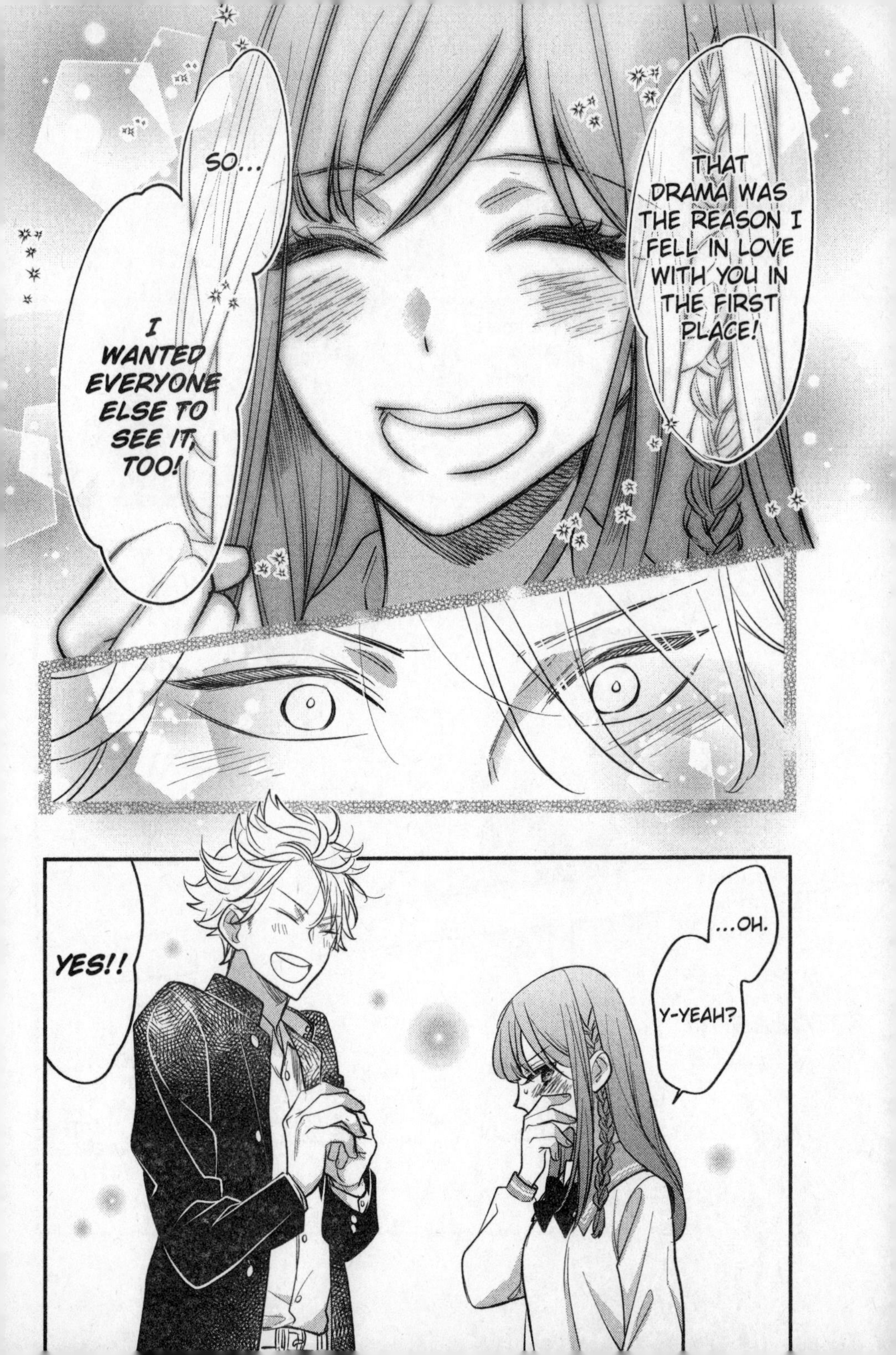
THAT DRAMA WAS THE REASON I FELL IN LOVE WITH YOU IN THE FIRST PLACE!
SO...
I WANTED EVERYONE ELSE TO SEE IT, TOO!
...OH.
Y-YEAH?
YES!!

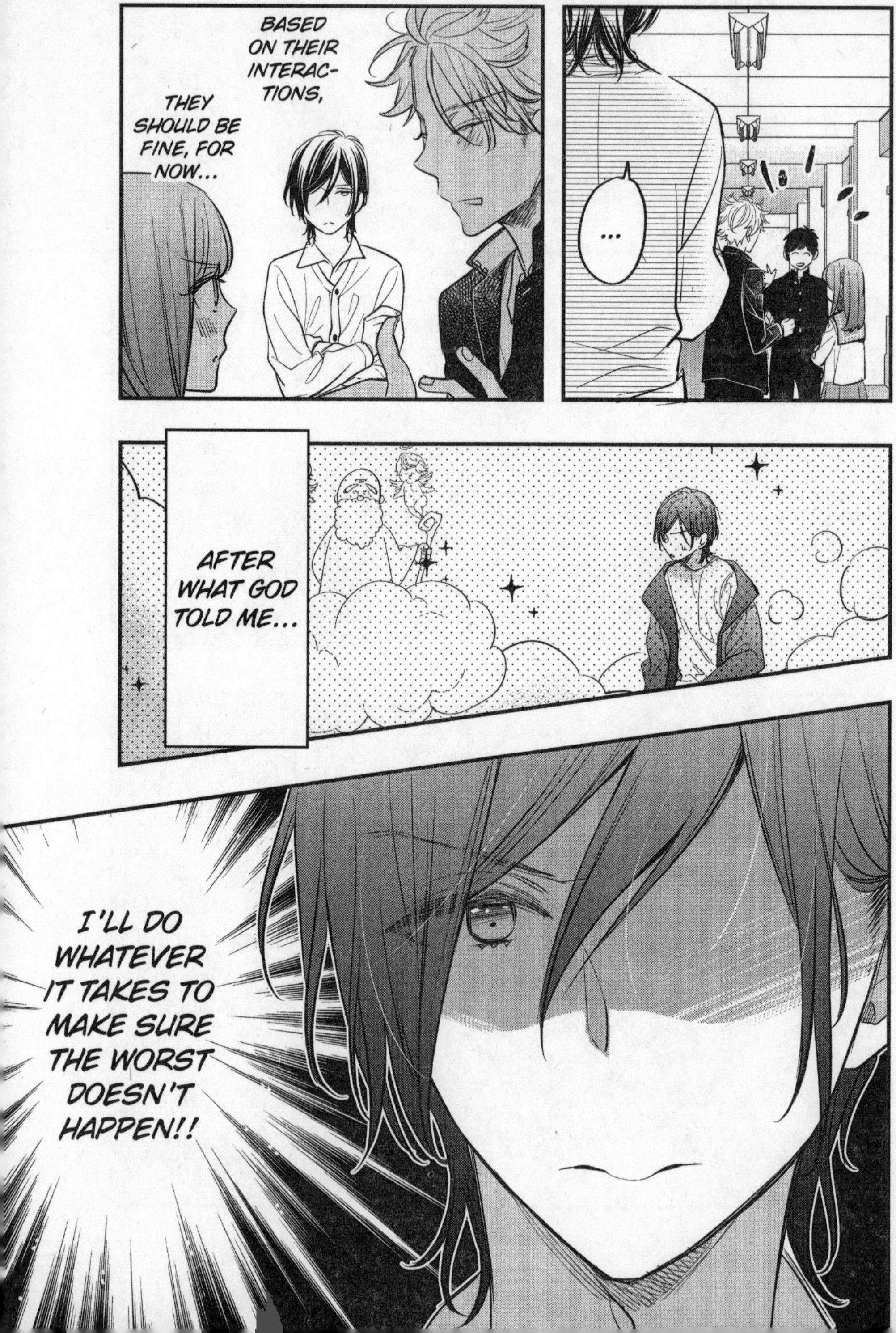
...
BASED ON THEIR INTERACTIONS,
THEY SHOULD BE FINE, FOR NOW...
AFTER WHAT GOD TOLD ME...
I'LL DO WHATEVER IT TAKES TO MAKE SURE THE WORST DOESN'T HAPPEN!!

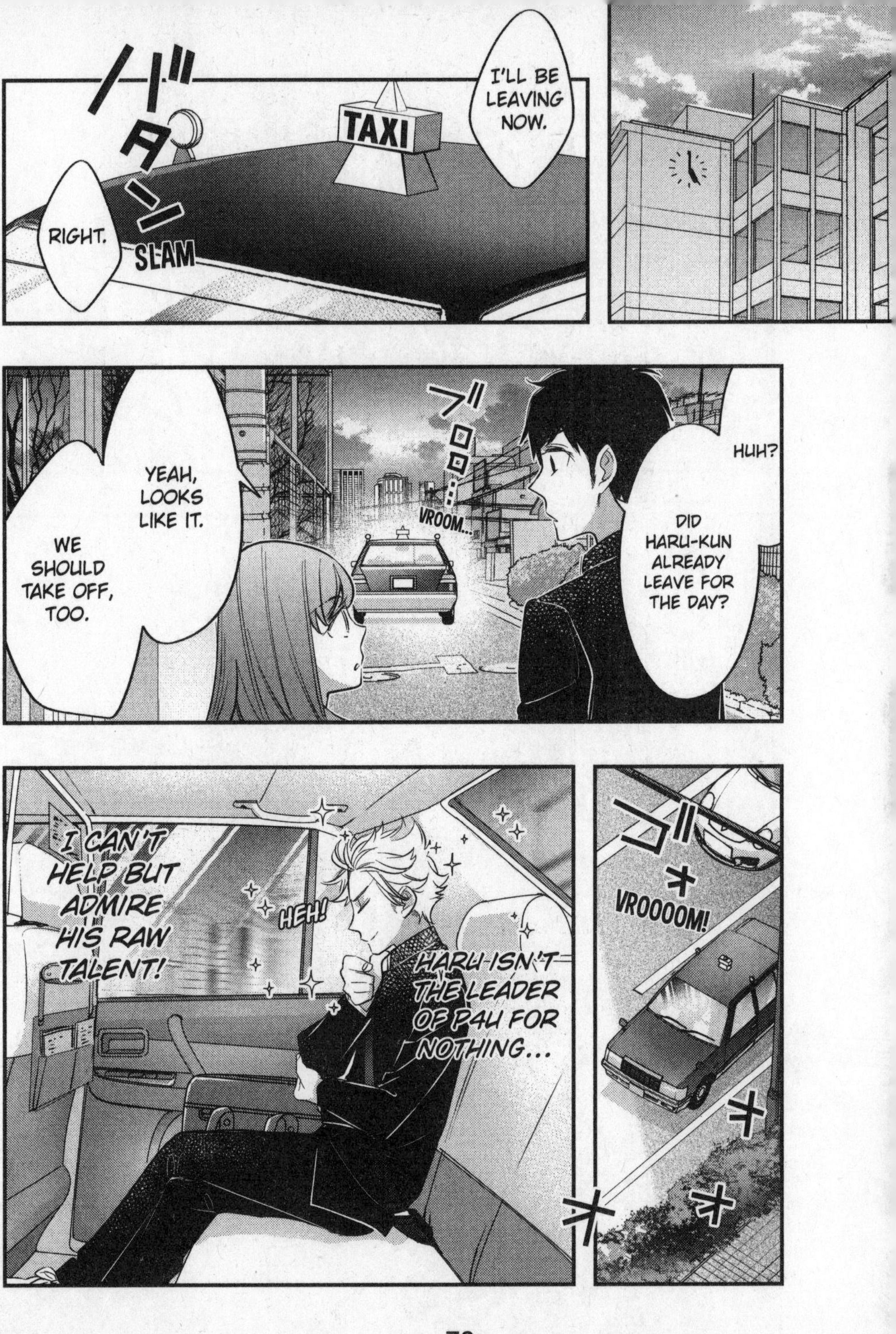
I'LL BE LEAVING NOW.
RIGHT.
SLAM
HUH?
DID HARU-KUN ALREADY LEAVE FOR THE DAY?
VROOM...
YEAH, LOOKS LIKE IT.
WE SHOULD TAKE OFF, TOO.
VROOOOM!
HARU ISN'T THE LEADER OF P4U FOR NOTHING...
HEH!
I CAN'T HELP BUT ADMIRE HIS RAW TALENT!

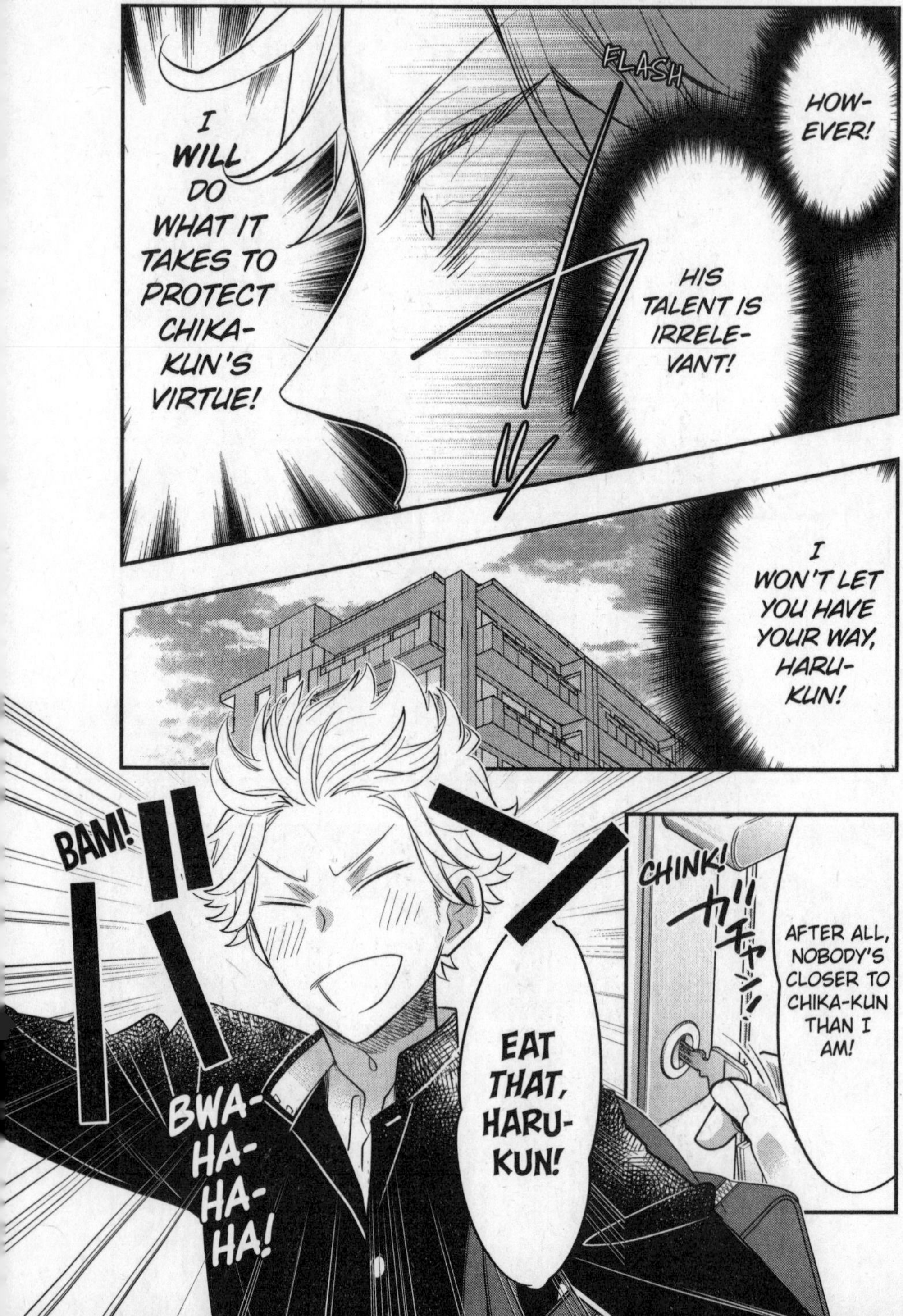
HOW-EVER!
FLASH
HIS TALENT IS IRRELE-VANT!
I WILL DO WHAT IT TAKES TO PROTECT CHIKA-KUN'S VIRTUE!
I WON'T LET YOU HAVE YOUR WAY, HARU-KUN!
CHINK!
ガチャン
AFTER ALL, NOBODY'S CLOSER TO CHIKA-KUN THAN I AM!
EAT THAT, HARU-KUN!
BAM!
BWA-HA-HA-HA!

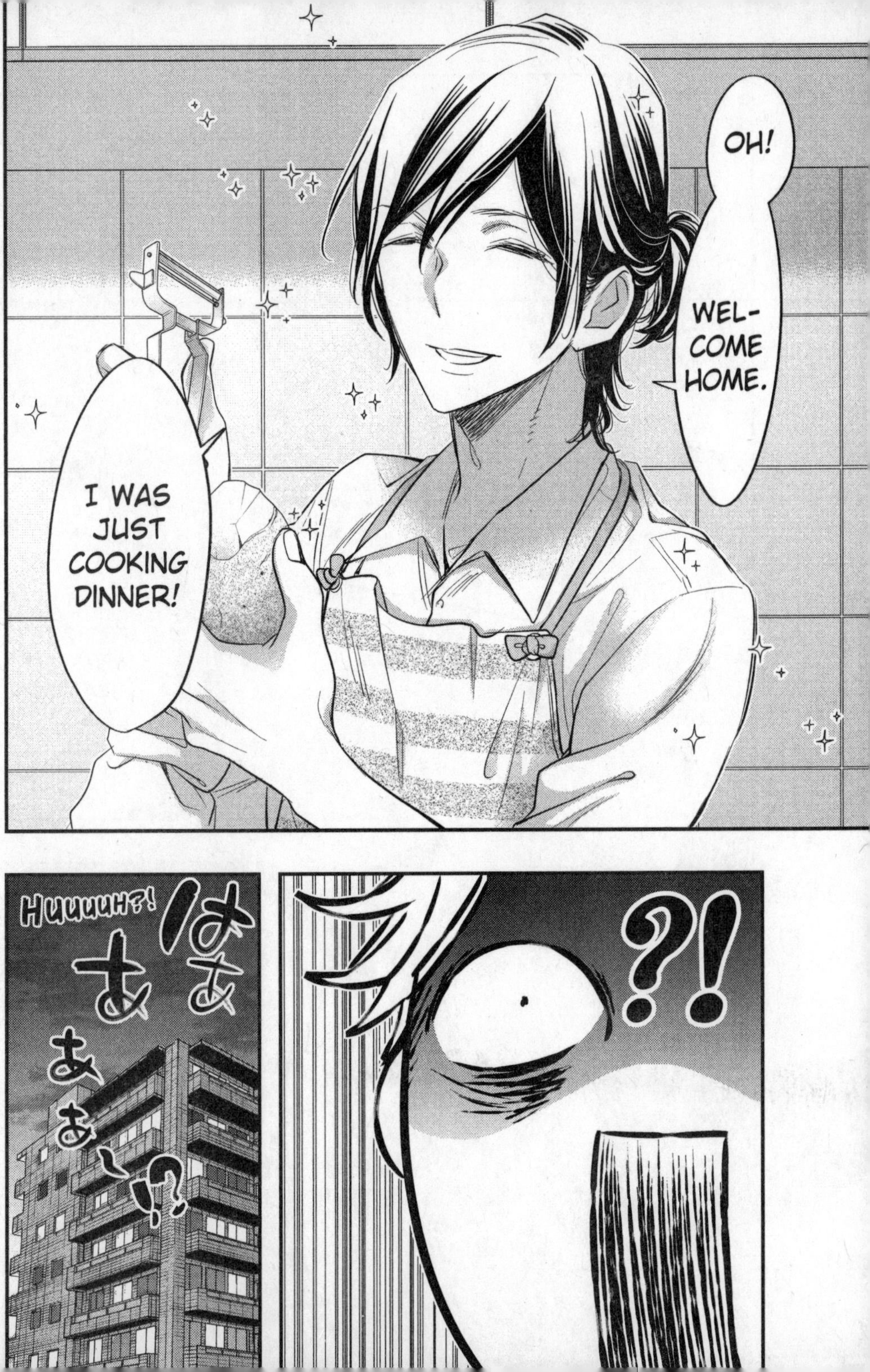
OH!
WEL-COME HOME.
I WAS JUST COOKING DINNER!
?!
Huuuuh?!

R⇄CROSS

D!! STAR

AR⇄CROS

CROSSED

⇄CROSSE

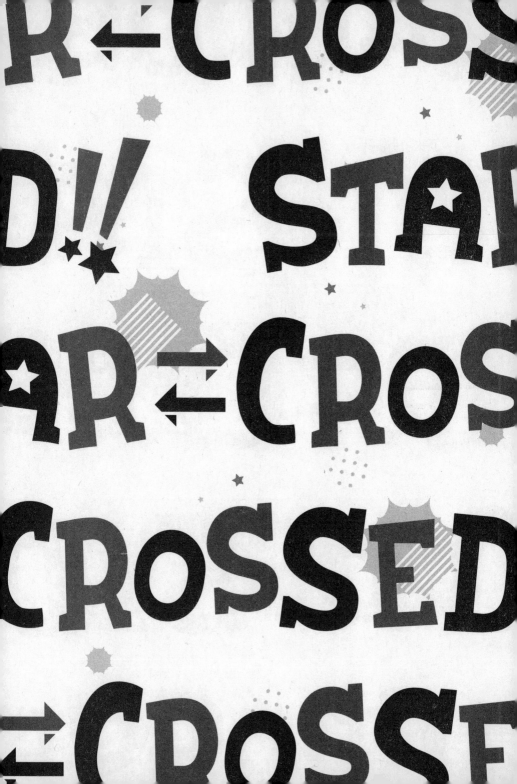

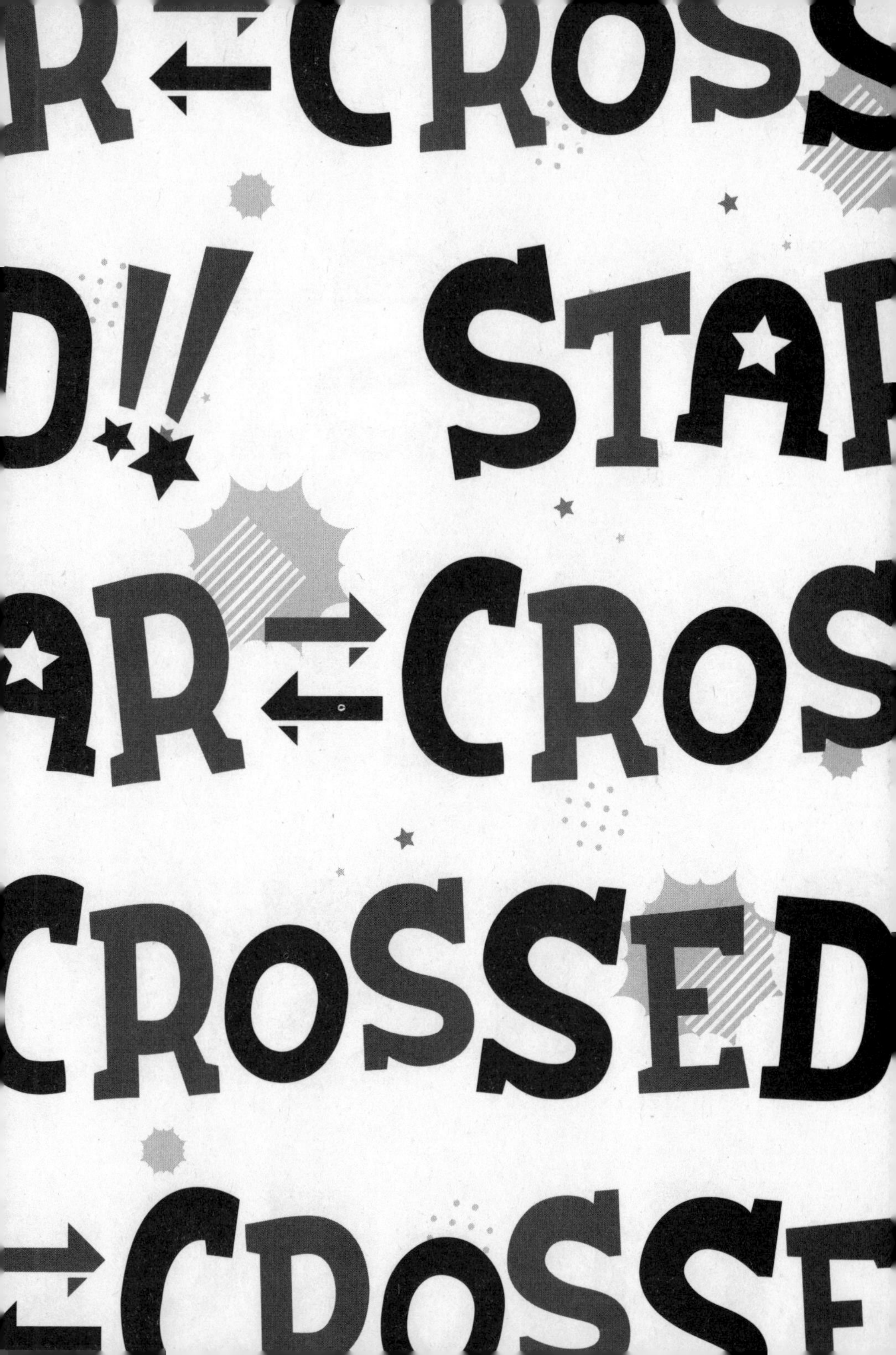
R⇄CROS
D!! STAR
AR⇄CROS
CROSSED
⇄CROSSE

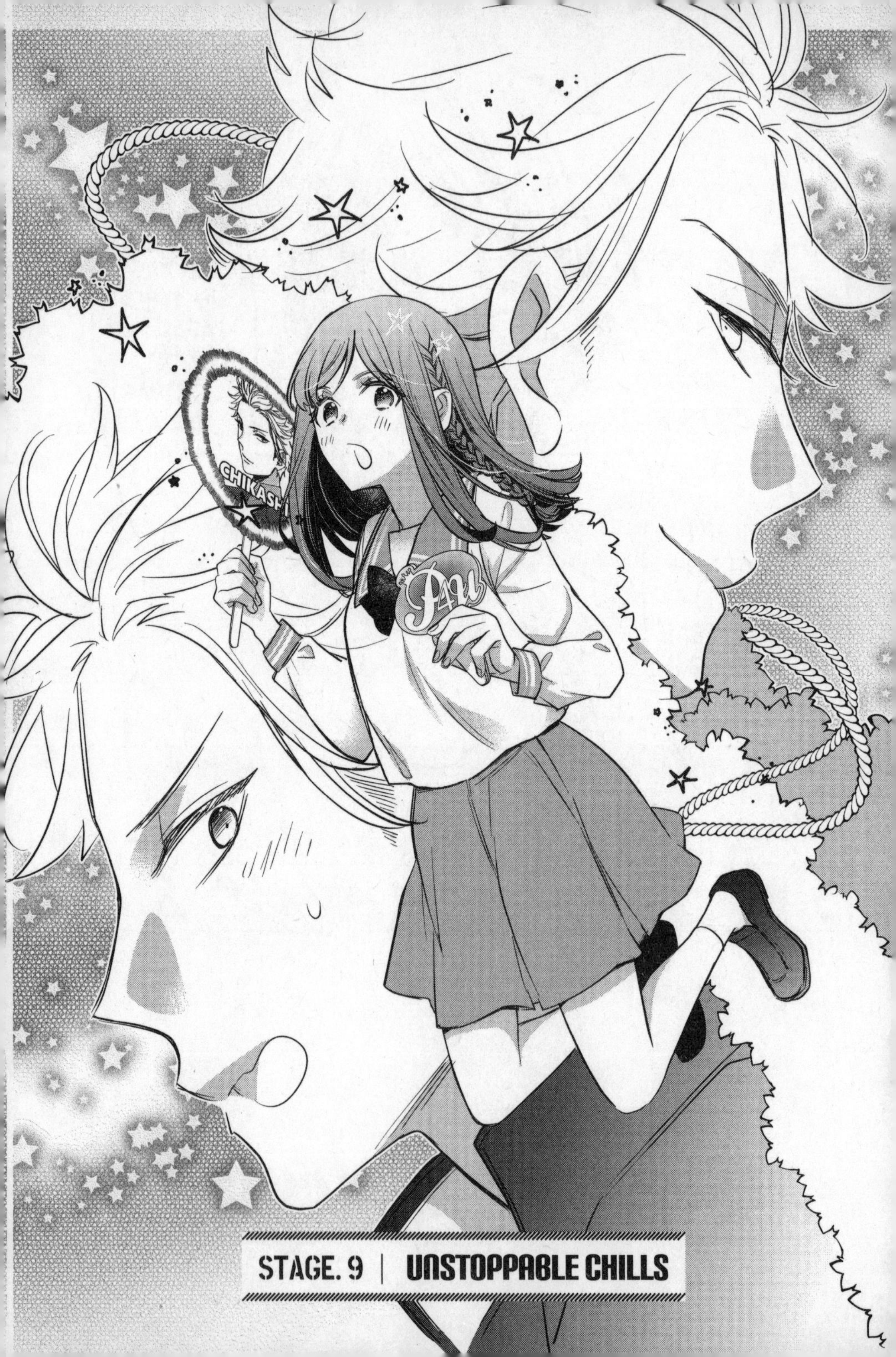
CHIKASHI
P4U
STAGE. 9 | UNSTOPPABLE CHILLS

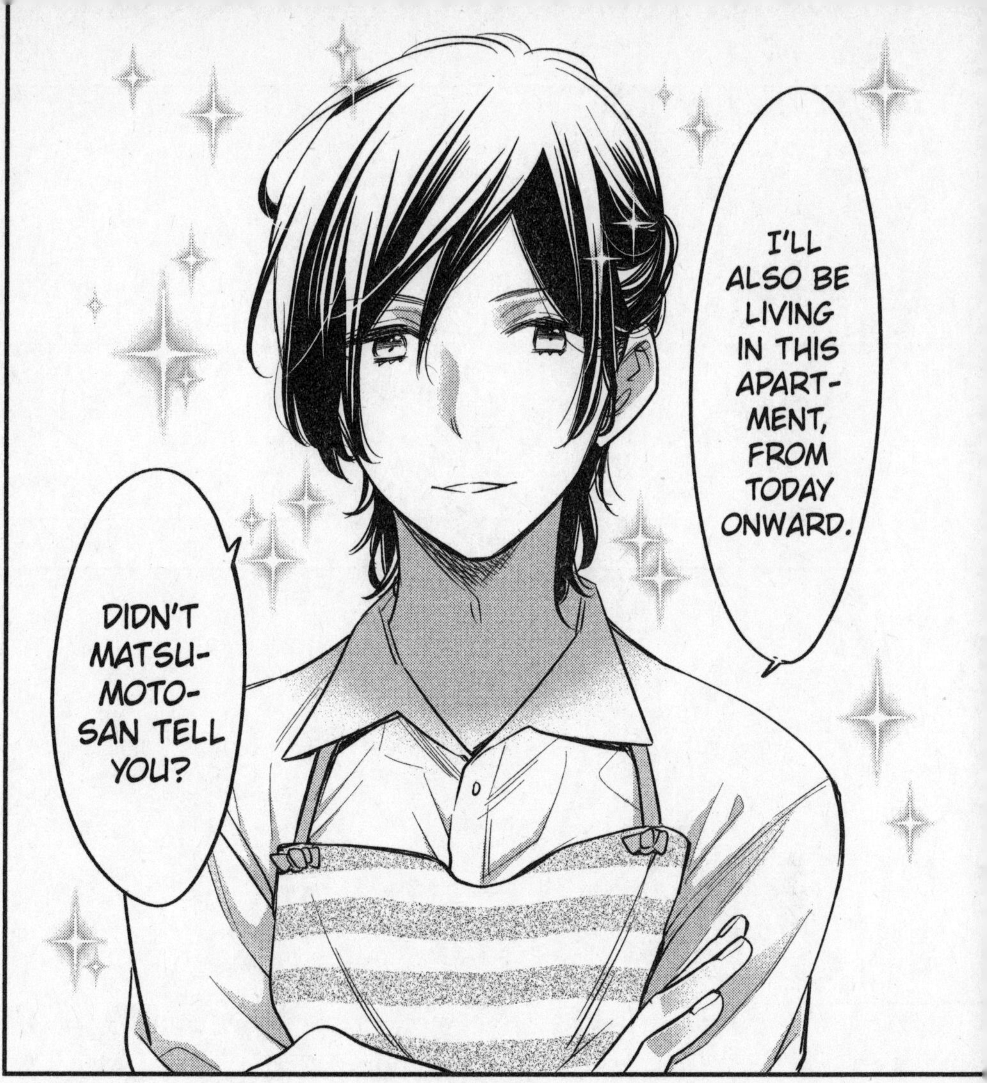
I'LL ALSO BE LIVING IN THIS APART- MENT, FROM TODAY ONWARD.
DIDN'T MATSU- MOTO- SAN TELL YOU?

STAR⇄CROSSED!!

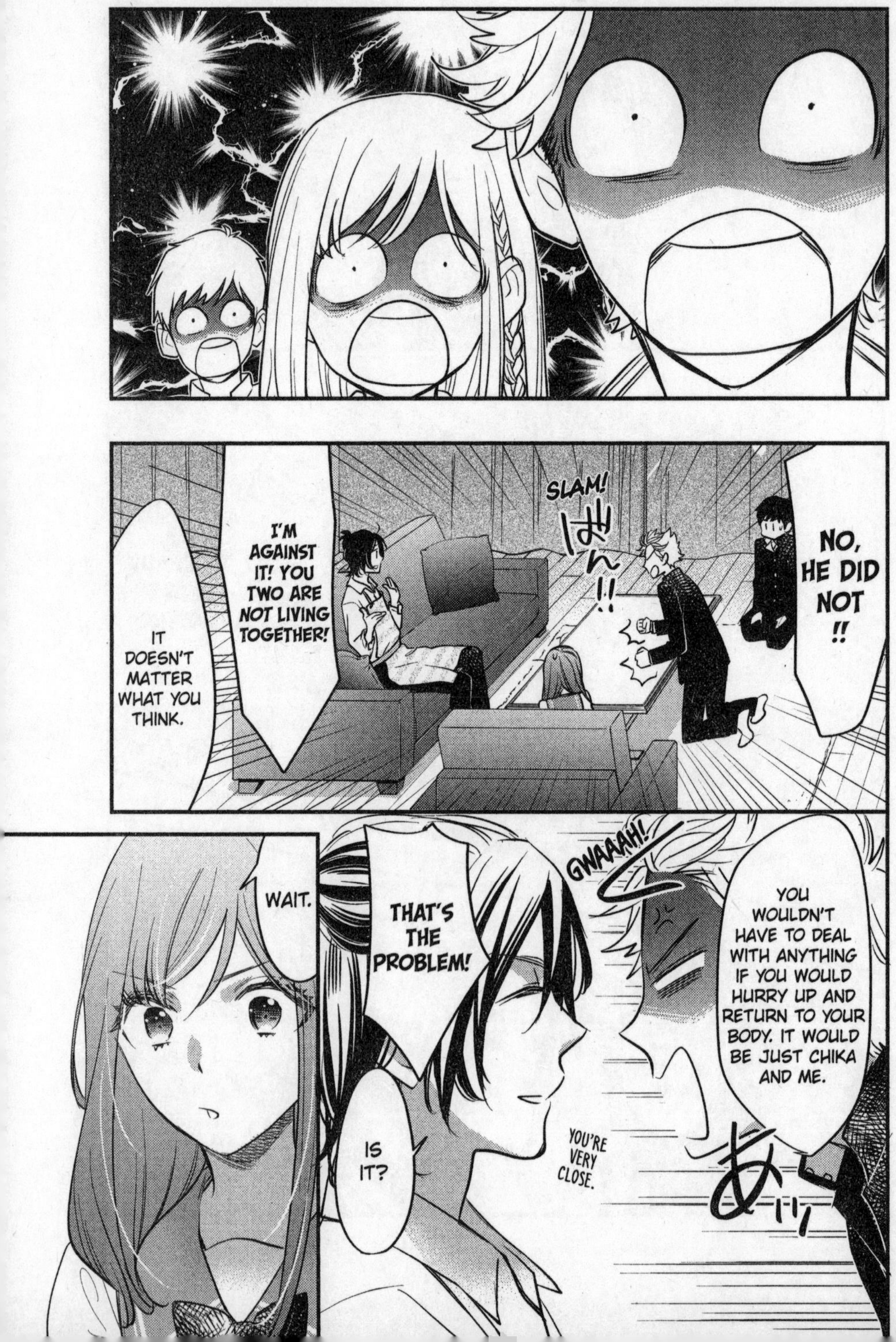

NO, HE DID NOT !!
SLAM!
ばん!!
I'M AGAINST IT! YOU TWO ARE NOT LIVING TOGETHER!
IT DOESN'T MATTER WHAT YOU THINK.
YOU WOULDN'T HAVE TO DEAL WITH ANYTHING IF YOU WOULD HURRY UP AND RETURN TO YOUR BODY. IT WOULD BE JUST CHIKA AND ME.
GWAAAH!
あ
YOU'RE VERY CLOSE.
THAT'S THE PROBLEM!
IS IT?
WAIT.

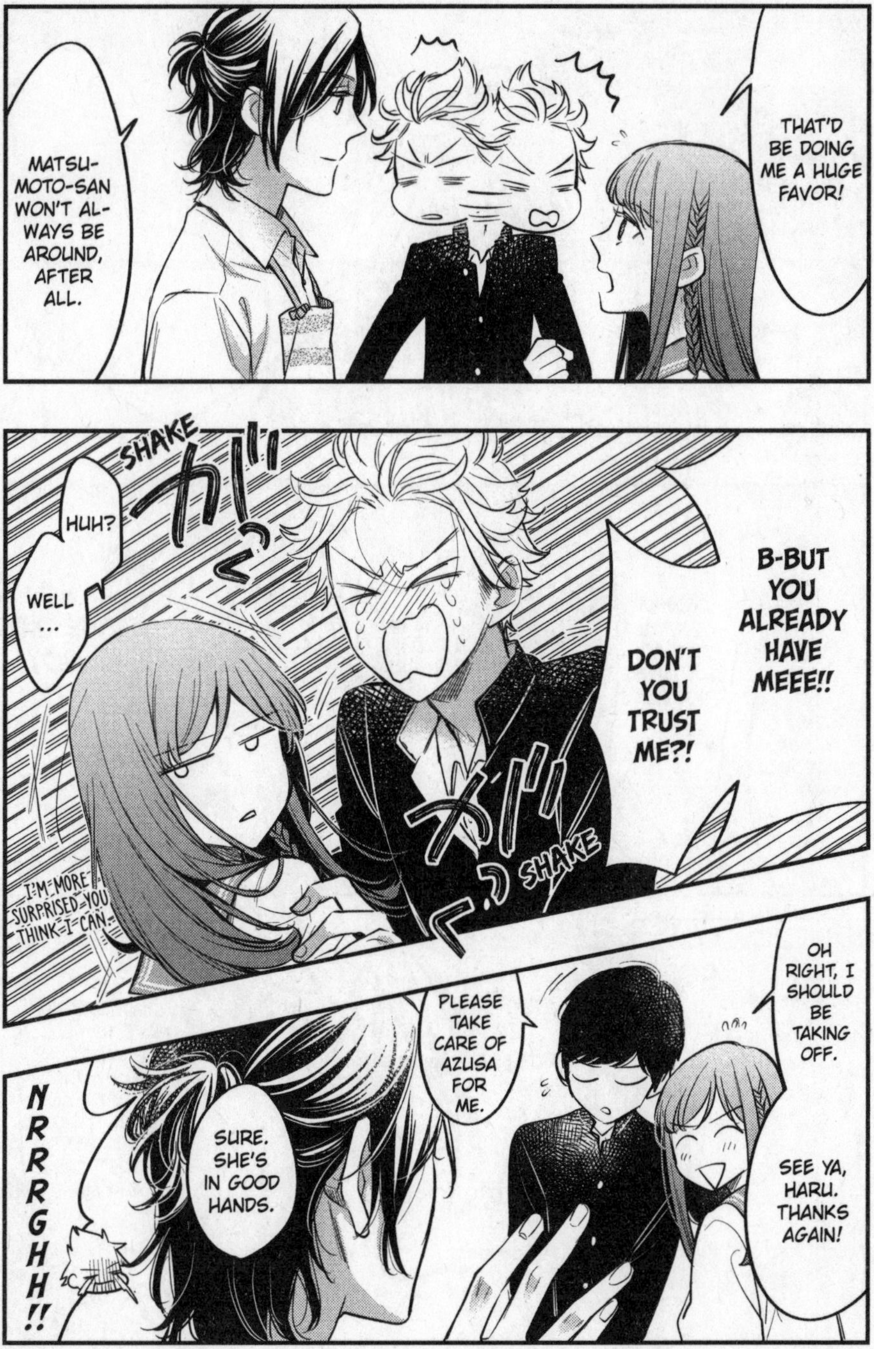
THAT'D BE DOING ME A HUGE FAVOR!
MATSU-MOTO-SAN WON'T ALWAYS BE AROUND, AFTER ALL.
B-BUT YOU ALREADY HAVE MEEE!!
DON'T YOU TRUST ME?!
SHAKE
SHAKE
HUH?
WELL ...
I'M MORE SURPRISED YOU THINK I CAN.
OH RIGHT, I SHOULD BE TAKING OFF.
SEE YA, HARU. THANKS AGAIN!
PLEASE TAKE CARE OF AZUSA FOR ME.
SURE. SHE'S IN GOOD HANDS.
NRRRGHH!!

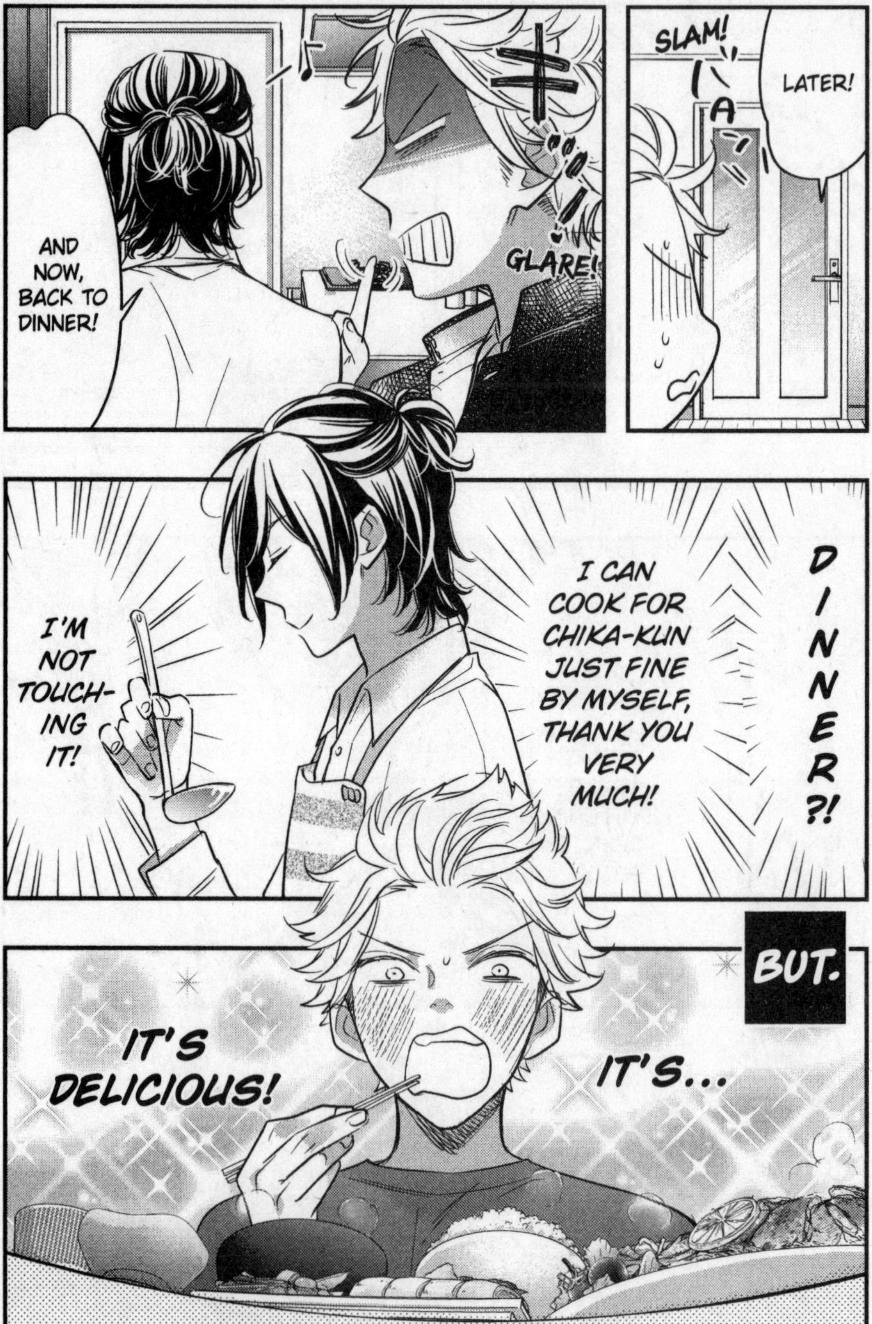
LATER!
SLAM!
GLARE!
AND NOW, BACK TO DINNER!
DINNER?!
I CAN COOK FOR CHIKA-KUN JUST FINE BY MYSELF, THANK YOU VERY MUCH!
I'M NOT TOUCHING IT!
BUT.
IT'S...
IT'S DELICIOUS!

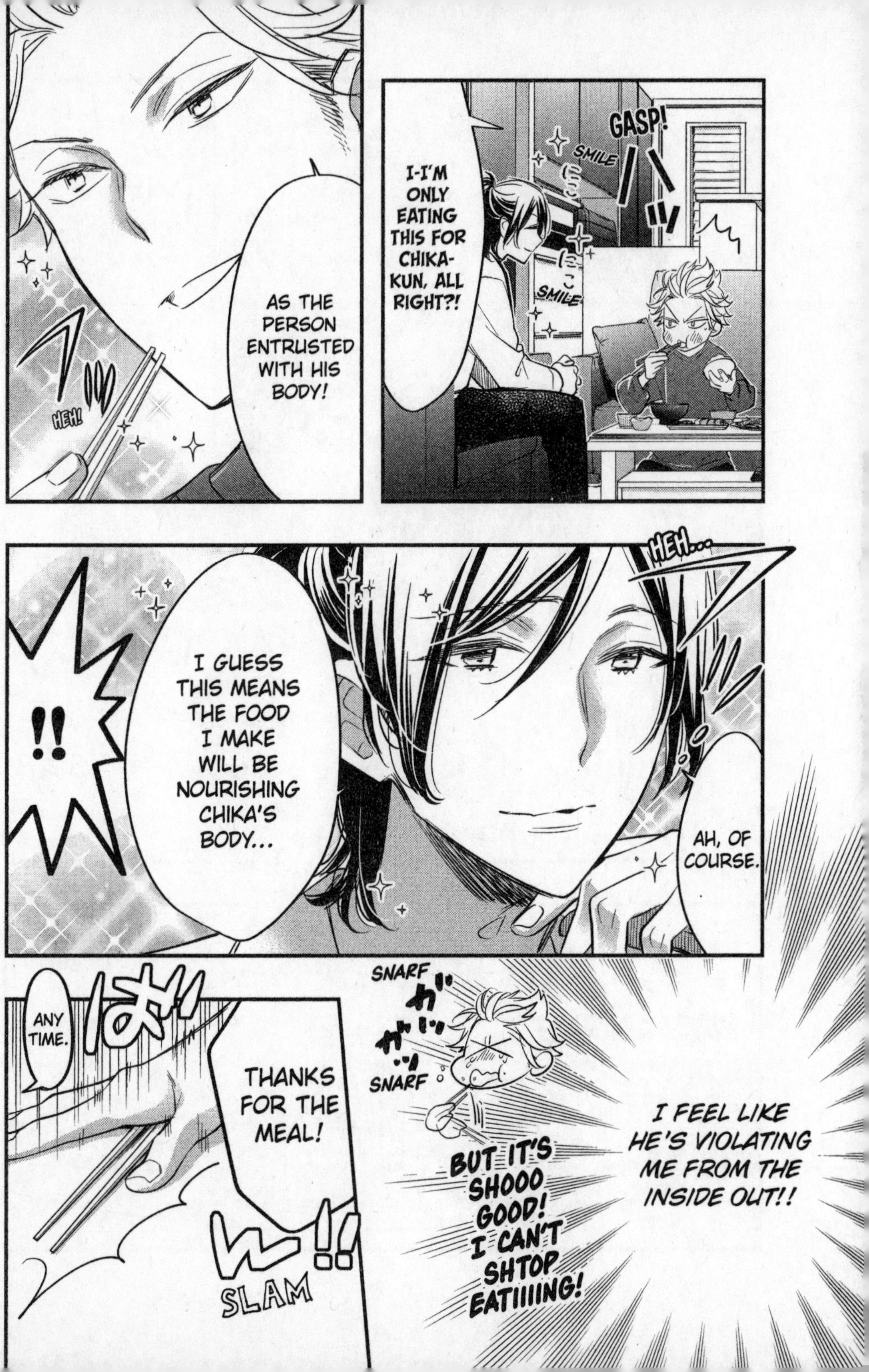
GASP!
SMILE
I-I'M ONLY EATING THIS FOR CHIKA-KUN, ALL RIGHT?!
SMILE
AS THE PERSON ENTRUSTED WITH HIS BODY!
HEH!
HEH...
AH, OF COURSE.
I GUESS THIS MEANS THE FOOD I MAKE WILL BE NOURISHING CHIKA'S BODY...
!!
I FEEL LIKE HE'S VIOLATING ME FROM THE INSIDE OUT!!
SNARF
SNARF
BUT IT'S SHOOO GOOD! I CAN'T SHTOP EATIIIING!
THANKS FOR THE MEAL!
ANY TIME.
SLAM

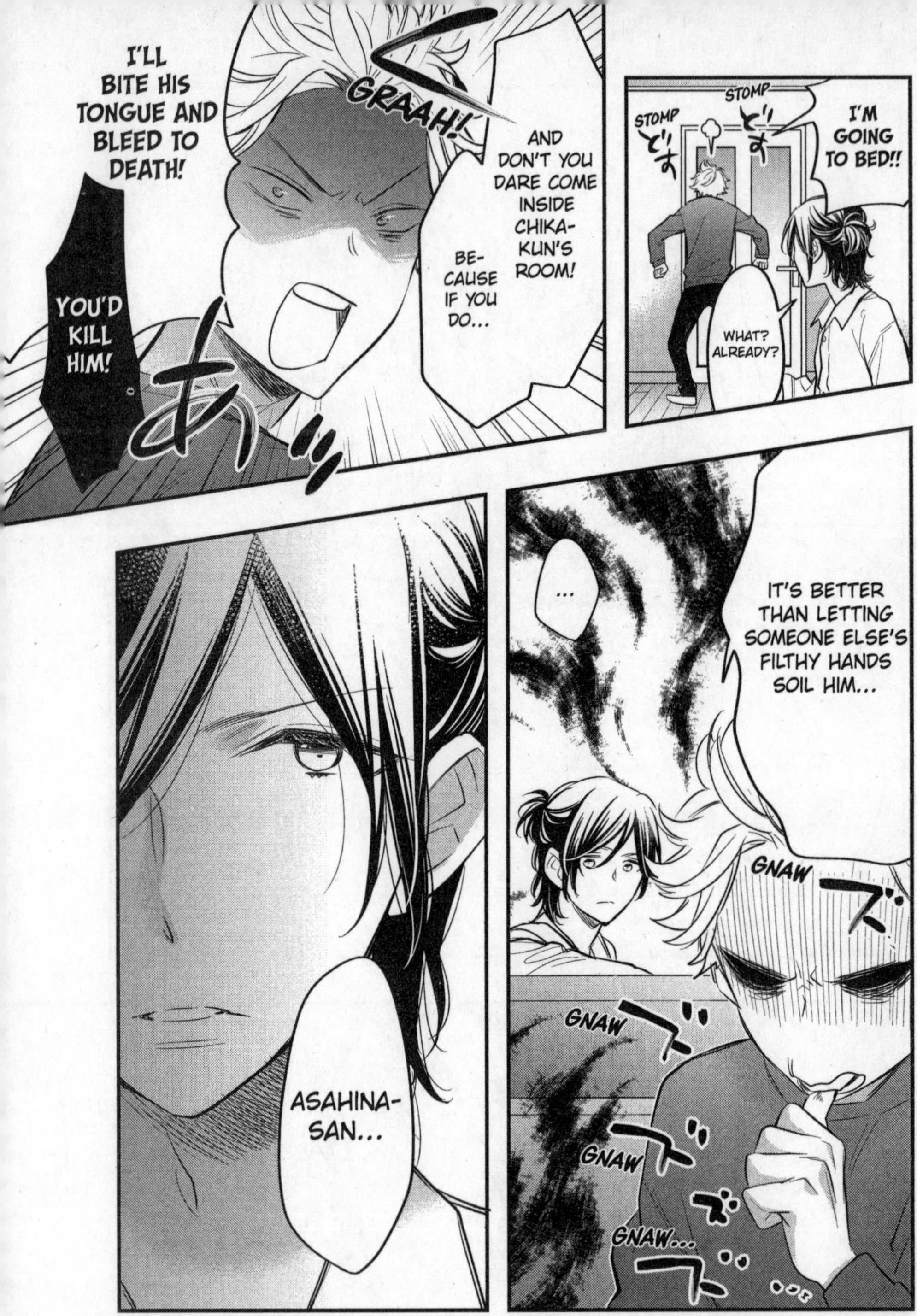
STOMP
STOMP
I'M GOING TO BED!!
WHAT? ALREADY?
AND DON'T YOU DARE COME INSIDE CHIKA-KUN'S ROOM!
BE-CAUSE IF YOU DO...
GRAAH!
I'LL BITE HIS TONGUE AND BLEED TO DEATH!
YOU'D KILL HIM!
IT'S BETTER THAN LETTING SOMEONE ELSE'S FILTHY HANDS SOIL HIM...
...
GNAW
GNAW
GNAW
GNAW...
ASAHINA-SAN...

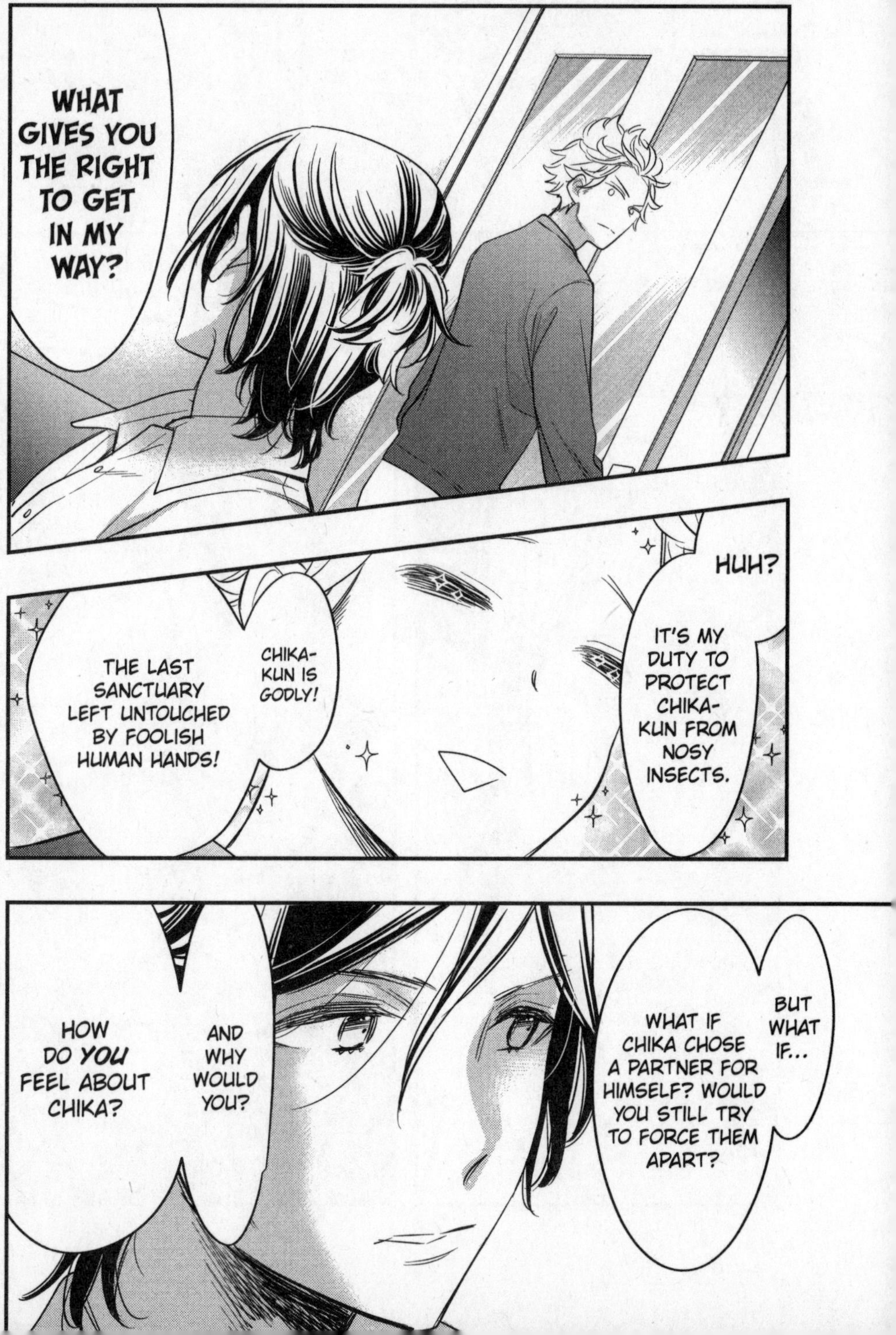
WHAT GIVES YOU THE RIGHT TO GET IN MY WAY?
HUH?
IT'S MY DUTY TO PROTECT CHIKA-KUN FROM NOSY INSECTS.
CHIKA-KUN IS GODLY!
THE LAST SANCTUARY LEFT UNTOUCHED BY FOOLISH HUMAN HANDS!
BUT WHAT IF...
WHAT IF CHIKA CHOSE A PARTNER FOR HIMSELF? WOULD YOU STILL TRY TO FORCE THEM APART?
AND WHY WOULD YOU?
HOW DO *YOU* FEEL ABOUT CHIKA?

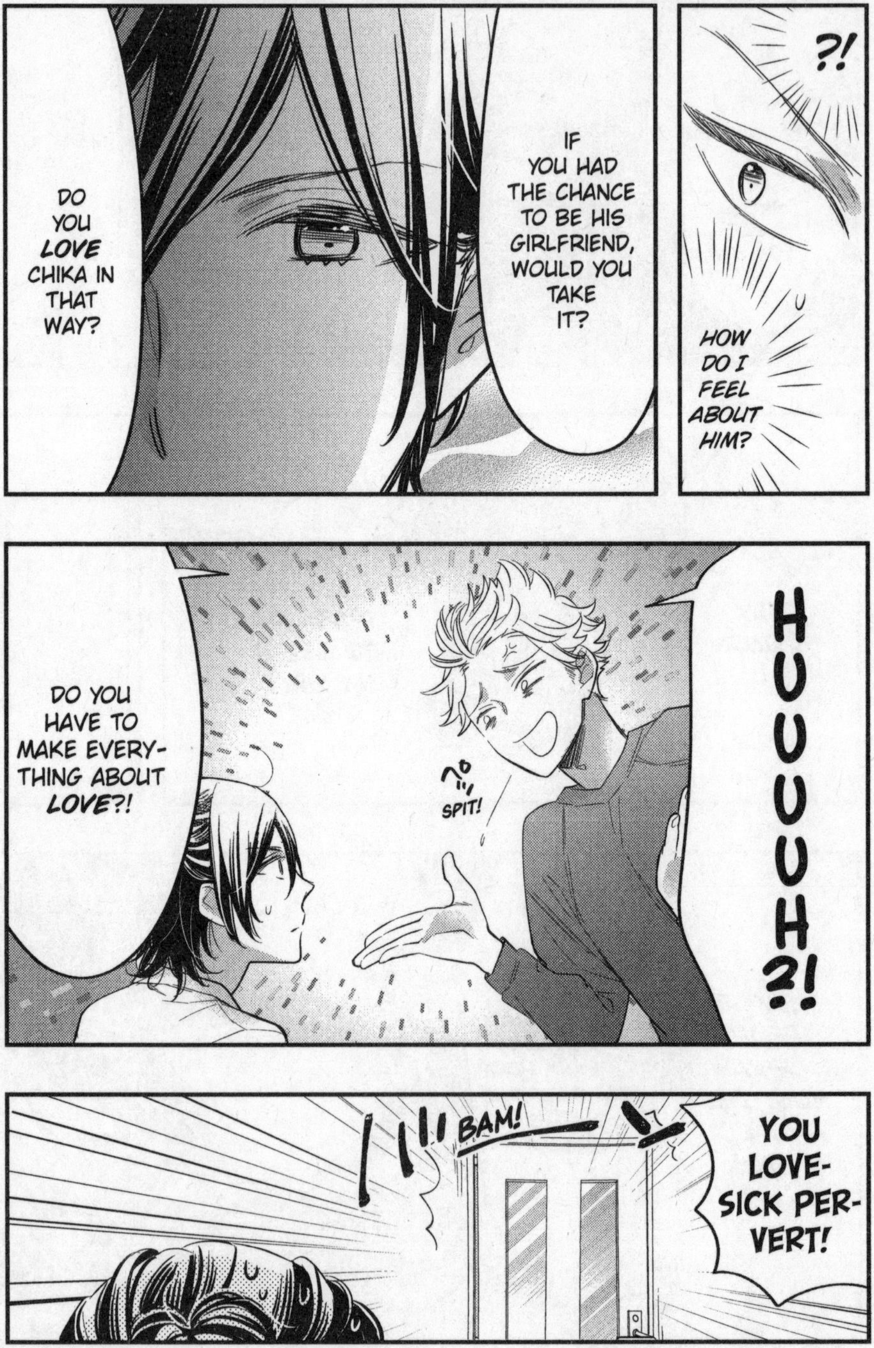
?!
HOW DO I FEEL ABOUT HIM?
IF YOU HAD THE CHANCE TO BE HIS GIRLFRIEND, WOULD YOU TAKE IT?
DO YOU *LOVE* CHIKA IN THAT WAY?
HUUUUH?!
ペッ
SPIT!
DO YOU HAVE TO MAKE EVERY-THING ABOUT *LOVE*?!
YOU LOVE-SICK PER-VERT!
BAM!

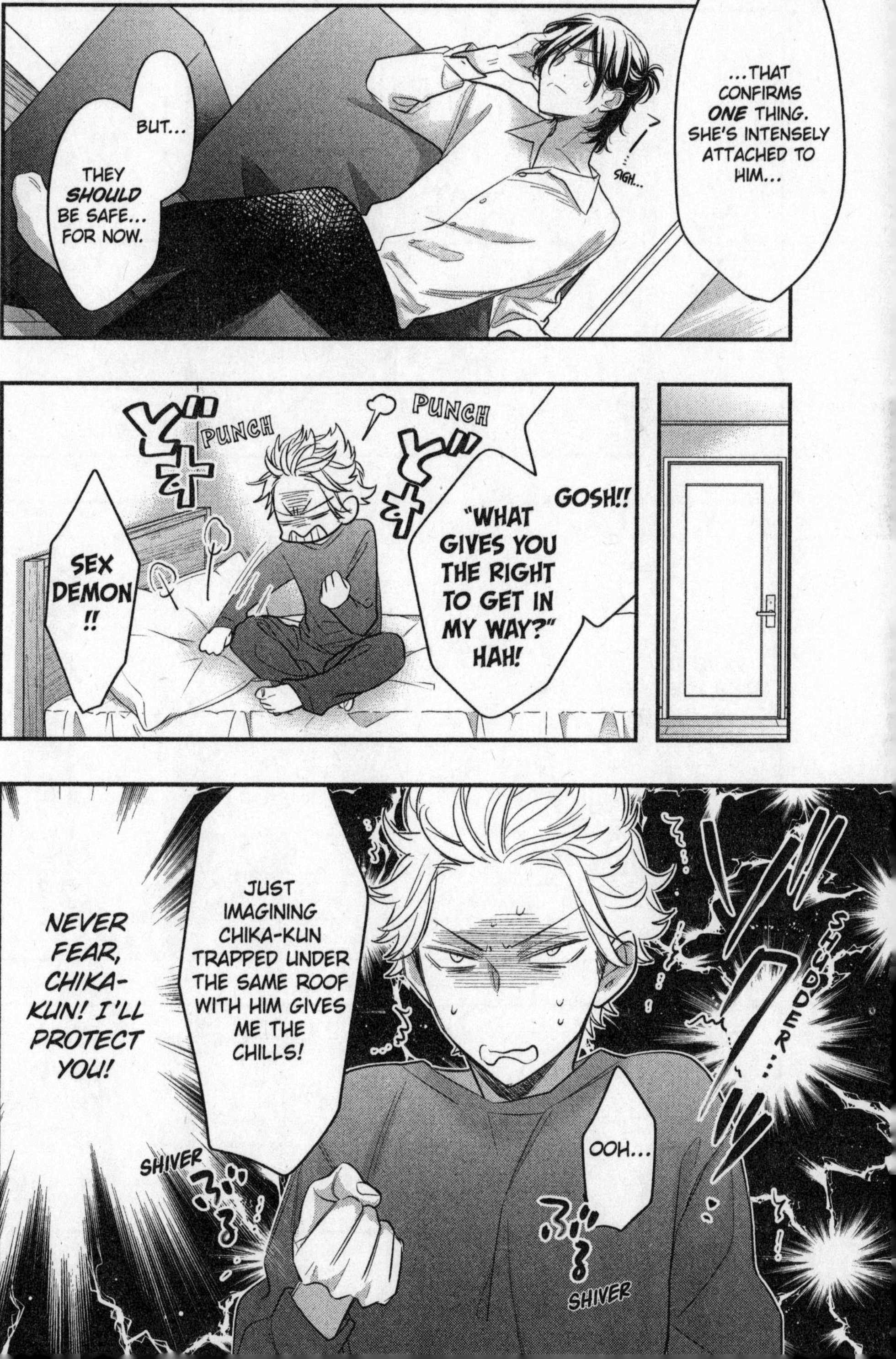

...THAT CONFIRMS ONE THING. SHE'S INTENSELY ATTACHED TO HIM...
SIGH...
BUT...
THEY SHOULD BE SAFE... FOR NOW.
GOSH!!
"WHAT GIVES YOU THE RIGHT TO GET IN MY WAY?" HAH!
PUNCH
PUNCH
SEX DEMON!!
SHUDDER...
OOH...
JUST IMAGINING CHIKA-KUN TRAPPED UNDER THE SAME ROOF WITH HIM GIVES ME THE CHILLS!
SHIVER
NEVER FEAR, CHIKA-KUN! I'LL PROTECT YOU!
SHIVER

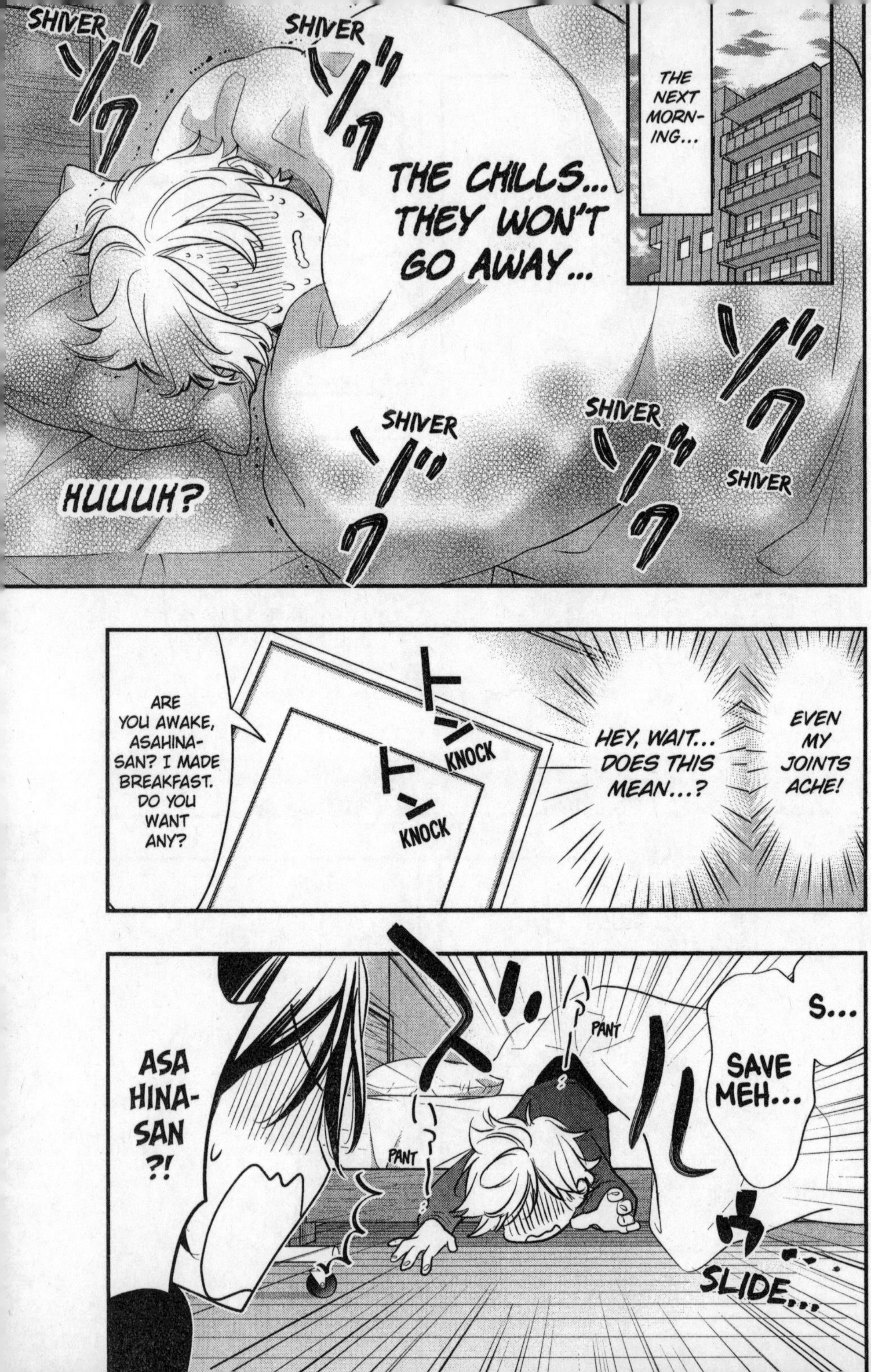
THE NEXT MORNING...
SHIVER
SHIVER
THE CHILLS... THEY WON'T GO AWAY...
SHIVER
SHIVER
SHIVER
HUUUH?
EVEN MY JOINTS ACHE!
HEY, WAIT... DOES THIS MEAN...?
KNOCK
KNOCK
ARE YOU AWAKE, ASAHINA-SAN? I MADE BREAKFAST. DO YOU WANT ANY?
S...
SAVE MEH...
SLIDE...
PANT
PANT
ASAHINA-SAN?!

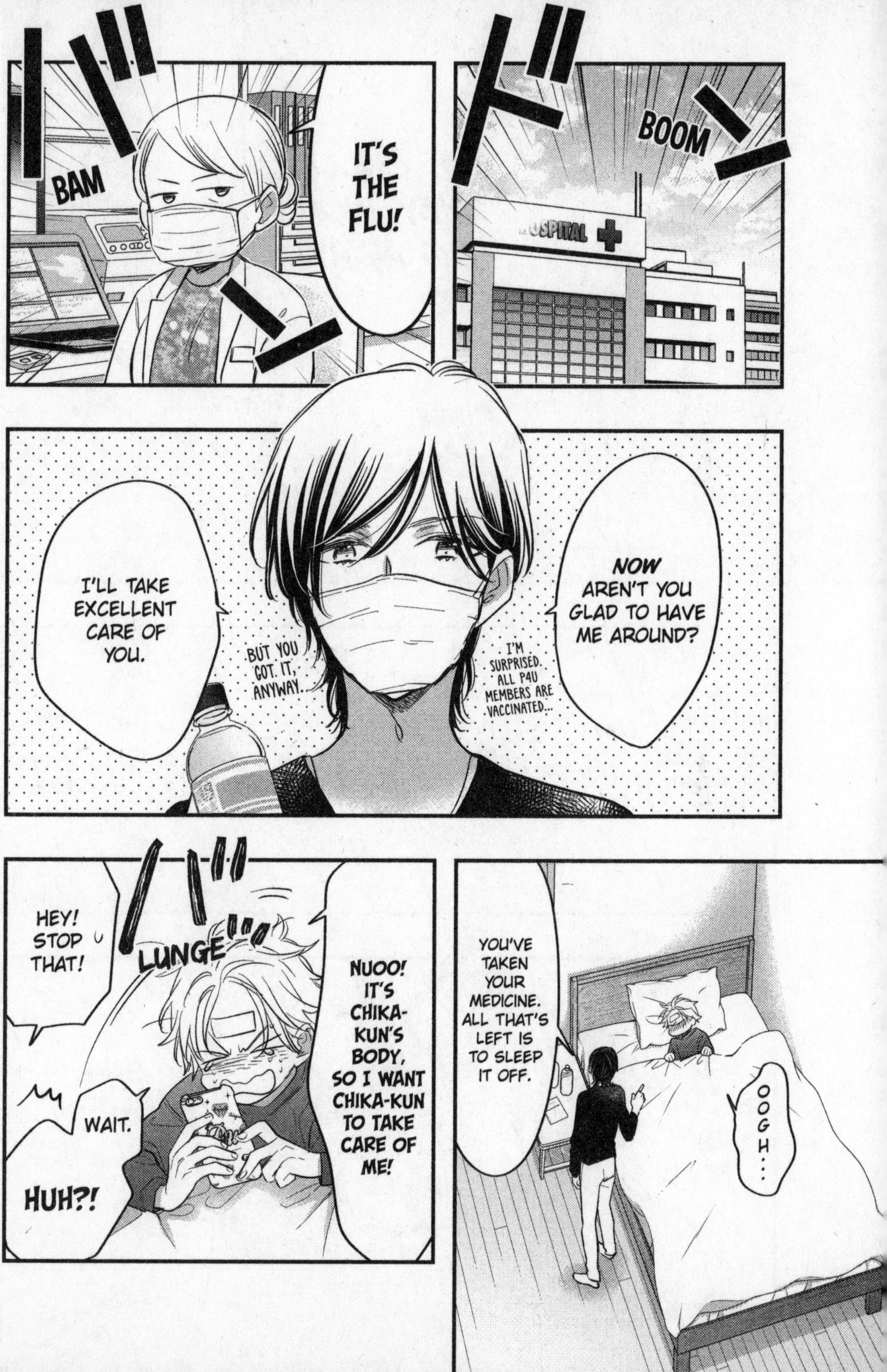
BOOM
IT'S THE FLU!
BAM
NOW AREN'T YOU GLAD TO HAVE ME AROUND?
I'M SURPRISED. ALL P4U MEMBERS ARE VACCINATED...
BUT YOU GOT IT, ANYWAY.
I'LL TAKE EXCELLENT CARE OF YOU.
YOU'VE TAKEN YOUR MEDICINE. ALL THAT'S LEFT IS TO SLEEP IT OFF.
OOGH...
NUOO! IT'S CHIKA-KUN'S BODY, SO I WANT CHIKA-KUN TO TAKE CARE OF ME!
LUNGE
HEY! STOP THAT!
WAIT.
HUH?!

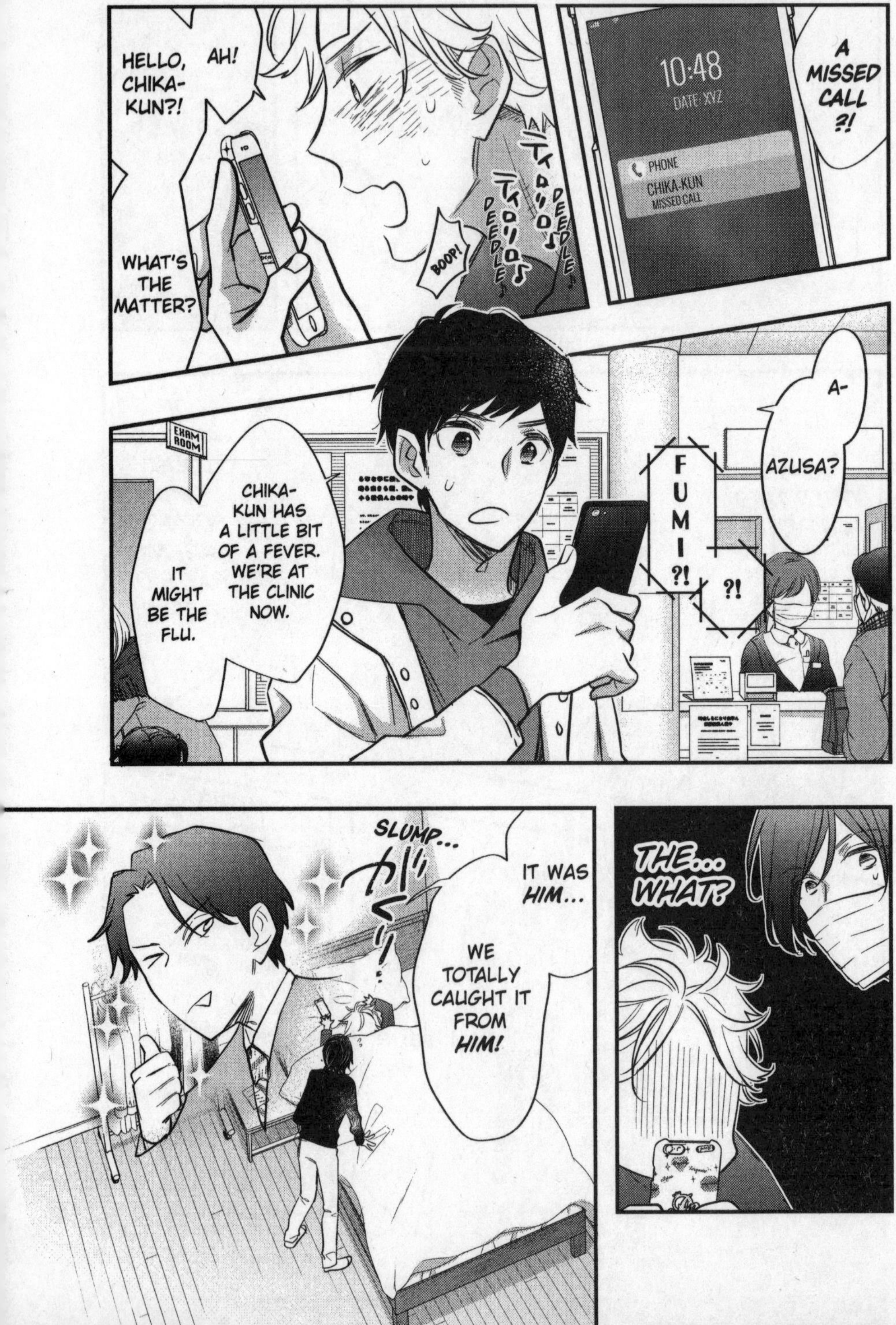
10:48
DATE XYZ
PHONE
CHIKA-KUN
MISSED CALL
A MISSED CALL ?!
DEEDLE DEEDLE♪
DEEDLE DEEDLE♪
BOOP!
AH!
HELLO, CHIKA-KUN?!
WHAT'S THE MATTER?
A- AZUSA?
FUMI ?!
?!
EXAM ROOM
CHIKA-KUN HAS A LITTLE BIT OF A FEVER. WE'RE AT THE CLINIC NOW.
IT MIGHT BE THE FLU.
THE... WHAT?
IT WAS HIM...
WE TOTALLY CAUGHT IT FROM HIM!
SLUMP...

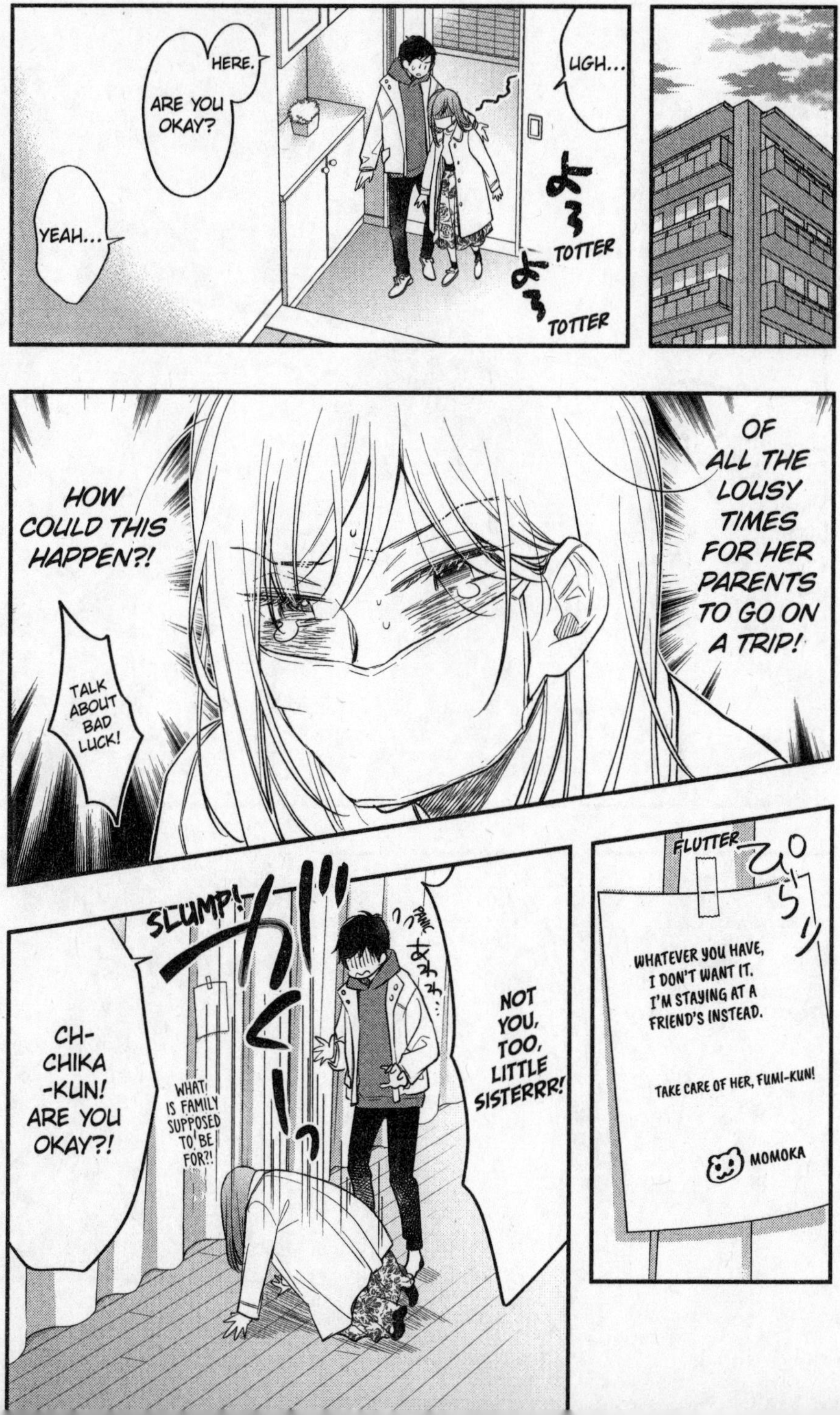

UGH...
HERE.
ARE YOU OKAY?
TOTTER
TOTTER
YEAH...
OF ALL THE LOUSY TIMES FOR HER PARENTS TO GO ON A TRIP!
HOW COULD THIS HAPPEN?!
TALK ABOUT BAD LUCK!
FLUTTER
WHATEVER YOU HAVE, I DON'T WANT IT. I'M STAYING AT A FRIEND'S INSTEAD.
TAKE CARE OF HER, FUMI-KUN!
MOMOKA
SLUMP!
PANIC
NOT YOU, TOO, LITTLE SISTERRR!
WHAT IS FAMILY SUPPOSED TO BE FOR?!
CH-CHIKA-KUN! ARE YOU OKAY?!

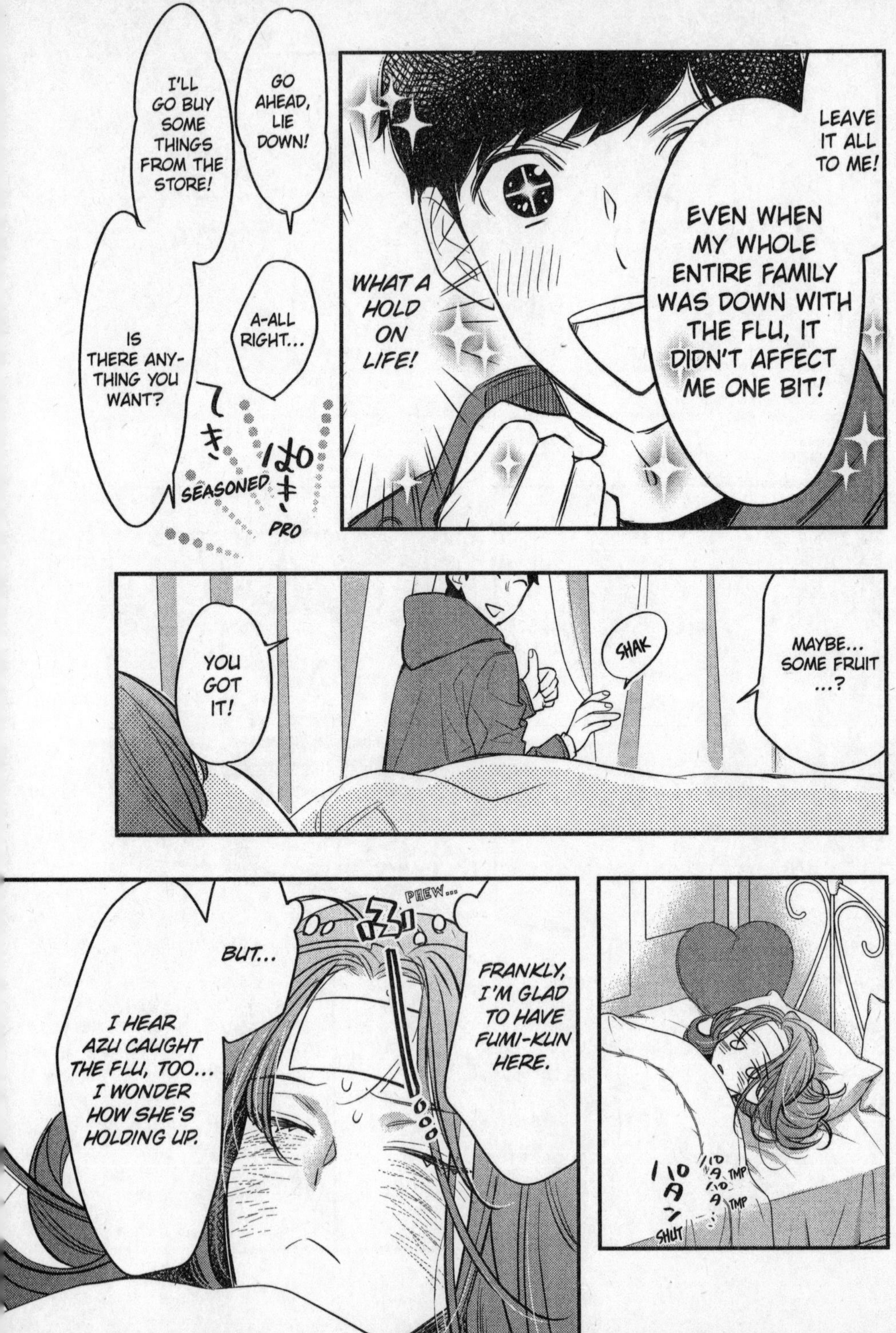
LEAVE IT ALL TO ME!
EVEN WHEN MY WHOLE ENTIRE FAMILY WAS DOWN WITH THE FLU, IT DIDN'T AFFECT ME ONE BIT!
WHAT A HOLD ON LIFE!
GO AHEAD, LIE DOWN!
I'LL GO BUY SOME THINGS FROM THE STORE!
A-ALL RIGHT...
IS THERE ANYTHING YOU WANT?
SEASONED PRO
MAYBE... SOME FRUIT ...?
SHAK
YOU GOT IT!
SHUT
TMP
TMP
PHEW...
FRANKLY, I'M GLAD TO HAVE FUMI-KUN HERE.
BUT...
I HEAR AZU CAUGHT THE FLU, TOO... I WONDER HOW SHE'S HOLDING UP.

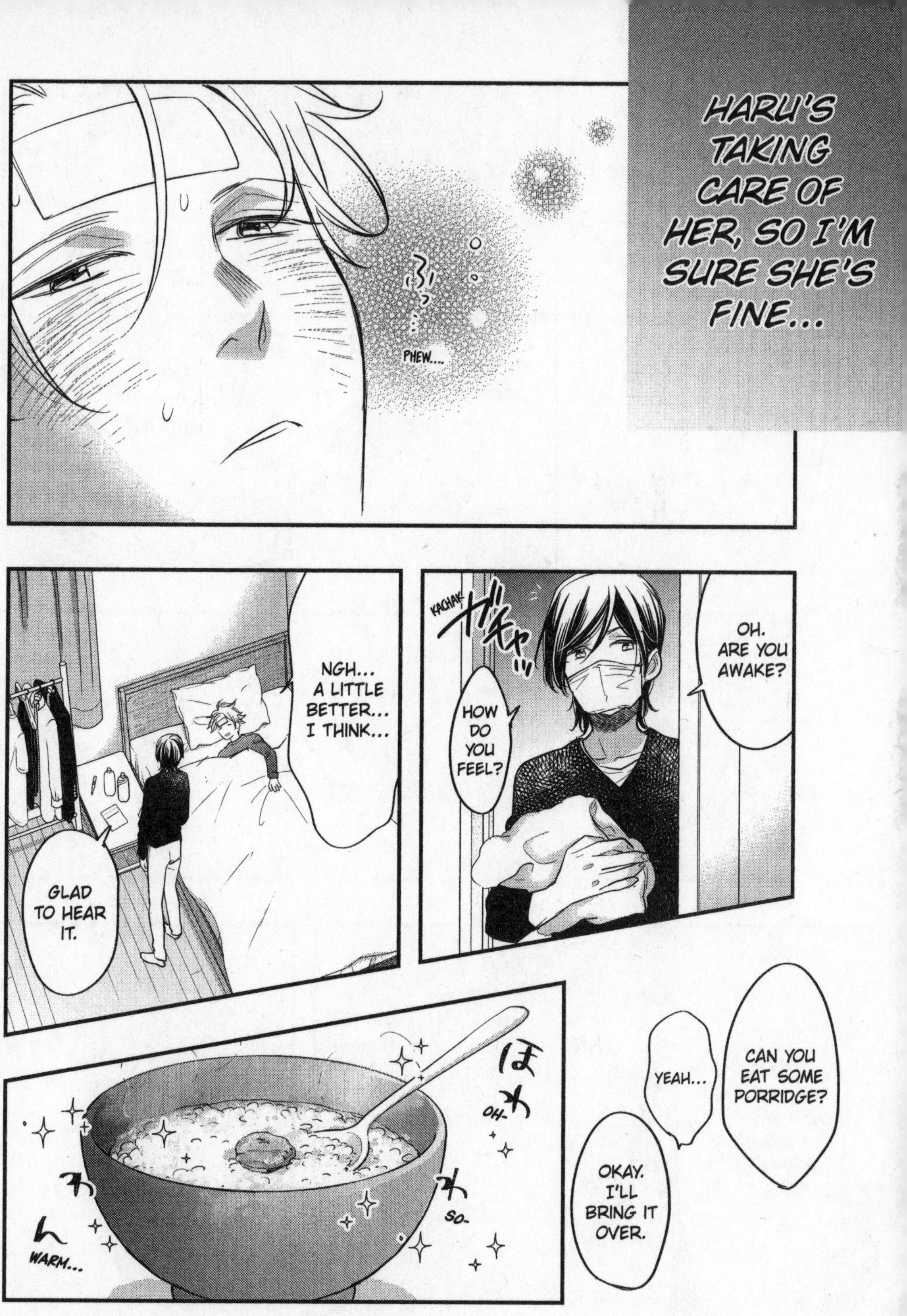
HARU'S TAKING CARE OF HER, SO I'M SURE SHE'S FINE...
PHEW....
ガチャッ
KACHAK
OH. ARE YOU AWAKE?
HOW DO YOU FEEL?
NGH... A LITTLE BETTER... I THINK...
GLAD TO HEAR IT.
CAN YOU EAT SOME PORRIDGE?
YEAH...
OKAY. I'LL BRING IT OVER.
OH-
SO-
WARM...

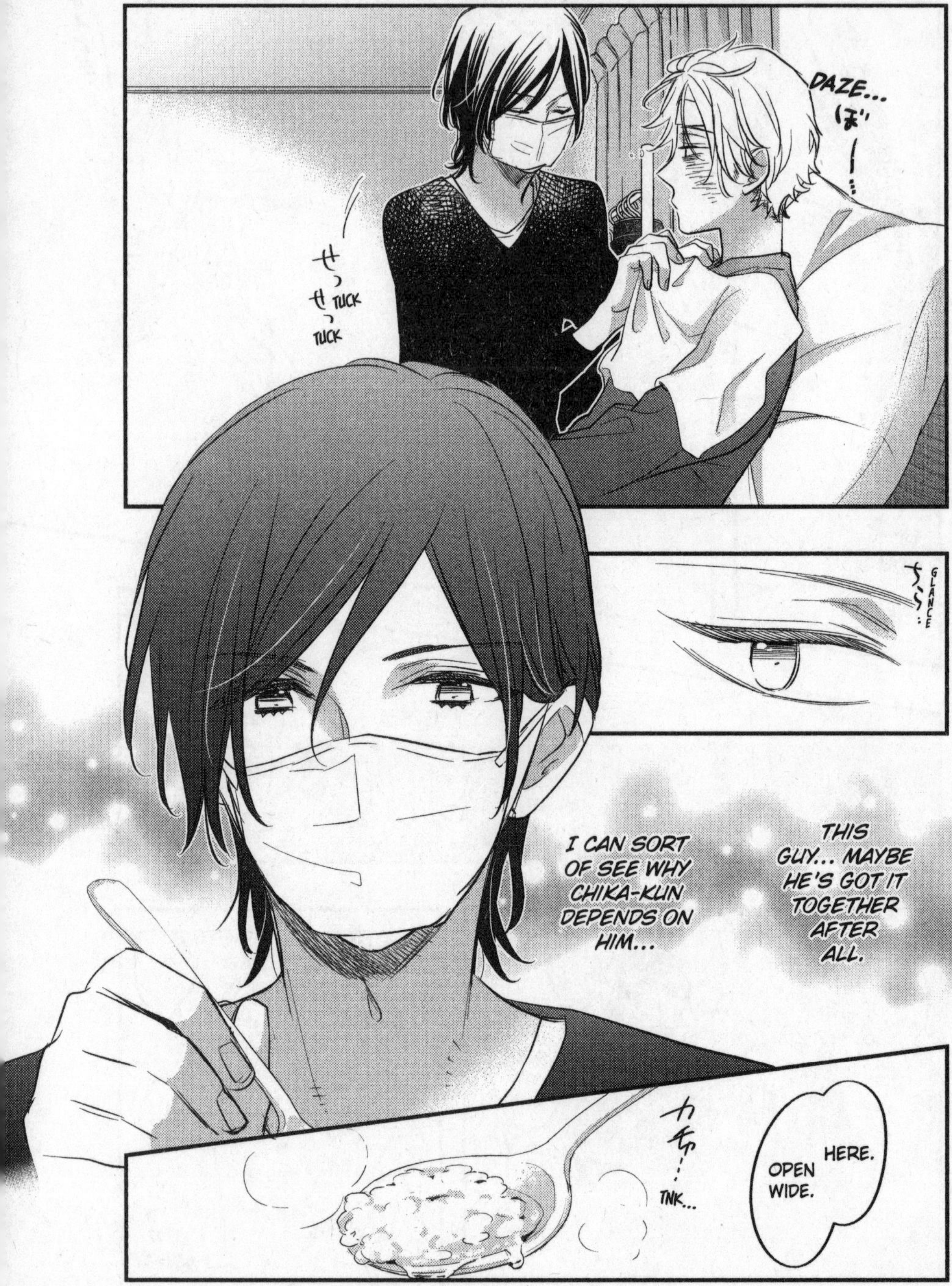
DAZE...
ぼー…
せっせっ
TUCK
TUCK
ちら…
GLANCE
THIS GUY... MAYBE HE'S GOT IT TOGETHER AFTER ALL.
I CAN SORT OF SEE WHY CHIKA-KUN DEPENDS ON HIM...
HERE. OPEN WIDE.
カチ…
TNK...

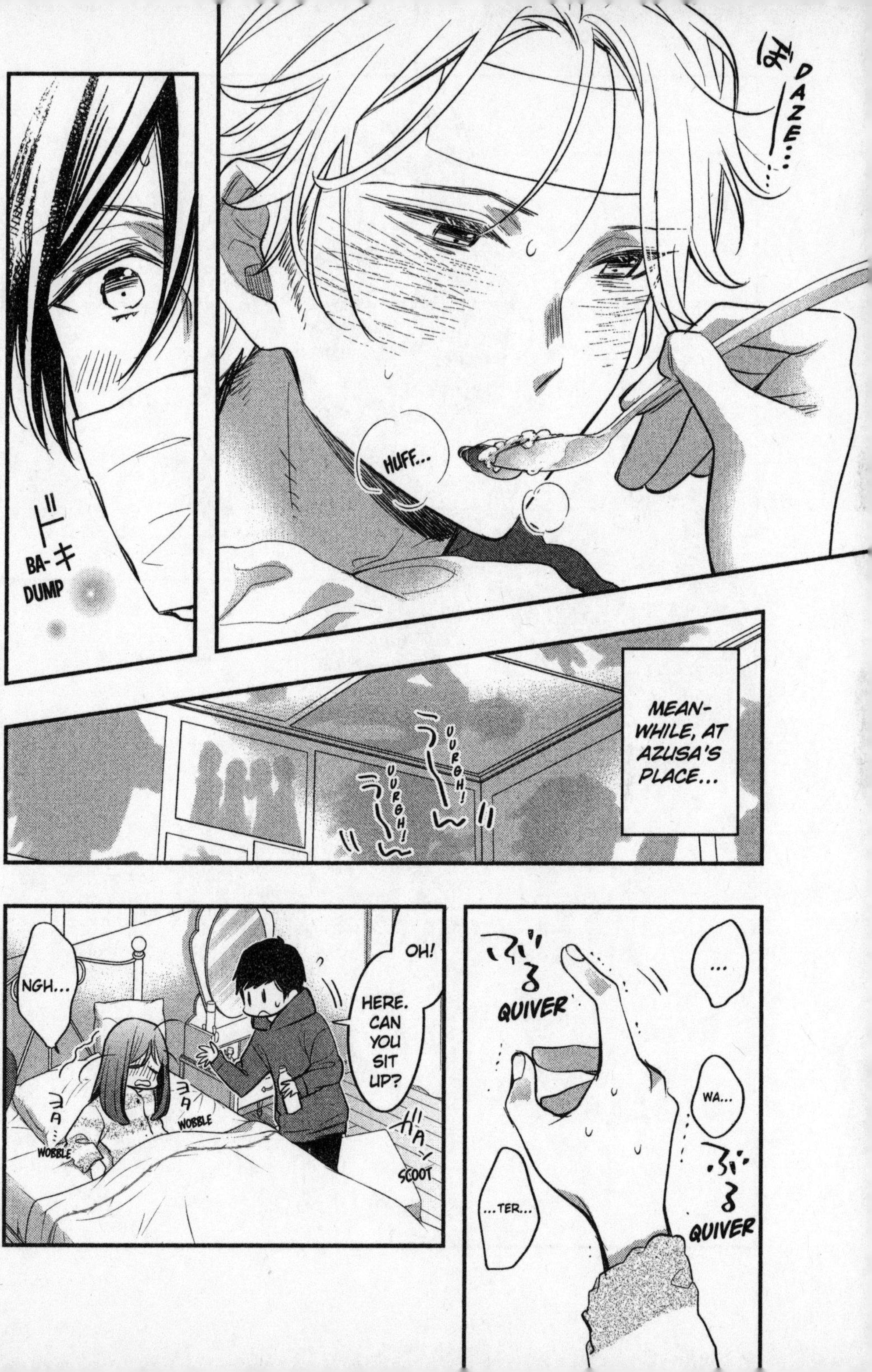
DAZE...
HUFF...
ドキ
BA-DUMP
MEAN-WHILE, AT AZUSA'S PLACE...
URGH!
URGH!
...
ぶる
QUIVER
WA...
ぶる
QUIVER
...TER...
OH!
HERE. CAN YOU SIT UP?
SCOOT
WOBBLE
NGH...
WOBBLE

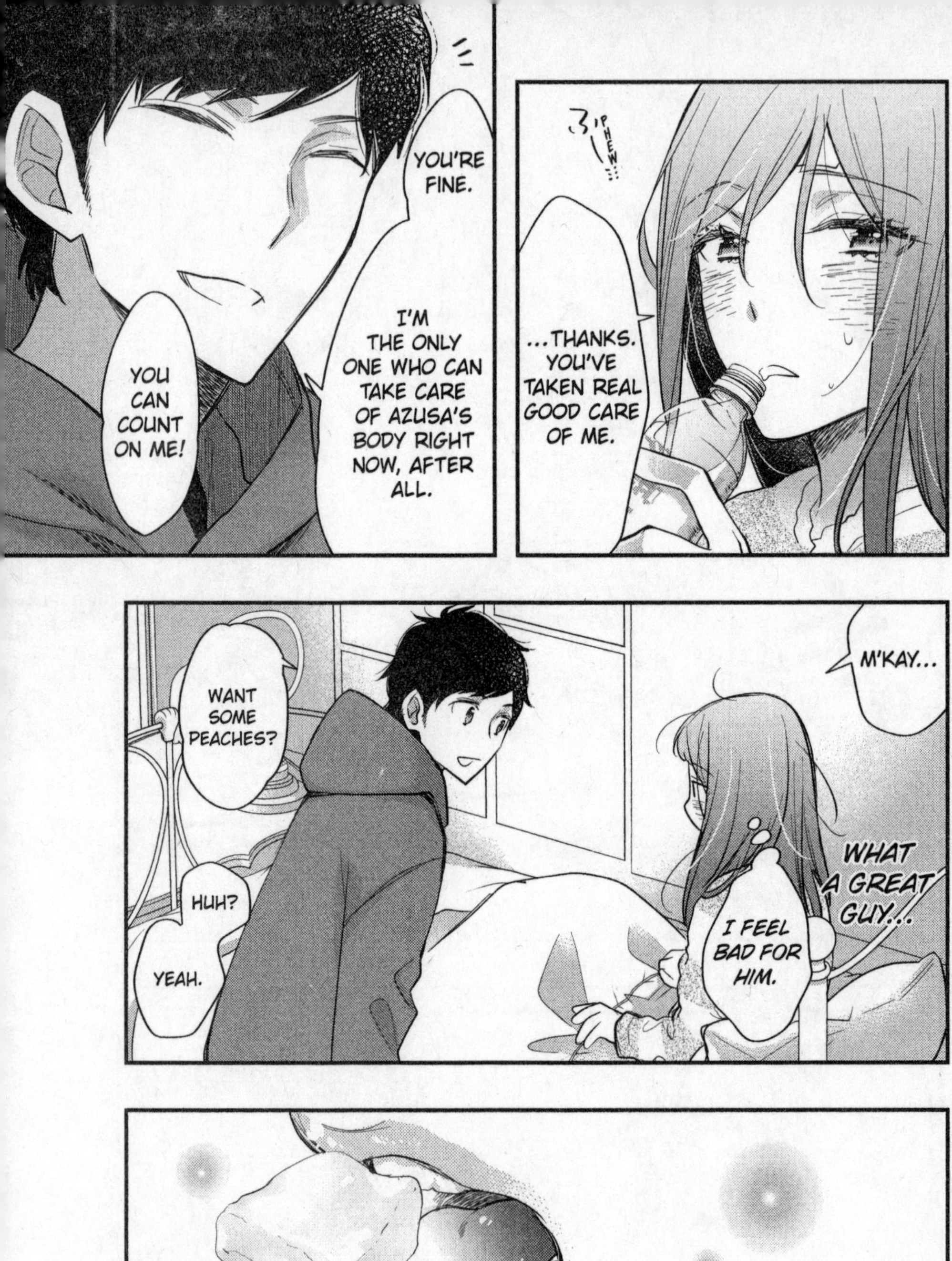
PHEW...
...THANKS. YOU'VE TAKEN REAL GOOD CARE OF ME.
YOU'RE FINE.
I'M THE ONLY ONE WHO CAN TAKE CARE OF AZUSA'S BODY RIGHT NOW, AFTER ALL.
YOU CAN COUNT ON ME!
M'KAY...
WHAT A GREAT GUY...
I FEEL BAD FOR HIM.
WANT SOME PEACHES?
HUH?
YEAH.

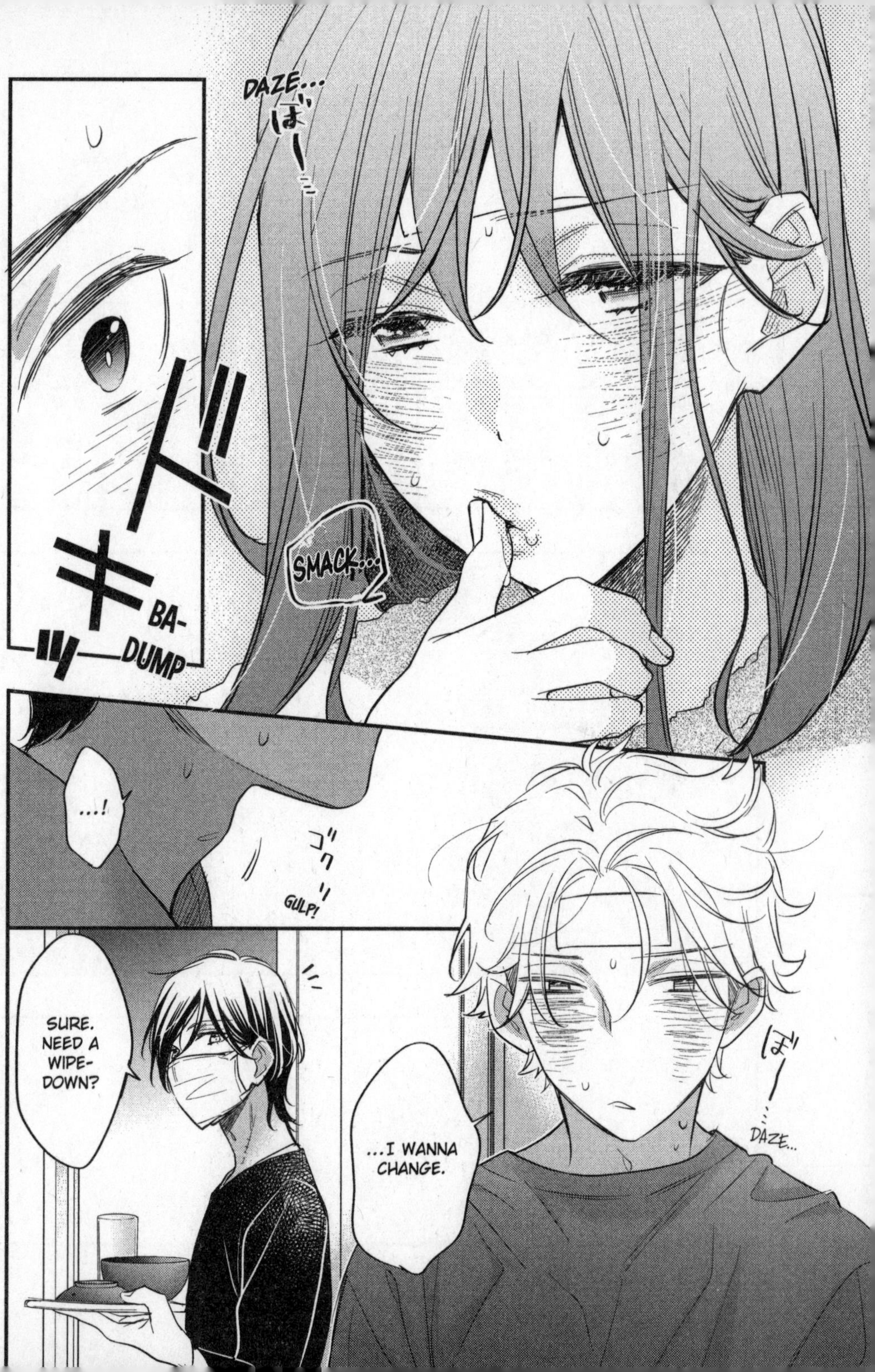
DAZE...
ぼー…
SMACK...
ドキッ
BA-DUMP
...!
ゴクッ
GULP!
ぼー…
DAZE...
...I WANNA CHANGE.
SURE. NEED A WIPE-DOWN?

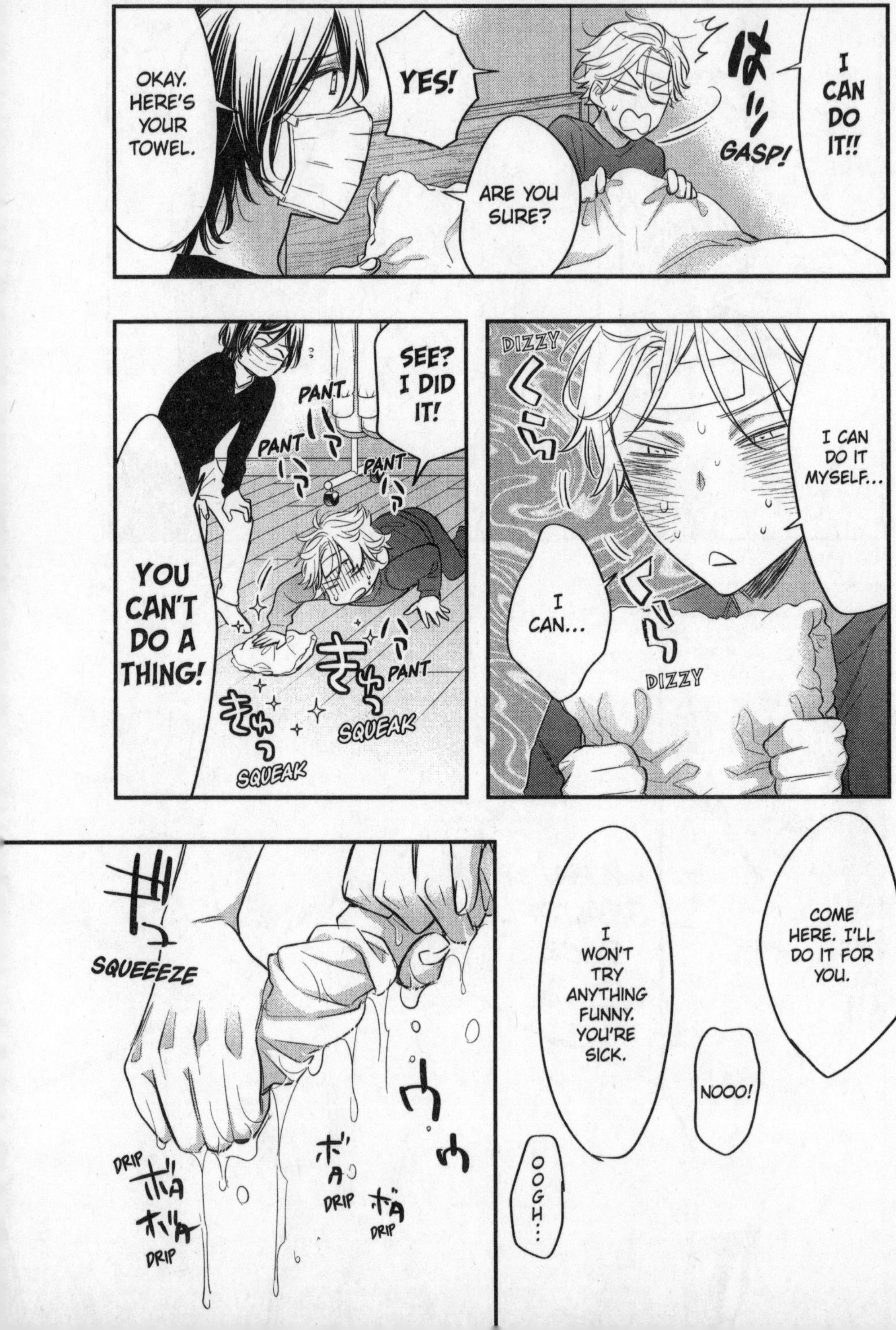
I CAN DO IT!!
GASP!
ARE YOU SURE?
YES!
OKAY. HERE'S YOUR TOWEL.
I CAN DO IT MYSELF...
DIZZY
I CAN...
DIZZY
SEE? I DID IT!
PANT
PANT
PANT
PANT
SQUEAK
SQUEAK
YOU CAN'T DO A THING!
COME HERE. I'LL DO IT FOR YOU.
NOOO!
I WON'T TRY ANYTHING FUNNY. YOU'RE SICK.
OOGH...
SQUEEEZE
DRIP
DRIP
DRIP
DRIP

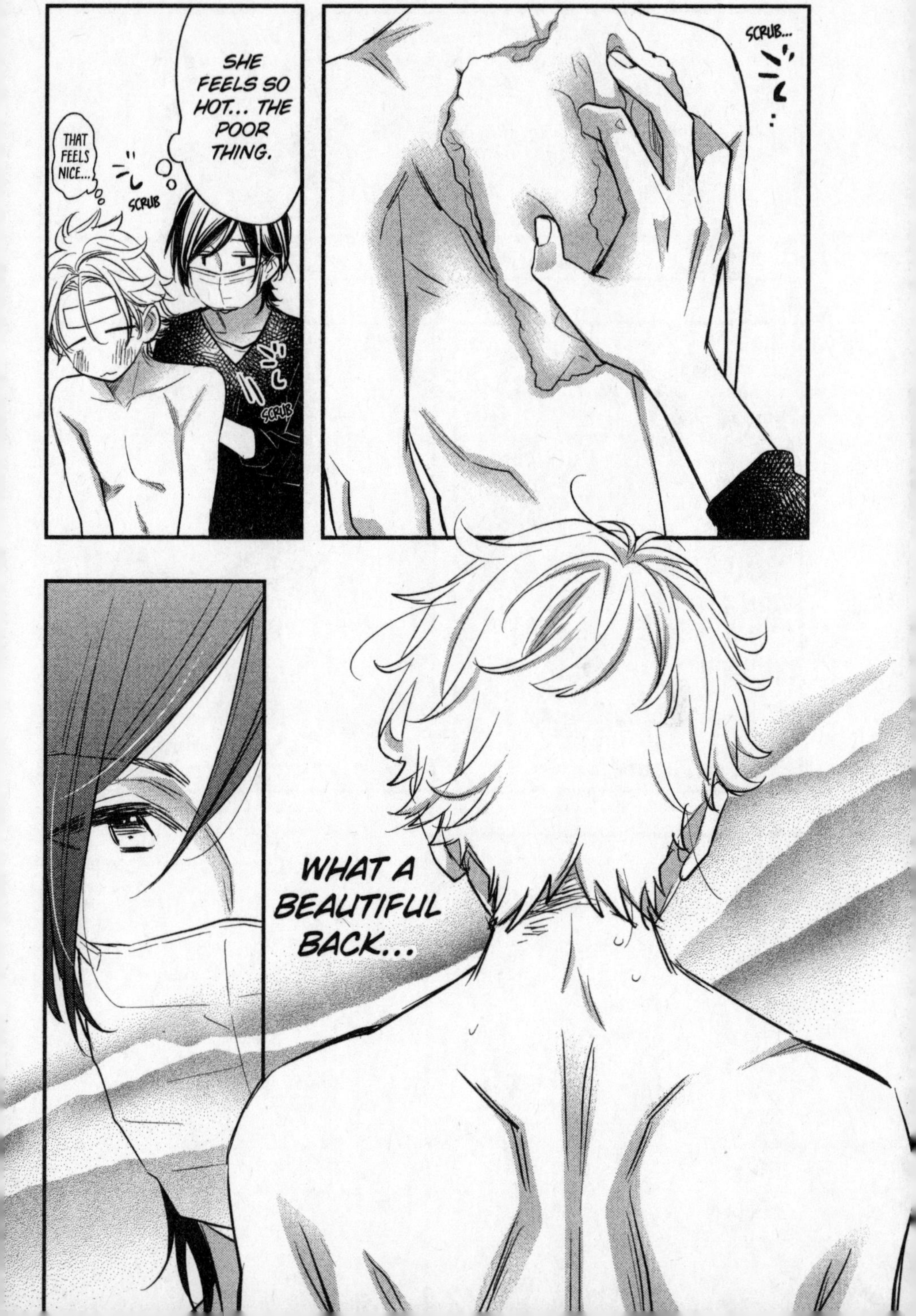
SCRUB...
SHE FEELS SO HOT... THE POOR THING.
THAT FEELS NICE...
SCRUB
SCRUB
WHAT A BEAUTIFUL BACK...

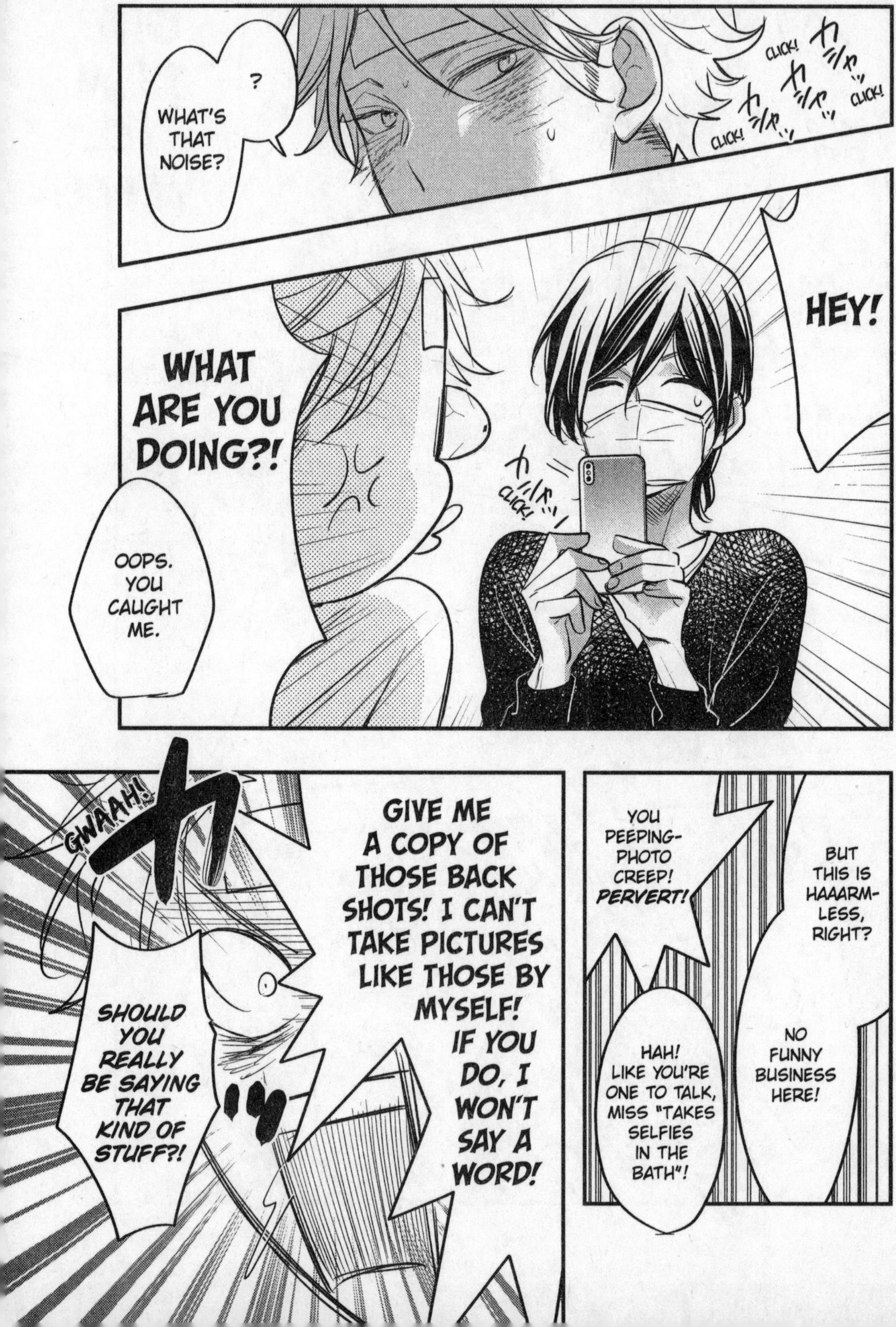
CLICK!
CLICK!
CLICK!
?
WHAT'S THAT NOISE?
HEY!
WHAT ARE YOU DOING?!
CLICK!
OOPS. YOU CAUGHT ME.
YOU PEEPING-PHOTO CREEP! PERVERT!
BUT THIS IS HAAARMLESS, RIGHT?
NO FUNNY BUSINESS HERE!
HAH! LIKE YOU'RE ONE TO TALK, MISS "TAKES SELFIES IN THE BATH"!
GWAAAH!
GIVE ME A COPY OF THOSE BACK SHOTS! I CAN'T TAKE PICTURES LIKE THOSE BY MYSELF! IF YOU DO, I WON'T SAY A WORD!
SHOULD YOU REALLY BE SAYING THAT KIND OF STUFF?!

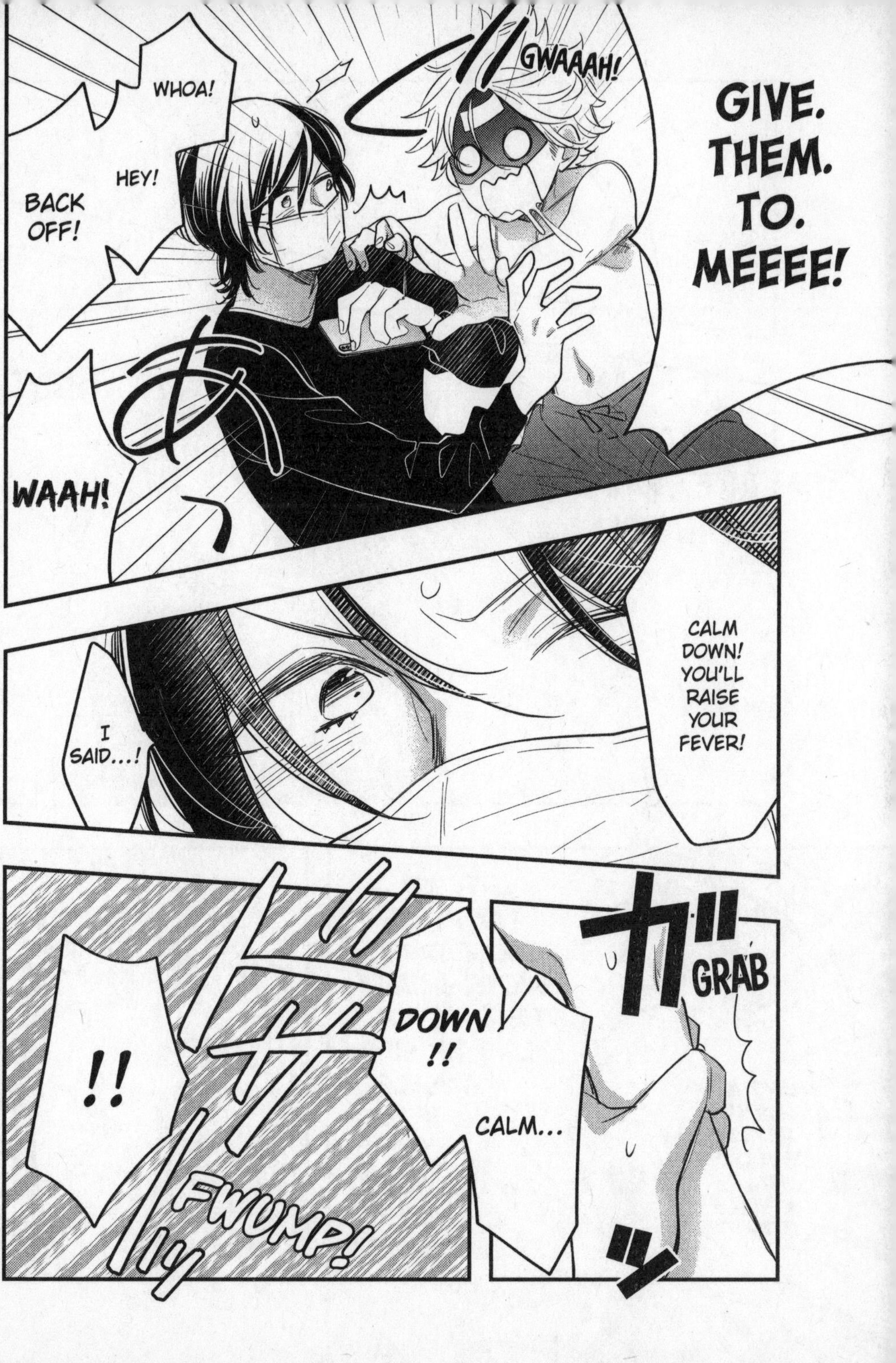
GIVE. THEM. TO. MEEEE!
GWAAAH!
WHOA!
HEY!
BACK OFF!
WAAH!
CALM DOWN! YOU'LL RAISE YOUR FEVER!
I SAID...!
GRAB
CALM...
DOWN!!
!!
FWUMP!

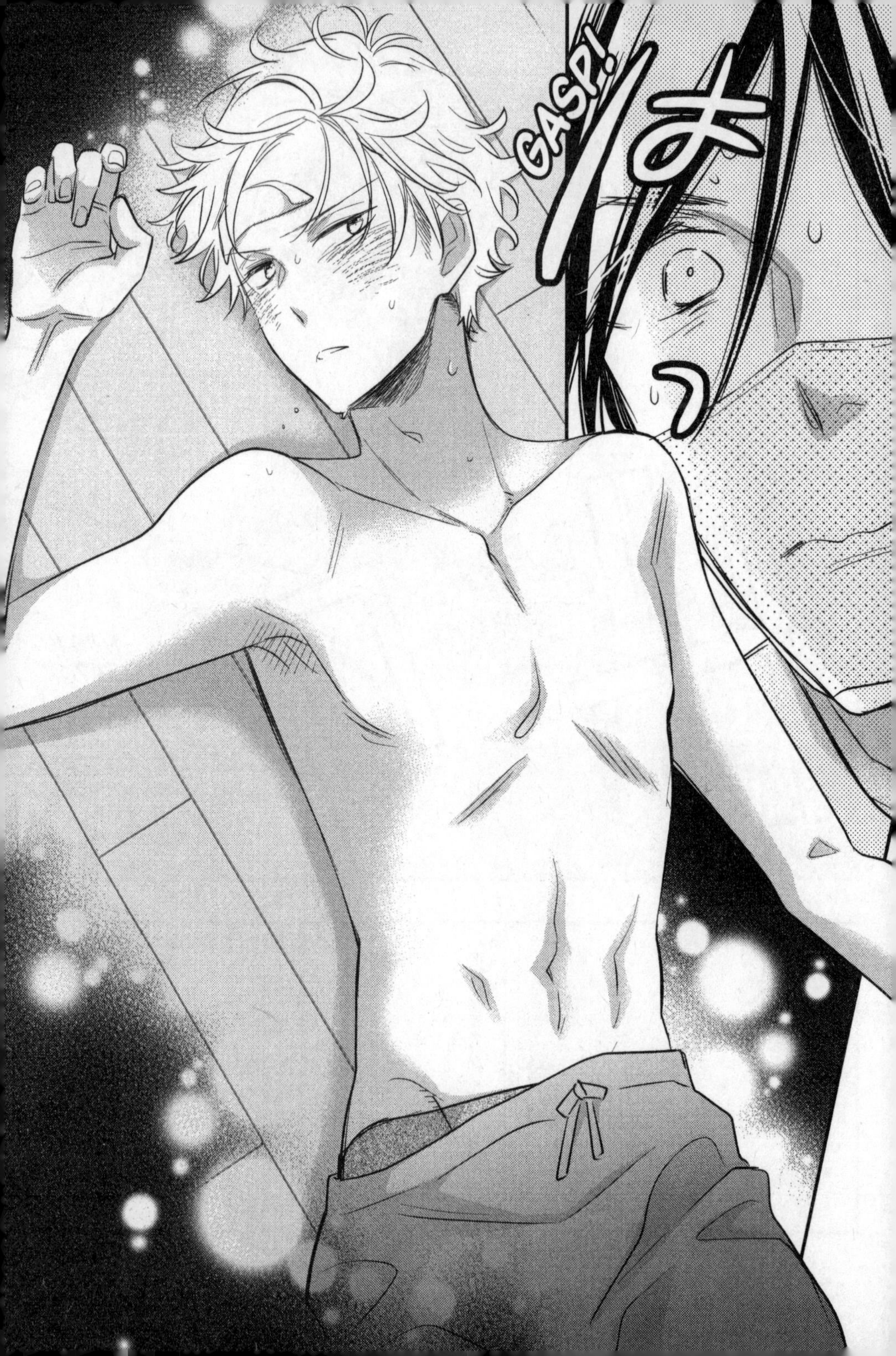
GASP!
まっ

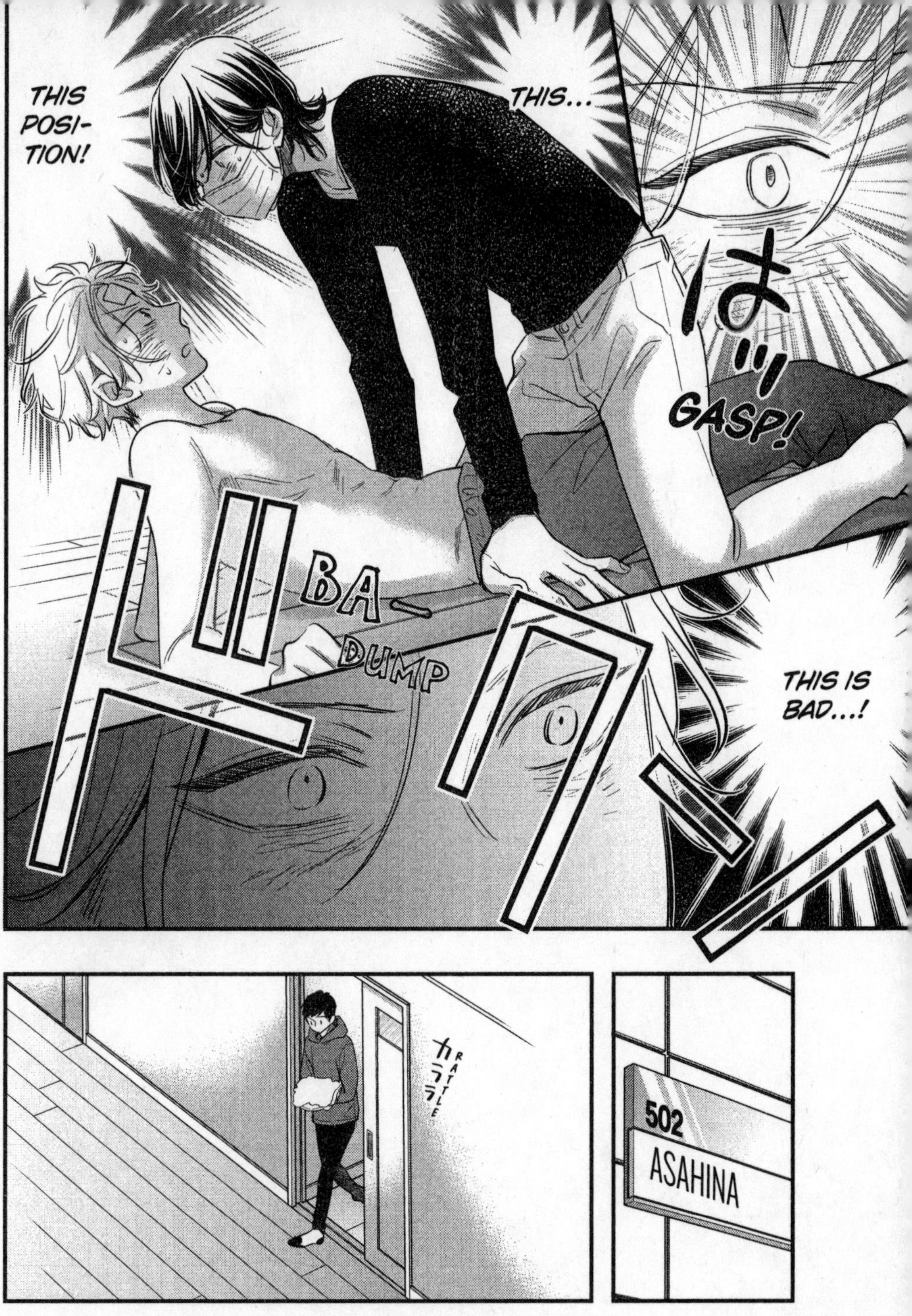
はっ
GASP!
THIS...
THIS POSITION!
THIS IS BAD...!
BA-DUMP
502
ASAHINA
カラララ
RATTLE

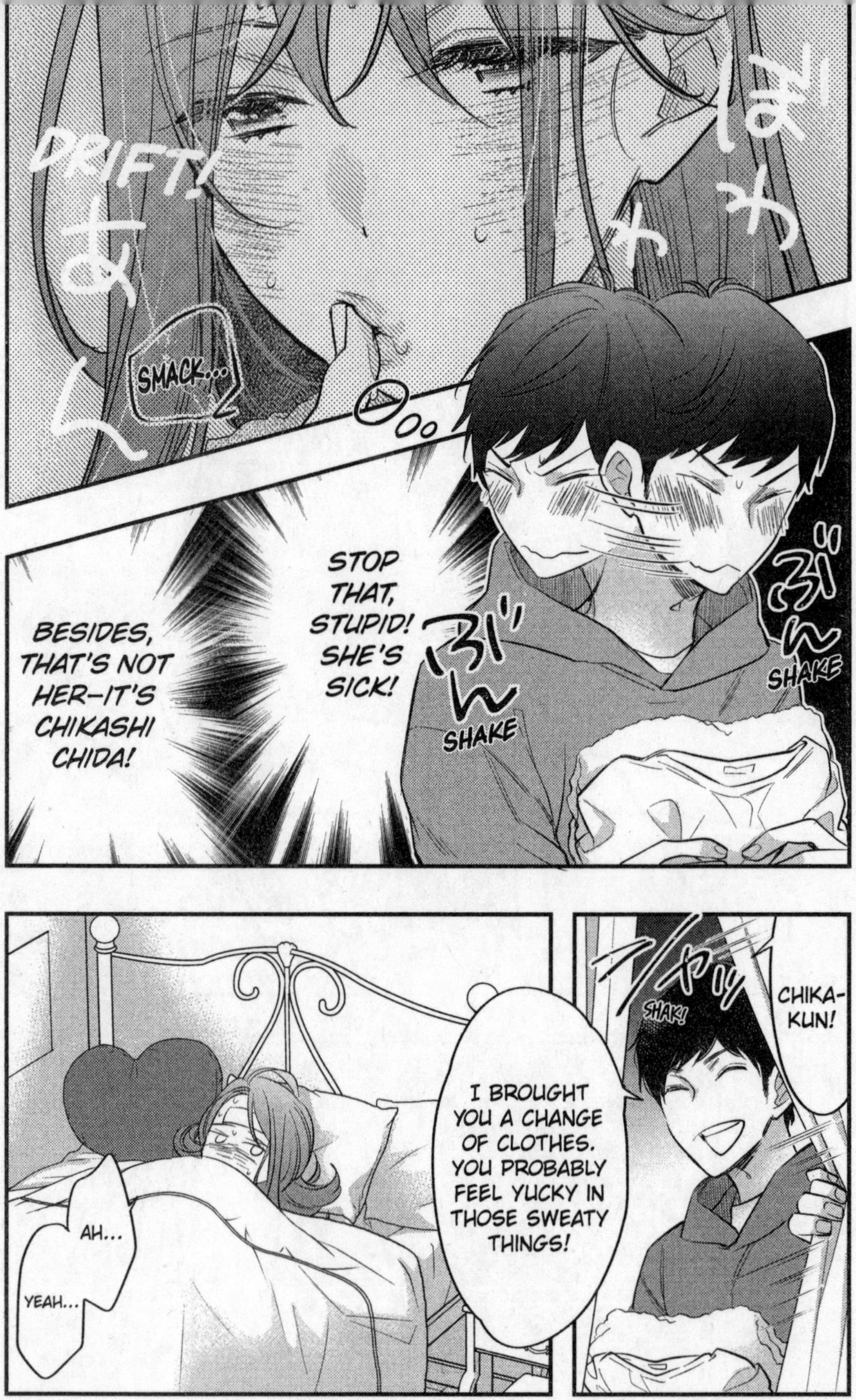
DRIFT!
SMACK...
SHAKE
STOP THAT, STUPID! SHE'S SICK!
SHAKE
BESIDES, THAT'S NOT HER—IT'S CHIKASHI CHIDA!
CHIKA-KUN!
SHAK!
I BROUGHT YOU A CHANGE OF CLOTHES. YOU PROBABLY FEEL YUCKY IN THOSE SWEATY THINGS!
AH...
YEAH...

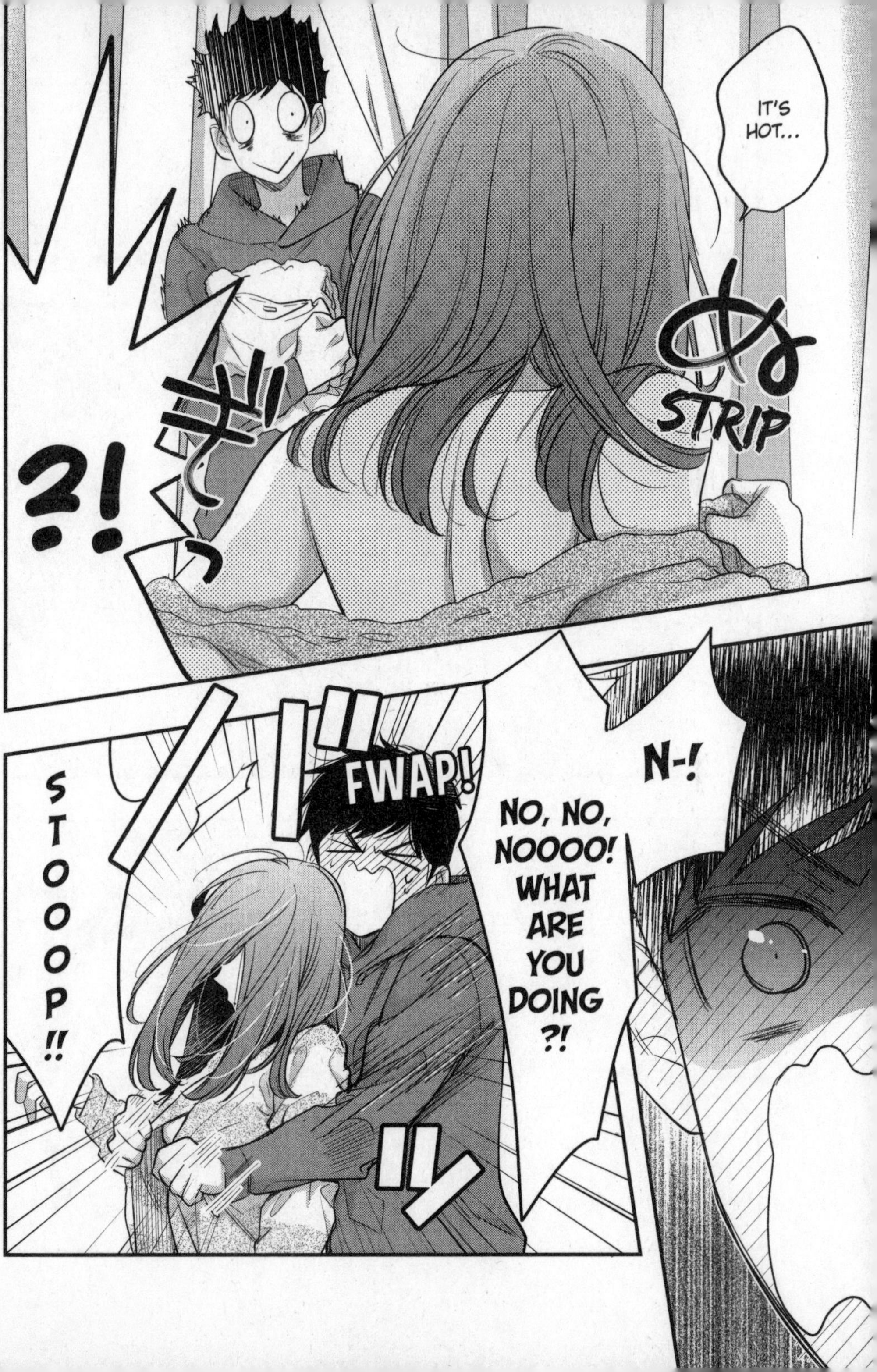
IT'S HOT...
STRIP
?!
N-!
NO, NO, NOOOO! WHAT ARE YOU DOING ?!
FWAP!
STOOOOP!!

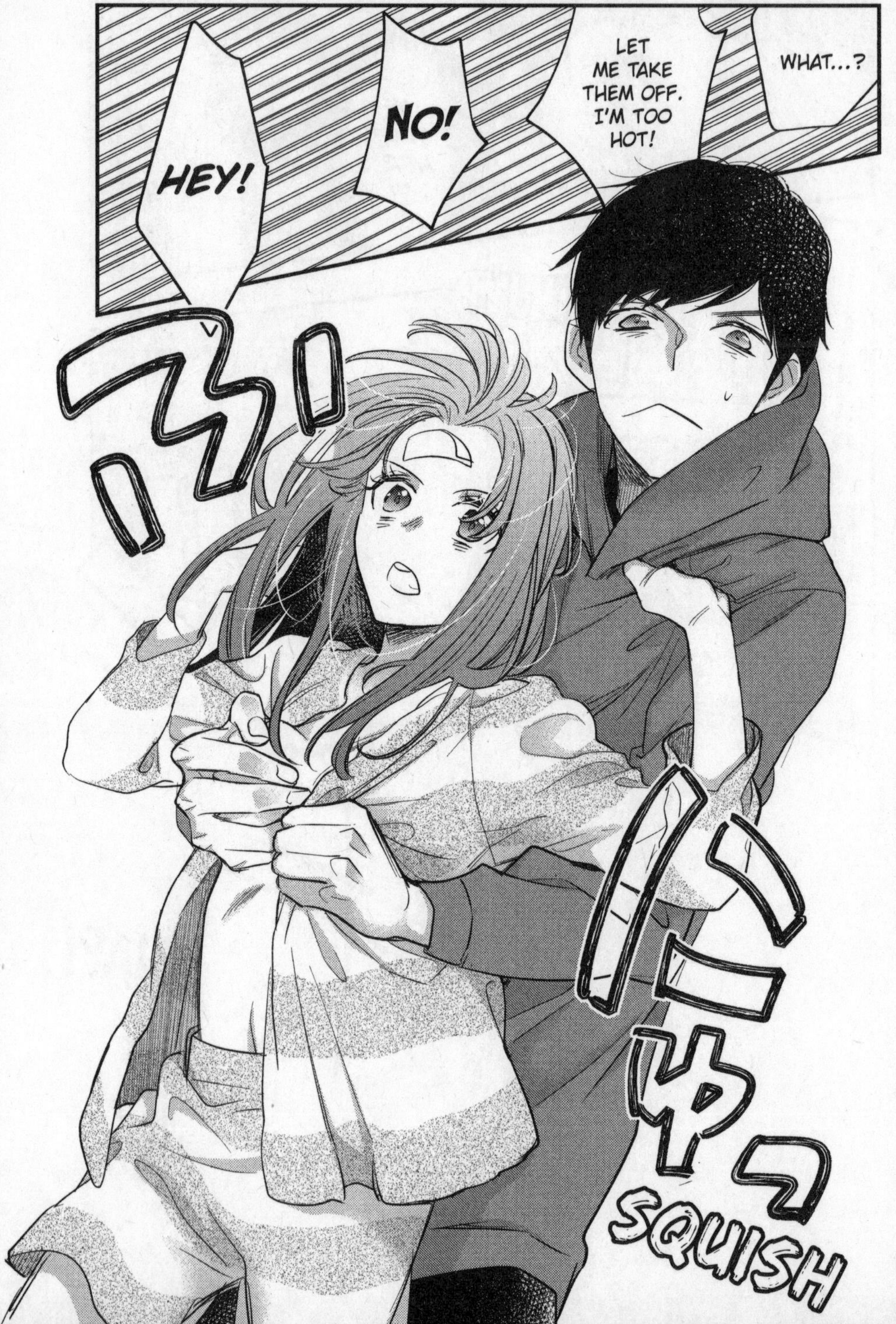
WHAT...?
LET ME TAKE THEM OFF. I'M TOO HOT!
NO!
HEY!
SQUISH

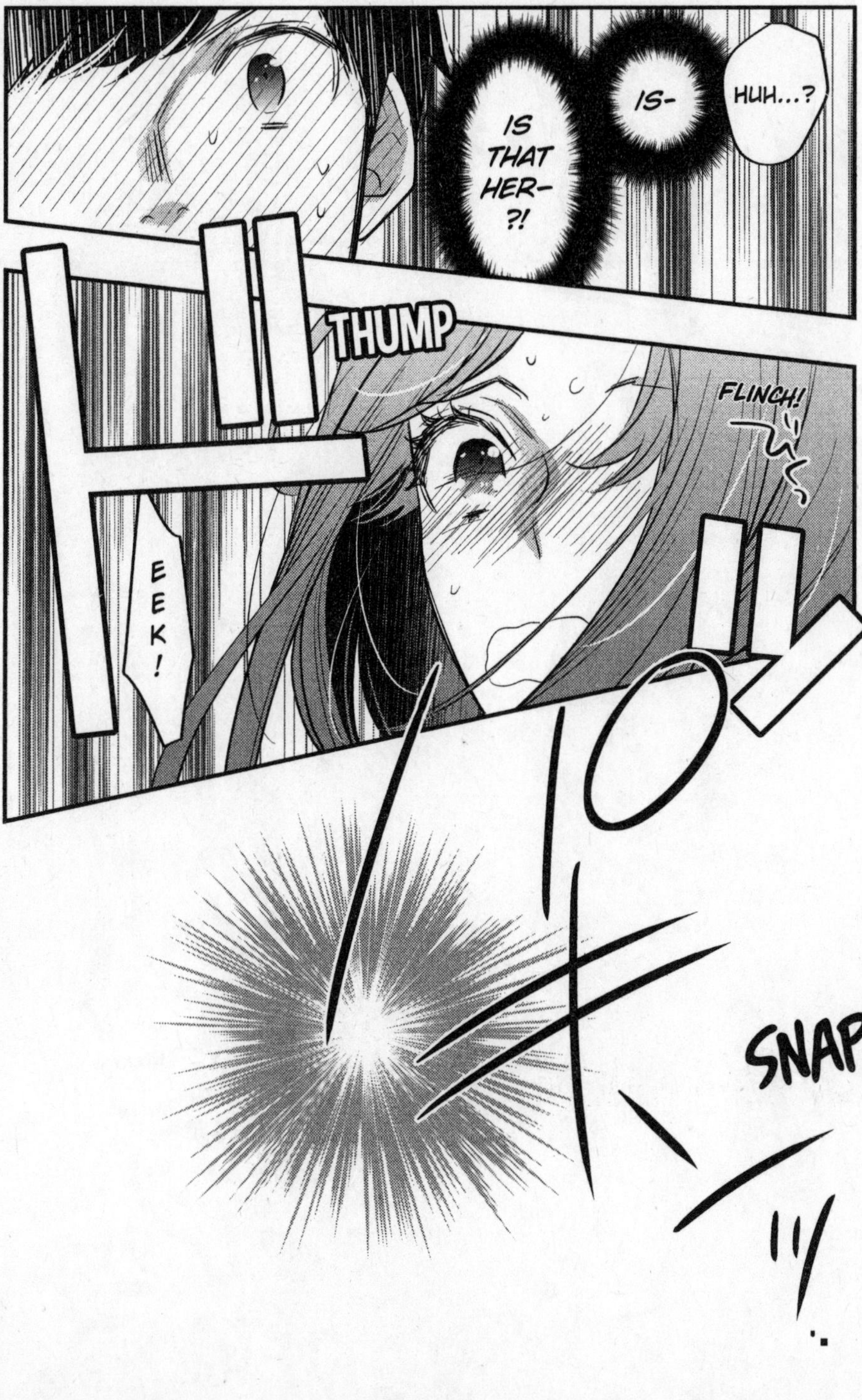
HUH...?
IS-
IS THAT HER-?!
FLINCH!
THUMP
EEK!
SNAP!

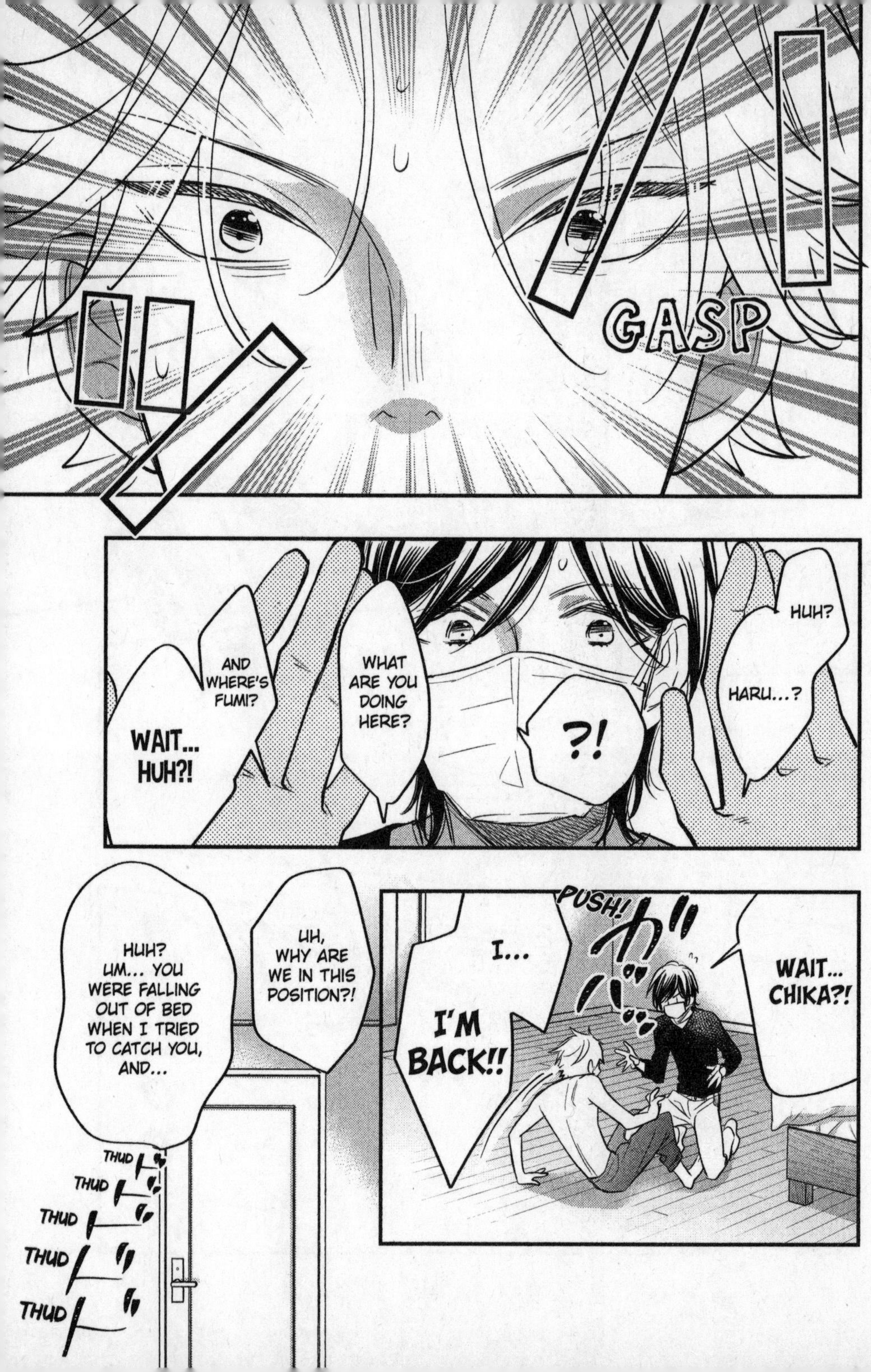
GASP
HUH?
HARU...?
?!
WHAT ARE YOU DOING HERE?
AND WHERE'S FUMI?
WAIT... HUH?!
WAIT... CHIKA?!
PUSH!
I...
I'M BACK!!
UH, WHY ARE WE IN THIS POSITION?!
HUH? UM... YOU WERE FALLING OUT OF BED WHEN I TRIED TO CATCH YOU, AND...
THUD
THUD
THUD
THUD
THUD

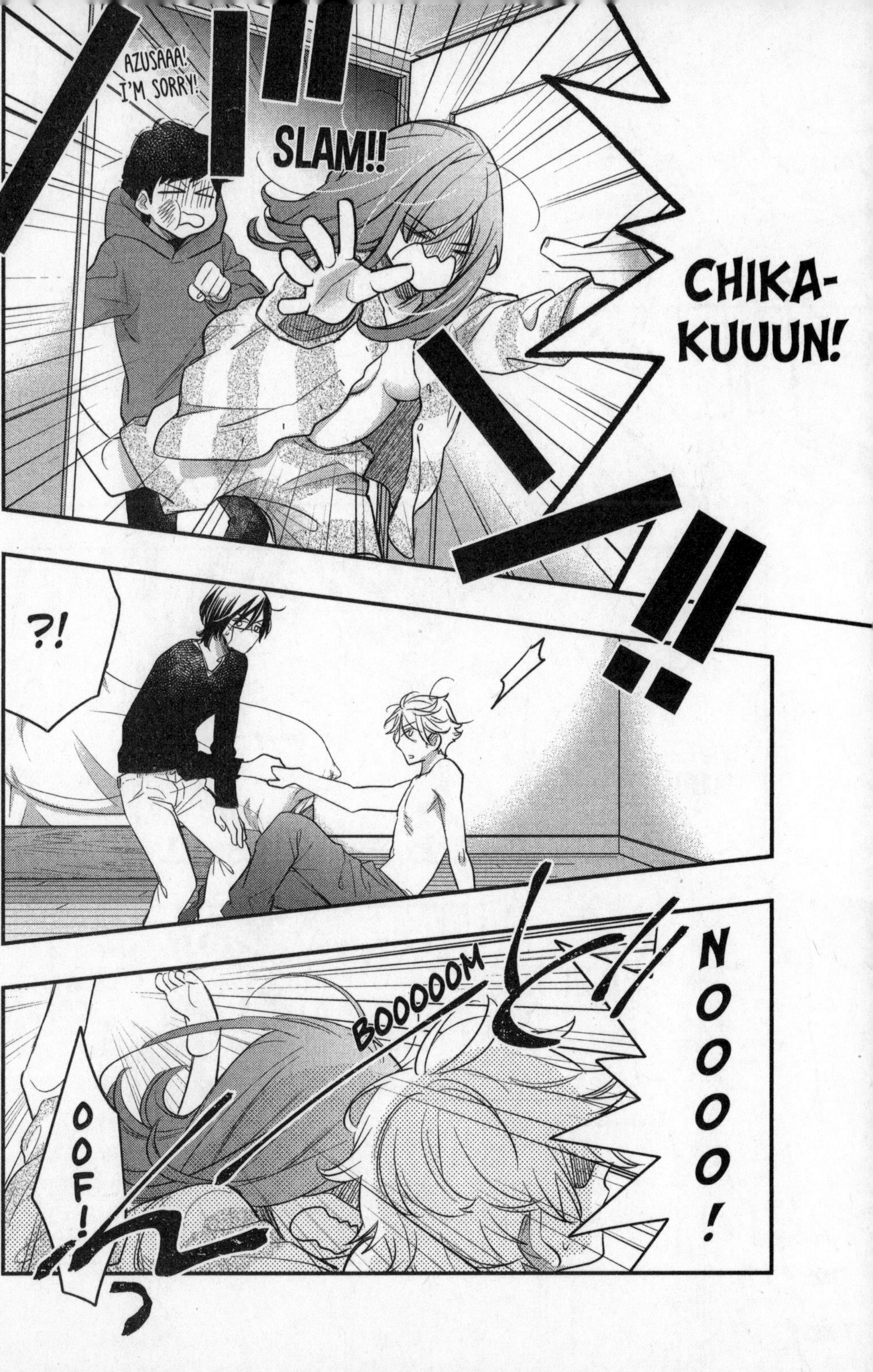
CHIKA-KUUUN!
SLAM!!
AZUSAAA! I'M SORRY!
?!
NOOOOO!
BOOOOOM
OOF!

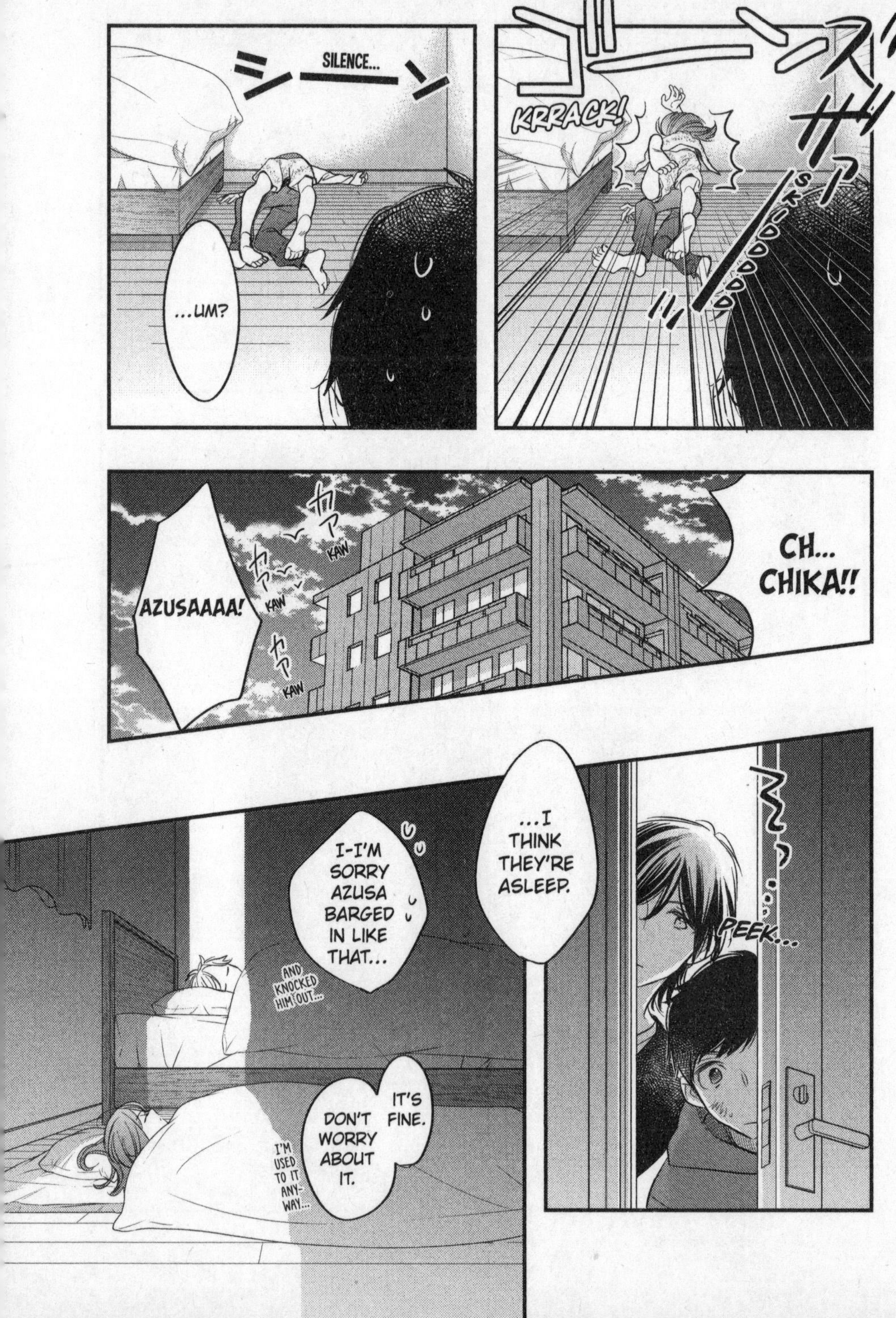
KRRACK!
SKIDDDDDDD
SILENCE...
...UM?
CH... CHIKA!!
KAW
KAW
KAW
AZUSAAAA!
PEEK...
...I THINK THEY'RE ASLEEP.
I-I'M SORRY AZUSA BARGED IN LIKE THAT...
AND KNOCKED HIM OUT...
IT'S FINE.
DON'T WORRY ABOUT IT.
I'M USED TO IT ANYWAY...

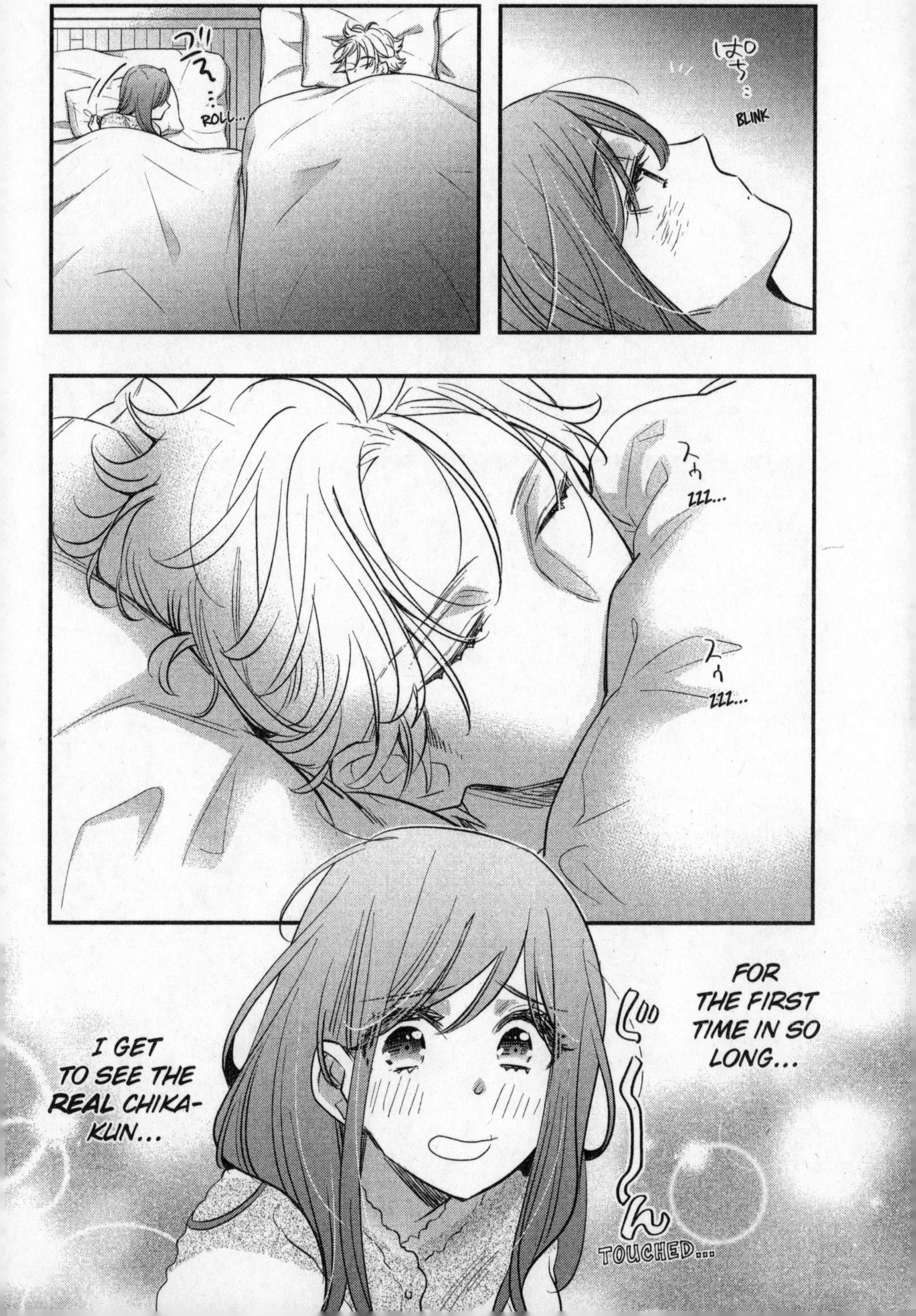
ぱちっ
BLINK
ごろ…
ROLL…
スゥ
ZZZ…
スゥ
ZZZ…
FOR THE FIRST TIME IN SO LONG…
I GET TO SEE THE REAL CHIKA-KUN…
じーん
TOUCHED…

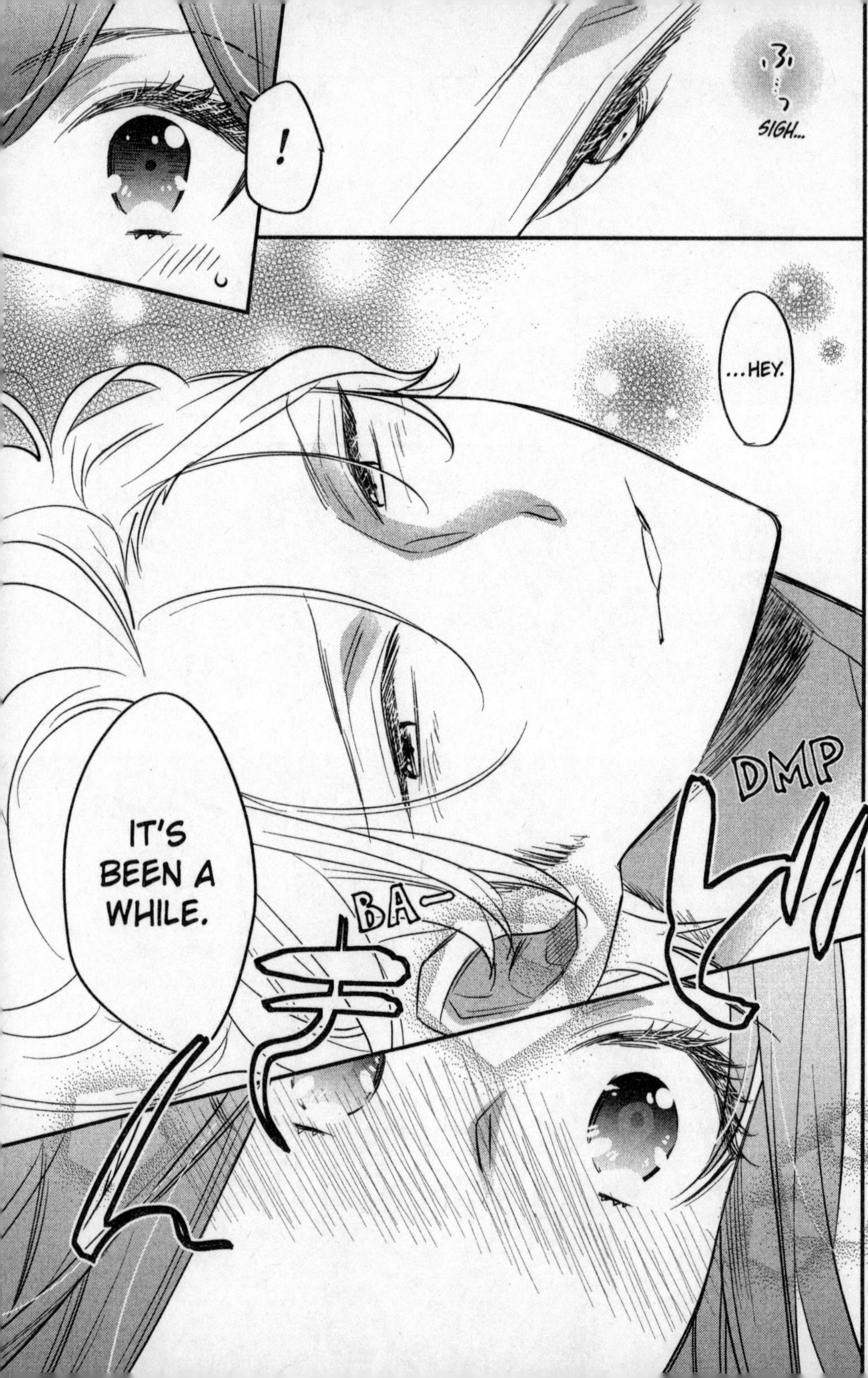
SIGH...
!
...HEY.
DMP
BA-
IT'S BEEN A WHILE.

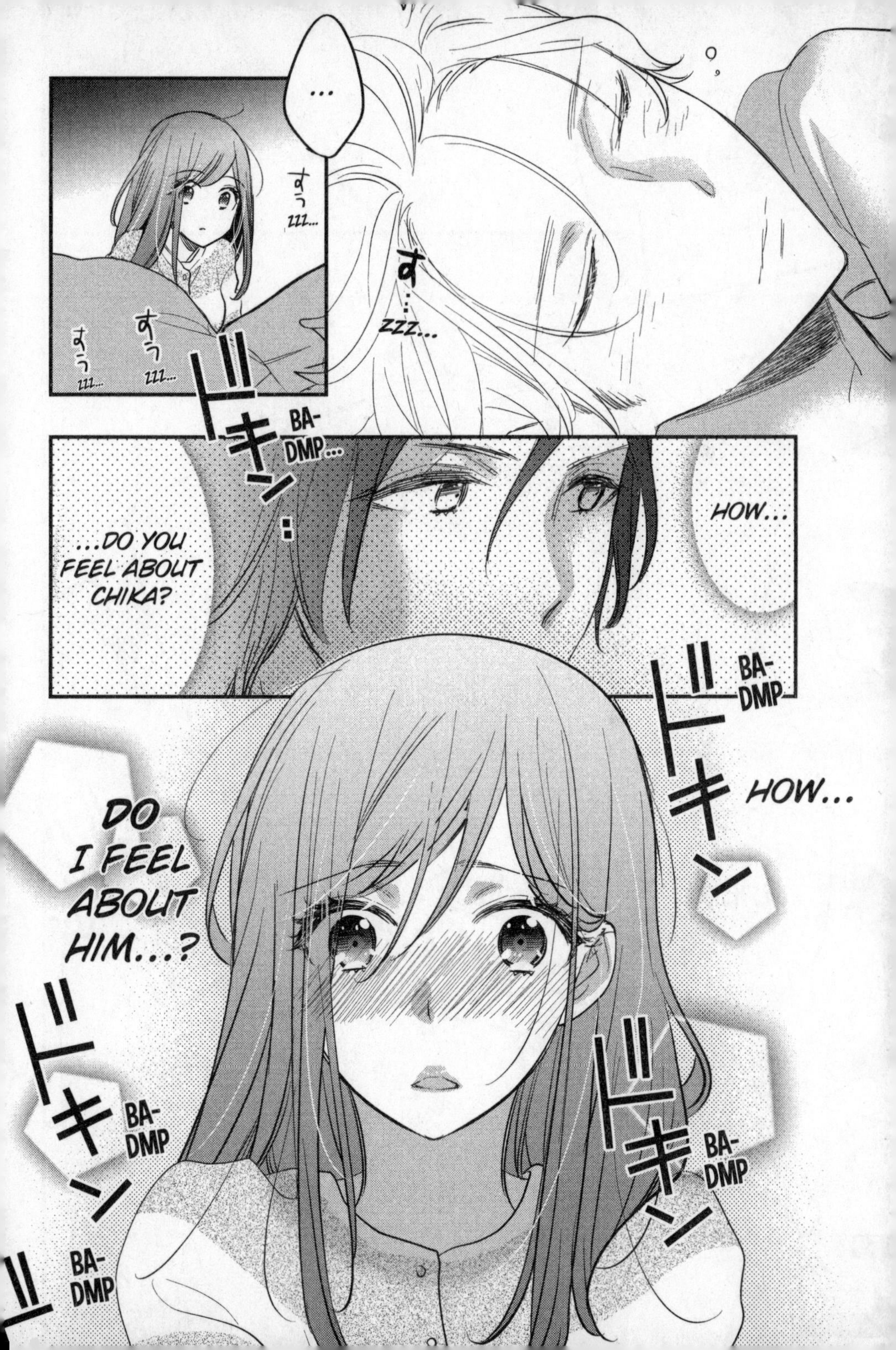

す…
ZZZ…
…
すぅ
ZZZ…
すぅ
ZZZ…
すぅ
ZZZ…
ドキン
BA-DMP…
HOW…
…DO YOU FEEL ABOUT CHIKA?
ドキン
BA-DMP
HOW…
DO I FEEL ABOUT HIM…?
ドキン
BA-DMP
ドキン
BA-DMP
BA-DMP

R⇄CROSS

D!! STAR

AR⇄CROS

CROSSED

⇄CROSSE

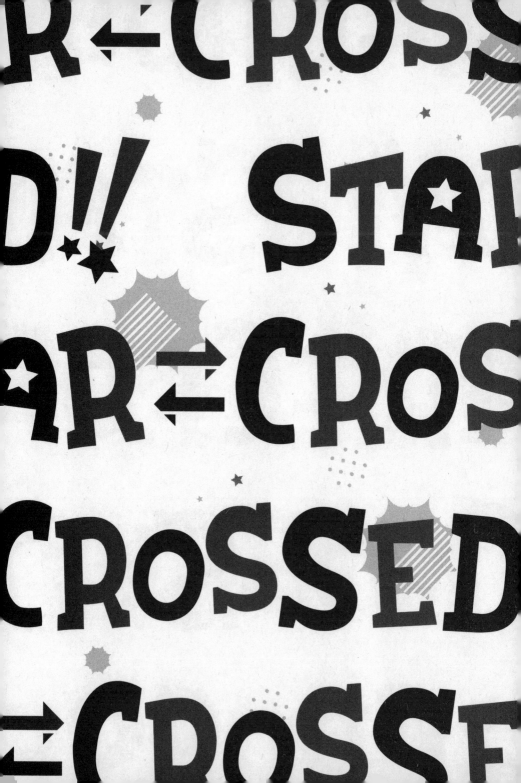

R⇄CROSS
D!! STAR
AR⇄CROS
CROSSED
⇄CROSSE

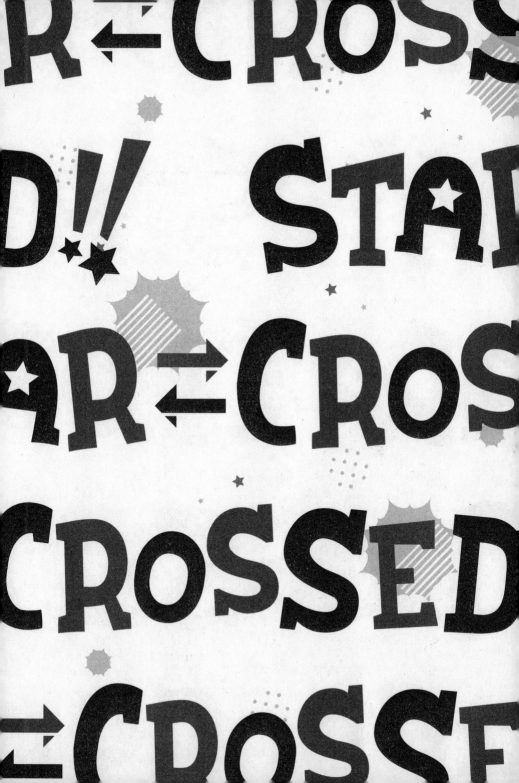

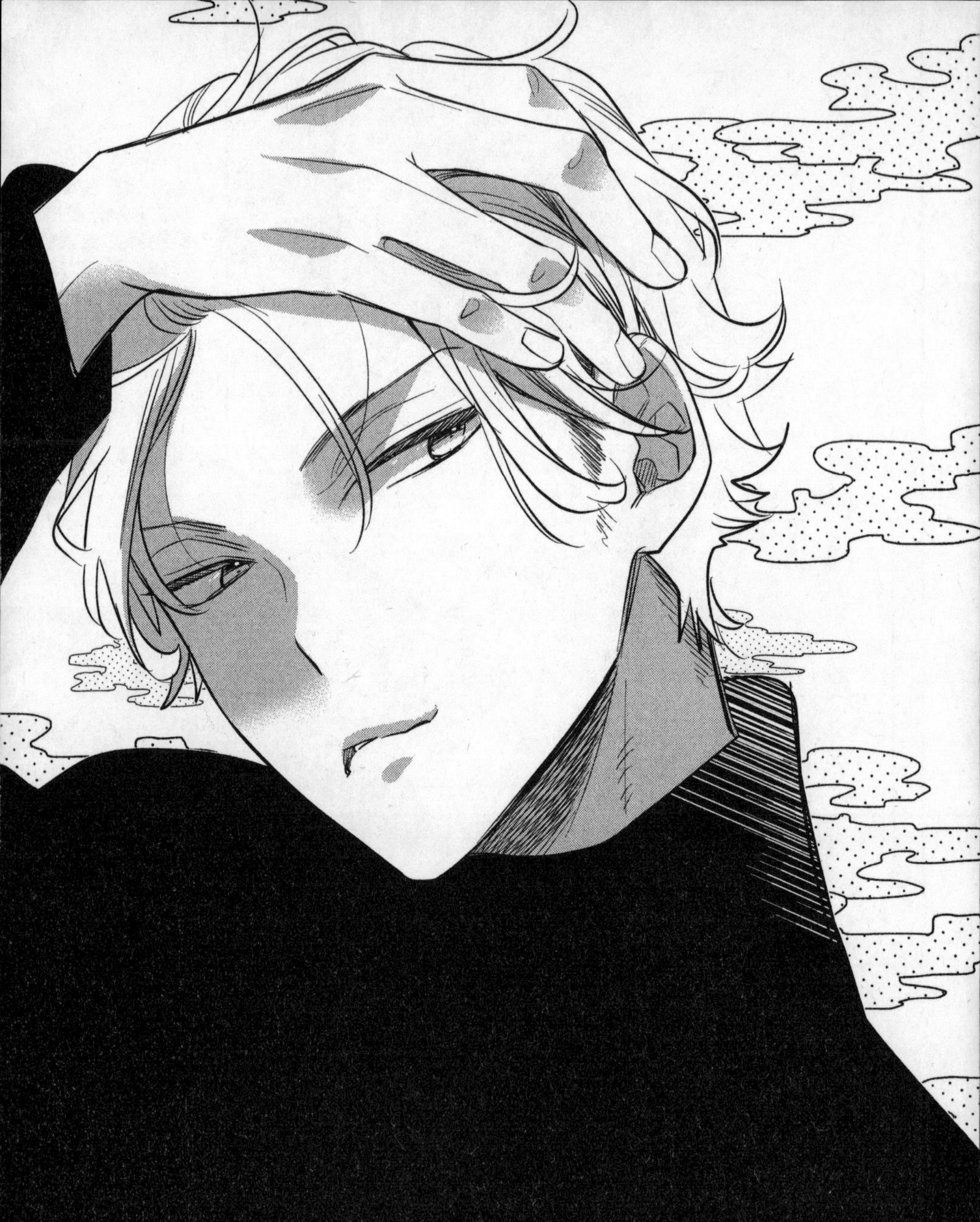

STAGE. 10 | I WANT TO OVERCOME THIS

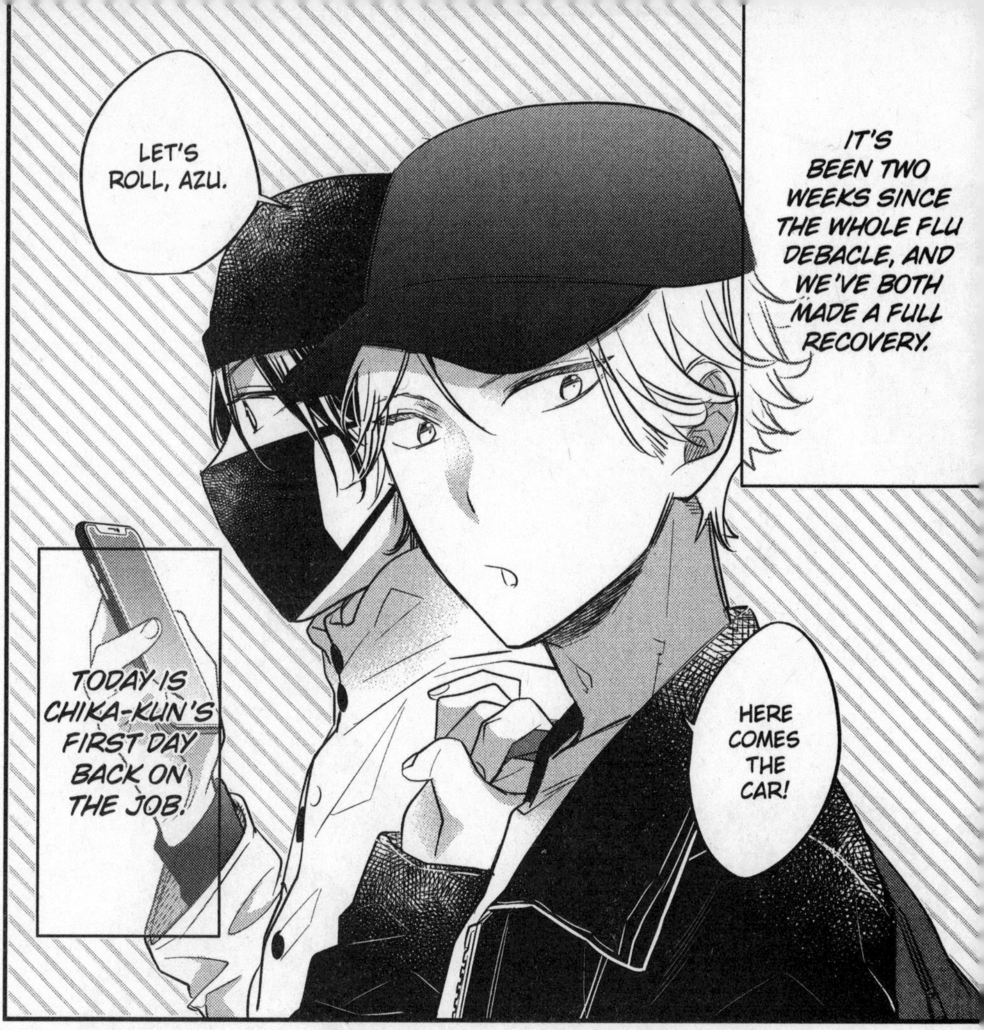
IT'S BEEN TWO WEEKS SINCE THE WHOLE FLU DEBACLE, AND WE'VE BOTH MADE A FULL RECOVERY.
LET'S ROLL, AZU.
HERE COMES THE CAR!
TODAY IS CHIKA-KUN'S FIRST DAY BACK ON THE JOB.

STAR⇄CROSSED!!

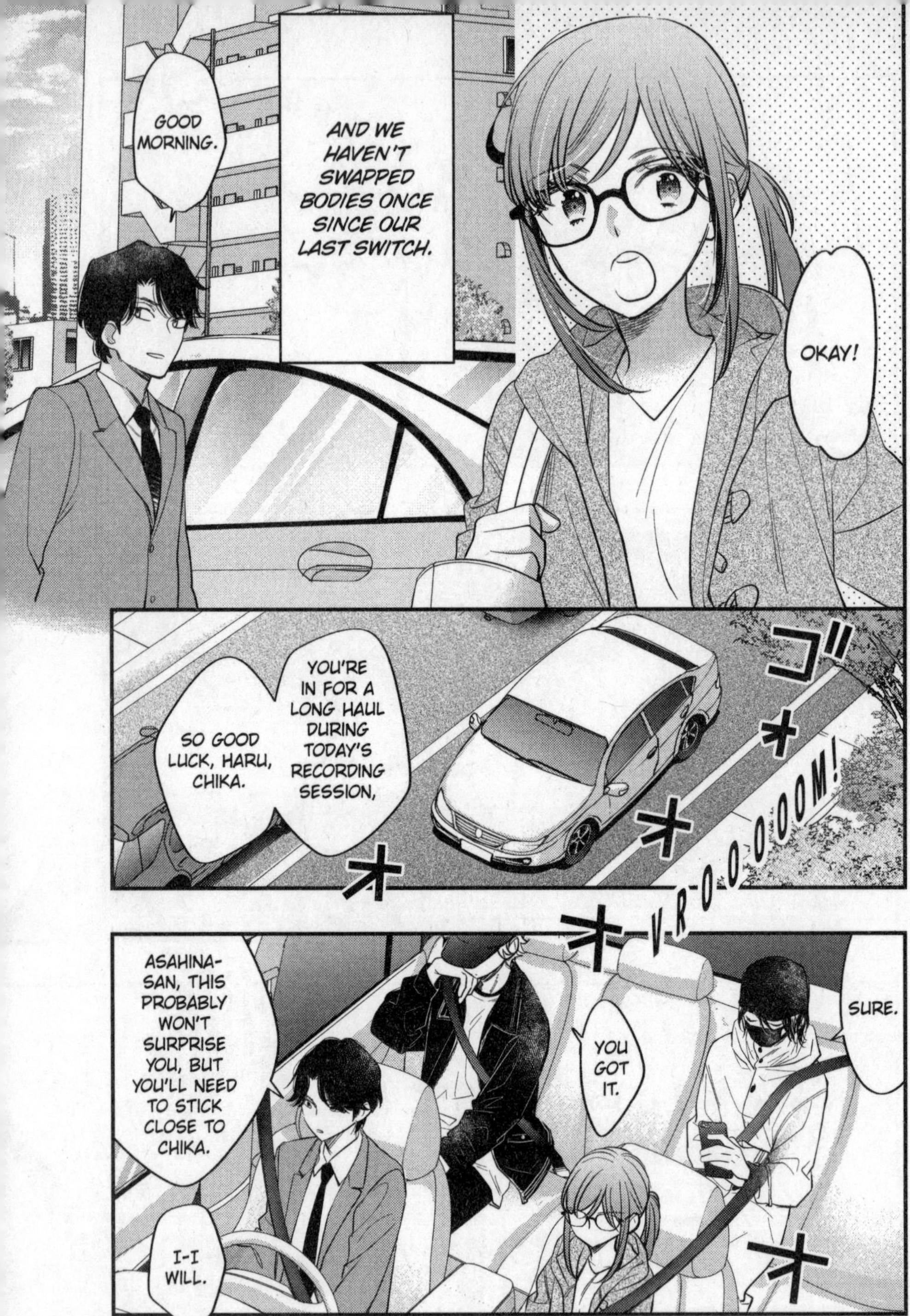
AND WE HAVEN'T SWAPPED BODIES ONCE SINCE OUR LAST SWITCH.
OKAY!
GOOD MORNING.
YOU'RE IN FOR A LONG HAUL DURING TODAY'S RECORDING SESSION,
SO GOOD LUCK, HARU, CHIKA.
ゴ
VROOOOOOM!
SURE.
YOU GOT IT.
ASAHINA-SAN, THIS PROBABLY WON'T SURPRISE YOU, BUT YOU'LL NEED TO STICK CLOSE TO CHIKA.
I-I WILL.

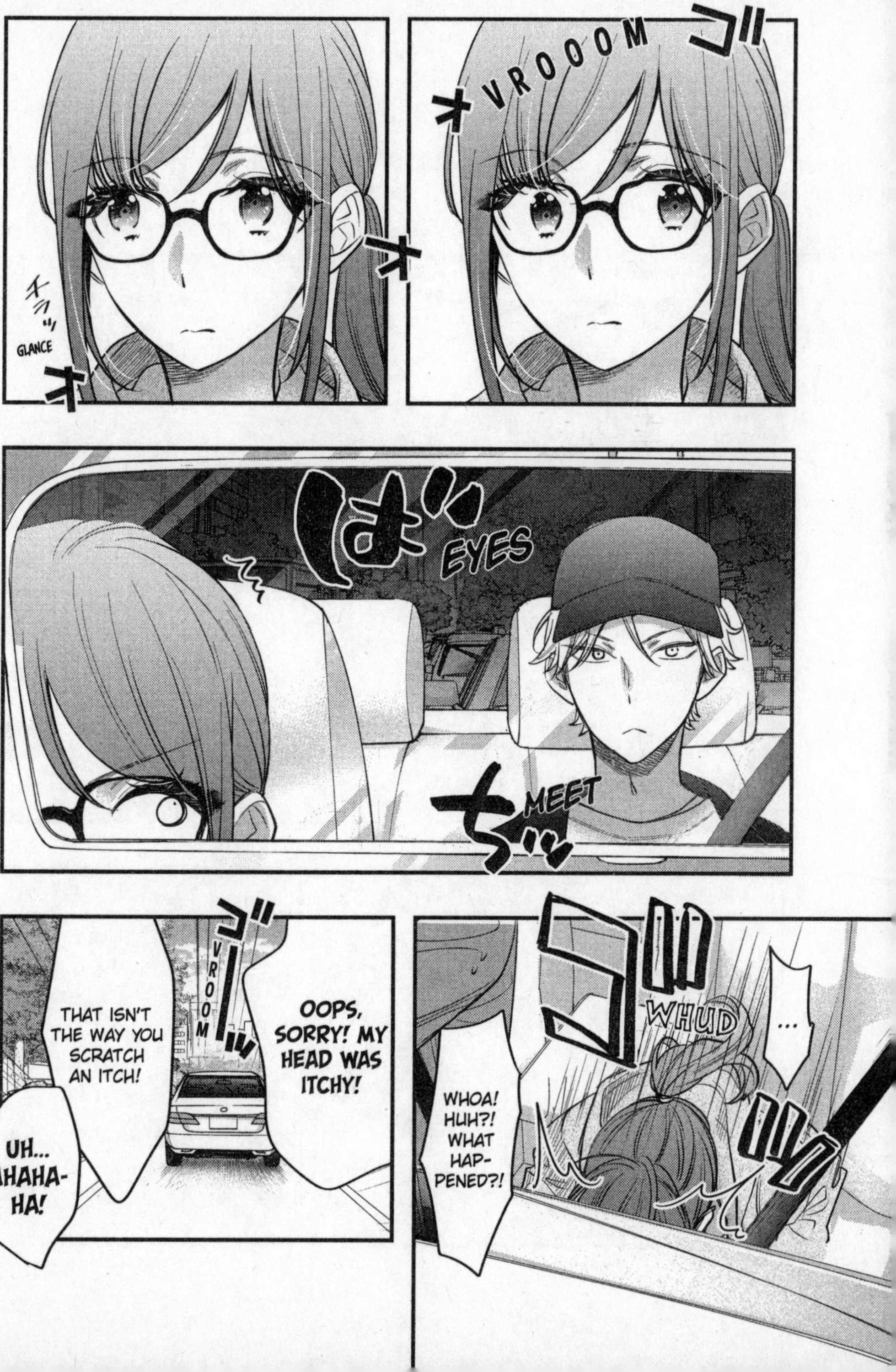
VROOOM
GLANCE
EYES
MEET
WHUD
...
WHOA! HUH?! WHAT HAPPENED?!
VROOM
OOPS, SORRY! MY HEAD WAS ITCHY!
THAT ISN'T THE WAY YOU SCRATCH AN ITCH!
UH... AHAHAHA!

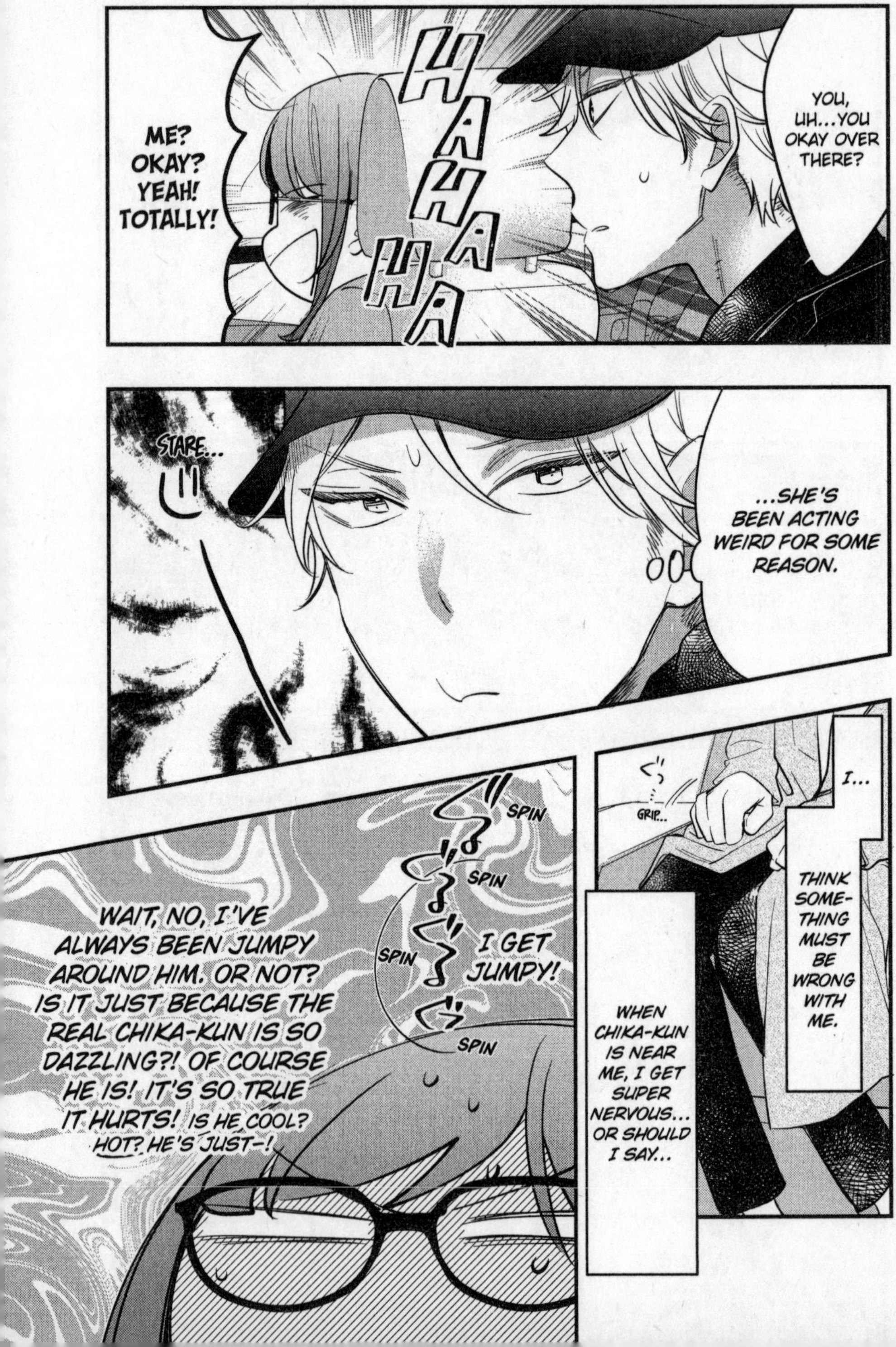
YOU, UH...YOU OKAY OVER THERE?
HAHAHAHA
ME? OKAY? YEAH! TOTALLY!
...SHE'S BEEN ACTING WEIRD FOR SOME REASON.
STARE...
I...
GRIP...
THINK SOMETHING MUST BE WRONG WITH ME.
WHEN CHIKA-KUN IS NEAR ME, I GET SUPER NERVOUS... OR SHOULD I SAY...
SPIN
SPIN
I GET JUMPY!
SPIN
SPIN
WAIT, NO, I'VE ALWAYS BEEN JUMPY AROUND HIM. OR NOT? IS IT JUST BECAUSE THE REAL CHIKA-KUN IS SO DAZZLING?! OF COURSE HE IS! IT'S SO TRUE IT HURTS! IS HE COOL? HOT? HE'S JUST-!

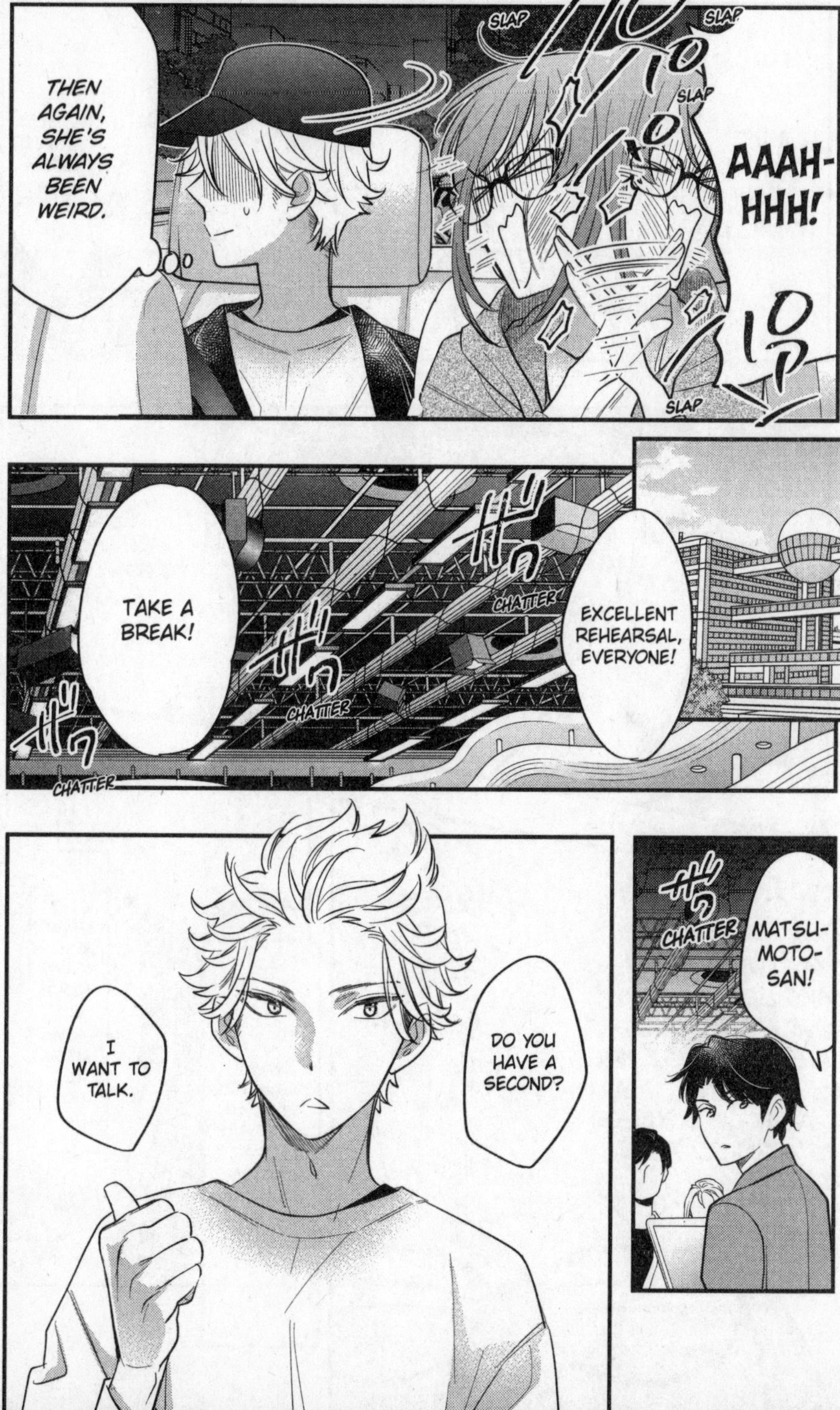
SLAP
AAAH-HHH!
SLAP
SLAP
SLAP
THEN AGAIN, SHE'S ALWAYS BEEN WEIRD.
EXCELLENT REHEARSAL, EVERYONE!
CHATTER
TAKE A BREAK!
CHATTER
CHATTER
MATSU-MOTO-SAN!
CHATTER
DO YOU HAVE A SECOND?
I WANT TO TALK.

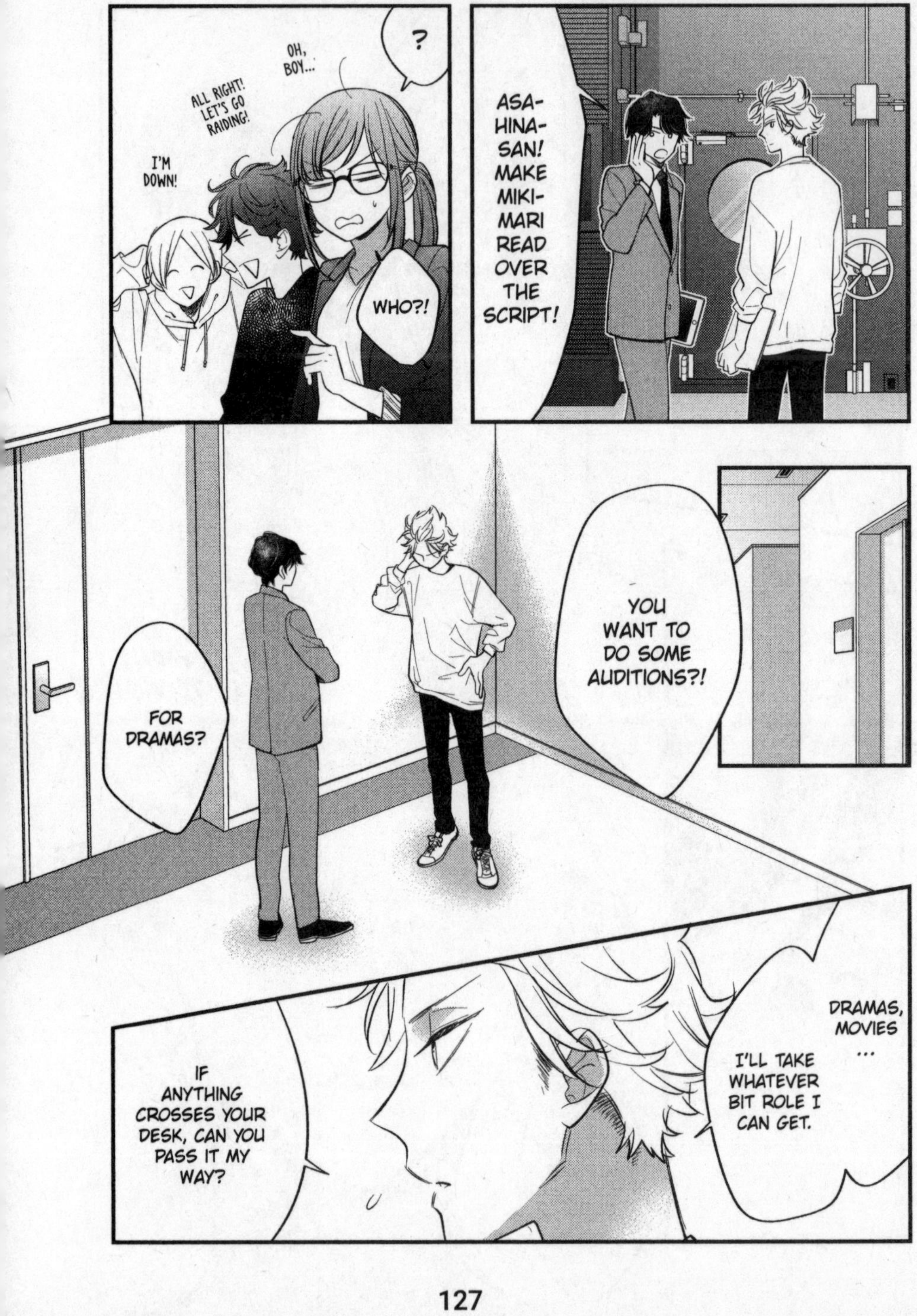
ASA-HINA-SAN! MAKE MIKI-MARI READ OVER THE SCRIPT!
?
OH, BOY...
ALL RIGHT! LET'S GO RAIDING!
I'M DOWN!
WHO?!
YOU WANT TO DO SOME AUDITIONS?!
FOR DRAMAS?
DRAMAS, MOVIES ...
I'LL TAKE WHATEVER BIT ROLE I CAN GET.
IF ANYTHING CROSSES YOUR DESK, CAN YOU PASS IT MY WAY?

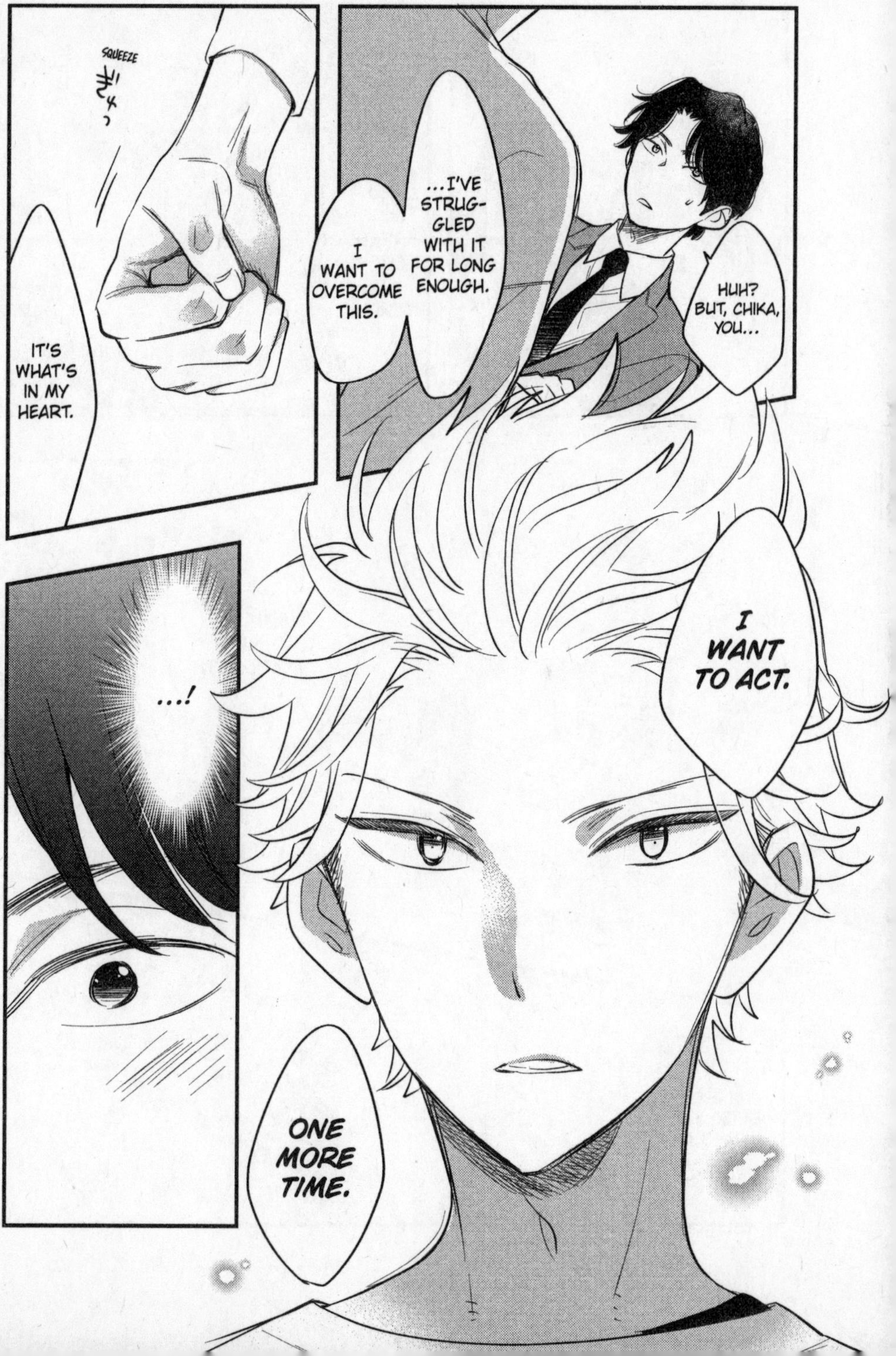
HUH? BUT, CHIKA, YOU...
...I'VE STRUGGLED WITH IT FOR LONG ENOUGH.
I WANT TO OVERCOME THIS.
SQUEEZE
IT'S WHAT'S IN MY HEART.
I WANT TO ACT.
ONE MORE TIME.
...!

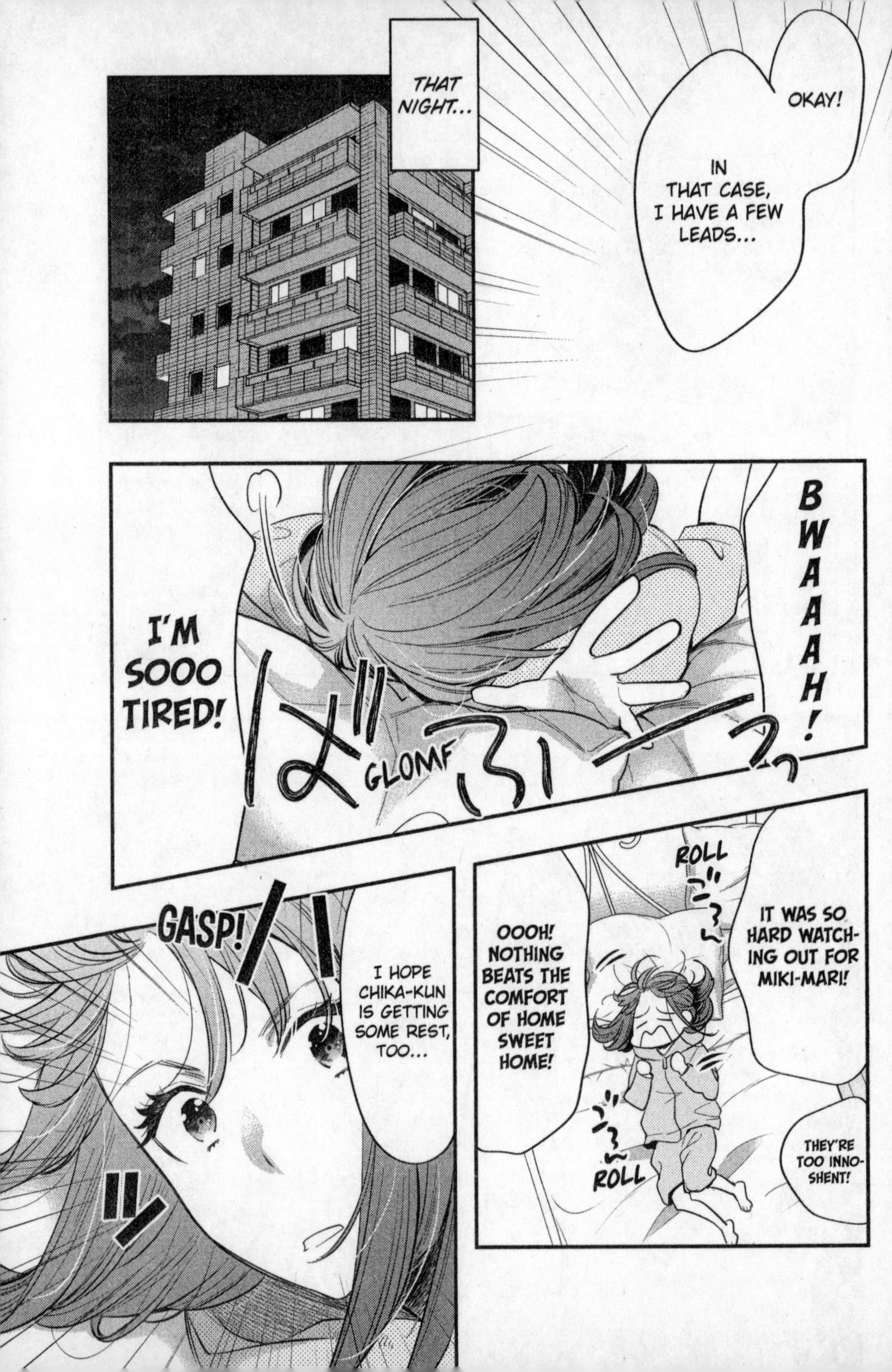
OKAY!
IN THAT CASE, I HAVE A FEW LEADS...
THAT NIGHT...
BWAAAAH!
I'M SOOO TIRED!
GLOMF
ROLL
IT WAS SO HARD WATCHING OUT FOR MIKI-MARI!
OOOH! NOTHING BEATS THE COMFORT OF HOME SWEET HOME!
ROLL
THEY'RE TOO INNO-SHENT!
GASP!
I HOPE CHIKA-KUN IS GETTING SOME REST, TOO...

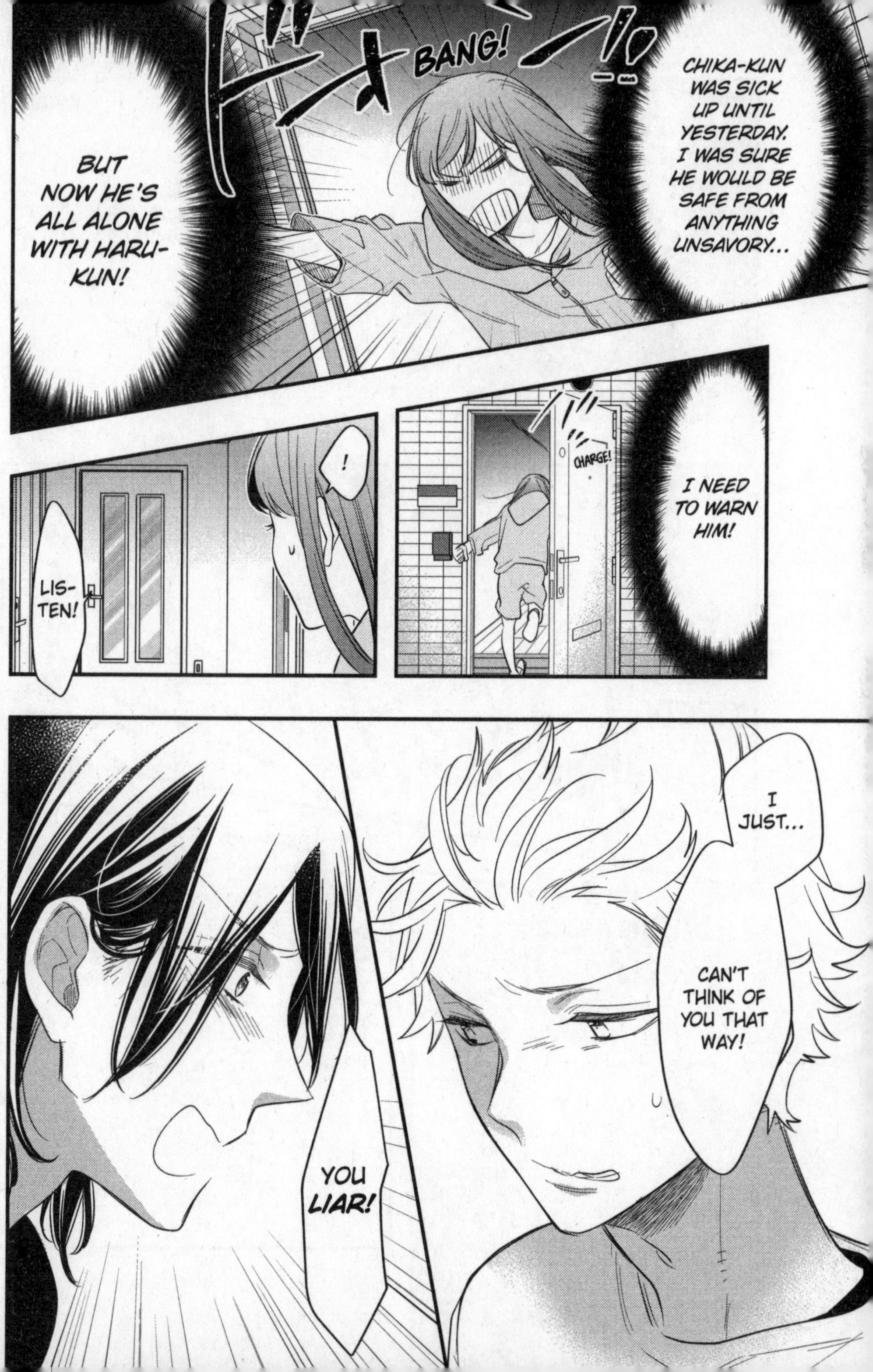
CHIKA-KUN WAS SICK UP UNTIL YESTERDAY. I WAS SURE HE WOULD BE SAFE FROM ANYTHING UNSAVORY...
BANG!
BUT NOW HE'S ALL ALONE WITH HARU-KUN!
I NEED TO WARN HIM!
CHARGE!
!
LIS-TEN!
I JUST...
CAN'T THINK OF YOU THAT WAY!
YOU LIAR!

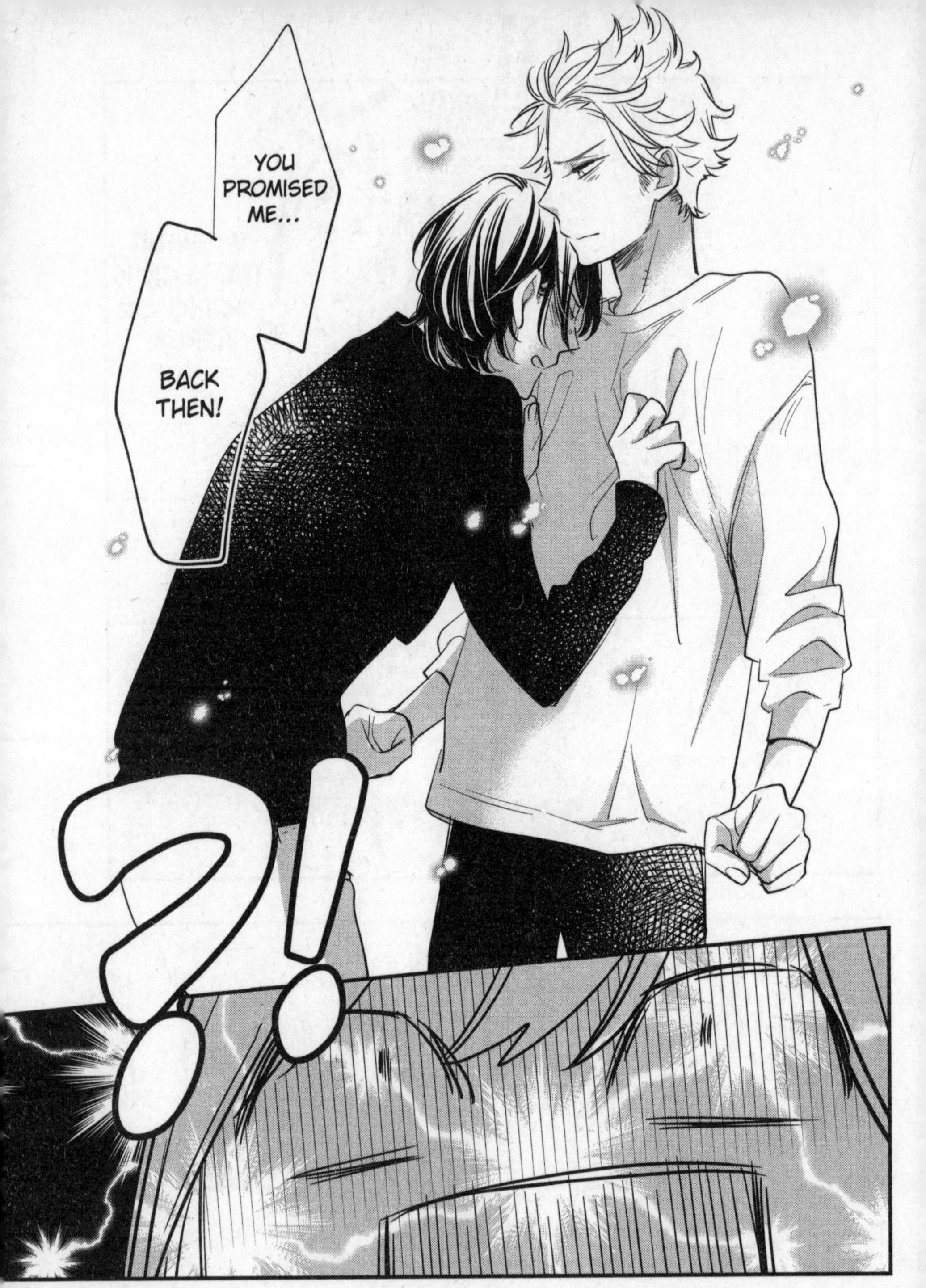
YOU PROMISED ME...
BACK THEN!
?!

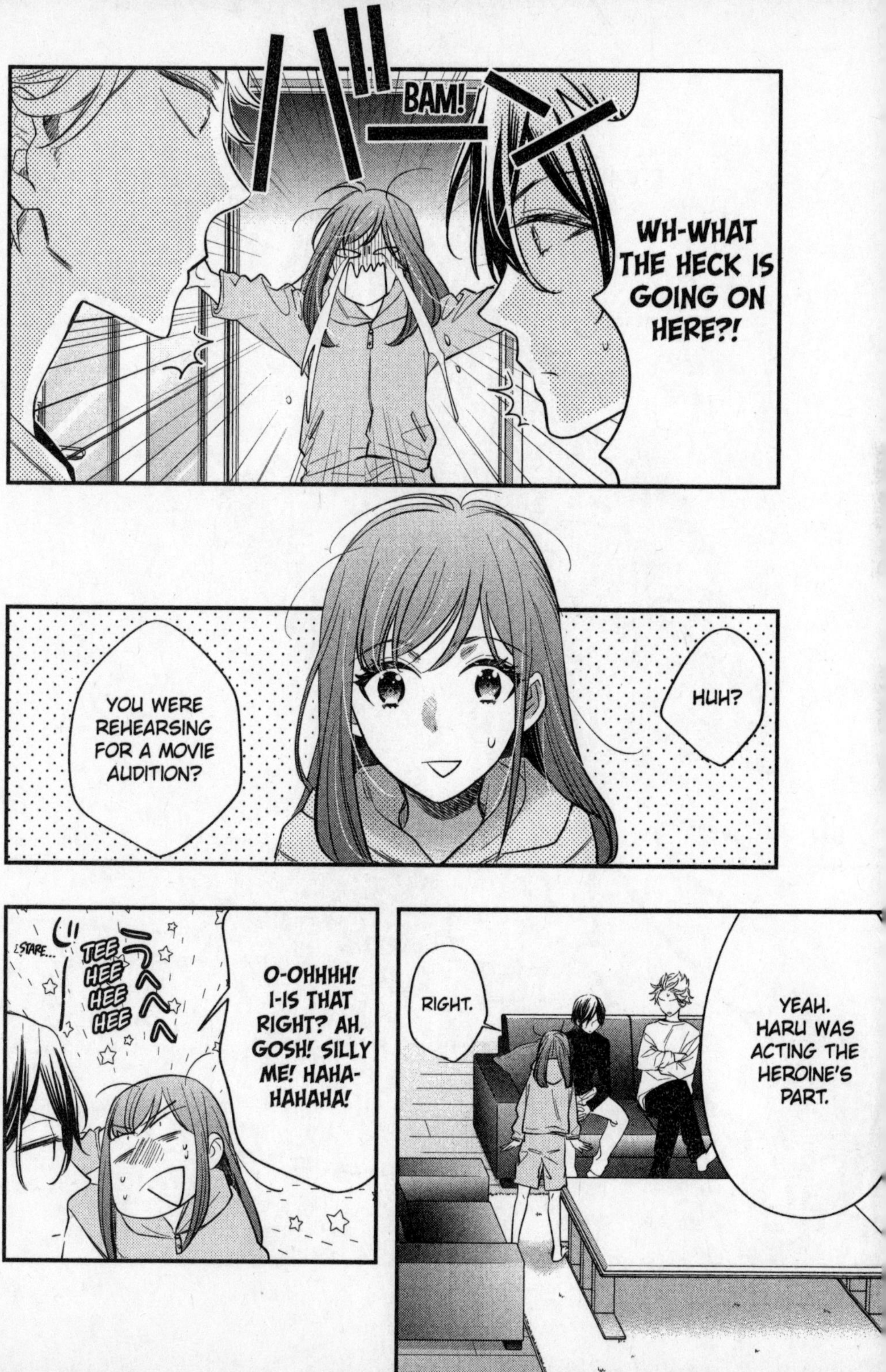
BAM!
WH-WHAT THE HECK IS GOING ON HERE?!
HUH?
YOU WERE REHEARSING FOR A MOVIE AUDITION?
YEAH. HARU WAS ACTING THE HEROINE'S PART.
RIGHT.
O-OHHHH! I-IS THAT RIGHT? AH, GOSH! SILLY ME! HAHA-HAHAHA!
TEE HEE HEE HEE
STARE...

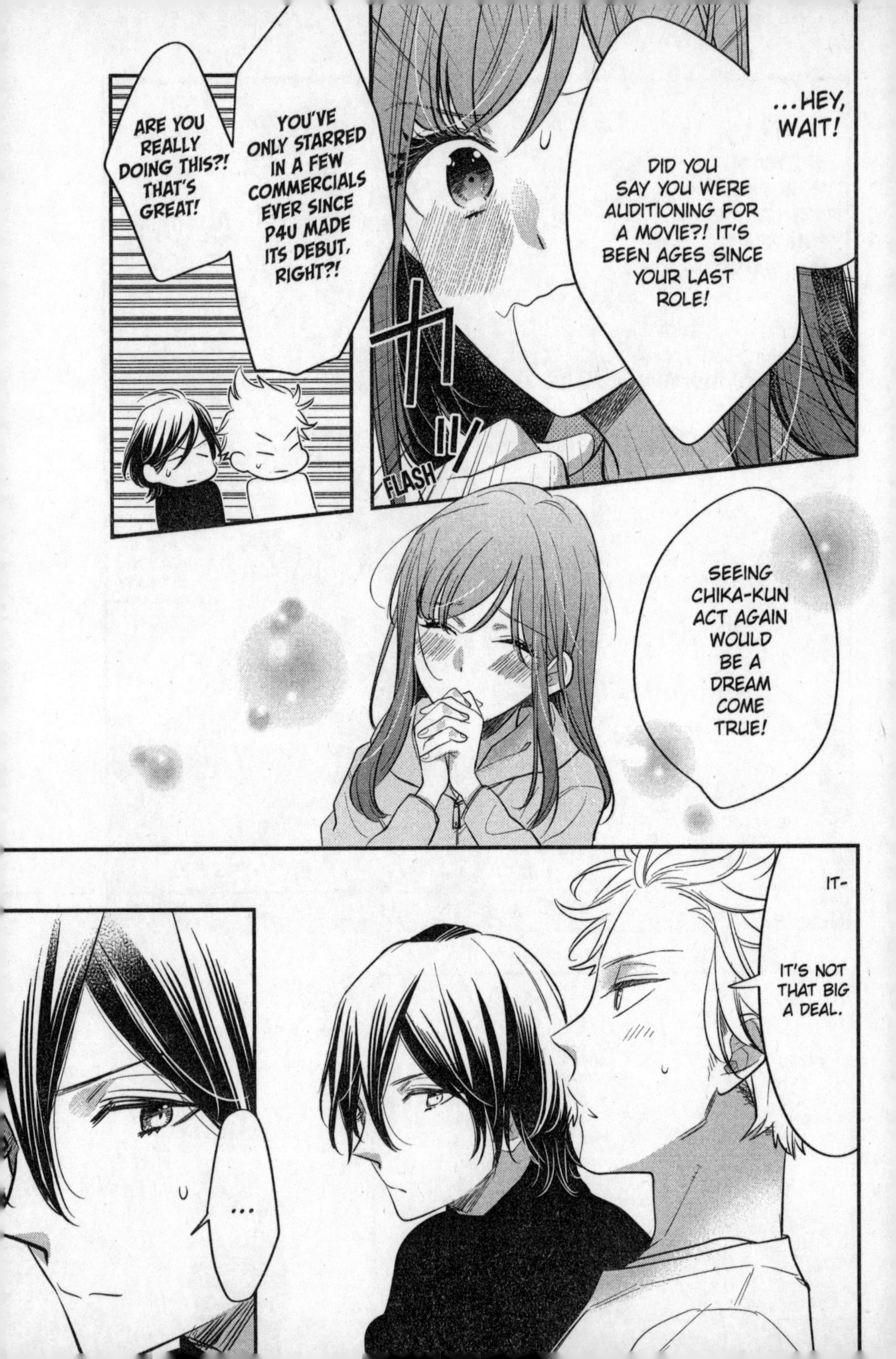
...HEY, WAIT!
DID YOU SAY YOU WERE AUDITIONING FOR A MOVIE?! IT'S BEEN AGES SINCE YOUR LAST ROLE!
FLASH
YOU'VE ONLY STARRED IN A FEW COMMERCIALS EVER SINCE P4U MADE ITS DEBUT, RIGHT?!
ARE YOU REALLY DOING THIS?! THAT'S GREAT!
SEEING CHIKA-KUN ACT AGAIN WOULD BE A DREAM COME TRUE!
IT-
IT'S NOT THAT BIG A DEAL.
...

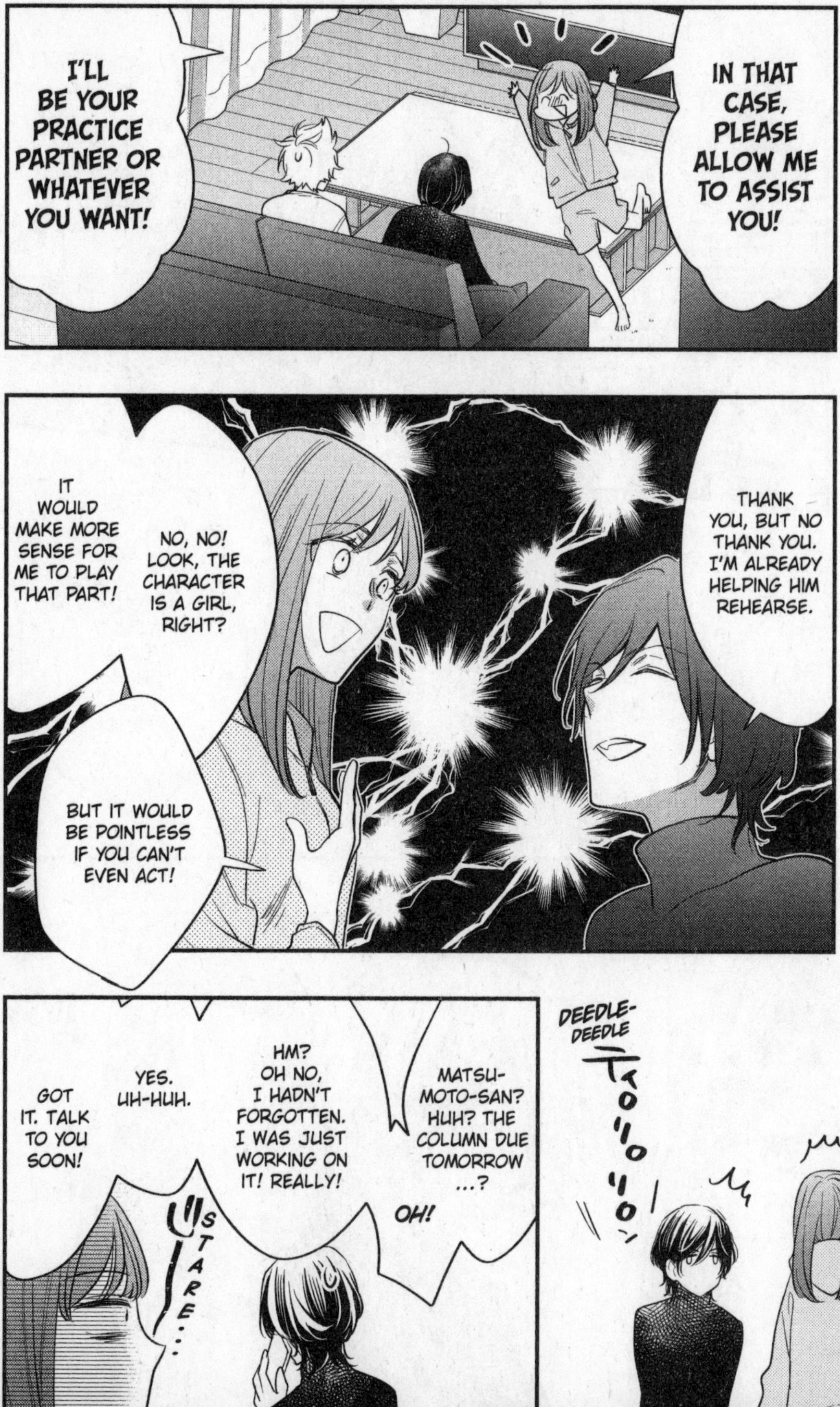
IN THAT CASE, PLEASE ALLOW ME TO ASSIST YOU!
I'LL BE YOUR PRACTICE PARTNER OR WHATEVER YOU WANT!
THANK YOU, BUT NO THANK YOU. I'M ALREADY HELPING HIM REHEARSE.
NO, NO! LOOK, THE CHARACTER IS A GIRL, RIGHT?
IT WOULD MAKE MORE SENSE FOR ME TO PLAY THAT PART!
BUT IT WOULD BE POINTLESS IF YOU CAN'T EVEN ACT!
DEEDLE-DEEDLE
MATSU-MOTO-SAN? HUH? THE COLUMN DUE TOMORROW ...?
OH!
HM? OH NO, I HADN'T FORGOTTEN. I WAS JUST WORKING ON IT! REALLY!
YES. UH-HUH.
GOT IT. TALK TO YOU SOON!
STARE...

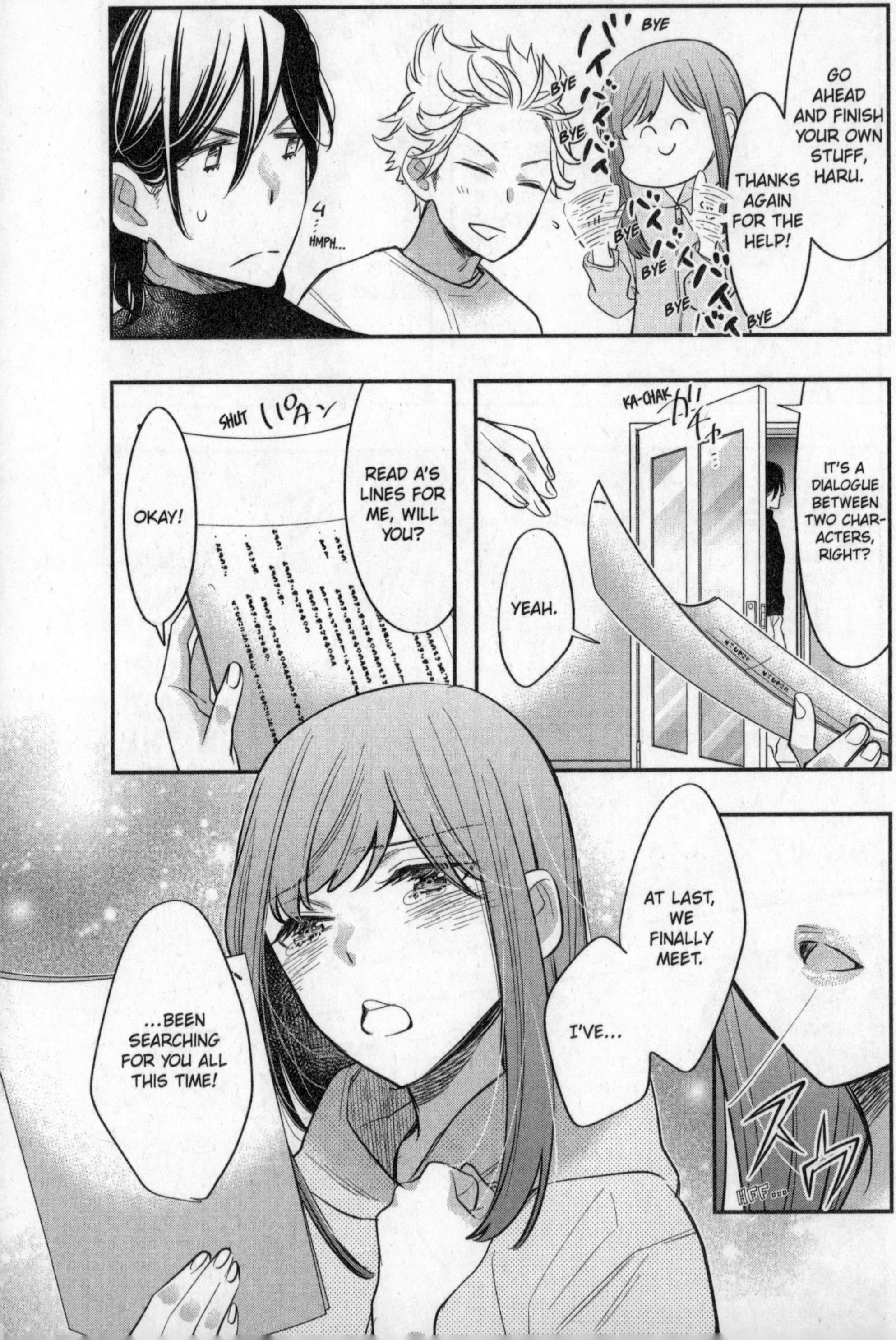
GO AHEAD AND FINISH YOUR OWN STUFF, HARU.
THANKS AGAIN FOR THE HELP!
BYE
BYE
BYE
BYE
BYE
BYE
BYE
HMPH...
IT'S A DIALOGUE BETWEEN TWO CHARACTERS, RIGHT?
KA-CHAK
YEAH.
READ A'S LINES FOR ME, WILL YOU?
SHUT
OKAY!
AT LAST, WE FINALLY MEET.
HFF...
I'VE...
...BEEN SEARCHING FOR YOU ALL THIS TIME!

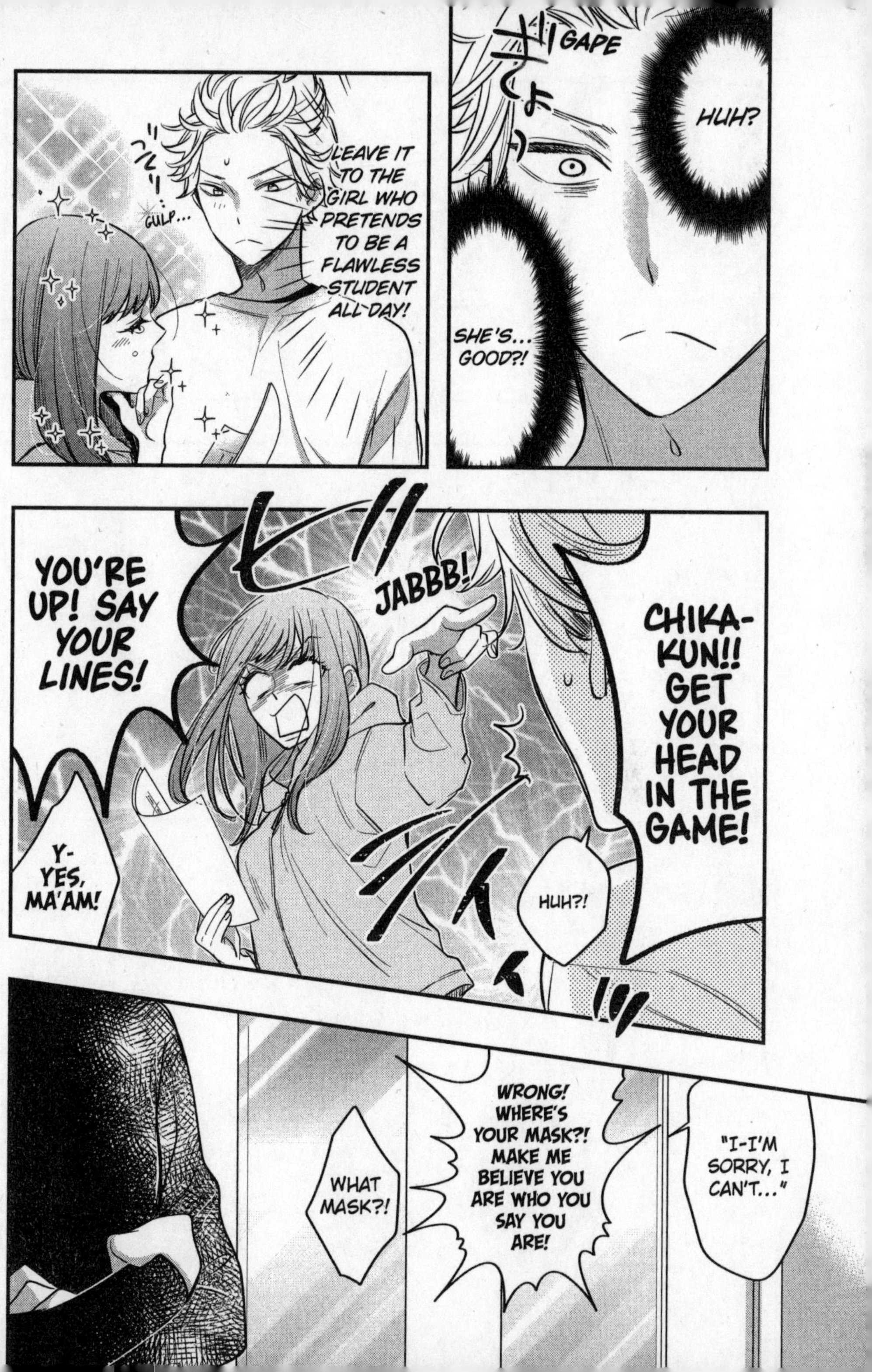
GAPE
HUH?
SHE'S... GOOD?!
GULP...
LEAVE IT TO THE GIRL WHO PRETENDS TO BE A FLAWLESS STUDENT ALL DAY!
CHIKA-KUN!! GET YOUR HEAD IN THE GAME!
JABBB!
YOU'RE UP! SAY YOUR LINES!
HUH?!
Y-YES, MA'AM!
"I-I'M SORRY, I CAN'T..."
WRONG! WHERE'S YOUR MASK?! MAKE ME BELIEVE YOU ARE WHO YOU SAY YOU ARE!
WHAT MASK?!

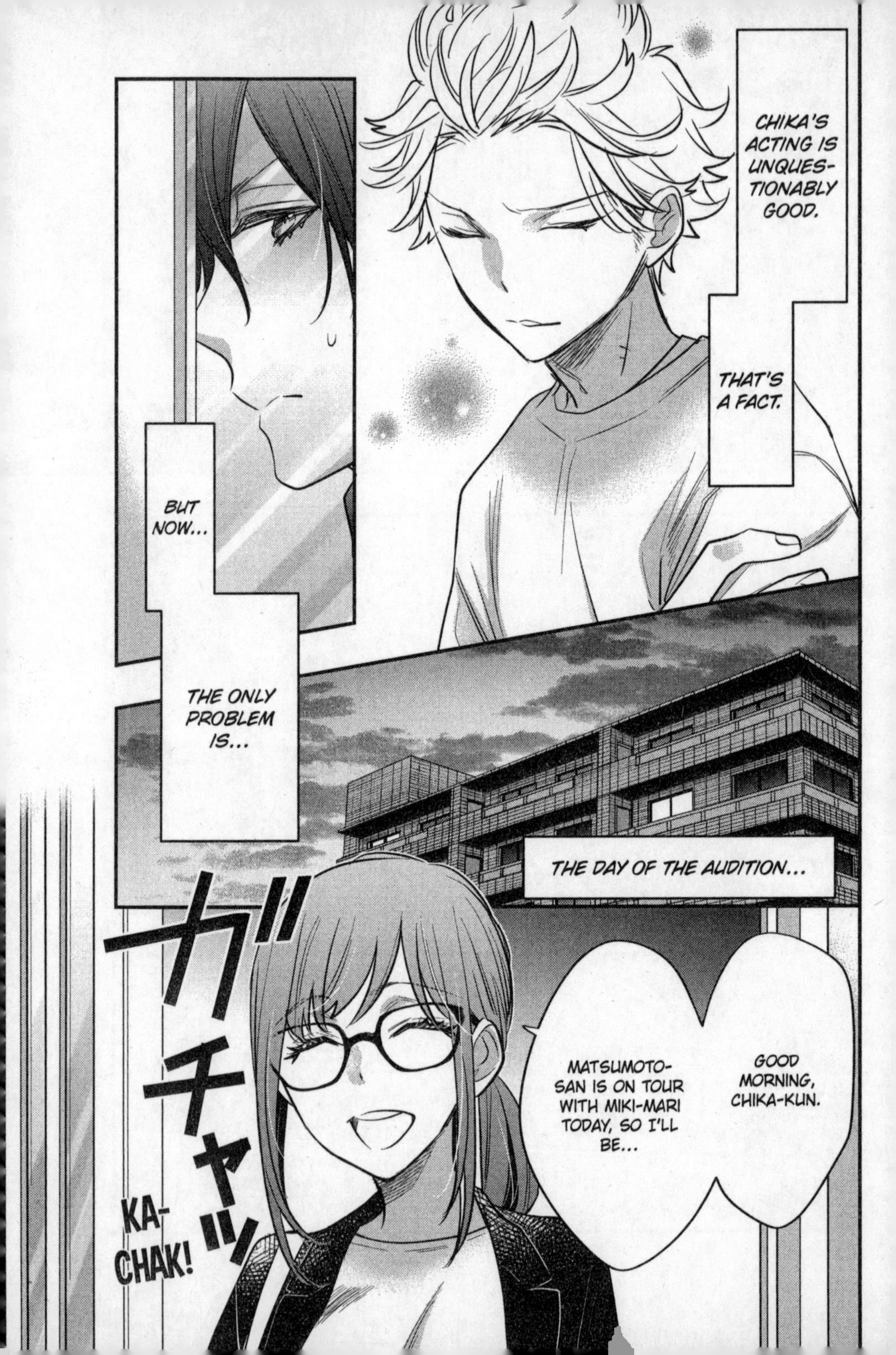
CHIKA'S ACTING IS UNQUES-TIONABLY GOOD.
THAT'S A FACT.
BUT NOW...
THE ONLY PROBLEM IS...
THE DAY OF THE AUDITION...
ガチャッ
GOOD MORNING, CHIKA-KUN.
MATSUMOTO-SAN IS ON TOUR WITH MIKI-MARI TODAY, SO I'LL BE...
KA-CHAK!

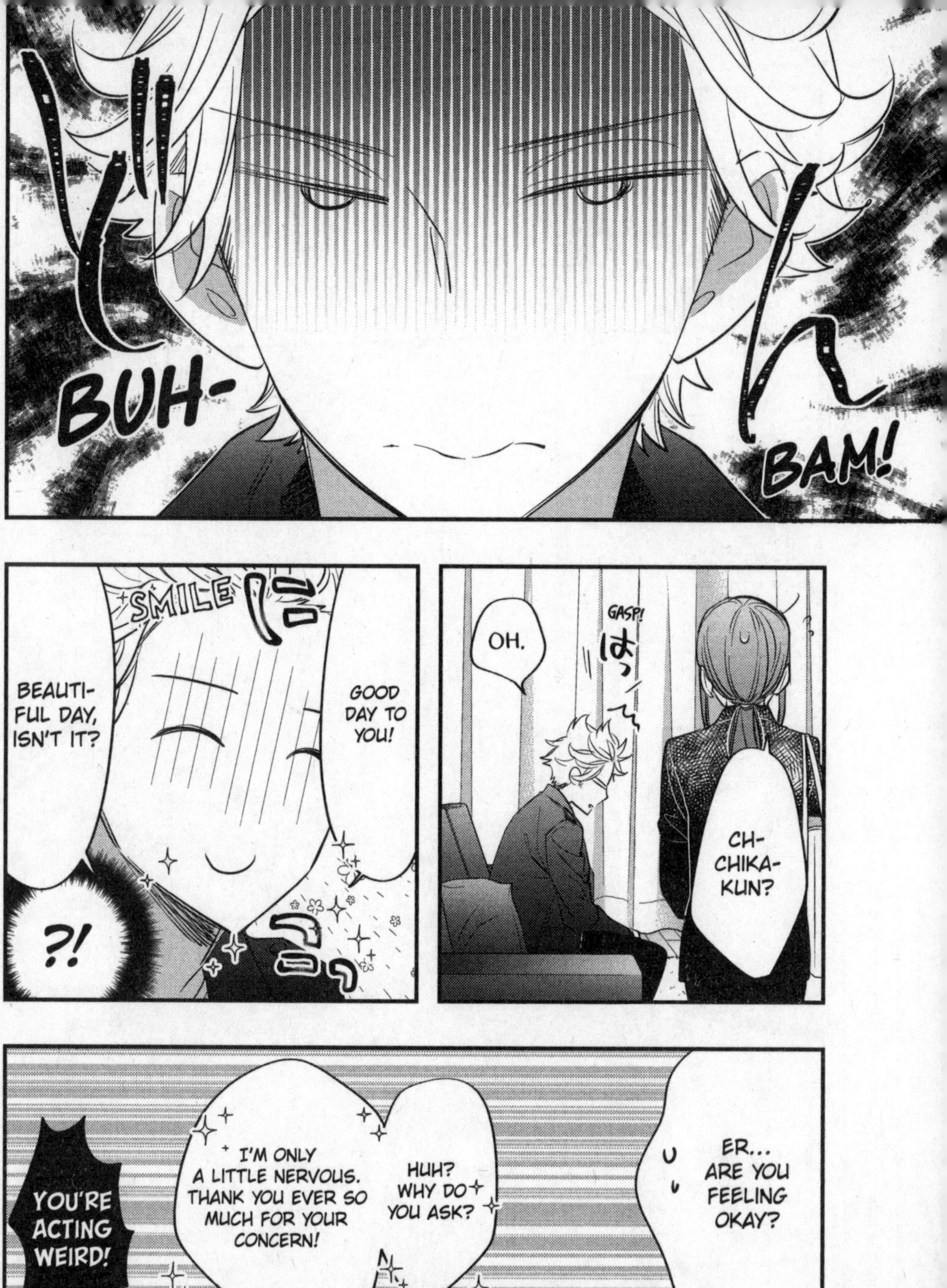
BUH-
BAM!
GASP!
CH-CHIKA-KUN?
OH.
GOOD DAY TO YOU!
BEAUTIFUL DAY, ISN'T IT?
SMILE
?!
ER... ARE YOU FEELING OKAY?
HUH? WHY DO YOU ASK?
I'M ONLY A LITTLE NERVOUS. THANK YOU EVER SO MUCH FOR YOUR CONCERN!
YOU'RE ACTING WEIRD!

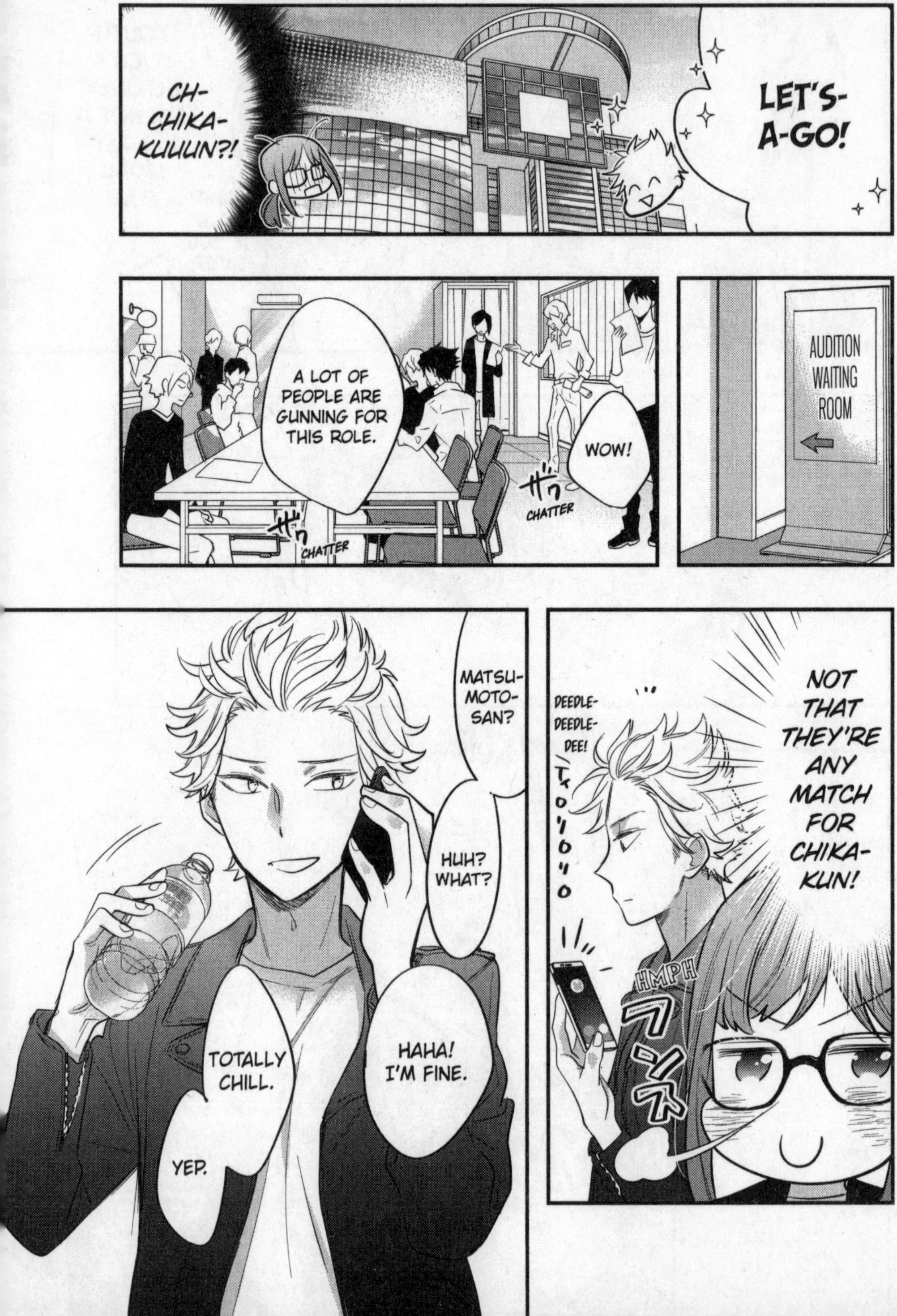
LET'S-A-GO!
CH-CHIKA-KUUUN?!
AUDITION WAITING ROOM
A LOT OF PEOPLE ARE GUNNING FOR THIS ROLE.
WOW!
CHATTER
CHATTER
NOT THAT THEY'RE ANY MATCH FOR CHIKA-KUN!
HMPH
...
DEEDLE-DEEDLE-DEE!
MATSU-MOTO-SAN?
HUH? WHAT?
HAHA! I'M FINE.
TOTALLY CHILL.
YEP.

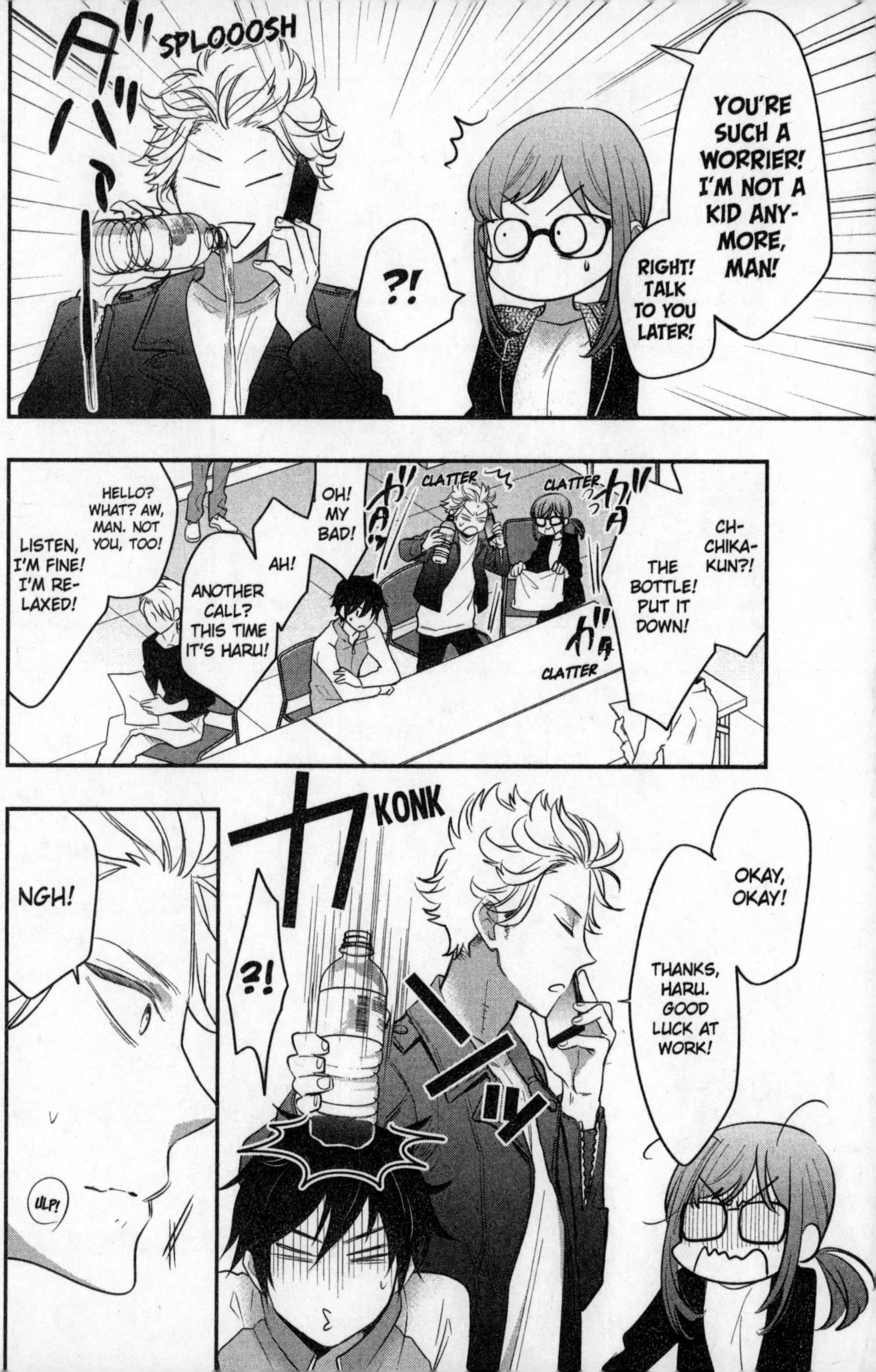
YOU'RE SUCH A WORRIER! I'M NOT A KID ANY-MORE, MAN!
RIGHT! TALK TO YOU LATER!
?!
SPLOOOSH
CH-CHIKA-KUN?!
THE BOTTLE! PUT IT DOWN!
CLATTER
CLATTER
CLATTER
OH! MY BAD!
AH!
ANOTHER CALL? THIS TIME IT'S HARU!
HELLO? WHAT? AW, MAN. NOT YOU, TOO!
LISTEN, I'M FINE! I'M RE-LAXED!
OKAY, OKAY!
THANKS, HARU. GOOD LUCK AT WORK!
KONK
?!
NGH!
ULP!

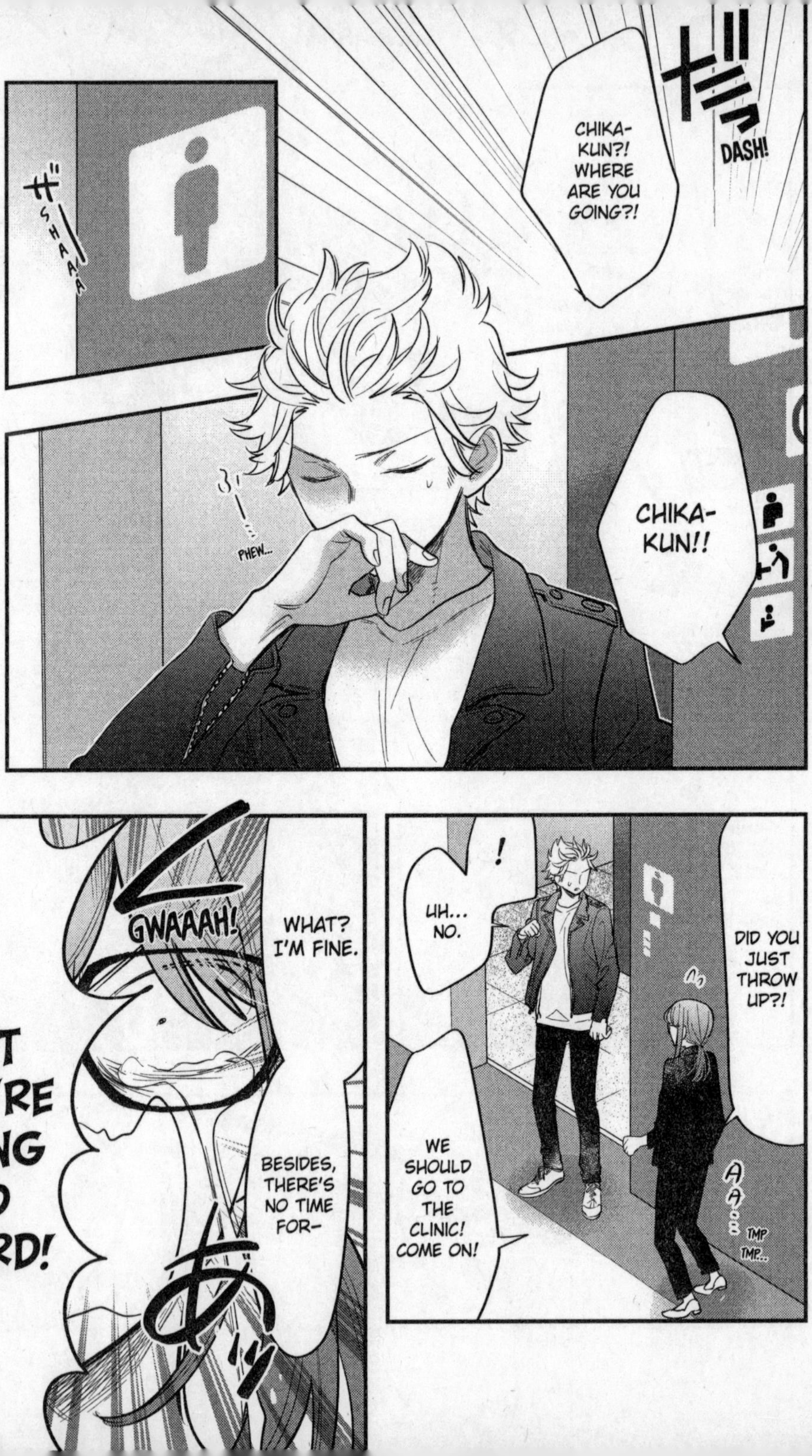

SHAAAA
CHIKA-KUN?! WHERE ARE YOU GOING?!
DASH!
CHIKA-KUN!!
PHEW...
DID YOU JUST THROW UP?!
TMP TMP...
!
UH... NO.
WE SHOULD GO TO THE CLINIC! COME ON!
WHAT? I'M FINE.
BESIDES, THERE'S NO TIME FOR-
GWAAAH!
BUT YOU'RE BEING SO WEIRD!

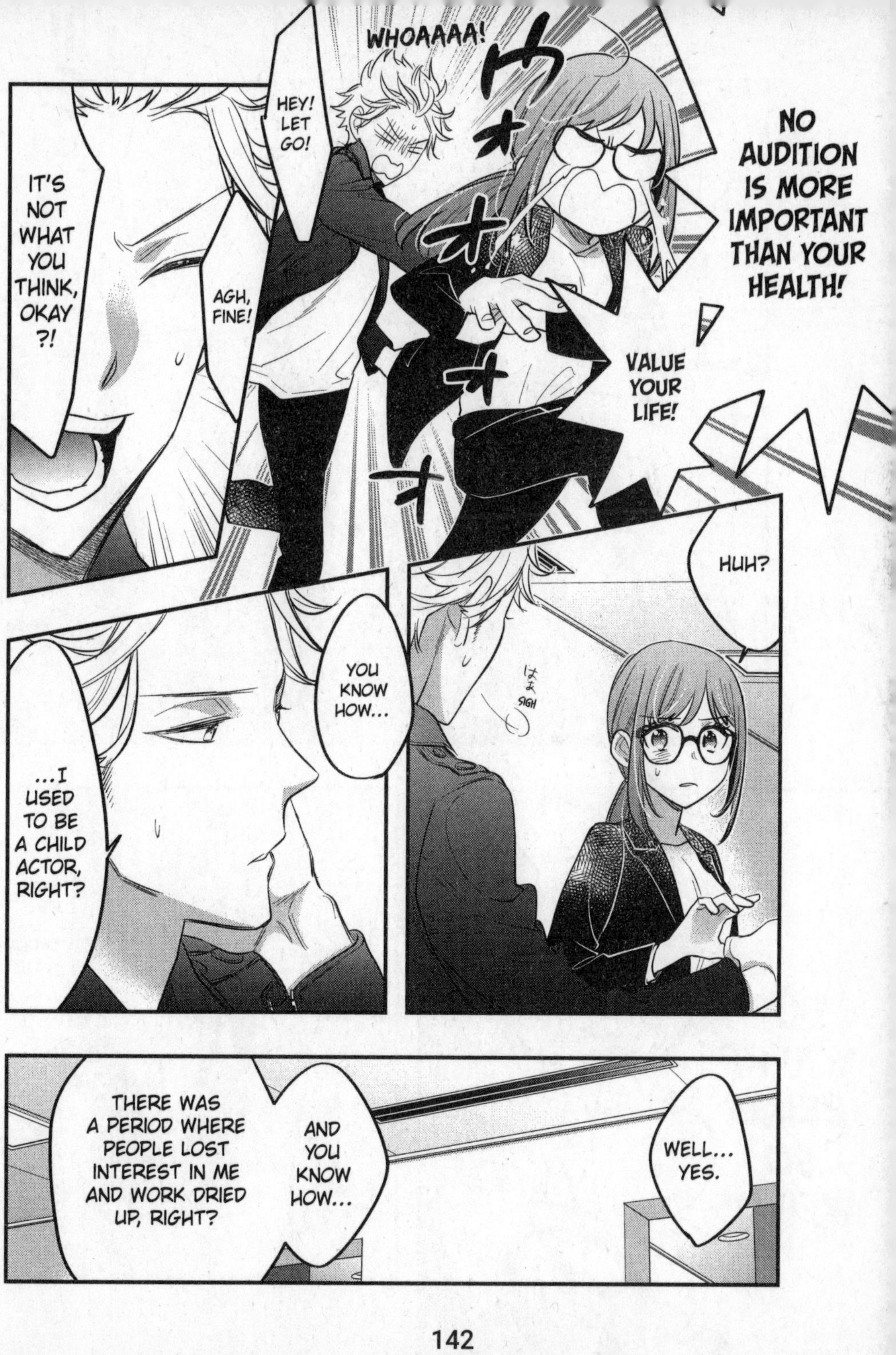
NO AUDITION IS MORE IMPORTANT THAN YOUR HEALTH!
WHOAAAA!
HEY! LET GO!
VALUE YOUR LIFE!
AGH, FINE!
IT'S NOT WHAT YOU THINK, OKAY?!
HUH?
はぁ SIGH
YOU KNOW HOW...
...I USED TO BE A CHILD ACTOR, RIGHT?
WELL... YES.
AND YOU KNOW HOW...
THERE WAS A PERIOD WHERE PEOPLE LOST INTEREST IN ME AND WORK DRIED UP, RIGHT?

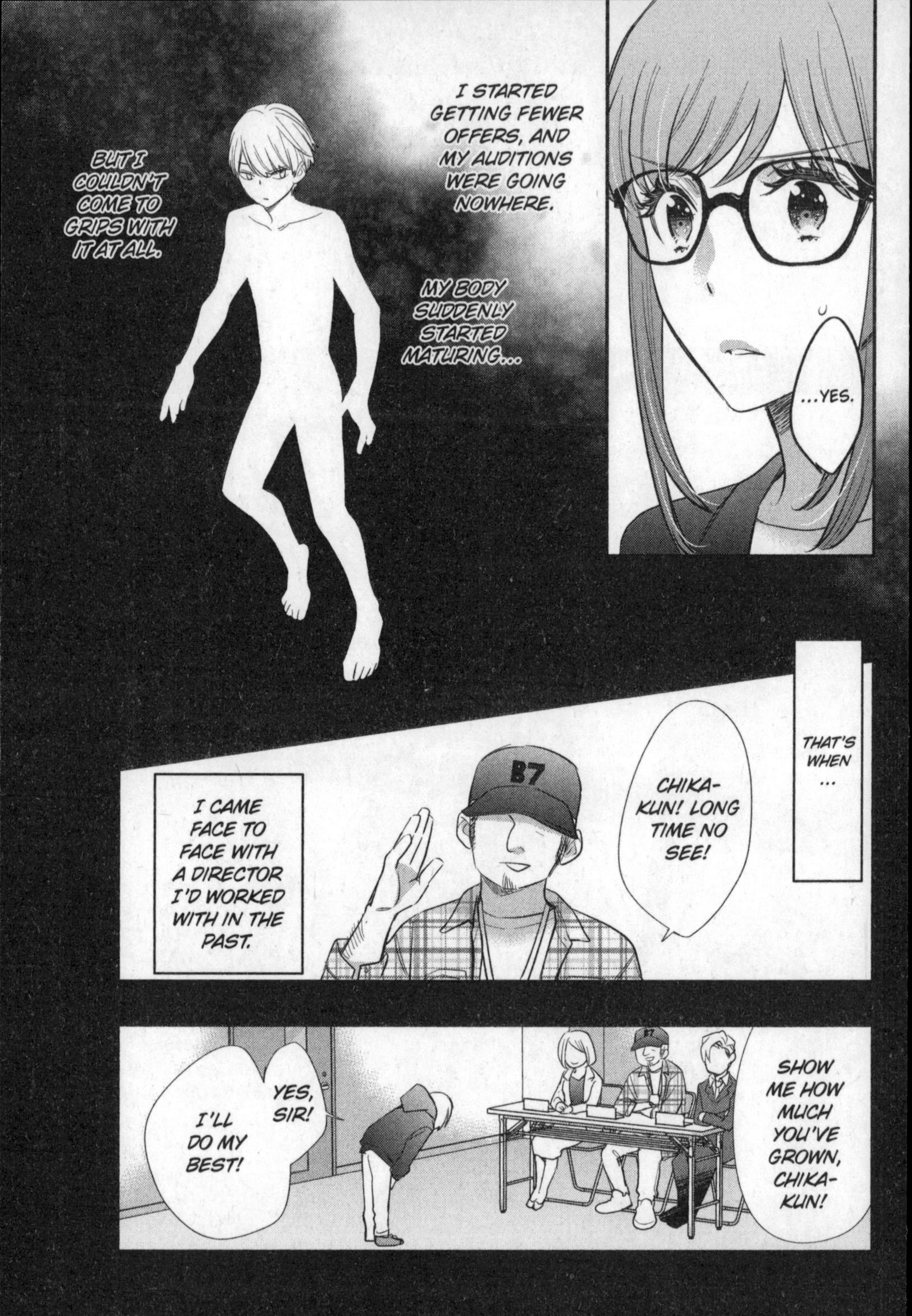
...YES.
I STARTED GETTING FEWER OFFERS, AND MY AUDITIONS WERE GOING NOWHERE.
MY BODY SUDDENLY STARTED MATURING...
BUT I COULDN'T COME TO GRIPS WITH IT AT ALL.
THAT'S WHEN ...
CHIKA-KUN! LONG TIME NO SEE!
I CAME FACE TO FACE WITH A DIRECTOR I'D WORKED WITH IN THE PAST.
SHOW ME HOW MUCH YOU'VE GROWN, CHIKA-KUN!
YES, SIR!
I'LL DO MY BEST!

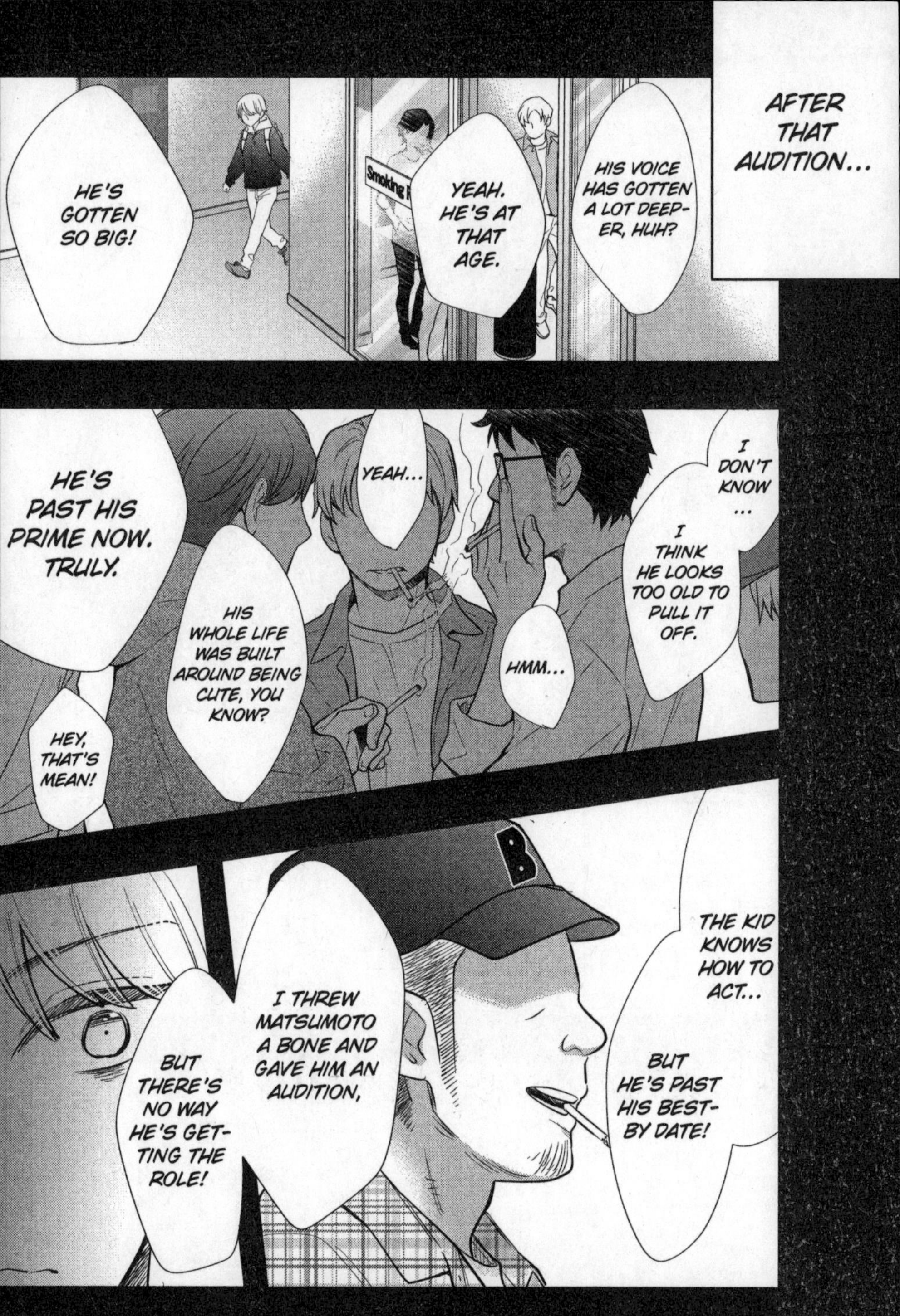
AFTER THAT AUDITION...
HIS VOICE HAS GOTTEN A LOT DEEPER, HUH?
YEAH. HE'S AT THAT AGE.
HE'S GOTTEN SO BIG!
I DON'T KNOW...
YEAH...
HE'S PAST HIS PRIME NOW. TRULY.
I THINK HE LOOKS TOO OLD TO PULL IT OFF.
HMM...
HIS WHOLE LIFE WAS BUILT AROUND BEING CUTE, YOU KNOW?
HEY, THAT'S MEAN!
THE KID KNOWS HOW TO ACT...
BUT HE'S PAST HIS BEST-BY DATE!
I THREW MATSUMOTO A BONE AND GAVE HIM AN AUDITION,
BUT THERE'S NO WAY HE'S GETTING THE ROLE!

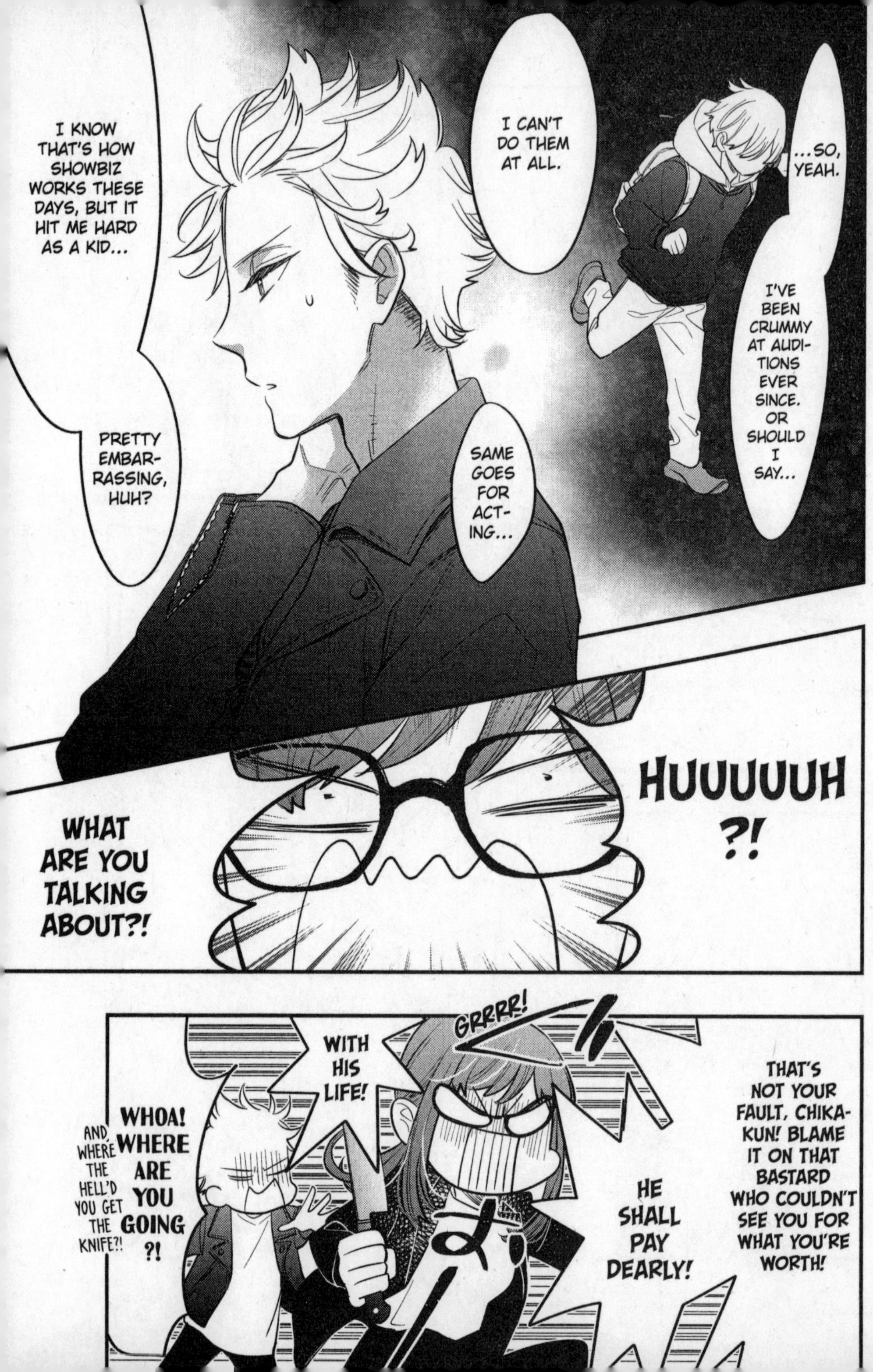
...SO, YEAH.
I'VE BEEN CRUMMY AT AUDITIONS EVER SINCE. OR SHOULD I SAY...
I CAN'T DO THEM AT ALL.
SAME GOES FOR ACTING...
I KNOW THAT'S HOW SHOWBIZ WORKS THESE DAYS, BUT IT HIT ME HARD AS A KID...
PRETTY EMBARRASSING, HUH?
HUUUUUH ?!
WHAT ARE YOU TALKING ABOUT?!
THAT'S NOT YOUR FAULT, CHIKA-KUN! BLAME IT ON THAT BASTARD WHO COULDN'T SEE YOU FOR WHAT YOU'RE WORTH!
HE SHALL PAY DEARLY!
GRRRR!
WITH HIS LIFE!
WHOA! WHERE ARE YOU GOING ?!
AND WHERE THE HELL'D YOU GET THE KNIFE?!

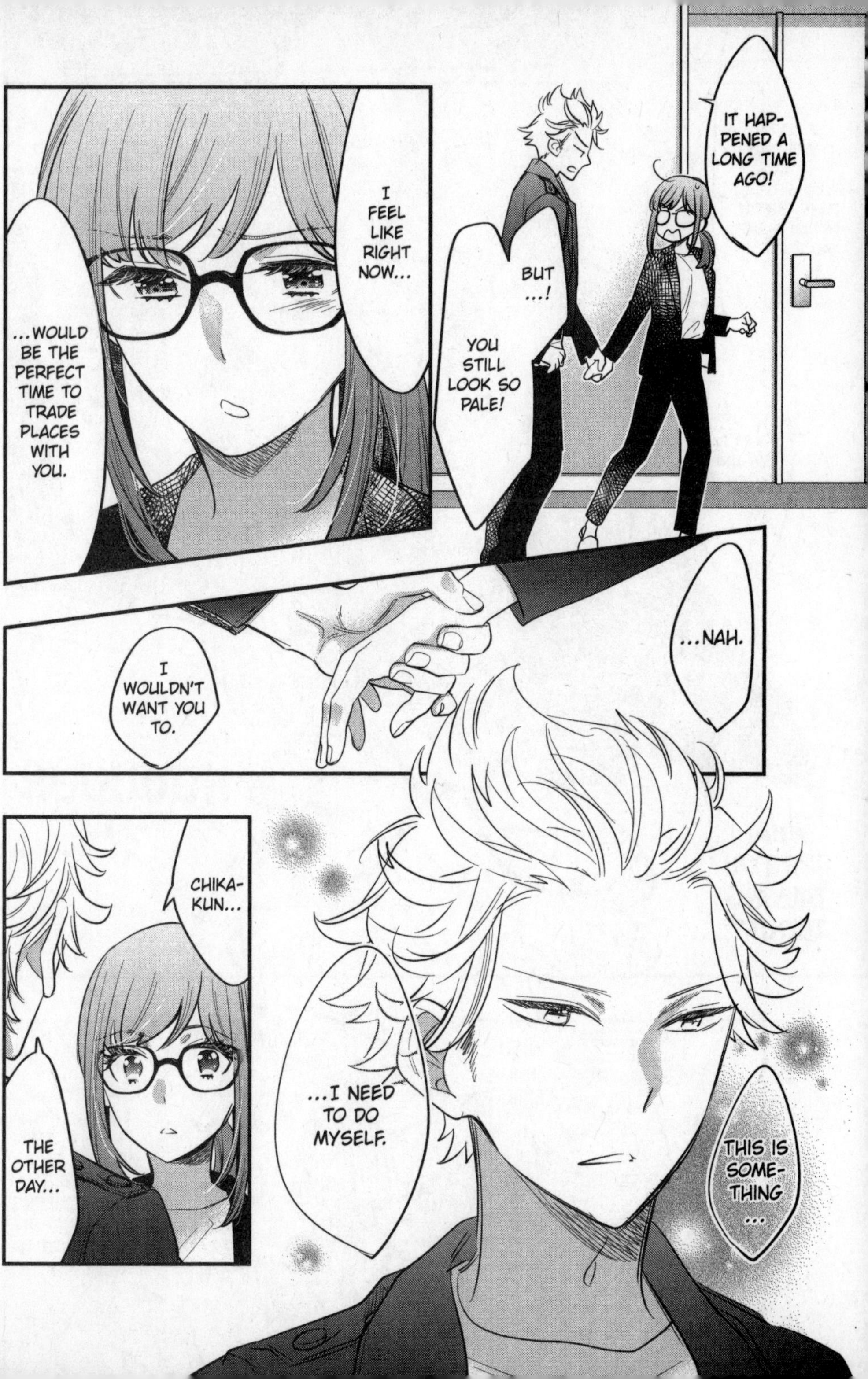
IT HAPPENED A LONG TIME AGO!
BUT ...!
YOU STILL LOOK SO PALE!
I FEEL LIKE RIGHT NOW...
...WOULD BE THE PERFECT TIME TO TRADE PLACES WITH YOU.
...NAH.
I WOULDN'T WANT YOU TO.
THIS IS SOMETHING ...
...I NEED TO DO MYSELF.
CHIKA-KUN...
THE OTHER DAY...

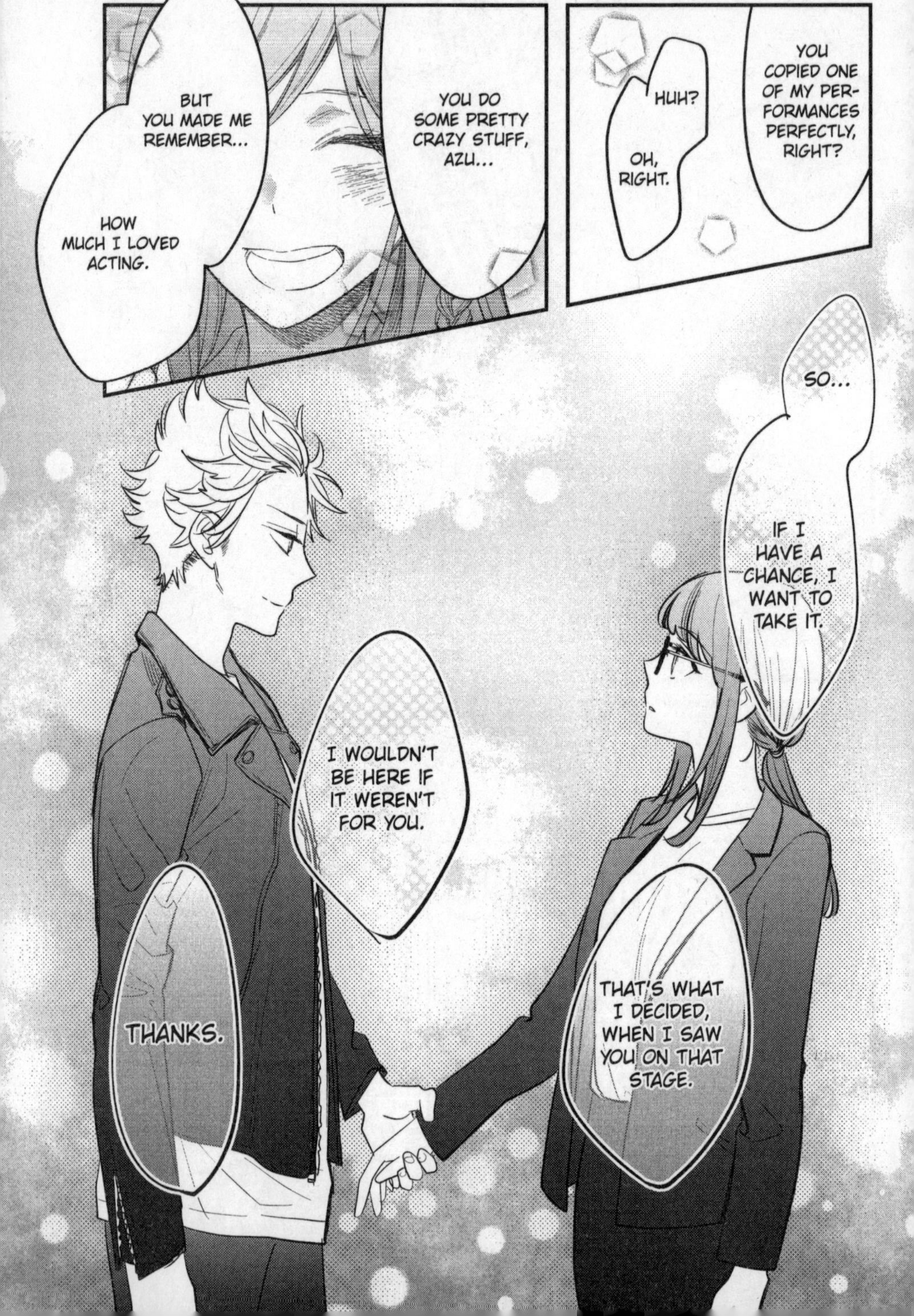
YOU COPIED ONE OF MY PERFORMANCES PERFECTLY, RIGHT?
HUH?
OH, RIGHT.
YOU DO SOME PRETTY CRAZY STUFF, AZU...
BUT YOU MADE ME REMEMBER...
HOW MUCH I LOVED ACTING.
SO...
IF I HAVE A CHANCE, I WANT TO TAKE IT.
THAT'S WHAT I DECIDED, WHEN I SAW YOU ON THAT STAGE.
I WOULDN'T BE HERE IF IT WEREN'T FOR YOU.
THANKS.

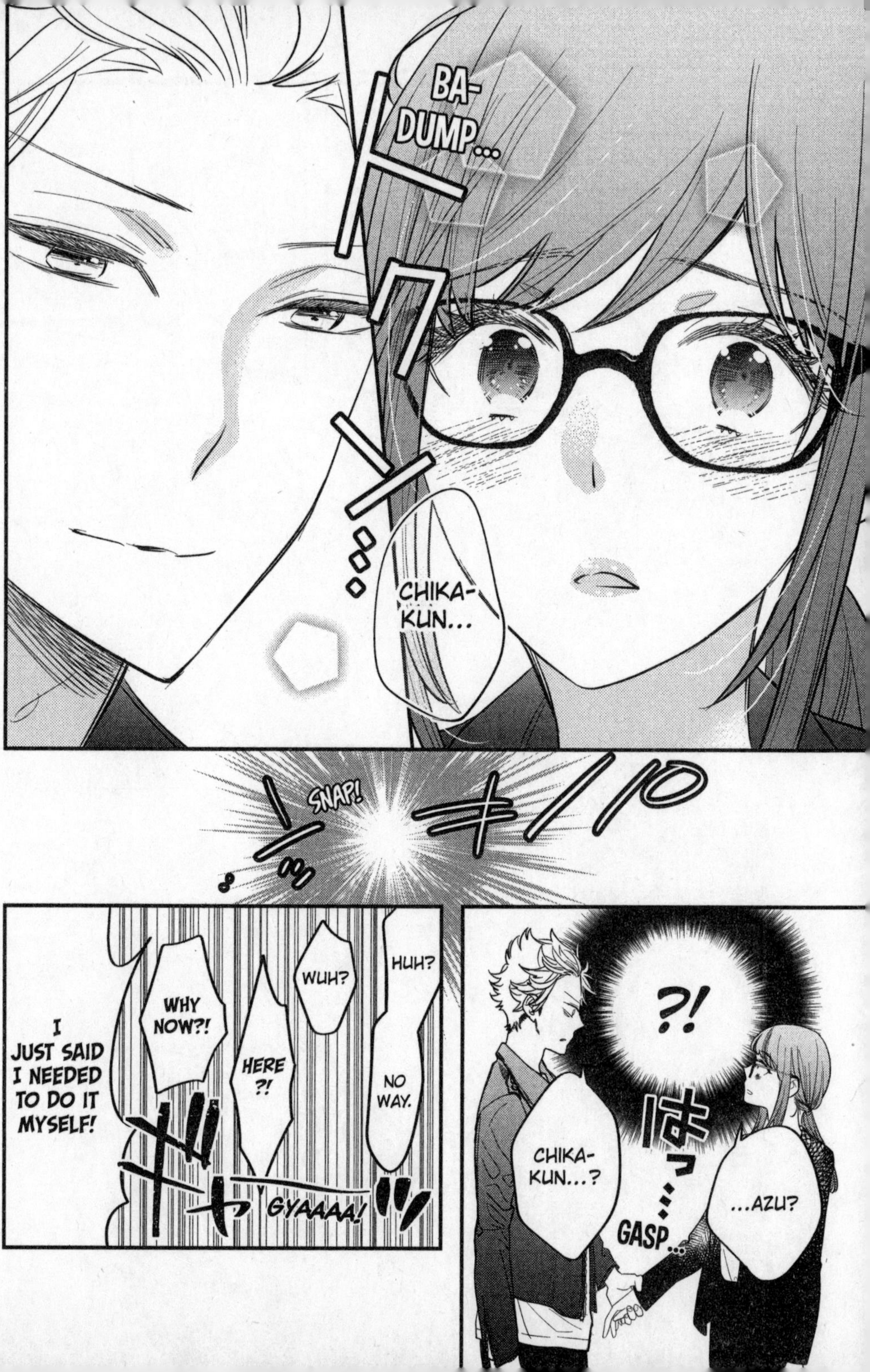
BA-DUMP...
CHIKA-KUN...
SNAP!
?!
...AZU?
CHIKA-KUN...?
GASP...
HUH?
NO WAY.
WUH?
HERE?!
WHY NOW?!
I JUST SAID I NEEDED TO DO IT MYSELF!
GYAAAA!

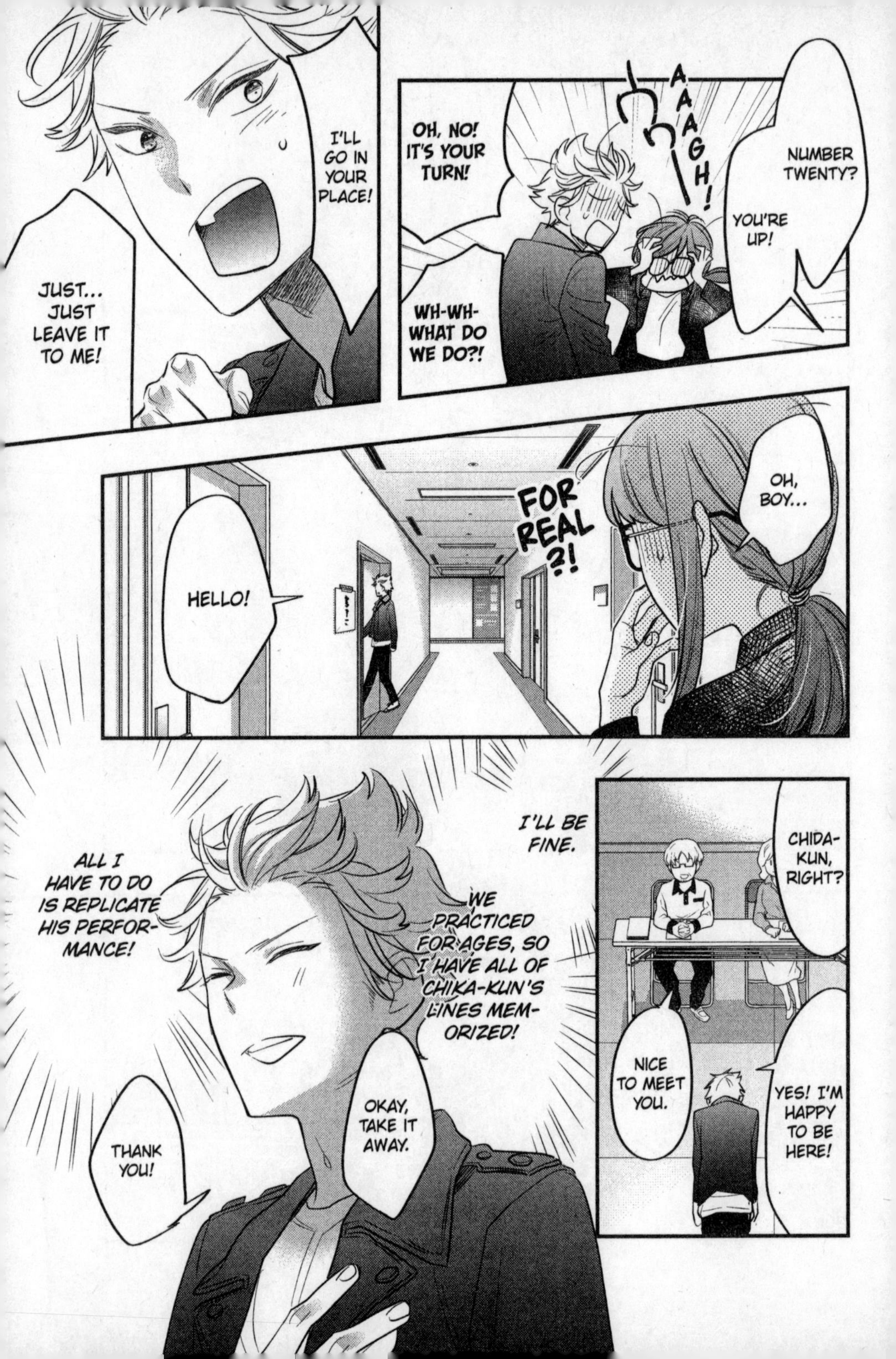
NUMBER TWENTY?
YOU'RE UP!
AAAGH!
OH, NO! IT'S YOUR TURN!
WH-WH-WHAT DO WE DO?!
I'LL GO IN YOUR PLACE!
JUST... JUST LEAVE IT TO ME!
OH, BOY...
FOR REAL?!
HELLO!
CHIDA-KUN, RIGHT?
YES! I'M HAPPY TO BE HERE!
NICE TO MEET YOU.
I'LL BE FINE.
WE PRACTICED FOR AGES, SO I HAVE ALL OF CHIKA-KUN'S LINES MEMORIZED!
ALL I HAVE TO DO IS REPLICATE HIS PERFORMANCE!
OKAY, TAKE IT AWAY.
THANK YOU!

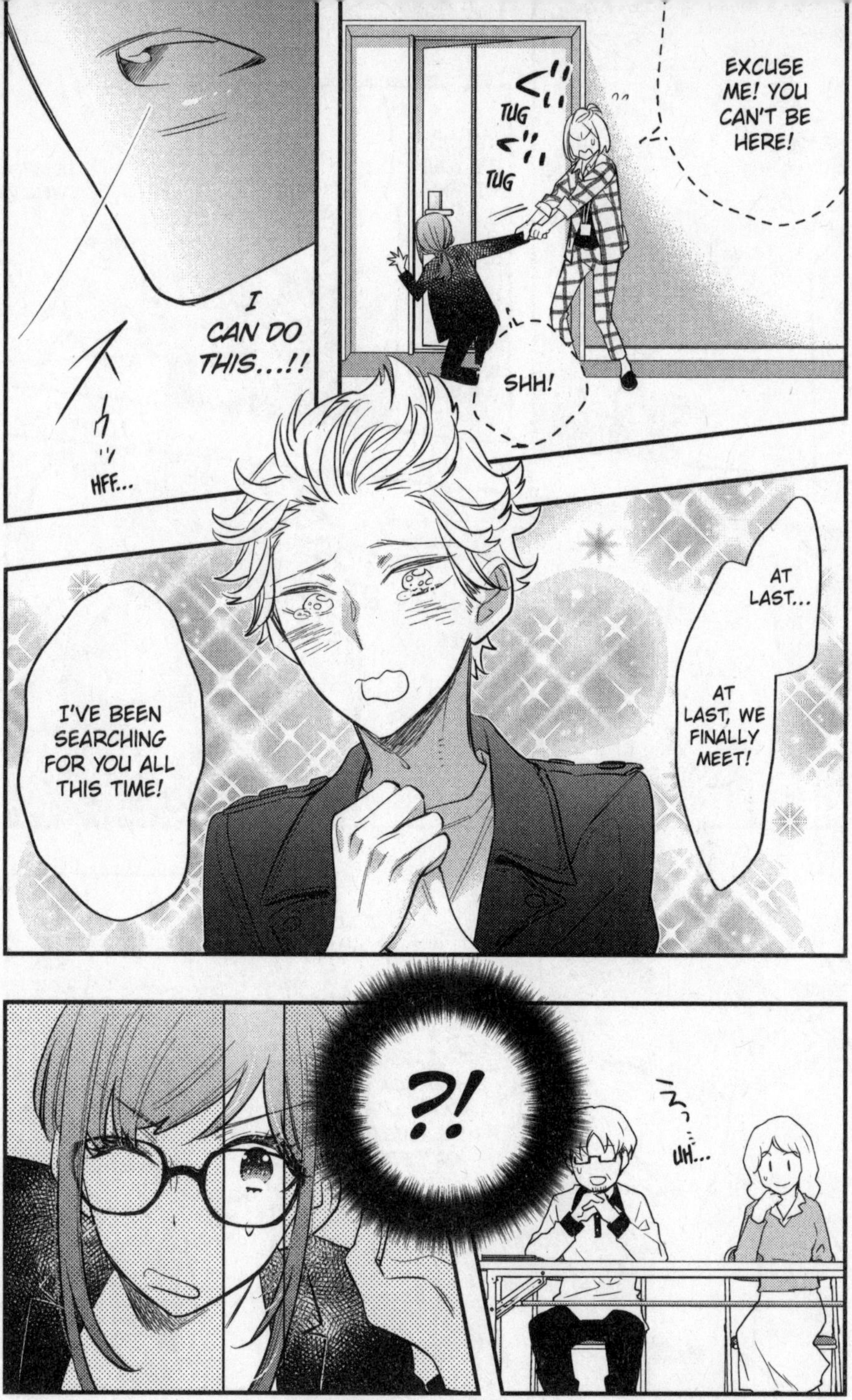
EXCUSE ME! YOU CAN'T BE HERE!
TUG
TUG
SHH!
I CAN DO THIS...!!
HFF...
AT LAST...
AT LAST, WE FINALLY MEET!
I'VE BEEN SEARCHING FOR YOU ALL THIS TIME!
UH...
?!

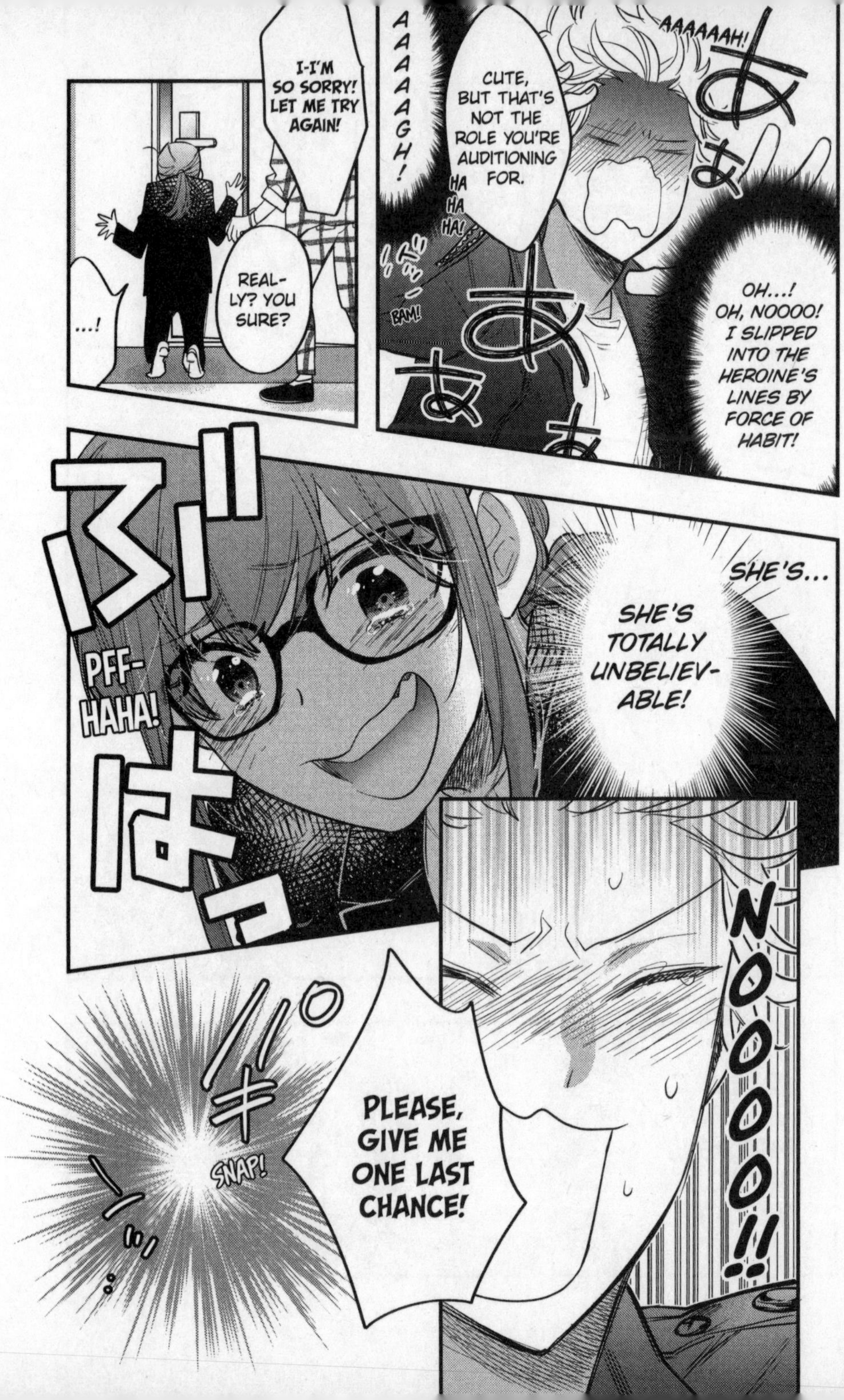
AAAAAAH!
OH...! OH, NOOOO! I SLIPPED INTO THE HEROINE'S LINES BY FORCE OF HABIT!
CUTE, BUT THAT'S NOT THE ROLE YOU'RE AUDITIONING FOR.
HA HA HA!
AAAAAAGH!
BAM!
I-I'M SO SORRY! LET ME TRY AGAIN!
REAL-LY? YOU SURE?
...!
SHE'S...
SHE'S TOTALLY UNBELIEV-ABLE!
PFF-HAHA!
NOOOOO!!
PLEASE, GIVE ME ONE LAST CHANCE!
SNAP!

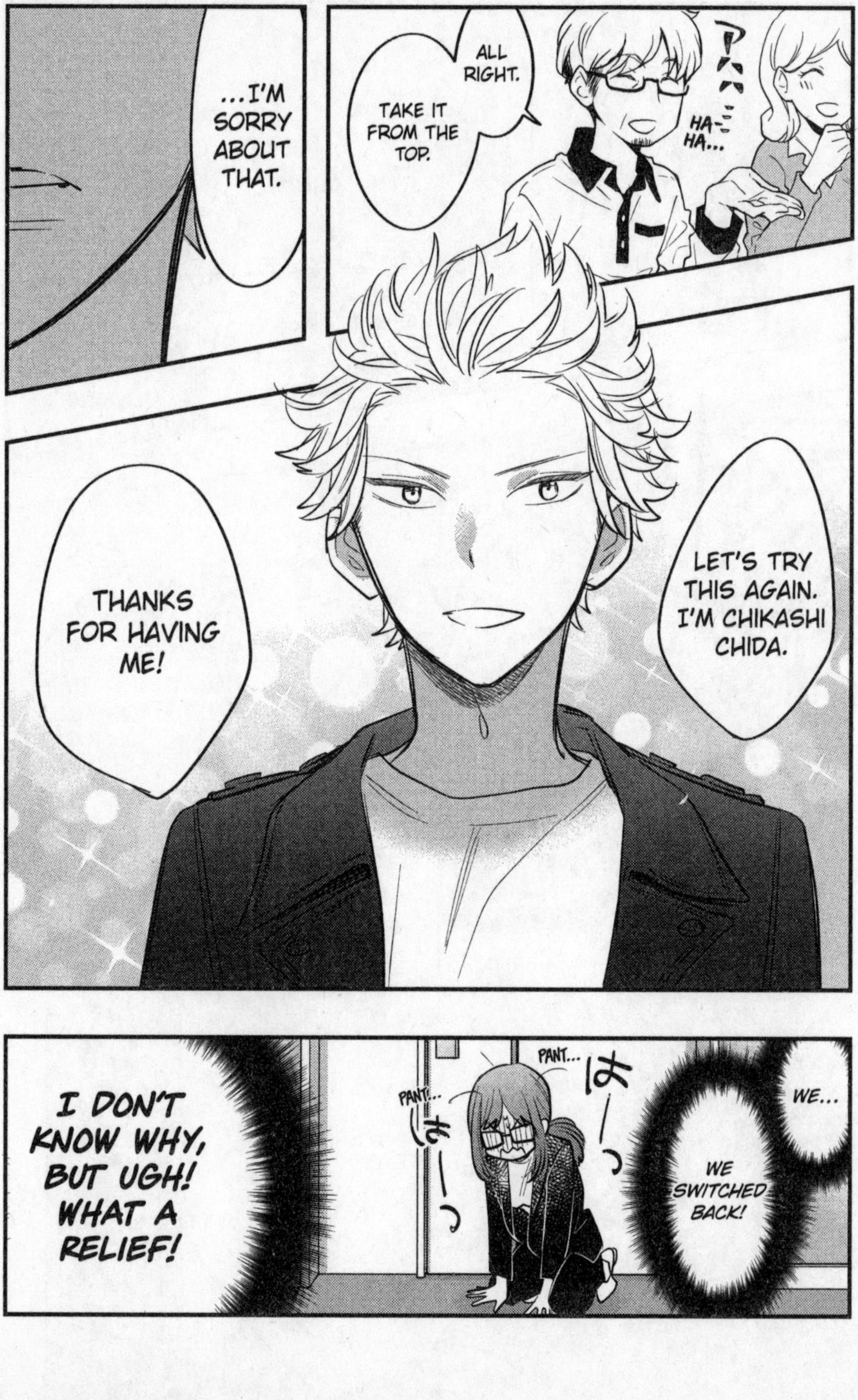
ALL RIGHT.
TAKE IT FROM THE TOP.
アハハ…
HA HA HA...
...I'M SORRY ABOUT THAT.
LET'S TRY THIS AGAIN. I'M CHIKASHI CHIDA.
THANKS FOR HAVING ME!
WE...
WE SWITCHED BACK!
PANT...
はーっ
PANT...
はーっ
I DON'T KNOW WHY, BUT UGH! WHAT A RELIEF!

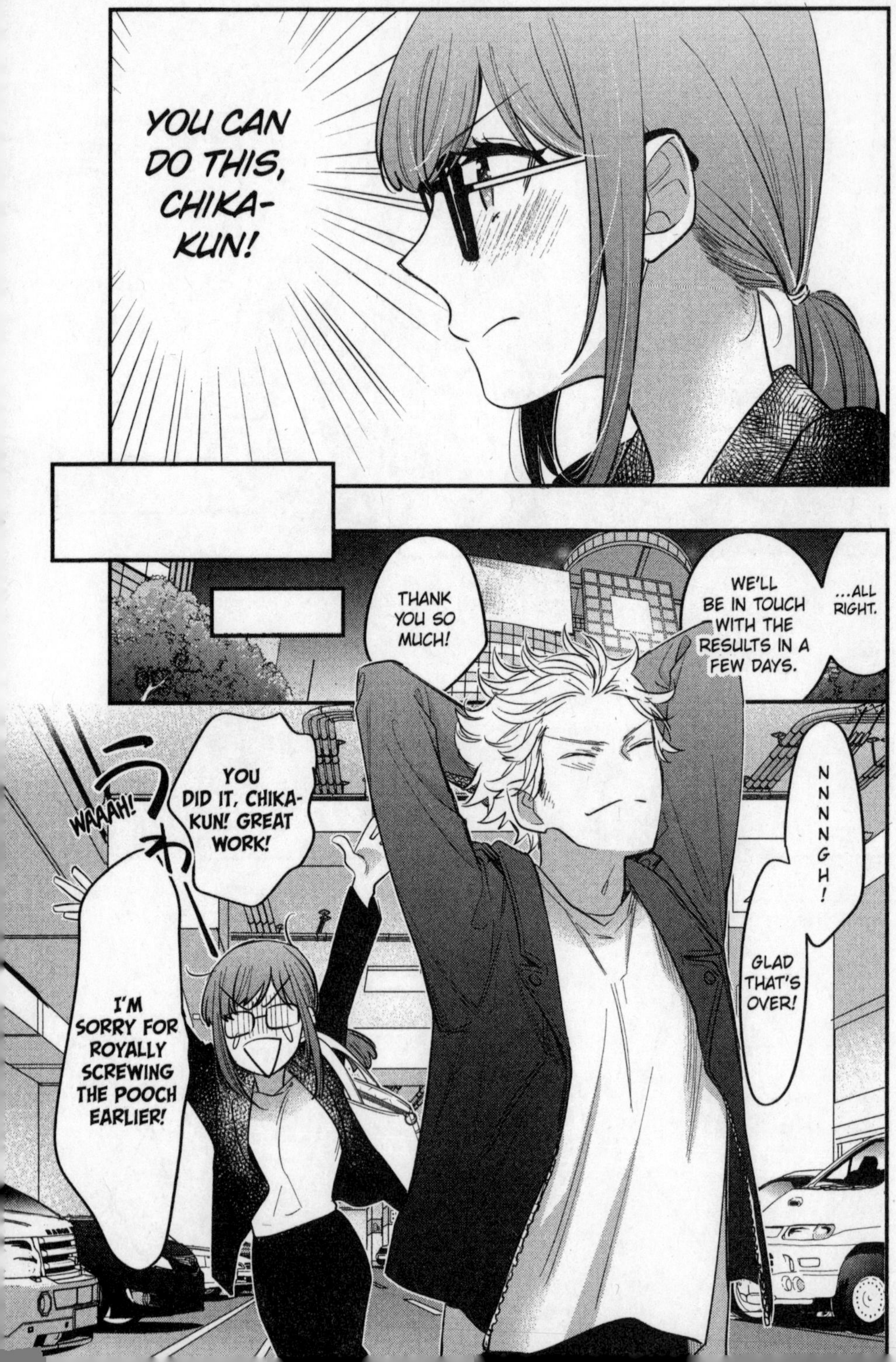
YOU CAN DO THIS, CHIKA-KUN!
WE'LL BE IN TOUCH WITH THE RESULTS IN A FEW DAYS.
...ALL RIGHT.
THANK YOU SO MUCH!
NNNNGH!
GLAD THAT'S OVER!
YOU DID IT, CHIKA-KUN! GREAT WORK!
うわ
WAAAH!
I'M SORRY FOR ROYALLY SCREWING THE POOCH EARLIER!

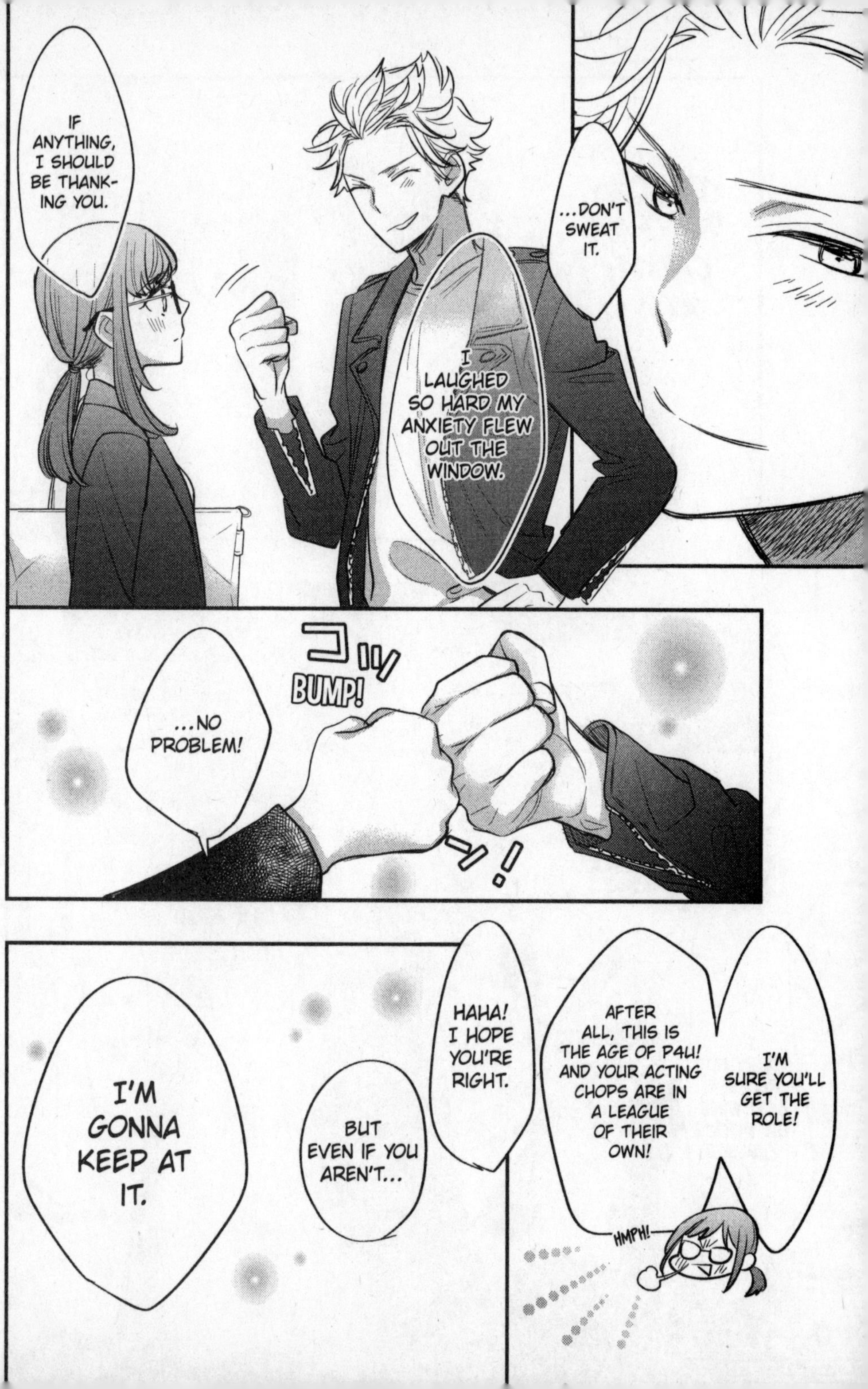
...DON'T SWEAT IT.
IF ANYTHING, I SHOULD BE THANKING YOU.
I LAUGHED SO HARD MY ANXIETY FLEW OUT THE WINDOW.
BUMP!
...NO PROBLEM!
I'M SURE YOU'LL GET THE ROLE!
AFTER ALL, THIS IS THE AGE OF P4U! AND YOUR ACTING CHOPS ARE IN A LEAGUE OF THEIR OWN!
HMPH!
HAHA! I HOPE YOU'RE RIGHT.
BUT EVEN IF YOU AREN'T...
I'M GONNA KEEP AT IT.

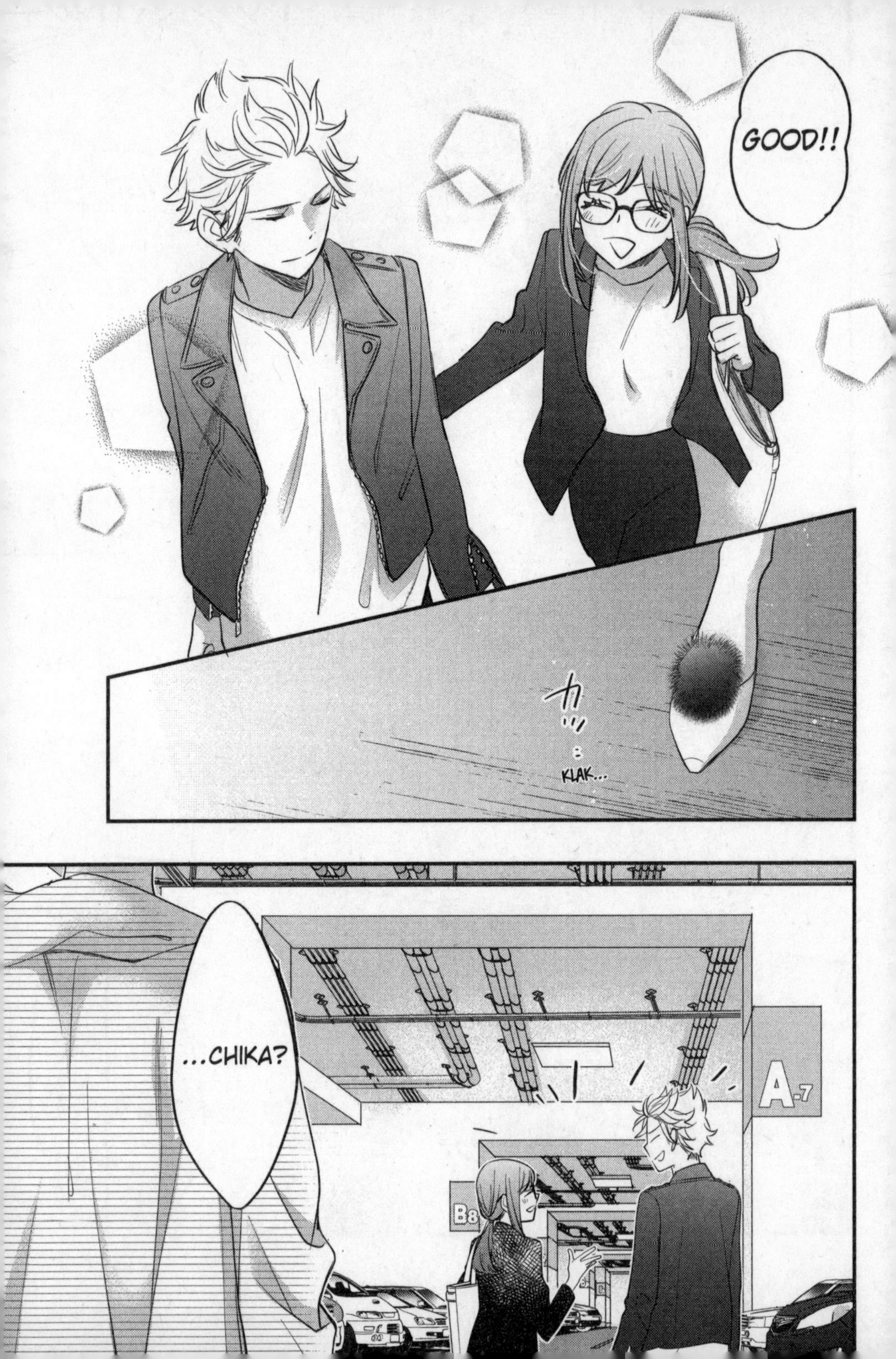
GOOD!!
KLAK...
...CHIKA?

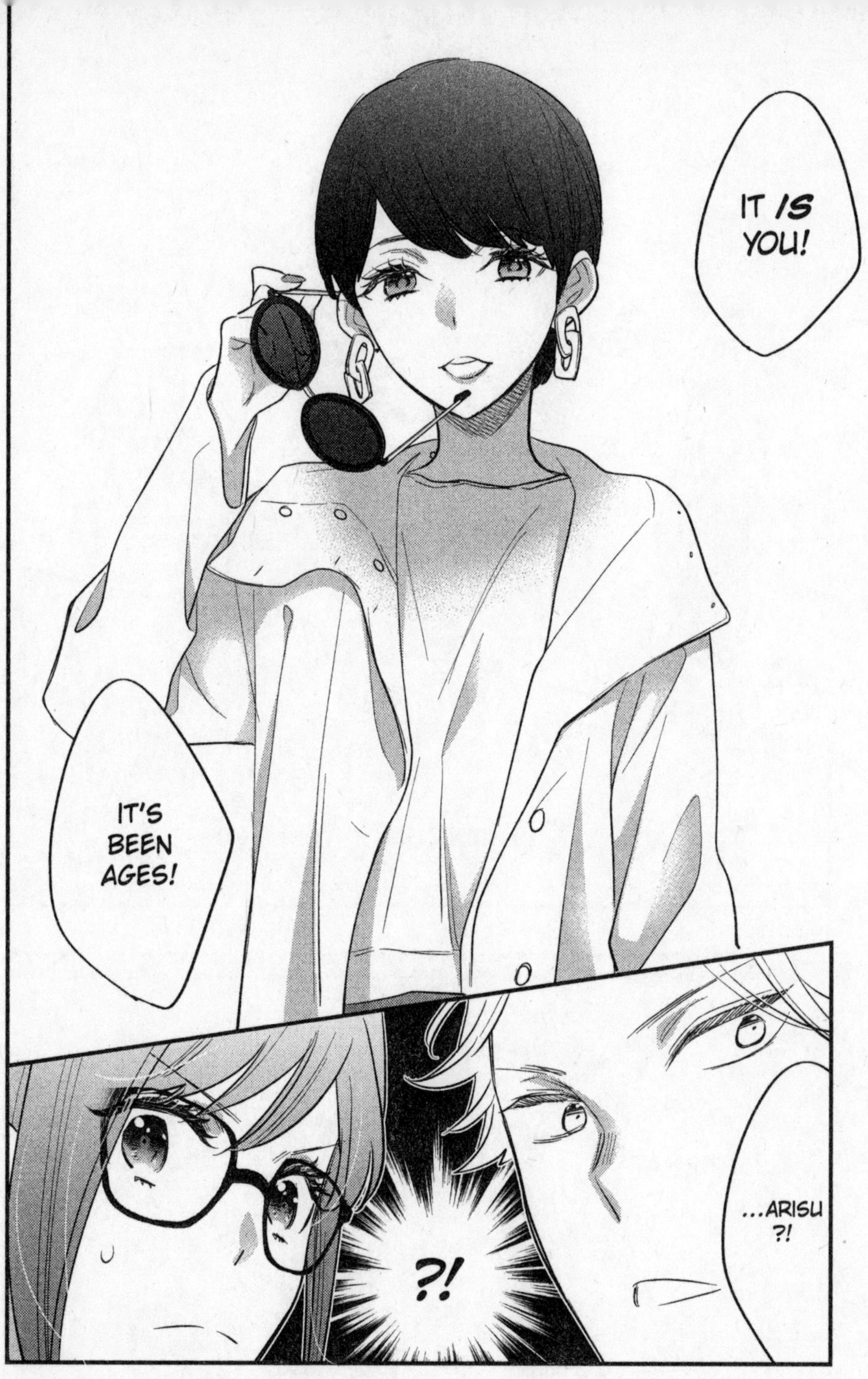
IT *IS* YOU!
IT'S BEEN AGES!
...ARISU ?!
?!

STAR⇄CROSSED!!

← To be continued in Volume 4

R⇄CROSS

D!! STAR

AR⇄CROS

CROSSED

⇄CROSSE

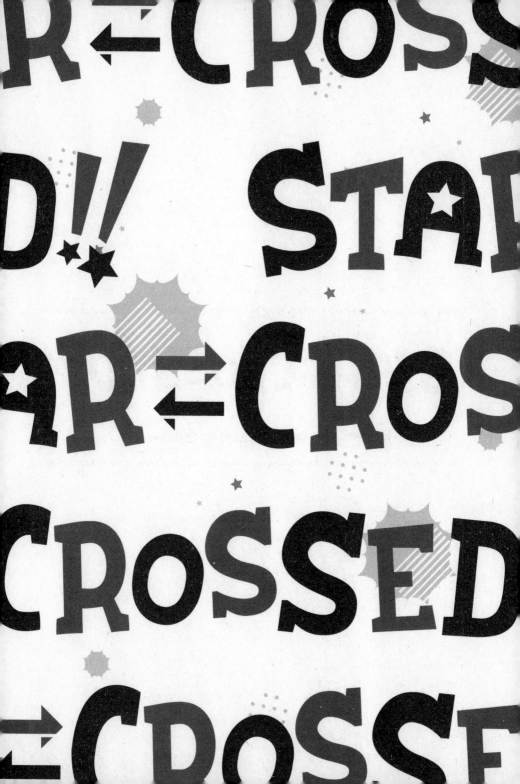

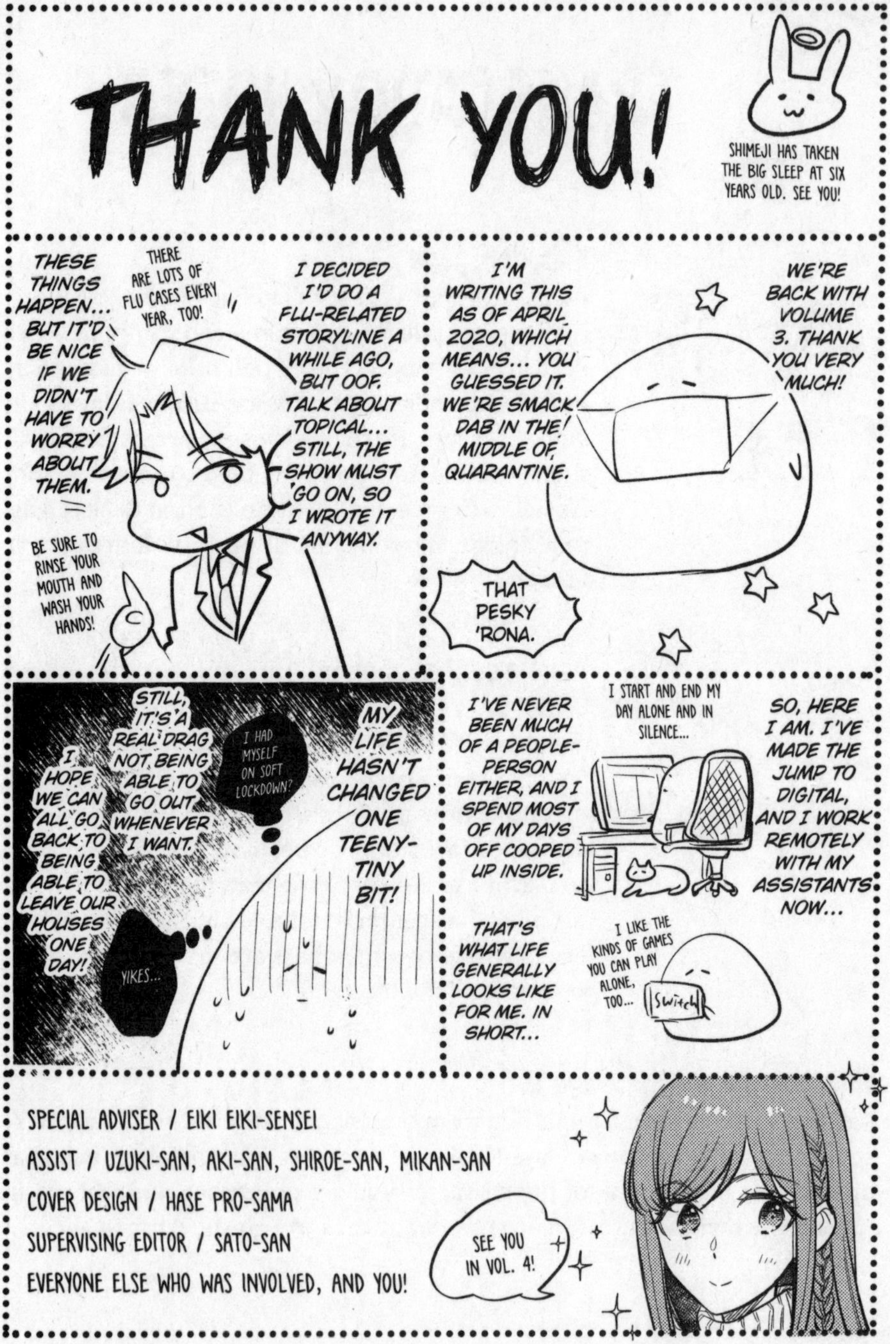
THANK YOU!
SHIMEJI HAS TAKEN THE BIG SLEEP AT SIX YEARS OLD. SEE YOU!
WE'RE BACK WITH VOLUME 3. THANK YOU VERY MUCH!
I'M WRITING THIS AS OF APRIL 2020, WHICH MEANS... YOU GUESSED IT. WE'RE SMACK DAB IN THE MIDDLE OF QUARANTINE.
THAT PESKY 'RONA.
I DECIDED I'D DO A FLU-RELATED STORYLINE A WHILE AGO, BUT OOF. TALK ABOUT TOPICAL... STILL, THE SHOW MUST GO ON, SO I WROTE IT ANYWAY.
THERE ARE LOTS OF FLU CASES EVERY YEAR, TOO!
THESE THINGS HAPPEN... BUT IT'D BE NICE IF WE DIDN'T HAVE TO WORRY ABOUT THEM.
BE SURE TO RINSE YOUR MOUTH AND WASH YOUR HANDS!
SO, HERE I AM. I'VE MADE THE JUMP TO DIGITAL, AND I WORK REMOTELY WITH MY ASSISTANTS NOW...
I START AND END MY DAY ALONE AND IN SILENCE...
I'VE NEVER BEEN MUCH OF A PEOPLE-PERSON EITHER, AND I SPEND MOST OF MY DAYS OFF COOPED UP INSIDE.
I LIKE THE KINDS OF GAMES YOU CAN PLAY ALONE, TOO...
Switch
THAT'S WHAT LIFE GENERALLY LOOKS LIKE FOR ME. IN SHORT...
MY LIFE HASN'T CHANGED ONE TEENY-TINY BIT!
I HAD MYSELF ON SOFT LOCKDOWN?
STILL, IT'S A REAL DRAG NOT BEING ABLE TO GO OUT WHENEVER I WANT.
I HOPE WE CAN ALL GO BACK TO BEING ABLE TO LEAVE OUR HOUSES ONE DAY!
YIKES...
SPECIAL ADVISER / EIKI EIKI-SENSEI
ASSIST / UZUKI-SAN, AKI-SAN, SHIROE-SAN, MIKAN-SAN
COVER DESIGN / HASE PRO-SAMA
SUPERVISING EDITOR / SATO-SAN
EVERYONE ELSE WHO WAS INVOLVED, AND YOU!
SEE YOU IN VOL. 4!

TRANSLATION NOTES

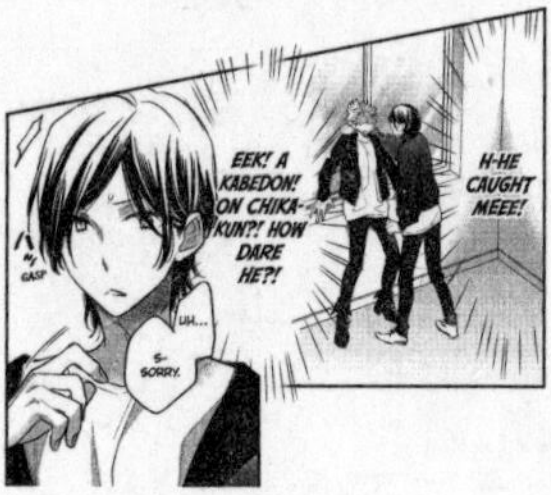
H-HE CAUGHT MEEE!
EEK! A KABEDON! ON CHIKA-KUN?! HOW DARE HE?!
GASP
UH...
S-SORRY.

Kabedon, page 27

Also known as "wall slam" in English, the kabedon is a trope popularized in anime and manga in which Person A will pound their open palm or fist into a wall directly adjacent to Person B, thus bringing the individuals into extremely close quarters. Because the sudden sound and closeness tend to cause Person B's heart to race, the situation is often depicted as awakening their romantic or physical desires toward Person A.

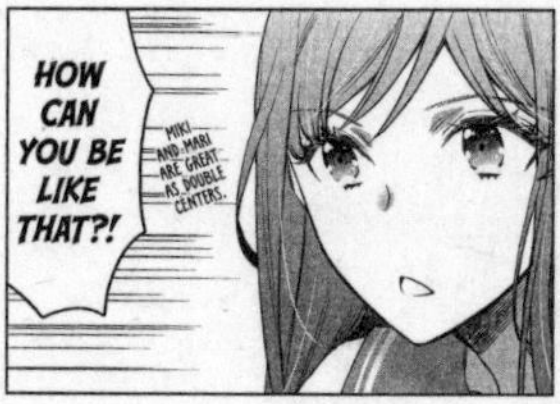
MIKI AND MARI ARE GREAT AS DOUBLE CENTERS.
HOW CAN YOU BE LIKE THAT?!

Double center, page 54

In idol or pop groups in which there are multiple members, it is common practice to feature certain members for a particular single or activity by having them sing primary vocals, appear in the middle of the dance formation, or promote the single in other media. In a single center format, the featured member is simply the "center." However, in cases like Miki and Mari's where two members are featured, they are known as a "double center."

Where's your mask?, page 136

Azusa is referencing a famous line from the anime/manga series Glass Mask, spoken by the protagonist Maya Kitajima. The series conceptualizes acting as donning the fragile mask of the character you are portraying, and that mask is "broken" when the actor's true self penetrates through the performance.

R⇄CROSS

D!! STA

AR⇄CROS

CROSSED

⇄CROSS

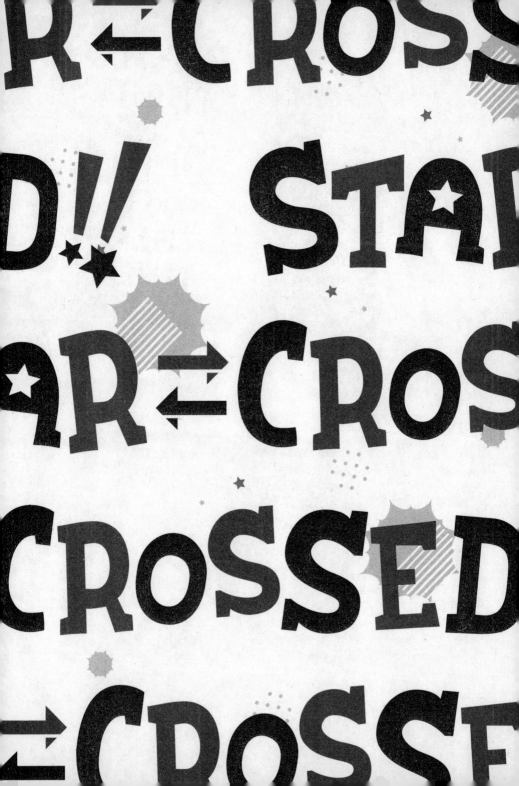

PERFECT WORLD

Rie Aruga

A TOUCHING NEW SERIES ABOUT LOVE AND COPING WITH DISABILITY

An office party reunites Tsugumi with her high school crush Itsuki. He's realized his dream of becoming an architect, but along the way, he experienced a spinal injury that put him in a wheelchair. Now Tsugumi's rekindled feelings will butt up against prejudices she never considered — and Itsuki will have to decide if he's ready to let someone into his heart...

"Depicts with great delicacy and courage the difficulties some with disabilities experience getting involved in romantic relationships... Rie Aruga refuses to romanticize, pushing her heroine to face the reality of disability. She invites her readers to the same tasks of empathy, knowledge and recognition."
—Slate.fr

"An important entry [in manga romance]... The emotional core of both plot and characters indicates thoughtfulness... [Aruga's] research is readily apparent in the text and artwork, making this feel like a real story."
—Anime News Network

KC KODANSHA COMICS

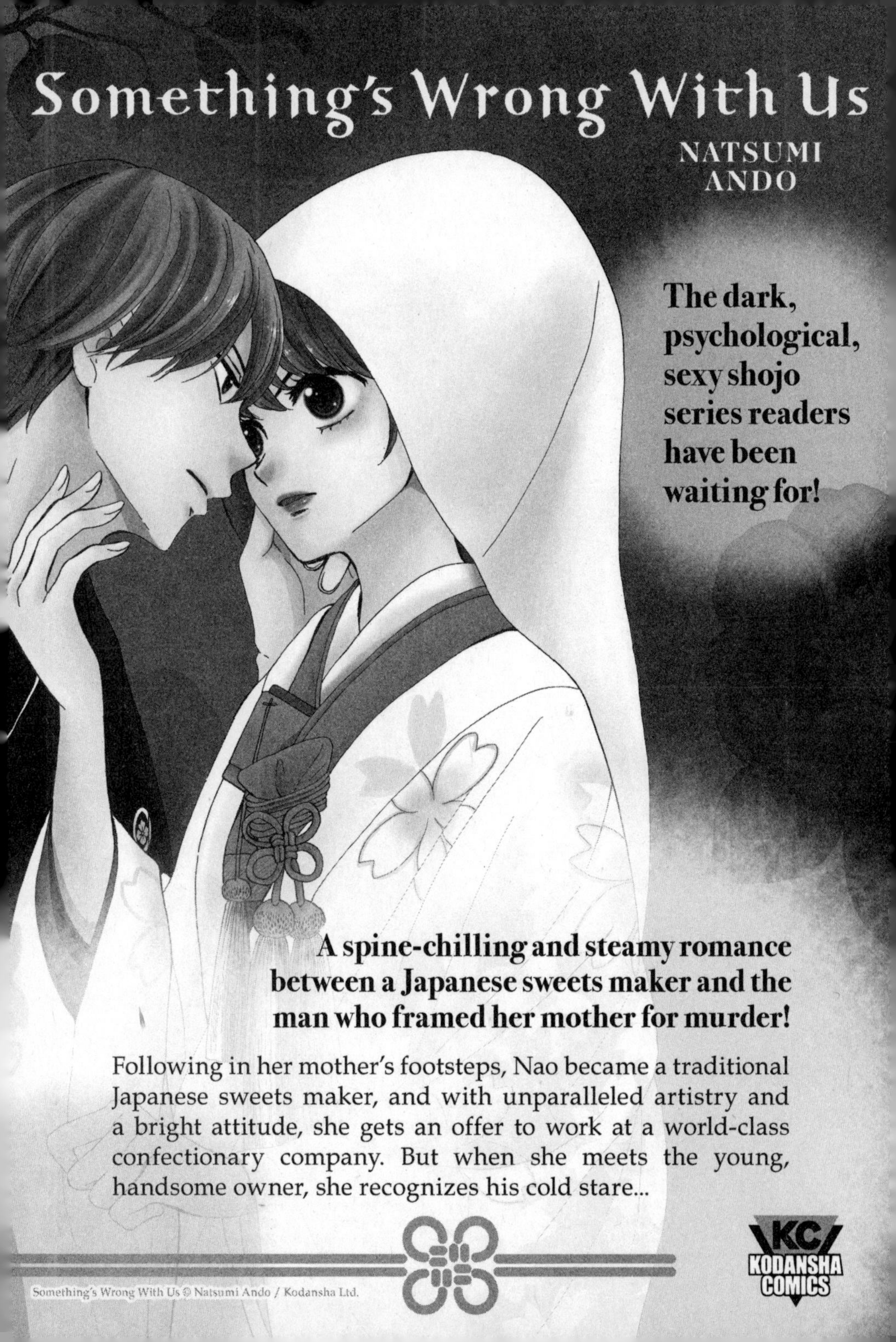
Something's Wrong With Us
NATSUMI ANDO
The dark, psychological, sexy shojo series readers have been waiting for!
A spine-chilling and steamy romance between a Japanese sweets maker and the man who framed her mother for murder!
Following in her mother's footsteps, Nao became a traditional Japanese sweets maker, and with unparalleled artistry and a bright attitude, she gets an offer to work at a world-class confectionary company. But when she meets the young, handsome owner, she recognizes his cold stare...
Something's Wrong With Us © Natsumi Ando / Kodansha Ltd.
KC
KODANSHA COMICS